LYND

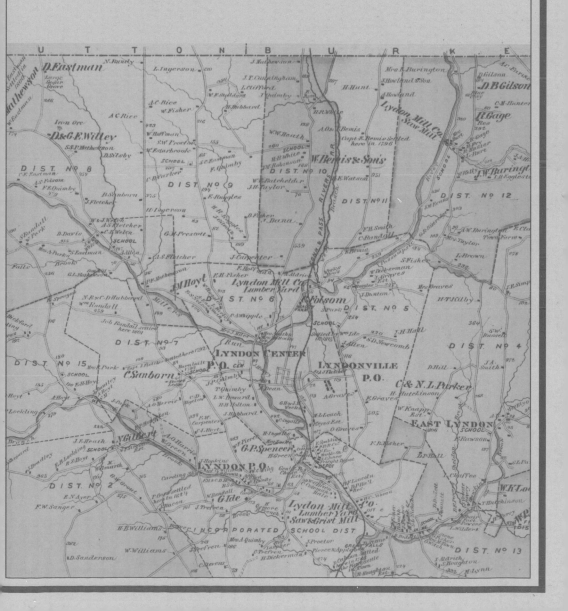

Lyndon: Gem in the Green

LYNDON

GEM IN THE GREEN

by

Venila Lovina Shores, PH.D., LITT.D.

Compiled and Edited by

Ruth Hopkins McCarty

TOWN OF LYNDON
Lyndonville, Vermont
1986

Official Seal of Town of Lyndon

On the official seal of the Town of Lyndon is a picture of the old "Pierce" House.

Although it was impossible to verify at the time the seal was made, there seems to be no doubt that the Old Pierce House was the first log cabin erected within the limits of what is now Lyndonville.

It is believed that the house was erected prior to 1825, and was deeded to Sophia Pierce, wife of Roswell Pierce, by Joel Aldrich in January 1832. It was located on "about three-fourths of an acre lying between the road leading from Lyndon Center easterly and the road leading from Lyndon Center southerly to Lyndon Corner, for a consideration of $8.00". Later the house owned by Buckley and Shattuck was located on the same spot. Two conveyances of this lot have been made since 1832, one to Ellen Pierce McFarland for $450 by the administrator of Sophia Pierce's estate. It was deeded by Mrs. Ellen Pierce McFarland and her husband in 1911 to Buckley and Shattuck.

If information is correct the old log cabin was destroyed by fire July 4, 1893. Several pieces of furniture that were in it were reported to be in the possession of H. H. Butterfield, a great-grandson of Mr. and Mrs. Roswell Pierce.

Rendering of official seal on front cover by A. McDonald.

TITLE PAGE: Meeting House, Horse Sheds, Graded School, Universalist Church, Burying Ground, June Training Ground (*Dorothy Walter and Elizabeth Nelson*)

ENDLEAVES: Lyndon, showing early School Districts (*Vermont Historical Society*); Map of Vermont (*The National Survey*)

Approximately 660 words passim from *Theodore N. Vail: A Biography* by Albert Bigelow Paine. Copyright 1921 by Albert Bigelow Paine. Renewed 1949 by Louise Paine Moore, Joy Paine Cushman and Frances Paine Wade. Reprinted by permission of Harper & Row, Publishers, Inc.

Table of Contents

Foreword

AT THE TIME of her death, Dr. Shores was in the process of preparing the Lyndon Town History for publishing. Much of the material was in the form in which it now appears in this book. This, along with her notes, and other pertinent information was deposited in the Lyndon town vault. Her copious notes consisted of many boxes of material, each page of which was dated and the source of information cited. These had been collected over a period of twenty-five years.

Therefore, when asked by the Lyndon Town Selectmen to get the town history ready for publishing, this editor decided that the work of Dr. Shores should be preserved whenever possible, in the belief that the townspeople would like to see her work.

Dr. Venila L. Shores was a true historian dedicated to the task of tracking down any elusive information pertaining to the early days of the town. This pursuit involved perusing many volumes of town, state, and national archives; of reading many newspapers and other publications; of studying private letters and papers; and in interviewing many people having knowledge of Lyndon's earlier days.

It would be impossible to list all the many people who have offered help and encouragement in the task of readying this information for publication. However, a special thanks should go to the following, who many times have helped to solve some difficult problem: The Lyndon Town Selectmen; Town Clerk, Robert Lawrence, and his Staff; Mrs. Elizabeth Wylie of the Cobleigh Library; the Lyndon State College Librarian and Staff; the Librarian and Staff of the Vermont Historical Library; the Librarian and Staff of the St. Johnsbury Atheneum; the University of Vermont Archivist; Mrs. Harriet Fisher; Edwin Houghton; Richard Lawrence; Rev. Jeanette McKnight; Paul

Aubin, Gerald Aubin; Mrs. Sheila Fors of the Shores Memorial Museum; George Hopkins; Lucille Powers; and the many, many citizens of Lyndon, who have, when asked, cheerfully aided in tracking down bits of necessary information. Without their generous help this book would never have been published.

A special thanks also goes to those who have loaned their pictures for use in the history, their names appear under the pictures.

Since this is the first of two volumes, some information of interest does not appear in Volume I.

Ruth H. McCarty

Preface

IN THE WARNING for the annual March town meeting in 1958, Article 12 was as follows: "Shall the town authorize the Selectmen to name five citizens to serve on a special committee to take the necessary steps, subject to the approval of the Selectmen, to have a town history compiled, and that the Selectmen be further authorized to allocate a sum of money to make this possible?"

Article 13 read: "Shall the town vote to appropriate a sum of money to sponsor locally an observance of the Champlain Festival? If so, how much?"

Action on these two articles was affirmative, and the two projects were combined under the responsibility of a single committee; the selectmen appointed Kenneth Hoffman, chairman, John B. Chase, W. Arthur Simpson, Ruth E. Johnson, and Dexter H. Simpson. The observance of the Champlain Festival was staged successfully in the summer of 1959. In August 1959, Mr. Hoffman resigned, and in late September this writer reluctantly accepted appointment to fill the vacancy. There was time for only one committee meeting before my return to my Florida home; the committee divided the town's history into four areas, promising to have them ready for editing on my return the following spring. Now, more than fifteen years later, I am still awaiting the fulfillment of that promise.

This history is at times somewhat fragmentary. The construction of a composite or even a complete picture of the rise and growth of the town of Lyndon is impossible because of, first, the unavailability of material and, second, the way in which the town has developed and the intense persistence of the individuality of the various localities. There has been not only Lyndon Corner, Lyndon Center, and Lyndonville, but also numerous neighborhoods therein: East Lyndon, Red Village, Hall's Mills, Mt. Hunger, Squabble Hollow, Pudding Hill, Egypt, Hadleyville, Hog Street, Bundyville, Mosquito District, Cold Hill, Owlsboro, Shadyville, and others that have been less cohesive and so have survived less long. Perhaps one of the reasons for survival of the town's sections has been the reluctance to permit the establishment of "consolidated" schools. In some periods the individual localities have established churches, contributing even further to the division. Rivalry between the districts appeared, descending at times to the bitterest jealousy. Only in the matter of government, and of political organization in those matters equally concerning all parts of the town, has there been cohesion through town meetings and town officials.

The first published history of the settlement of the town of Lyndon was Zadock Thompson's 1824 *Gazetteer of Vermont*.[1] This was followed in 1842 by the same author's *History of Vermont*,[2] in which the account was somewhat expanded. John Hayward included Lyndon in his consideration of the various towns in the state in 1849.[3]

At the town meeting of 1852, it was voted "to appoint a committee of four to take into consideration a sketch of the Town of Lyndon written by Reverend Jonathan Greenleaf of Brooklyn, New York, and by him presented to the town for their use." The committee was to report at the next meeting what action the town would take in regard to the same. The committee chosen consisted of George A. Bingham, Charles Roberts, Silas Houghton, and E. A. Cahoon. The next meeting of the voters occurred on September 2, when a laudatory report was given. The committee recommended that:

> something like a permanent character may be given to its existence, by enrolling it upon the town books, and by *printing* in pamphlet form sufficient number of copies to furnish one to each head of a family in town, fifty to be deposited in the Clerk's office for use as the town shall prescribe, and 25 to be presented to Mr. Greenleaf. They further recommended a vote of thanks to the Rev[d] Jonathan Greenleaf, and that the Clerk be instructed to communicate to him such vote, together with a copy of this report and the action of the town thereon.

The committee report[4] was adopted and Reverend Greenleaf graciously accepted the courtesy. No record has been found to prove that the vote was fulfilled, but since several copies of the pamphlet have survived, that may be accepted as circumstantial evidence of compliance with the vote.

The next account of the history of the town appeared in the *Vermont Quarterly Gazetteer: A Historical Magazine*, edited by Abby Maria Hemenway and published in Ludlow (1862). This account was written by George C. Cahoon, a grandson of Daniel Cahoon, Sr., who was a lawyer in Lyndon for some fifty-five years; "Lyndon" originally appeared in the April 1862 issue of the magazine (pp. 338–56). At the town meeting of March 1, 1881, the purchase of a copy was authorized.

In mid-1887, Editor Chase reported in the *Vermont Union* that M. L. Stedman of West Bloomfield, N.Y., the agent for Child's *Gazetteer of Caledonia and Essex Counties*,[5] had completed his task of delivering "197 copies in Lyndon, in Kirby 18, in Burke 97, in St. Johnsbury East 17" at a price of $5.50 each. The article on Lyndon, credited to George C. Cahoon, contains many similarities to the one that had appeared in Hemenway.

In preparing this history of the town of Lyndon, I have had access to all the above accounts. Fortunately, too, the minutes of the town meetings and the records of land transactions have been faithfully and legibly preserved. However, reports of committees or town officers, though noted in the minutes as having been made, were neither incorporated in the minutes nor preserved elsewhere. Records of expenditure of money are nonexistent prior to 1886, when the first town report was printed; and even thereafter, hard work, imagination, and ingenuity are often employed without extracting unquestionable evidence. For instance, at the town meetings of 1843, 1844, 1845, 1848, and 1851 the minutes report the instruction of the selectmen to "lot out" the cemetery. The sexton's report of March 1852 shows it to have been finally accomplished in that year.

We know that at one time there was a mass of material that would have answered such questions as these. In 1905, when Mr. and Mrs. Martin Daniels moved into the house long the home of Isaac W.

Sanborn (44 years Lyndon Town clerk), they found many barrels and chests in the shed-chamber[6] containing papers of various sizes;[7] these were the original reports made to the town clerk. Mr. Daniels consulted the selectmen, who felt the documents were of no value, believing their substance had been copied in the town record books.[8] So as storage space was needed, Mr. Daniels emptied barrels and burned papers.

Finally, O. D. Mathewson became the next-door neighbor. Knowing his interest in such things, Daniels asked if he would be interested in looking at some of the remaining papers. The answer was affirmative, so they were moved to the Mathewson home. Years passed, and after Mr. Mathewson's death, Mrs. Mathewson decided to clean the remaining barrel! We are deeply indebted to her for saving so many of these papers and making them available for our use. They have been the only source of information and proof of many events in the early history of the town. The minutes make note of a report having been presented and acted upon, and through the notation on the back of these originals[9] we can relate them unequivocably to the notation in the minutes.

We are deeply indebted to the late Charles M. Chase (1829–1902), founder and longtime editor of the *Vermont Union*, for preserving so many reports of the activities of the town's people as well as so many of his own reminiscences.[10] His son, John B. Chase (1872–1960), possessed a wealth of memories that contributed much subject matter, and his enthusiasm restored my courage many times in the face of disheartening reverses, especially during the early days of the quest.

Another useful source of information has been the *St. Johnsbury Republican*, in the management of which D. P. Hall and his son-in-law, C. T. Walter, both Lyndon residents, were so long active. The granddaughters of Mr. Hall, the late Dorothy C. Walter, Elizabeth Walter Nelson, and Alice Walter Fulton, have been most gracious in sharing with this writer not only their bound files of the *Republican* but also the many hundreds of family papers, books, and pictures, and—especially—their own reminiscences.

Newspapers never can be considered truly reliable sources of material for historical writing. However, they have been the only available material for much of the history of the town of Lyndon. Cross-checking and verification have been impossible for lack of other sources. We can only hope that their reporting was more accurate than has been true in our own time.

The disastrous fires of 1894 and 1924 destroyed records of many organizations and fraternal groups, leaving no possible way of bridging those gaps in information. Private collections of records, diaries, account books, and correspondence have been sacrificed to the passing of time.

Though it is impossible to name all the very many people who have carried on an endless search for material, this writer is most humbly and deeply grateful and heavily indebted to all of them. A few have been especially faithful in their efforts and encouragement: the town clerks and their staffs, the late S. R. Lang and Ashley Jewell, the selectmen, Grace Mathewson (Mrs. O. D.), Ethel Blake (Mrs. Harry), Harriet Fisher (Mrs. Paul), Edwin Houghton, the members of the various town history committees, and the staff at the Vermont Historical Society Library and at Cobleigh Public Library.

It is my most sincere hope that posterity will find a minimum of factual error in the material here presented, and will remember that such errors as do occur were due to lack of available information and were made by accident rather than by intent. I also hope that some younger person may find something here that provides the inspiration to carry on the endless, and often fruitless, quest to complete the task here begun.

I

The Township

THE TOWN OF LYNDON is located in the upper Piedmont area
of Vermont. It was a part of Orange County until 1792, when the
Caledonia County was formed. When surveyors first looked on the
territory later to be known as Lyndon, they saw a heavily forested,
uninhabited land dominated by the Passumpsic River and its
tributaries. Level lands along the river formed the basis for meadow-
lands; terraced hills along its sides followed the riverbeds and showed
the surveyors the lay of the land.

The Passumpsic River—the name is Abnaki for "clear waters"—
runs through the center of town and has several major tributaries
within the town. They are South Branch, west of Lyndon Corner;
Hawkins Brook, east of Lyndon Corner; Miller's Run, north of
Lyndon Center; and West Branch and East Branch, north of Lyndonville. During the early 1860s someone called the Passumpsic a "liquid
corkscrew." The appropriateness of this nickname was borne out
when the railroad was built. In a distance of twenty-five miles it
crossed the river about twenty times. One seven-mile section of
railroad is said to have contained eleven bridges; the river wandered
about thirty-five miles within that stretch.

The forty-three-mile–long Passumpsic follows the topography as
it drains an area of about 507 square miles. Its flood plain is usually
rather narrow; in the Lyndon–St. Johnsbury area, however, it sometimes reaches about a thousand feet in width. Prior to the settlement
of the area, leaves, limbs, and logs helped to control the runoff, so
less flooding occurred and streams were more stable in size. Since
the area's settlement, flooding has at times been a major problem.

Near the southern border of the town are Great and Little Falls.

One requirement of the original charter was that these be included within the boundaries of the new town. Great Falls descended a distance of sixty-five feet within a distance of about thirty rods. Little Falls, located about a mile above Great Falls, descended about twenty feet. These provided abundant waterpower, allowing the area eventually to set up its own electric company. In the early days the Falls provided adequate power for mills located in the Lyndon Corner area.

Early Indians are known to have hunted and fished in the area of the Great and Little Falls. Little is known of these people, but they are believed to have been members of the Abnaki tribes. Early Indian migration routes followed the Passumpsic River from its junction with the Connecticut River north through Lyndon; the Indians would then portage across to the Barton River and follow waterways to Lake Memphremagog and the St. Francis River and Canada.

Few Indian artifacts have been found in the area, probably due to the flooding over the years, and to the fact that few archaeological digs were made in Vermont before 1968. The fact that signs of Indian culture have been located in nearby towns suggests that Indians also traversed this area in early days. With the advent of the Interstate 91, a few digs were made. Only within the last few years has an interest in the archaeology of the area been shown. Evidence indicates that Archaic sites along the Passumpsic River may exist at altitudes above an elevation of 598 feet; most lower sites are thought to have been destroyed by flooding. Early home sites and abandoned farms and communities have much to offer as archaeologists continue to delve into the past of the Northeast Kingdom.

II

The Lyndon Grant

W HEN THE KING OF ENGLAND established the boundaries in
the charters of the thirteen American colonies, knowledge was limited concerning the lands involved, and grants were made in such
general terms that the boundary claims overlapped. Throughout the
sessions of the Continental Congresses, one of the major points of
friction was the land claims of the various colonies. One of the most
bitterly contested of these tracts was that known as the "New Hampshire Grants," the land lying between the Hudson and Connecticut
rivers. This land was claimed by both New York and New Hampshire,
and for many years the governors of the two colonies issued charters
conveying parts of it—sometimes the same land—to individuals or
groups of individuals.[1] Some of the southern part of the tract was
claimed by Massachusetts and was included in some of the charters
that colony granted. Furthermore, all the other ten colonies considered the "New Hampshire Grants" as public domain; in other words,
it belonged to the Union of Colonies in equal shares.

On January 16, 1777, residents of the New Hampshire Grants,
having been duly elected as delegates, met at Westminster and pro-
claimed the territory to be a free and independent state that in the
future would be known as "NEW CONNECTICUT[2] ALIAS VER-
MONT—an independent REPUBLIC." They drafted a formal declaration to that effect, and also a petition to Congress for admission
of their representatives to seats in that body, thus launching the
long struggle for admission to the Union of American Colonies.
This independent status came to an end only in 1791, when Vermont
submerged its independence and joined the other thirteen states.

During this fourteen-year period, the leaders of the Republic of

Vermont were concerned with many types of problems. (1) Without funds or tax-levying machinery, the equipment for an army[3] had to be provided. The British were a threat on the north, as the colonial army was on the west, so a careful balance had to be maintained between the two. (2) Law and order had to be preserved within the republic. (3) As a means of raising money, further settlement had to be encouraged, and thus a demand developed for the purchase of land, the only real source of revenue. (4) The favorable attitude of the members of Congress must be cultivated in the interest of eventual admission to the Union. (5) Tensions, constantly bordering on bloodshed, continued to exist with both New York and New Hampshire as each attempted to enforce its authority. (6) One of the most dreaded threats was that those two colonies would compromise their dispute, divide Vermont between them, and place their joint boundary on the crest of the Green Mountains.

Agents[4] — "observers," as they were called — were sent to the various colonial legislatures and to Philadelphia to curry favor and make friends for the Republic of Vermont. These agents not only made friends but generously broadcast blank petitions for grants of land which were returnable to the governor and council of the Republic.[5] They also publicized the policy so ably stated by Ira Allen:[6] "In consequence of internal divisions, and to make government popular, it was thought good policy not to lay any taxes on the people, but to raise a sufficient revenue out of the property confiscated, and the ungranted lands."

Companies interested in acquiring Vermont lands were formed in New Hampshire, Massachusetts, Connecticut, and Rhode Island. Officers and members of both the Continental army and the Continental Congress also formed such associations. These companies usually had about sixty-five members who, under the leadership of one of their number, petitioned for the grant of a township of land. In considering the requests for grants, the governor and council appear to have examined with great care the personnel of each applying group, for the republic needed not only money but — perhaps even more important — influence.[7] Throughout the fourteen years of Vermont's efforts to be recognized as a state and a member of the Union,

Rhode Island and Connecticut remained staunch supporters of all the republic's petitions.

When the petition[8] for the grant of the township of Lyndon was made or who the petitioners were is not known, but it appears to have been purely a business adventure, a land speculation. On November 2, 1780, a committee of the General Assembly on ungranted lands in Vermont recommended to the governor and council that a grant be made

> . . . to Jonathan Arnold and sixty associates as laid down and described on the plan exhibited by the Surveyor Gen[l] marked N°
> 25 (provided the said described and marked tract aforesaid shall on examination be found to include the upper great falls on the Massumsick (alias Passumpsick) river; but if not, said township to be bounded so as to include said falls if said falls be found to be contained in the now vacant or unappropriated lands as appears by said plan) containing twenty-three thousand and forty acres. . . .[9]

The following day a resolution was adopted approving the grant,[10] stating the number of prospective proprietors as sixty-four, the size and the name of the prospective township, the price to be paid, and the conditions of settlement to be fulfilled.

The charter[11] of the town of Lyndon, signed by Governor Chittenden on November 20, 1780, included the provisions of the November 3 resolution and listed the names of fifty-three proprietors. It provided that the township was to be six miles square and divided into seventy rights of 329$\frac{1}{7}$ acres each, 9$\frac{1}{7}$ acres of each right being reserved for roads and highways. Each proprietor was to receive one right, with these exceptions: Jonathan Arnold was to have five, Joseph Brown and Asa Kimball three each, and John Innes Clark, Joseph Nightingale, and Daniel Owen two each.[12] Six rights were reserved for public uses: one right each was reserved for a seminary or college, a county grammar school, an English or common school, the settlement of a minister, the support of the "social worship of God in the township," and a gristmill and sawmill. The rights for the college and the county grammar school were reserved in perpetuity to the state, the other three to the town. The proprietors were given the responsibility of locating each of these reserved rights where they "will least incommode the general settlement of the said Township." The proprietors were also "impowered to dispose of in such manner as they shall judge best for the encouragement of erecting the first grist Mill and Saw Mill in said township"—the mill right," as it has always been called.

The charter established another reservation: ". . . all Pine Timber suitable for a navy to be reserved to the use and benefit of the Freemen of this State agreeable to an act of the legislature of said State passed at their session Oct[r] 1781."[13] Furthermore, each proprietor was obligated, under the provisions of the charter, to

> plant and cultivate five acres of Land and build a house at least eighteen feet square on the floor or have one family settled on each respective right . . . within the term of four years next, after the circumstances of war will permit of settlement with safety, on penalty of forfeiture of each right . . . not so improved . . . the same to revert to the freemen of the State to be by their representatives regranted. . . .

On January 1, 1781, a little more than a month after the official signature had been affixed to the charter of the town of Lyndon, the proprietors met in Providence, R.I.[14] Lt. Col. Jeremiah Olney was chosen moderator. The morning meeting was adjourned until three o'clock in the afternoon, when Olney Winsor was chosen "clerk to the proprietors." Several votes were taken that had significance in settling the new town:

Each proprietor was obligated to pay one-half the granting fees and the arrearages of expenses on his right, or rights, on or before February 1, 1781. The committee was instructed to "strike their name out for so many rights as they shall be deficient on that day."[15] The balance of the granting fees had to be paid by April 15, "and in case of failure of the last payment . . . the committee [was to] return the names of those deficient to the Governor and Council of the State of Vermont . . . as defaulters in order that they may be left out of the Charter for s[d] Township."

This committee was empowered to insert in the charter the names of any persons who paid the delinquent right charges on February 1. In accepting these delinquent payments, preference was to be given to persons who were already proprietors and had paid their own quotas. In case these new proprietors made their payment promptly, their names were to be sent to the governor and council for inclusion in the charter. Those whose names appear in the final charter list "shall pay down all Monies which have been advanced in procuring the same [the charter] by such defaulters in whose names they may be inserted to the Clerk, previous to their being so returned, which Monies shall be by him repaid to such defaulters." The committee elected to perform these functions was John Innes Clark and David Howell, Esqrs., and Olney Winsor, who were also given the task of settling accounts with Jonathan Arnold.

Also at this meeting, a committee was selected to draft instructions to the committee to whom would be entrusted responsibility "to locate, bound, and survey s^d Township of Lyndon." This instruction committee consisted of Jonathan Arnold, Esq., Col. Israel Angell, and Olney Winsor. Following this action the meeting was adjourned until the following morning at ten o'clock.

The first business of this adjourned session was receipt of the report of the committee on instructions. Next, it was voted that "Jonathan Arnold and Daniel Owen Esqrs. with one of the following, viz. Daniel Cahoon,[16] Jonathan Jenks and Joel Mathews Esqrs . . . be the committee to locate, bound, and survey s^d Township of Lyndon agreeable to instructions voted for that purpose." The proprietors voted that payment of the granting fee should be

> in Silver or Gold, or in Continental Money at the exchange of not less than seventy-five for One — The Proprietors who pay in Continental Money to be obligated to make up any deficiency that there may be on Account of the rise of the exchange for Silver; and that they have the benefit of a Refund if the Money is received for the Grant at any less exchange.

The money received by the clerk in the first payments of granting fees was to be paid to Jonathan Arnold "Ag^t for the Propriety [*sic*] to & for their use he to be accountable." Arnold was to be paid nine shillings per day "silver money" for his services in obtaining the grant of the township plus his necessary expenses. Furthermore, the proprietor of each right was obligated to advance "five Silver dollars" to defray the expenses of the committee to locate the township. This was to be paid to the clerk when the last payment on the granting fees was made.

The instructions drafted by the committee and approved by the proprietors directed the committee on location (Jonathan Arnold, Daniel Owen, and Daniel Cahoon) to fix upon a beginning boundary,[17] then with the assistance of the surveyor general or his deputy or "some other surveyor of ability & character . . . run the Outlines of the s^d Town, fixing such Bounds & Monuments, as you may judge necessary to ascertain & perpetuate the same." This being done, the committee was instructed to "perambulate & view the Lands contained" within the bounds set: it was thought that this would provide information concerning the "general Quality of the Soil, Situation and other Advantages for Settlement." The committee was then charged to "lay out the several Rights, Public and Private. . . ."

This committee was directed to designate an appropriate location for the five rights[18] reserved for public use, then to divide "the rest of the Land into the number of Lots there are Private Rights in the said Township. . . ." The three men were also responsible for fixing the necessary monuments to designate the bounds of the private rights. To complete its task, the committee was instructed to "cause a Plan or Map of s^d Township to be drawn as accurately as possible describing the situation of each Lot & the size thereof & having marked off the Public Rights & Lots laid as aforesaid, number the rest according to the Number of Rights belonging to the Proprietors, viz. Sixty-four. . . ." The men were authorized to lay out land for a sawmill and a gristmill and assign it on the map of the town. They were also authorized to make a written contract, on behalf of the proprietors with someone to build a gristmill and sawmill; if they thought it wise, the contract could include time limits on construction. When the committee had completed these tasks, it was to report to the proprietors, draw names and rights, and record the results of those drawings on the map of the township.[19]

On August 2, 1781, the proprietors met in Providence, with Joseph Brown as moderator. The report of the locating committee was read and adopted.

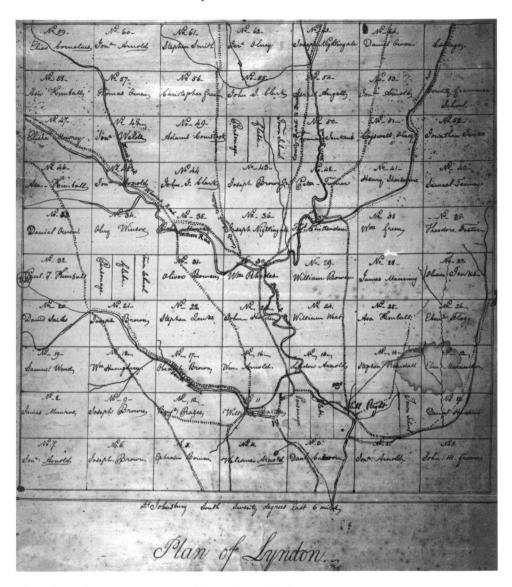

Plan of Lyndon showing original Proprietors Rights
(*Vermont Historical Society*)

The meeting accordingly proceeded to draught the several Rights, in manner & form of a lottery—viz. The names of each Proprietor was written and roled up & put into a Hat, & the number of each Right roled up into another Hat, & each of them drawn out by the Committee agreeable to the former directions of the Proprietors.

This task having been completed, the proprietors passed several resolutions: a committee consisting of Jonathan Arnold, Joseph Brown, John I. Clark, Daniel Owen, and Daniel Cahoon "or any three of them" was charged with the responsibility of reporting to the Vermont General Assembly the division that had taken place, and asking for the passage of an act of the Assembly confirming the action taken. The committee was empowered to do anything relative to laying out the town that seemed to need doing. The second resolution[20] provided (1) for paying Johnathan Arnold 51£ 14s 8d for the balance due on his account; (2) paying Daniel Owen 22£ 4s 6d for the balance due on his account; and (3) in compensation for his services to the proprietors, to give Olney Winsor the horse Arnold had purchased for the use of the survey committee, and that "both bills presented by him that day should be settled and Ballanced." The final action of the meeting was a vote to establish a tax "to the amount of the several Ballances due from the Proprietors . . . after deducting what is yet due on the Rights . . . payable to Olney Winsor . . . on or before the Tenth day of September next." As a penalty for nonpayment of the tax, this action called for the sale of "so much of his [the proprietor's right] in s^d Township at public Vendue as will pay the Taxes thereon assessed."

The last meeting of the proprietors of which record has survived was held February 2, 1784, at the house of "Mr. Peter Chandler, Inn Holder in Providence" with Theodore Foster, Esq. as moderator. The proprietors voted to assign the mill right to Daniel Cahoon "on the Conditions expressed in the Instructions to the Committee for locating said Township." Jonathan Jenks and Jonathan Arnold were designated a

> committee to confer with the said Daniel Cahoon Esq.:
> and in case he shall agree to erect the Mills upon the said Conditions,
> to enter into an Agreement in Writing Obligatory for his performing

the same, within such time as the said Committee shall think best to promote an early settlement of s^d Township, on or before the last day of October A.D. 1785.

These same two men were charged with the responsibility to formulate and carry into execution "such Measures to promote Settlement in the Township as they may judge proper"; roads and the establishment of lot lines were suggested.[21] They were also charged

> to sowe or cause to be sowed within said Township a sufficient Quantity of Apple Seeds to furnish a Nursery of Apple Trees sufficient in Number to furnish, at least, One hundred apple Trees to each Proprietor's Right, and cause the Lands whereon they are sown to be well fenced, in order to secure them to the Benefit of the Proprietors, from the Owner of the Right on which they may be sown as shall be effectual for the purpose.

From the accounts of Olney Winsor (treasurer) in the Proprietors' Book of Reccord it appears that the following were the costs to the Proprietors:[22] Nineteen proprietors appear to have qualified as officers of the "Rhode Island Line" and so paid as granting fees 7£ each for the twenty-three rights they purchased; thirty-three proprietors purchased the remaining forty-one rights at 8£ 10s each — a total of 509£ 10s ($1747.54). In addition to his payment of this "granting fee," each proprietor was obligated to pay 10s 2d on each right as "expense of procuring the grant" and 1£ 10s as "locating advancement," making a total of 2£ 2d. Thus, the total payment on each right was 9£ 2d for the "Rhode Island Line" proprietors, and 10£ 2d for the others. In the summary account of Olney Winsor with the town of Lyndon, some entries imply his payment for lead, but the record is not clear.

There is no entry in the minutes of the meetings of the proprietors reporting any consideration as to the name of the town. In Rev. Jonathan Greenleaf's "Sketch of the Settlement of the Town of Lyndon in the County of Caledonia and State of Vermont" (1852) the statement is made (p. 7) that the town was named for Josias Lyndon Arnold, the son of Jonathan Arnold. This statement probably is not correct. This young man was born April 22, 1768, and was named for his father's friend who had been elected governor of Rhode Island a few days before the child's birth. Thus, when the charter was *granted*, Lyndon Arnold would have been twelve years of age, but he was some years younger when the petition for the charter was made, at which time the desired name for the town appears to have been stated. The great majority of the prospective proprietors were men active in Rhode Island politics. It seems much more likely, then, that the name was chosen to honor Josias Lyndon, who would have been a distinguished political associate of most of them and ex-governor of their home state.

Construction on the mill right was made urgent by the fact that it was necessary to travel some distance—to St. Johnsbury or Barnet—for some kinds of mill service. As early as 1793 Jonathan Arnold had built a mill on the Branch[23] in Little York, but it was not acceptable to the early settlers. They agreed to quit claim their title to the mill right to William Cahoon if he would build acceptable mills[24] at the Little Falls, thus giving him full title of ownership of this right. (For more information on this subject, see "Lyndon Corner," below.) There must have been keen rivalry between the Arnold and Cahoon mills, although the only evidence is an occasional word in the proprietors' quit claim deed. A few years later the Cahoons built a residence a short distance to the east of the mills.[25]

III

The Settlement of the Town

THE SURVEY OF THE TOWN and of the individual rights was made by James Whitelaw, surveyor-general of Vermont, a close friend of both Jonathan Arnold and Daniel Cahoon. The first notes[1] of his survey of the town are dated June 11, 1781, whereas the survey of the individual rights was postponed for seven years, beginning September 16, 1788, near the middle of the southern boundary of Right 3. This was the right drawn to Daniel Cahoon and sold[2] by him to his son, Daniel Jr., for 18£ in 1788. It was on this right that Daniel Cahoon, Jr., felled the first trees during the summer of 1788, and here built the first log house in the town.[3] According to local tradition, Cahoon was not alone in his first summer's activity, for John Davis, Nathan Hines, and Daniel Hall were clearing land nearby. None of them ventured to stay through the winter, but all returned early the following spring (1789). At that time Davis was accompanied by his wife, the first woman resident in town, and they are said to have lived in the Cahoon log house for a time.

The requirement set by the charter—that there be immediate use of every right—resulted in clearings being scattered throughout the township. Since the proprietors did not intend to become residents of the town and wished to protect their land from default of title, it became common practice to deed a portion of each right to someone who was willing to accept responsibility for fulfillment of the "settling duty." The amount of land so deeded varied from 40 to 100 acres. In some instances a man accepted responsibility for performing "settling duty"[4] on several rights, then transferred, perhaps sold, the land and responsibility to someone else. As most of the proprietors were residents of Rhode Island, so many of the first settlers were Rhode Islanders.

By 1790 it was possible for the first federal census[5] to count twelve heads of family and fifty-nine residents, listing the following:

	Free white males 16 + years of age including heads of family	Free white males under 16	Free white females including heads of family
Cahoon, Daniel [Jr.?]	5		2
Davis, Jonathan	1		1
Hacket, Stilson	1	2	2
Hall, Daniel	2	2	4
Hervey, Daniel [Harvey?]	2		
Hines, Nathan	4	1	1
McGaffey, Andrew	4	1	3
Reniff, Daniel	1	1	2
Robert, Charles	2		
Spooner, James	3	2	3
Sprague, Jonas	2	1	2
Thurston, Thomas	2		

It is interesting that though the 1800 census reported 94 heads of family and a total population of 542, only 5 of the 1790 heads of family remained in the town to be counted: Stilson Hackett, Andrew McGaffey, Daniel Reniff, Jonas Sprague, and Thomas Thurston.

Due to the requirement in the township grant that there must be cultivation of, or building on, every right within four years, multiple road and bridge building was forced on the town from the very beginning. As early as 1789 Jonathan Arnold petitioned[6] the General Assembly for the improvement of roads and communication facilities in the northern part of the state. Apparently this was not the beginning of his appeals. A letter from Arnold to James Whitelaw,[7] dated from Bennington on March 8, 1787, begins:

> The Surveyor General having appointed me to look out, cut & make a Road from the North westerly part of Littleton to the Northern or Northwestern corner of the Township of Lyndon . . . Also a Road from the West line of St. Johnsbury . . . and thence crossing the Passumpsick River at or as near as the Land will suit the best falls in s^d River . . . to the west line of Lunenburg. . . .

In 1790 the General Assembly passed a resolution ordering the surveyor-general to prepare a map of the state. To fulfill this resolution[8] the selectmen of the various towns were ordered

> to make out and send to the surveyor general before the first day of August next a proper plan of their several towns exhibiting the courses and lengths of the several streams with their names, public roads and where they lead to, the situation of meeting houses, mills and other public buildings, also the situation and names of ponds, mountains, and everything necessary to make a complete map. . . .

If compliance with this order was delayed until after March 1, 1794, there was a penalty. The map[9] for Lyndon, preserved in the office of the secretary of state (Montpelier), is signed by James Whitelaw, Esq., and by "Daniel Cahoon Town Clerk and Selectman of Lyndon." The maps received as a result of this order provided the material for what is known as the "Whitelaw Map of 1796," the first official map of the state. Since this Cahoon map is the earliest one found and it shows three roads[10] in the town, it is reasonable to assume that they were the first roads. They are identified as the East Road, the Middle Road, and the West Road, and all extend north to south. The terminals of all of them are the Arnold Mill on the South Branch of the Passumpsic and the Cahoon Mill in Billymead (Sutton). The East Road followed the height of land immediately east of the present Lyndonville.[11] The Middle Road also followed a height of land over Fletcher Hill[12] to the south end of Squabble Hollow, then turned due north over the western side of Pudding Hill to Billymead; this was later known as the County Road. The West Road followed another height of land over Diamond Hill, through Mosquito District down the hill into the north end of Squabble Hollow (past the present site of the schoolhouse) over Mathewson Hill into Billymead. Interstate 91 now crosses the latter two roads, so their identity will be largely obliterated for future generations. Interestingly enough, this first map shows no east-west road, nor does one appear on any map until the "county map" of the H. E. Walling Company in 1858.

A study of the town deed books shows that there was a rapid exchange of land titles in some parts of the town during its early years. The William Barton right (11), on which the village of Lyndon Corner developed, was divided into the smallest tracts and changed hands most frequently. This was followed in frequency of transference by the Rhodes right (30) on which the village of Lyndon Centre grew up. The rights to which Jonathan Arnold had title were also sold often. The regions which have come to be known as Bemis Hill (rights 42 and 50), Squabble Hollow (45), East Lyndon (13), Mt. Hunger (51), and Pudding Hill (44) changed hands rapidly, and from the deeds one might gather that these were the more heavily populated portions of the town during its first fifty years of existence. In some instances one is tempted to infer that the prime interest in land was to remove the lumber rather than to clear it with the intent of cultivation or of building a home. Land acquisition almost invariably was accomplished through small down payments plus mortgages secured by several small notes, often $25 or $50 denomination. In many instances, title to the land was sold before the mortgage had been liquidated, so that the new owner assumed completion of that obligation. Ownership of these mortgages and notes was reassigned frequently to new holders, sometimes in fulfillment of business obligations or as security for new purchases of land. They seem to have been used much like paper money of a later time.

Especially during the early years of the town, vendues of land for taxes, either for special levies or for the regular annual assessment, were a common procedure. The sale of a whole right (320 acres) for $5 or $6 seems unbelieveable, but apparently that was the way farms were enlarged or added investments made.

The first child born in town was Lyndon Hines, son of Nathan Hines, on February 9, 1791; in October of the same year Benjamin Parker Cahoon arrived, the son of Daniel Cahoon, Jr., and his wife, Judith. The first girl to come was Lydia Wilder on September 14, 1792, daughter of Zebina Wilder. The first death in town was that of Daniel Cahoon, Jr., on June 11, 1793; several other deaths soon followed, including that of Elder Hines, a suicide. The first marriage in town was that of Jeremiah Washburn and Hannah Orcutt from Billymead on June 26, 1794, performed by Daniel Cahoon, Sr., justice of the peace. The first grand list for taxation in the town was 359 covering "30 polls (28 being taxed), 22 oxen, 22 cows, 6 three-year-olds, 7 two-year-olds, 2 yearlings, and 11 horses."

During the first century of the occupation of the town of Lyndon, the life of the citizens was related directly or indirectly to some aspect of agriculture. At first life was dominated by the struggle for mere existence: clearing land, erecting shelter for man and beast, plus planting and harvesting food for their survival. The clearing of the heavily forested land provided logs—hand-hewn at first—for the construction of homes and barns. After sawmills were erected, logs were made into planks; then came boards, and buildings were framed. According to Jonathan Greenleaf, Daniel Cahoon, Jr., built the first framed barn in 1789, and Nathaniel Jenks raised the first framed house in 1795. In clearing the land for cultivation, many more trees were cut than could be used for houses and barns. However, if burned, potash and pearlash were created[13], and these constituted, for many years, the major materials to be exchanged for commodities unavailable from home industry. A large number of potash pits must have existed. This writer has been able to establish, with a fair degree of certainty, the location of only two: one was in the south end of the ravine on the west side of Main Street in Lyndon Corner, and one seems to have been on the west side of the County Road in Lyndon Center opposite the Bemis store—which must have placed it near the Parade Ground and not far south of the Meeting House.

Early in the 19th century surplus food stuffs were added to the potash and pearlash being freighted to Boston or Portland: butter, cheese, and pork were the major products, and all traveled well. Locomotion at first was furnished by oxen,[14] but by the early 1800s there were ample horses for the four-, six-, and eight-horse teams which moved these loads, so "freighting" became a well-established industry. Winter seems to have been the best time for this business. Both men and beasts were less needed in work on the land, winter vehicles were more adaptable, and the commodities of trade were less likely to spoil on the way. The usual charge was 65¢ to 75¢ per hundredweight. It was common for several drivers to go at the same time, often making a caravan a mile or more in length. The return load included salt, fish, molasses, tobacco, commodities for store trade, or luxuries on some private family order. Some freighters are said to have made 50 to 100 trips per winter. Livestock, especially cattle, sheep, and sometimes turkeys, were driven to market in Brighton or Boston once or twice a year; these "drives" were not wholly popular because the livestock lost so much weight on the way.

In the same era that "freighting" became a profitable industry, passenger travel via stagecoach became common. The Tavern (Hotel Lyndon)[15] — built in 1807 by Capt. Alfred Fletcher for John Johnson — became increasingly popular as an overnight stop on the way between Boston and Montreal.

Potatoes appear to have yielded a most generous return to the Lyndon farmers. Plantings yielded 300 to 400 bushels per acre, and potatoes sold for a shilling to a quarter per bushel. Many were shipped[16] to Boston and Portland. Many starch factories are also claimed to have flourished, and it has been said that wherever there was a starch factory[17] there was also a distillery. The Knapp place on Hawkins Brook and the Whipple establishment[18] on Whipple Brook have been cited most frequently as distillery locations, but no solid evidence exists to support the suspicion. Also mentioned has been Kathan's distillery, located near the present junction of South Wheelock Road and the road to Vail Hill.

Brick kilns were established early on in several places in the town. At least two existed in the Red Village area, one being on the flat north of the Cahoon house, and at least two more were located in Squabble Hollow. As late as 1870, T. A. Ceyr from St. Johnsbury leased a piece of land in Bundyville for five years on which to construct a brickyard. The schoolhouse building committee was responsible for this action; brick was needed for the new schoolhouse.

Thompson's Gazetteer, published in 1842, provides this statement on the prosperity of the town of Lyndon:

> Population 1753; cattle 3359; horses 546; sheep 8766; swine 1931; bushels of wheat 3370; barley 655; oats 35,376; rye 155; buckwheat 3350; Indian corn 7277; potatoes 113,934; hay, tons 6115; pounds maple sugar 68,364; wood 15,850.

?◐

Lyndon Corner

ABOUT 1792 MRS. CYNTHIA JENKS, widow of Jonathan Jenks,[19] and her two sons, Nehemiah and Brown, came to the town. She purchased land on the William Barton right (11), made a clearing, and built a log cabin a short distance northeast of the present-day junction of Main, Chapel, and York streets.[20] She died of "lockjaw," or tetanus, on August 12, 1794. Her sons soon left town, but the old log house remained for many years as common town property, being frequently characterized as "the door of the town" because so many of its settlers lived there for a short time before establishing the site for their permanent residence. Tradition has it that Rev. Abner Jones taught Lyndon's first school in this log house.

The town selectmen — Abel Carpenter, Isaiah Fisk, and Alpheus Houghton — established the limits and bounds of the village (Lyndon Corner) as the result of a petition made on January 15, 1820, by James Knapp, Daniel Kathan, Daniel Bowker, Warren Parker, Merrill Pillsbury, George A. Miller, Levi Cushing, Benjamin Ellis, Ephraim Chamberlin, Samuel Willard, Asahel Hubbard, Hubbard Field, and Richard Stone. ". . . it containing no more than ten dwelling houses according to a late act of the General Assembly," these bounds were set:[21]

> Beginning in the road 20 rods northwest of Gaius Peck's house, thence in a straight line easterly to the guide post near the Buckling barn, so-called, thence southerly in a straight line to the southeast corner of lot no. 11, thence on the south line of said lot westerly so far as that a line drawn due north and south will strike the bars in the bend of the road westerly of the schoolhouse in said village, thence in a straight line to the 1st mentioned bounds.

Businesses developed rapidly near the Tavern, and as a result Lyndon Corner became the real metropolis of the 19th-century town of Lyndon and the marketplace of the neighboring towns. It may have reached the peak of its prosperity in 1874, when Editor Chase reported in the *Vermont Union* that it had

> . . . three wideawake dry goods stores, two millinery establishments, the most extensive tin and hardware establishment in the county, two large wagon factories, shoe making shops, saddlers shops, two law shops, printing office, bank, hotel, a carding mill, a big lumber-mill and gristmill, two carpenter and joiner shops, meat market, a tailoring establishment, Grange, drug store, three blacksmith shops, a chair shop, two doctors, a jeweller, two churches and a whaling big school house.

Perhaps the first sawmill in Lyndon was built by the Arnolds near the north side of the present bridge[22] at the west end of York Street (Lyndon Corner). Their mills did not receive popular approval, according to a resolution adopted at the town meeting in 1796. Under the provisions of this same resolution,

> . . . if William Cahoon will go on and build a good gristmill and Sawmill on the Mill Right at the place called the Little Falls and Compleat the Same as soon as he conveneantly can, to the Acceptance of the Inhabitants there we will Assign to him the s^d William Cahoon all our Right and Title in and unto the s^d Mill Right by virtue of Being Proprietors and Landholders in s^d Town which is in the Proportion of on Seventieth Part of the land we hold in s^d Town and will confirm the same to him the s^d William his Heirs & Assigns by Deed of quit claim and use our Endeavor to get the other Proprietors to do the same.

At the 1797 town meeting it was voted to accept the mills built by William Cahoon at the Little Falls as full compensation for the mill right,[23] and quit claim deeds were soon drawn.

Though the Arnold Mills were not deemed worthy of receiving the mill right, their location proved desirable for many uses for more than 150 years. Ephraim Chamberlin built a gristmill here before 1817 and later added a sawmill; both were a part of his estate in the latter part of the 1830s. His son, Myron, continued to run the mills for a time, and built a new gristmill about 1840. In 1868 the *Union* reported

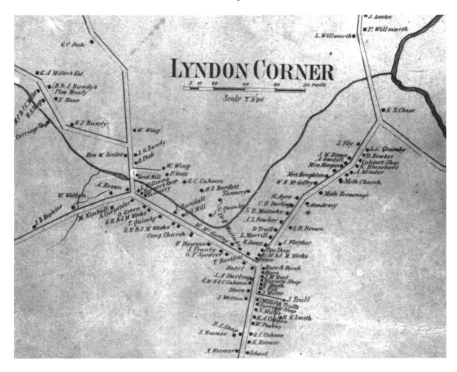

Lyndon Corner (*Vermont Historical Society*)

that "L. Soper who has been renovating feather beds in St. Johnsbury has rented the Chamberlin gristmill and will open business there next week. . . ." In 1870 Levi Cole advertised the mills for sale at auction. John Prescott of St. Johnsbury bought them for $900 and installed machinery to manufacture sash, doors, blinds, etc., plus a blacksmith shop. Prescott had learned his blacksmith's trade from Bradbury Richardson (one of the ablest blacksmiths ever in Lyndon), and he had been thirty-eight years in J. H. Paddock's mill at St. Johnsbury, so he was well equipped to succeed. In 1872 he advertised the mills for sale. By the next year Reuben Goodell was using part of the building as a cabinet shop, and A. Ballou had established a chair factory and was making basket-bottom chairs in another section of the building.

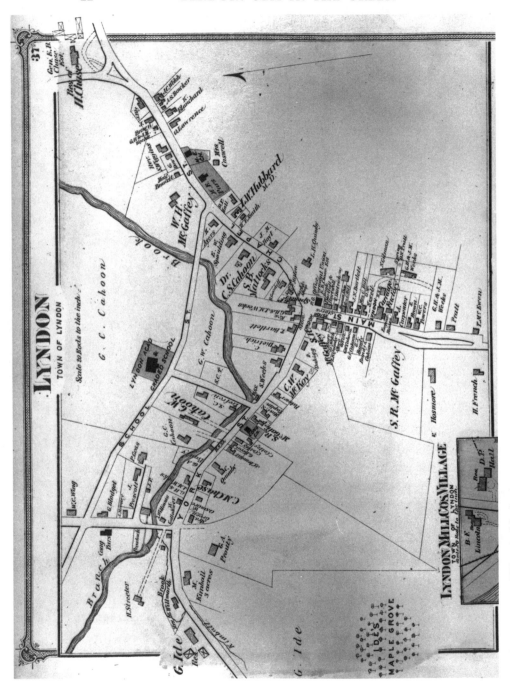

Lyndon (*Vermont Historical Society*)

In 1874 the Chamberlin sawmill was taken down "after some sixty years" of service. In the mid-1870s John Weeks of Danville used the place as a stone shed. The property was acquired in 1881 by D. N. Trull from E. A. Ward. It changed hands again in 1892, when Henry Ketteridge bought it and built a sawmill. J. G. Hadley leased the mill in 1895 and fitted it up as a dressing mill in order to meet the heavy demand for house finish caused by the new construction in Lyndonville that followed the 1894 fire. Daniel Paris, who purchased the property in 1900, constructed a new dam and penstock and continued furnishing house finish for the community. From 1905 to 1937 Harold Whitcomb owned the site. He remodeled the mill property and installed electricity in place of the waterpower; when he went to California he sold to Francis Nadeau, who owned the site until 1952. He was succeeded by Carlton Pearce, who sold to the Chester brothers. They had the remaining mill burned in 1962, feeling that it had become a public danger.

Through the many changes of ownership the name of Chamberlin has clung to this site, and the mills have been the Chamberlin Mills. The bridge nearby has always been known as the Chamberlin Bridge, except for part of the time that Whitcomb owned the mill. The old schoolhouse on the rise of ground south of the bridge was the Chamberlin School.[24] The Chamberlin residence at the corner of the road to South Wheelock has never completely lost its kinship to the family.

The Cahoon Mills were constructed at the Little Falls in the 1790s and run for a time by John Cahoon. He was followed by Gen. Wm Cahoon, who died in 1833. John Gates and his son Ezra were the millers for some years, followed in succession by Joel Harvey, John Knapp, John Hopkins, and Mr. Potter. About 1863 D. P. Hall invested some $25,000 in the property, rebuilt the dam, the gristmill, and the sawmill, and built two or three tenement houses. About the same time he purchased 4000 acres of timberland in East Haven, Newark, and Burke from which he secured logs.

In 1865 W. P. Fairbanks of St. Johnsbury acquired a half interest in the gristmill. Orren Chase and S. W. Russell were the millers until nearly 1880. The capacity of the mill was 3000 barrels of flour per year plus the custom work, which was heavy. The *Vermont Union* reported a single month's grinding for customers in 1877 as 4053 bushels of locally grown grain.

W. H. Goodrich bought an interest in the lumber business with Hall. The mill at East Burke was built, the two mills having a capacity of 2.5 million feet a year; half of this was cut at each mill. In 1866 B. F. Lincoln bought out Goodrich and a half interest in Hall's 4000 acres of timberland, the company becoming the lumber business. In August 1867 the lumber business was incorporated as the Lyndon Mill. Corp. with D. H. Hall, B. F. Lincoln, Geo. Ide, and S. S. Thompson as equal owners in the $100,000 capital stock of the gristmill and sawmill company. They gained possession of some 10,000 acres of timberland, located in East Haven, Burke, Newark, Victory, and Kirby in places convenient to the Passumpsic River. In 1872 they built the stave mill in Mt. Hunger,[25] "the best mill around," with a capacity of 20,000 feet a day making a total capacity of 7 million feet a year in the three mills. They also bought the Myron Smith Mill in East Haven.

An item in the *Vermont Union* of May 22, 1874, gives a hint of the activity of the company:

> The biggest drive of logs ever made on the Passumpsic River was made last week by D. P. Hall and a gang of about 25 hands. About 2,000,000 logs were in different places in Newark and East Haven rolled into the river, 5,000,000 were driven from Newark and East Haven to East Burke where George Ide with about 10 hands drove 3,000,000 to the New Mill in the north side of Lyndon, 1,500,000 passed the slide there and were driven to the mills near Lyndon.

The Lyndon Mill. Corp. was dissolved in 1883 and the property divided between the partners: Geo. Ide took the gristmill, the two tenement houses, and his balance in East Haven timberland, the company having at that time 7000 acres of virgin forest. D. P. Hall took the Lyndon sawmill and boarding house, the East Burke and East Haven mills, and 3000 acres of land, after buying 4000 more acres of land tributary to his mill. B. F. Lincoln took the Mt. Hunger mill, 3200 acres of land partly cut in Burke, Kirby, and Victory, and $10,000 in cash from Hall, who had taken that much more than his fourth of the property. Thompson took his quarter of the prop-

Lyndon Mill Company (*Vermont Historical Society*)

erty in Victory land. After the dissolution of the company, Hall and Lincoln became increasingly involved in their investments in the Michigan forests. Ide continued the gristmill activity, and Hall, with C. P. Chase as partner, continued the lumber business at Cahoon Falls until 1885.

In May 1892 disaster struck the Hall's Mills community when fire destroyed a four-tenement house belonging to the Hall estate and a dwelling house belonging to Ide. In 1898 fire struck again, this time destroying Don Gray's shingle mill at the Falls.

In 1900 the Hall and Lincoln sawmill was sold by the executors of the Hall estate to H. O. Cushman of Boston. The sale included half the water rights, the other half belonging to the gristmill property. Cushman remodeled the mill, converting it to the manufacture of leatherboard. When opened for business, it had the capacity of 1½ tons of stock per day.

In February 1905, George Ide sold his gristmill to E. T. and H. K. Ide of St. Johnsbury, who immediately began repairs on the property, extending the side track, installing a power elevator for unloading grain, and otherwise equipping themselves to serve the needs of local farmers with both grinding and store facilities. These repairs were nearly finished in May when fire destroyed both the gristmill and the leatherboard factory along with three frieght cars on the siding nearby and a considerable amount of stock in both mill and factory.

Perhaps the industry that brought the greatest distinction to Lyndon was the making of wagons and sleighs. In 1818 Anson Miller came from Dummerston, Vt., and built a wagon shop at the north end of the Chamberlin bridge, filling all the space between the bridge and the Chamberlin sawmill. In 1828 he moved to Cahoon Falls, where he built a new shop. Over the next ten years he was joined by his brother William and by his and William's sons. In 1838 fire destroyed the shop, tools, stock—everything. Courageously they reestablished the business. In 1842 Anson left the Cahoon Falls shop, moved back to the Corner, and started business in Bundyville in the shop abandoned by Bundy Plow Works Corporation. Here he built a home and carried on business until his death in 1855 at the age of sixty-five. His sons Myron and Charles carried on the business for a time. Then Myron went to Brattleboro, but Charles continued for several years to perform both repair work and new construction. William and his sons John D. and Norman remained at Cahoon Falls until 1848, when under the leadership of John D. they moved to the Corner and built a large house on Main Street. The north half was used as a residence for the family and the south half as a carriage shop.

The major difference between the Millers' "Lyndon Buggie" and the wagons commonly used was in weight; the "Lyndon Buggie" weighed 175 to 275 pounds, as opposed to 400 pounds or more, for the competition. The Millers' vehicles were soundly built. All parts were made by hand from raw materials. They used elm for hubs, and ash, maple, and basswood for fellies (wheel rims), gearing, and boxes; the company blacksmiths made all the braces, nuts and bolts, and bars and rods. Rather than merely putting together various parts obtained from elsewhere, they completely manufactured the vehicle from start to finish.

In 1851 a new carriage shop was built and machinery installed, with a twenty-horsepower steam engine taking the place of the family horse traveling around a post. A brick blacksmith shop with a half dozen forges was built for them by Carl Blanchard, a St. Johnsbury brick mason. In the beginning the Millers' work was largely repair, but soon they were creating vehicles on order. At the height of their prosperity they turned out 200 new buggies a year and an undetermined number of sleighs, while continuing their repair work. The work force comprised some 15 to 25 employees.

Each spring their salesmen started out with a number of buggies fastened together, and they did not return until the last one had been sold. An especially healthy market for Lyndon buggies existed in Georgia. After 1860 this southern trade decreased and collections stopped, however; this meant severe losses and, finally, failure. Miller soon moved to St. Johnsbury, where with the assistance of his father, brother Norman, and son Sidney, he built up a prosperous carriage manufacturing business under the name of Miller and Ryan.

After the failure of the John D. Miller business in Lyndon, the building was purchased by D. N. Trull and his brother-in-law, S. S. Mattocks. The business continued for about thirty years under various company names: Trull and Miller; John Darling; Darling, Hartwell, and Newton; Mattocks and Hartwell; Trull and Mattocks.

The highest prices prevailed from 1862 to 1873, when the open buggy easily brought $125 and the top buggy $175. Some years most of the buggies were sold before they were completed, but after 1873 this business, like most others, met with reverses.

On the South Wheelock road just beyond the Chamberlin Mills, the Bundy Foundry and Plow Shop did a lively business for several years, some of the time producing materials used in carriage construction. At the western edge of Bundyville in the early 1870's Guild, Drown and Company established a sleigh construction shop, but the partnership soon dissolved. However, the waterpower at this point continued in use for a mill until the flood of 1927 created damage too severe to repair. During many of these years Horace Guild and his son, Arthur, provided finish lumber for much of the house construction done in this and neighboring towns.

Next to the building of wagons and sleighs, the industry most prominent in early Lyndon was that of making tinware; this developed very rapidly after about 1836. Before that time utensils of wood, iron, and pewter provided for the needs of pioneers. The first tinsmith probably was Elisha Peck, followed by Jehial Applebee and then by Applebee's son, Cephas. The first tin shop, established soon after 1840 by John H. Skinner and Austin Foss, was in business for about 10 years.

About that time Cephas Applebee joined with L. K. Quimby in a new business venture. Soon they expanded their tinware production to include stoves, kitchenware, and farming tools, and the addition of one peddler laid the foundation for a barter business. Meanwhile, Erastaus Cobleigh joined the firm. By 1860, twenty peddlers in one-, two-, or even four-horse carts worked out of the store. They accepted hides, wool, rags, scrap iron, and junk in exchange for the new tin or notions in their carts. Their routes extended throughout rural northern Vermont and New Hampshire. Sometimes two or three weeks travel time would be needed to dispose of a load of new tinware valued at some $200 or $300. Wholly inexperienced at the start, the young cart drivers would have acquired much business savvy after two or three years of such trading. The pay was usually $20 to $40 per month.

B. F. Lincoln bought into the firm, permitting Quimby to favor his poor health, and for a few years the firm became Lincoln and Cobleigh. Then Lincoln sold half interest to his brother-in-law Julius C. Eaton, who had begun work for him in 1860. Ten years later Alvah Harvey came into the business when Quimby's health further declined, but this combination lasted only a short time, and the firm's name reverted to Quimby and Eaton.

In the late 1870s the company became involved in the maple sugar trade, buying and selling 100,000 to 500,000 pounds in a year.

In 1884 Quimby sold to his partner and retired permanently. The next year Haddon W. Lyster[26] joined Eaton, the firm becoming J. C. Eaton and Company. Under this name the firm handled a variety of commodities. For instance, in the summer and fall of 1875 the company bought and sold 90,000 pounds of dried raspberries, and in 1879 it paid 6¢ per pound for maple syrup (eleven pounds equal one gallon). The firm also became heavily involved in producing equipment for maple sugaring. In 1889 eight workmen were employed solely in making 40,000 sap spouts; in 1898 this work force had increased to thirteen men who worked day and night to turn out 40,000 cans and 10,000 pails before March. In 1904 a crew of twenty men made 100,000 sugar and syrup cans.

In the mid-1880s Homer C. Wilson and his father-in-law, B. F. Lincoln, opened a hardware store in the Nichols Block, Lyndonville. A couple of years later Eaton and Company bought them out and opened a branch of their Lyndon Store on the site.[27]

Another industry that extended over a period of many years was that of constructing basket-bottom chairs,[28] a business engaged in by three generations of the Powers family. The first to do so was Benjamin W. Powers, the husband of Lydia Wilder, the first white woman to be born (September 14, 1792) in the town of Lyndon, the daughter of Zebina Wilder. In 1814 Benjamin and Lydia built a small plank house; across the road on the bank of Hawkins Brook, Benjamin built his shop. After Benjamin's death (1866, age 78), his son Benjamin Franklin, carried on the family farm and chairmaking trade until his death (1897). The third generation involved was Henry G., Benjamin Franklin's son. He was not only a chairmaker but also a carpenter, a good butcher, and a mechanic. His death in 1901 was the result of a barn-raising accident in Concord.

The secret of the craftsmanship of the Powers chairs lay in the use of native green and dry woods. The wood to be used for the rounds and slats was dried; the wood for the posts, usually black cherry, was saturated with water. Characteristics of the Powers chairs were the bowed ash armrests, the pinched feet, and the back posts that were straight down to the seat but bent back slightly below the seat. A wooden mold filled with boiling water was used to accomplish the bending. Enough posts to make three or four chairs were placed in this rectangular tank, and a centered wooden screw did the bending. Slats were formed in a similar fashion. Finally, a groove was cut in the end of a dry rung to make a "shoulder," and the rung was driven into the wet post—creating a joint that, when dry, could not be separated except by breaking the post. By the same method the dry slats were driven into the wet posts, and square pegs were driven into the round holes bored through the slat end of the post.

The basket-bottom woven seats were made of brown and white ash. The logs were quartered and left soaking in "recking water." Later they were cut in one-inch strips, then hammered on a piece of railroad iron until the strips split; loose ends were shaved off, and the twelve-foot lengths were then ready to be woven, often in ingenious patterns. Before the chairs were stained or varnished the maker's name was stenciled on the back, usually on the middle slat. There were slight differences in the chairs made by the three generations. All the chairs are real antique treasures, and most have been carried out of the state by "collectors."

In the summer of 1876 the Wilder brothers (Charles T. and Herbert A.), paper manufacturers in Massachusetts, purchased the water privilege of the Great Falls plus seventy acres of adjoining land.[29] They announced plans to erect a paper pulp mill and eventually to install machinery for the manufacture of print paper. It was expected that the venture would require an investment of $50,000 and employ thirty to fifty workmen. The material to be used would be spruce, which the brothers considered to contain superior fiber for paper. The foundations of the mill were laid in October 1870 under the supervision of John Clement, a local expert in such work. The building was to be 40 x 80 feet and three stories high. Construction progressed successfully, and on February 23 the first sheet of pulp was made. The original capacity of the mill was six to eight tons of pulp per day.

Early in March 1877 the Wilders broke ground for a boarding house[30] 30 x 40 feet, located on a knoll west of the railroad track overlooking the highway on the west and the mill to the east. In the same month the mill was operating day and night, and in the last week of the month shipped out its first carload of paper pulp.

In September 1879 the *Union* reported that Wilder's four new houses at the mill were in the hands of the painter, G. S. Blodgett. Mother Nature was soon playing evil tricks, for in the fall of 1880 the water was so low that only about half the men and machines could work. By the end of December 1880, however, the mill was

John Chase and a Powers Chair (*Bessie Harris Brown*)

back on full time (night and day) and producing at the rate of 2 million feet of spruce logs per day, most of which came from Canada. By 1889 the Wilder Mill was shut down "for repairs"; for the next five years there were alternating rumors that the mill would and would not be reopened. Finally, in 1894, the machinery was removed, and five years later the 60-foot chimney was purchased and dropped for its used bricks at about $1 per thousand. In the fall of 1895 citizens of Lyndonville leased the Wilder privilege and thus began the Lyndonville Electric Plant.

The first lawyer in Lyndon was Nathaniel Goodhue, who came from Windham County in 1804 and remained for a few years. His brother S. B. Goodhue took his place and stayed until 1811, when Isaac Fletcher arrived and began his tenure as the only lawyer in town. During that time he developed an especially well-equipped office.

For fully fifty years, at least two young men were always "reading law" in the village. At first, it was in Fletcher's office; after his death (1835) it was with George Cahoon and Thomas Bartlett. Some of these fledgling lawyers returned to their home states to practice, and some stayed in town. Among the latter were George Cahoon, Thomas Bartlett, Edward A. Cahoon, William O. Fuller, Henry S. Bartlett, George W. Cahoon, and E. H. Hoffman—all served the community long and ably.

Early in the history of the town of Lyndon, stonecutting was in demand. According to Editor Charles Chase, among the best stonecutters in the state were John Winter and his son Charles E., G. P. Spencer and his two sons Frank and Fred, and A. S. Jones. Chase said that the father of the stonecutting business in Lyndon was John Winter, who came to town in 1856 from Lowell, Mass. He opened a shop under the name of Winter and Wheeler, but sold the business to S. C. Otis in 1858 and returned to Lowell. Otis continued in business alone for a couple of years before G. P. Spencer bought in. During the next twenty-five to thirty years Spencer and his sons maintained the trade in various locations, finally moving the business to their home on the back road between Lyndon Corner and Lyndon Center.

After an absence of some years A. S. Jones returned to Lyndon from Massachusetts and opened a stone shed in South Wheelock, where he worked alone for a time before taking Elijah Ward into the company. In 1883 Charles Winter bought out Jones and Ward. For a few years about 1900 Arthur Wiggin had a stone shed near the foot of Pudding Hill on the Wheelock road.

Information about the industry has been limited. Its period of prosperity appears to have been in the last half of the 19th century. During this time many monuments were placed in the cemetery; these are a lasting tribute to the skill of the local craftsmen. Unfortunately, their creators placed no mark of identification on the monuments.

The hides of the early town were never sent away for processing. The local tannery converted them into leather, and the village saddlers and shoemakers made them into harnesses, saddles, boots, and shoes. Probably the first tannery was that built in Little York by William Houghton about 1810. It was purchased by Jonathan Weeks about 1814, leased to his brother, Meyer, who was succeeded by Simeon Foster. The tannery, located near the east end of York Street, was equipped with forty vats plus the needed machinery. Its patronage was local, receiving hides from the surrounding butchers and farmers, buying some, tanning others to shares, supplying local shoemakers with stock. Even as late as the mid-nineteenth century many farmers kept leather in their homes to furnish stock for the itinerant shoemaker who travelled with bench and kit from house to house remaining long enough to make shoes and needed repairs for all the family. Often times, leather and measurements were left at the shoemaker's shop and he was paid only for his work in making the boots and shoes for the family. Their harnesses and saddles were made from their own leather in much the same way. In 1872 these vats were drained and filled with dirt.

There was another shorter lived tannery, located near the base of Prospect Hill, built by Squire Joseph Ingalls. This ceased to exist about 1830–1840. In writing of it Editor Charles Chase characterized it as "being headquarters for boys in the wood-chuck business because it paid six cents apiece for the hides". About 1840 Charles Ingalls, son of Joseph, built a tannery on the branch back of the family homestead (obliterated for Interstate #91), and still later built another on the southern edge of his farm on the road to Lyndon Center.

About twenty-five years before his death in 1836, Jonathan Weeks maintained his shoeshop at the south end of the tannery in which he employed three to six "crispins" or apprentice shoemakers. In that day and time all foot gear was made to measure. Other able shoemakers of this era were John W. and Albert Brown, William Bancroft, Kingsley Sawtelle, Eli Dunklee, Horace Randall, Giles Bradshaw, John Cassidy.

Also in Little York using the water power of the South Branch were a carding mill, a fulling mill, a bark mill, a saddler's shop, and an oil mill. There were at least two blacksmith shops in Lyndon Corner, and a great many in other parts of the town. Unfortunately, records of these various establishments have been completely illusive, so all we can say is that they existed for some years and carried on a thriving business.

In 1908 Elizabeth Chase and Gertrude Newton became active in directing the Home Garden Club work in cooperation with the Department of Agriculture. They worked with the boys and girls of town stimulating their interest in raising vegetables, fruits, and animals and in performing various home duties, including sewing. The Garden classes were given the use of a sugarplace, so Mrs. Chase's kitchen was used for making sugarcakes and simple maple candies. From this simple beginning developed the Elizabeth Chase Maple Candies, which were sold widely in the United States. For seventeen years they were annually displayed at the Boston Flower Show and also for many years at the New York and Chicago flower shows. In 1947 the business was sold to Carl Lyster, who reestablished it near the town line of St. Johnsbury and Lyndon and enlarged it to include a gift shop.

ॐ

Lyndon Center

LYNDON CENTER (or Lyndon Centre, as it was originally spelled) developed on Right 30, drawn to William Rhodes; nearly half (136 acres) of the right lay east of the Passumpsic River. The first entry in the Town Land Records concerning this right is the deed (September 17, 1794) conveying forty acres to William Fisher as compensation for performing the "settling duty." The second entry is a deed transferring 336 acres[31] from William Rhodes to Job Sheldon. In the early years of the town, more deeds concerning this right are recorded than of any other except the William Barton right (11) on which Lyndon Corner developed, and which was divided into the smallest tract in the town.

At a special town meeting on December 23, 1800, a committee was elected to seek a piece of land as near the center of the town as possible on which to build a meetinghouse. On May 31, 1801, Job Sheldon deeded six acres on Right 30 to the selectmen; part of the tract was to be used for the meetinghouse, part for a burial ground, and part for a parade ground. Though the building was not finished, the freeman's meeting of 1809 was held there.

Among the many entries relating to this right, it is not until 1812 that one mentions a building—the store of Josiah and Samuel Marsh.[32] The first mention of a dwelling house is one on the land sold by Philip Goss in 1815. It seems unlikely that no houses or other buildings had been constructed before this time.

The road from Lyndon Corner to Burke must have been opened early, as it is mentioned in some of the earliest deeds as a boundary. In the early years of Lyndon Centre there was a well-established tradition that the "highway from Lyndon Corner to Burke" had turned east off the Middle Road through the (then) Ingalls sugarplace, circled Harris Hill on its southeast side, and continued down the steep hill at the south end of the village's Main Street. This route was said to have been superceded by the construction of the locally known "back road to the Corner" and the road to Joel Fletcher's farm from the center of the village. In support of this tradition, it is positive that as late as the early 1900s a road could be clearly discerned in this location. Also, south and west of the sugarplace were cellar holes, apple trees, rose bushes, tansy and lily beds—all evidences of earlier homes. These facts may imply that the Middle Road was originally much farther east than it has been in recent years.

A "one-half acre plus 32 rods" tract in Lyndon Centre on the east side of this Lyndon-to-Burke highway changed hands many times, and frequently the deed mentions a store. This tract appears to have

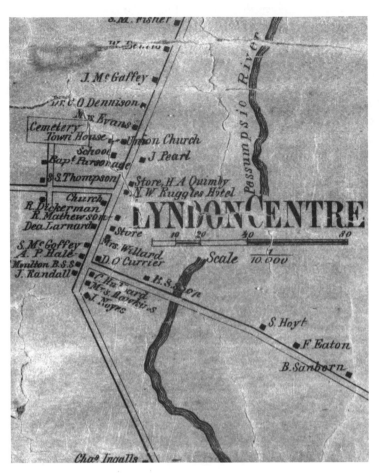

Lyndon Centre (*Vermont Historical Society*)

been near the spot occupied by the 20th-century store and post office.

Few business establishments[33] developed in early Lyndon Centre: two or three blacksmith shops, a combination saddler's shop and shoe shop, a couple of stores, and one or two taverns. On March 5, 1829, a post office was established at Lyndon Center with Elias Bemis, jr., as postmaster. On April 4, 1893, the post office department changed the spelling of the name to "Lyndon Center." No explanation or further information about this action has been available.

In 1835 selectmen Welcome Bemis, Paul Houghton, and Joseph Ingalls stated the bounds of the village as follows:

We, the Selectmen of Lyndon:

Agreeably to a petition of seven of the freeholders, inhabitants of said Town of Lyndon, do establish and lay out Village of Lyndon Centre (so-called) agreeable to an act of the Legislature of the State of Vermont, passed November 11, 1819, to restrain certain animals from running at large in said Village, as named and described in said act—bounded and described as follows, viz.—beginning at the store now owned and occupied by Nehemiah Fletcher, meaning to extend so far as the south end of said Fletcher's house, and from the aforesaid Store northerly on the road leading to Sutton and Burke so far as to enclose the house and out buildings owned and now occupied by David Whipple, and from said Store easterly on the road leading to Daniel Emery's so far as to enclose and take in the house and out buildings owned and now occupied by Benjamin Sanborn, & from said Store westerly on the road leading by Joel Fletcher's to the woods, where the 1st tree now stands on the road leading from the said Store, and to extend on the road from the said Store to Wheelock so far as to enclose and take in the house and out buildings now owned and occupied by Jedediah Skinner.

Lyndon, September 1, 1835   Welcome Bemiss
Paul Houghton
Joseph Ingalls
Selectmen[34]

The Baptist Church was first built about 1849 near the highway between Lyndon Corner and Burke. In the early 1870s it was moved to its present location and remodeled to its present form. The Baptist parsonage was first located[35] west of the parade ground, but was moved in 1870 when the land on which it stood was needed as part of the construction site for the Lyndon Literary and Biblical Institution.

In the late 1840s the Universalist Society built a chapel[36] a few feet north and east of the meetinghouse owned by the town. This was a famous landmark for many years because of the ornament—the "Angel Gabriel"—on top of its tower. This was such an outstanding piece of carving that people traveled long distances to see it; it was also the subject of repeated theft attempts, one of which was finally successful on the night of July 3, 1883.[37]

When the building ceased to be used for religious purposes is not

Universalist Church as training and livery stable, Lyndon Center
(*Mrs. Milton Kerr*)

known. It was neglected for some years, then sold to Edwin Fisher in 1887 and by him to A. W. Brockway, who used it as a paint shop before selling it in 1895 to the Lyndon Building Company. It was immediately remodeled into John Moulton's Training Stable, where for nearly ten years, the finest of Lyndon's horseflesh received its education.[38] Under two successive owners (Enos Phillips and J. A. McDowell) it was a livery stable before becoming the barn of a private residence. For a few years W. D. Hill used it as a workshop before fire destroyed it in 1938.

The Walling map of 1858 shows the village schoolhouse on the County Road, but south of the meetinghouse. However, there is good reason to believe a new schoolhouse was built north of the meetinghouse about 1857. One located there was used until 1900, when a new building[39] was erected between Sanborn Hall and the Baptist Church at a cost of $1441.08. This building has been enlarged, moved, and enlarged again as well as completely remodeled over the years, so that now it retains little that is recognizable from the first structure.

The existence and prosperity of the Free Baptist Church in Lyndon Centre was a major factor in the establishment of the Lyndon Literary and Biblical Institution here in 1867. This in turn has been important in preserving the residential character of the community.

ào

East Lyndon

LITTLE INFORMATION IS AVAILABLE on East Lyndon. The community of about eighty people appears to have developed early in the second half of the 19th century. Their major bonds seem to have been nearness of residence and common interests and activities. They developed a school as District 8 (1856) and later as District 4. John Smith, S. L. Parks, and Samuel Russell formed the committee to build their school, which was accomplished at a cost of about $700.

A Methodist church building, to accommodate about 200 people, was constructed at a cost of $1600; the building committee comprised F. B. Newton, N. L. Parker, and H. L. Wetherbee. The church was dedicated on July 15, 1877, at the morning service. Rev. W. R. Puffer gave the sermon, using Luke 24:46, 47 as a text; the afternoon sermon by Rev. W. J. Johnson used Isaiah 46:13. Most of the costs of building had been subscribed, but the remaining $400 was contributed before the end of the day of dedication, so the church began its work free from debt. During the succeeding years the pastoral leadership in the East Lyndon church experienced varied and changing associations with the Methodist churches in St. Johnsbury Center, Lyndon Corner, and Lyndonville. In its later years the church building was used as a community center. Soon after the union of the Methodist churches in town the contents of the East Lyndon church were sold at auction.

Family names in East Lyndon have changed through the years.

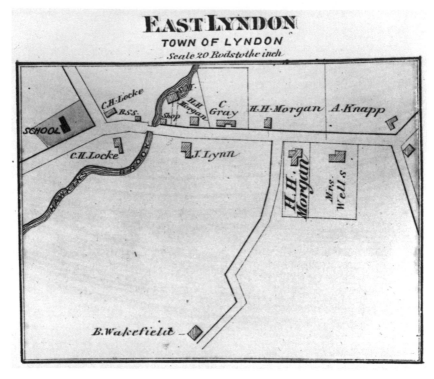

East Lyndon (*Vermont Historical Society*)

Early families here included Young, Smith, Parker, Wetherbee, Gorham, Mitcham, Brown, Perry, Pope, Chaffee, Clark, Locke, Morgan, Rawson, and Wilder. Most of these names are no longer heard.

In 1932, Editor John Chase, in a reminiscing mood, published in succeeding issues of the *Vermont Union Journal* two articles about East Lyndon that are worthy of quoting here as a means of preserving two fragments of history. The first appeared in the issue of November 23, 1932.

EAST LYNDON 35 YEARS AGO

Charles Locke has been in a profound study the past few days, caused by a retrospect of his school district of forty years ago. Charles moved to his present farm in April 1856, and found that community under the school division of District No. 8 since changed to No. 4 and composed of 21 families with a population of 80. There was the old saw mill, put in by William Morgan more than 40 years ago, and the blacksmith shop where Hollis Parker presided at the forge. The floods of the past summer (1897) swept away the shop and part of the mill. The present school house was built about 25 years ago on the site of the original, at a cost of $800. There was no church till about 20 years ago when the present neat edifice was built. Mr. Locke finds only two persons in his district who were there when he moved in, George M. Park and Miss Emily K. Hill, many having passed away and others moved away.

Here are the names of the heads of families at that time (1856) and also the present (1897) owners of the old homes: Charles Locke, who then bought the Tyler E. Parker farm, owned by him to this day; Joel Bronson, whose place is now occupied by Ed. Simpson; Rufus Chaffee who lived where Russell & Gage now live; Otis Lawrence occupied the farm owned now (1897) by John A. and F. D. Smith; Amasa Knapp's farm is now the home of J. E. Simpson; Betsey Brown owned the farm where William Webber lives; Nathan Wetherbee's old place is not occupied but is owned by Mrs. May Webber of Lyndon Center; Wm. Morgan's homestead is now the home of Charles Hall; Hollis Parker's farm is owned by Mrs. Josiah Brown; Thomas Carter lived on the farm occupied by Lyman Walter; Joseph Parker's farm is owned by Emily K. Hill, daughter of Daniel Hill; Enoch Carter lived where Thomas Bradshaw lives; Loren Chaffee owned Bine Laducer's place; Lincoln Park's farm is the home of his son, F. M. Park; Ward Knapp was on the hill where Calvin Hodgdon and son now live and his neighbor was Daniel Hill whose place is now occupied by Horace Graves; Nathan Parker's place, buildings now gone, occupied at that time by his widow, is now owned by Fred Hovey; Perry Cushing's old homestead, buildings now gone is a part of the present Smith farm; C. W. McCoy's old home is now the property of Geo. Kittredge and Jeff Welch but is not occupied; Carlos Parker's farm is now part of Fred Hovey's farm. This is East Lyndon of 1856, and, to see it as it is in 1897, add four new homes in which live Hoarace Jones, W. A. Eggleston, George Greenwood, the same number of families 21, a gain of 10 in population, 90 and two homes unoccupied.

It would now be interesting to have a list of the present owners of these farms and homes, after a period of 35 years.

The second article was the late W. Arthur Simpson's answer to the challenge of the first, published in the issue of November 30, 1932.

EAST LYNDON — 1932

My thanks to W. Arthur Simpson for the following article [Editor Chase's note]:

Your note in last week's paper on Charles Locke and the changes in East Lyndon from 1856 to 1897 (41 years) lead me to comment on those since that date.

My folks moved from where I now live to the Amasa Knapp farm in East Lyndon in 1894 when I was seven years old. My Grandfather Simpson moved from the Will Bean farm in the west of the town to the Bronson farm sometime in the early seventies. This place is still in the Simpson name. A. J. Mosher lives on the Russell and Gage farm of 1897 and this was the Chaffee farm in 1856. The Lawrence farm occupied by John A. and Fred Smith in 1897 is where Warren Drown now lives. My brothers live on our old farm, Thomas Stanhope on the Betsy Brown place and Willis Flint on the Nathan Wetherbee place.

The house where G. R. Dresser lives was built by Henry Morgan and when we moved to East Lyndon Jim Webber lived there and conducted a store. The Wm. Morgan place is owned by Bion Laducer. The Morgans were a prominent family here in the early days. In the Morgan Hall the Good Templar lodge and the East Lyndon Grange conducted their meetings.

Mrs. Eben Clark lived where Thomas Fitzpatrick now owns. She was one of the oldest inhabitants when I was a boy and a cousin of my Grandfather Wilder. She lived to nearly 100 years. She was sister to Hollis and Tyler Parker, Mrs. John Fisher and Mrs. Bradley, mother of Herman Bradley.

The Thomas Carter place occupied by Lyman Walter in 1897 is now occupied by Dana Smith. Fred Hovey lives on the Josiah Brown place that was once the Wakefield place. Mrs. Newman is on the Charles Locke farm, George Blood lives where Emily Hill lived and Charles Nickerson on the W. A. Eggleston place.

The Morgan sawmill was directly behind the Nickerson house. This was washed out in 1897 and never rebuilt but did a lively business in the early days. When washed out it was owned by a man by the name of Stone, father of Eugene and George Stone. The blacksmith shop was south and beside of the present cement bridge in the village.

The Carter farm occupied by Thomas Bradshaw in 1897 is where L. O. Sleep lives, the buildings burned many years ago. The Park farm where Howard Foster lives was in the Parks family for three generations. Lincoln Park came there with his bride and tradition has it that before the house was built they lived in a sap tub. The old gentleman was horribly burned in his old age by falling into a pan of hot sugar and his son, George bore the scars of burns which he received in rescuing his father. Mrs. Ed. Young is a daughter of George Park.

The Chaffee place is where Frank Randall lives, Titus Hutchinson lived where Paul Houghton resides and Will Jewell is on the Locklin farm. This is one of the oldest farms in the neighborhood and was in the Locklin family for three generations. Wallace Houghton lives where his father, William Houghton, lived 35 years ago. Scott Ranney was on the present James Robinson farm, that was the old John and Dexter Bly farm, and these old settlers are buried in the old part of the cemetery at the Center.

Where John Beattie lives was the old Powers place and in the old house lived Frank Powers. He was a son of Benjamin Powers and Lydia Wilder, the first female child born in Lyndon. Frank Powers and his son, Henry, built and operated the chair factory on Hawkins brook and there are many of the old Powers chairs still in use in this section. George Meserve lives in the Henry Aldrich house. The houses where Bailey and Frank Woodward lived were parts of one that once was situated on the other side of the road and moved by Solomon and Henry Stone. Bruce Wallace lives on the Henry Powers place and S. L. Taylor built and occupied the place where Charles Celley lives. John Watkins' place was the old Jehial Powers farm, occupied by Philo Graves when I was a boy. Eliphelas Graves came from Walpole, N.H. about 1800 and settled on what has long been known as the Shonyo farm. He was a great grandfather to Henry Graves and Ed. Graves.

Ed Hovey's farm was owned by John Fisher who operated a blacksmith shop near the turn in the New Boston road. Hoarace Jones lives on the Mike Lynn place and Milo Houghton on the old Houghton farm. The first Houghton, Alpheus, came from Rhode Island to St. Johnsbury about 1786 and twenty years later came to Lyndon. His son Paul was the father of the late Austin, William and

Dr. Silas. William was the father of Wallace Houghton and Dr. Silas the father of Milo and Paul Houghton who still live in the neighborhood, making one of the longest old time families in this section.

Back of the Red Village school are the cellar holes of the Dave Bodette place and in the Randall pasture the cellar holes of the old Porter place. The Ward Knapp farm, later the Hodgdon place, is no more and nearby was the farm on which Carlos Parker lived. Nathan Parker, his father, first located on the farm where Warren Drown now lives. He married three times and had eighteen children. His grandson, Carlos Parker, was grandfather to Elwin Parker of Lyndon Center.

My grandfather's grandfather Zebina Wilder, came to Lyndon in 1790 and purchased the Bemis farm on Bemis hill. He sold to Captain Bemis and bought the farm where Dale Roundy now lives. In 1809 he bought and built on the place where I live. The early house was over the hill in the pasture and another one, in which he died, was in the extreme south corner of the present field. The road came across the brook near John Beattie's, over the Hogback and through the field to the junction near Robinson's. Elias Wilder, my grandfather, was born here in 1833 and my story of these early days was largely derived from him.

Chronicles of the early days are soon forgotten and it may be that years from now this little account will be sought out in the old files of the Journal and prove of interest to some of our descendants.

W. Arthur Simpson

Other than farming, the only industry in East Lyndon of which mention has been found is that of stencil making in 1868. H. H. Morgan's stencils were used to mark grain bags, robes and blankets, boxes, and barrels and other containers of grain or flour.

Lyndonville

THE DESTRUCTION BY FIRE of the St. Johnsbury shops of the Connecticut and Passumpsic Rivers Railroad Company on March

21, 1866, motivated the construction of the new shops at Lyndon Center, begun later the same year. The architects of the company immediately surveyed the tract, carefully selecting the location for the shops and then plotting the remainder into (1) streets at right angles to the tract for the shops, (2) house lots, and (3) parks at strategic points. All streets were planned in uniform widths except Broadway—extending from the north side of Depot Street to South Street—which was much wider.

The first brick in the foundation of the new shops was laid at 3:57 on Wednesday afternoon, August 1, 1866—the "New Village" was begun. However, the community existed for almost two years without any other name. During this time there was serious and extensive discussion of a desirable name to be chosen by and for this fragment of Lyndon Center, and "Keyes Ville" seemed the most popular choice in honor of Henry Keyes, president of the railroad company. Suddenly George B. Walker, proprietor of the hotel, received a communication from the U.S. Post Office Department announcing his appointment as postmaster at Lyndonville on April 13, 1868. Without consulting the village it had been named!

As the community developed, the architects' plans were modified by usage. "Broadway" came to be "Broad Street" and lost most of its extra width from Center Street to South Street.[40] Depot and Main Streets were planned as the primary residential streets, with two-story dwellings placed 20 feet from the road; Center Street was intended to be the major business street.[41] After the fire of 1894, however, typical small stores were constructed along Depot Street, and the 20-foot area was swallowed up. This process was repeated after the fire of 1924, except that the building size was increased, with one building now taking the place of two or more of the earlier day.

On the hill east of the shops, employees of the railroad company early were set to creating a "water reservoir 50 x 80 feet and 7 feet deep thus capable of holding 2 to 300,000 gallons of water"[42] to be distributed via four-inch pipes not only to the shops but also to the community and to hydrants for fire protection.[43] George B. Walker bought the first building lot from the Railroad Company, at the southeast corner of Main and Depot streets, and J. E. Chesley paid

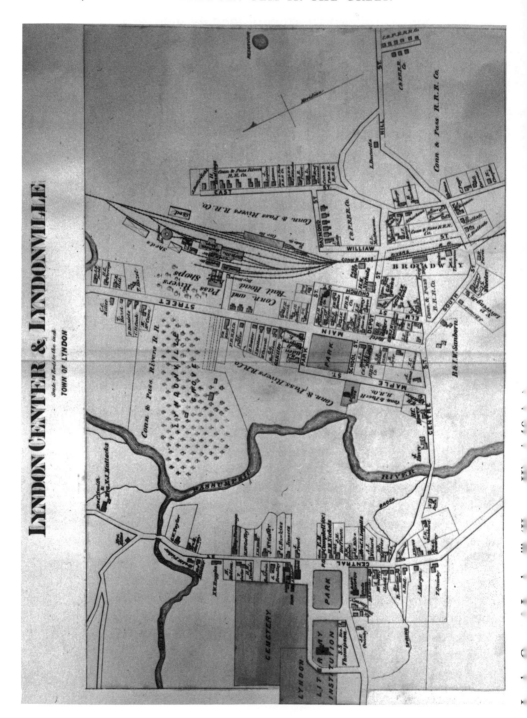

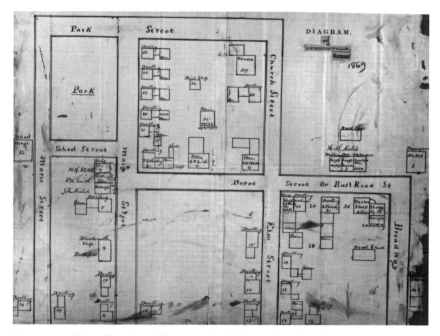

Surveyors Plat of Lyndonville made by Nelson Chamberlin, 1886
(*Town Clerk's Office*)

$450 for the second lot, at the northeast corner of the same two streets. Walker immediately built a hotel—capable of serving fifty or sixty people—for the convenience of the employees of the company. The first houses built by the company for rental to its employees were on East Street. Others soon followed on Raymond Street, on Main Street just south of Grove Street, and on Center Street between Broad and Elm streets. Even with the help of Walker's Hotel, these did not provide adequate living quarters for all, so on March 1, 1867, the "commuter train" to and from St. Johnsbury went into service.

Building lots along Main Street sold rapidly, and houses were soon constructed. The above-mentioned architects' plans—that all houses must be at least two stories in height, and not less than 20 feet from the street—were written into the lot deeds. The rapidity with which the company building developed is shown by its annual report of 1868:

Stove-Pipe City [Shantyville], now location of Catholic Cemetery; railroad laborers lived here in late 1850's (*Alfred Smith*)

Amount of rolling stock in the shop, wood etc., $439,242,00. Last year it was $357,764.64. The amount expended in Lyndon to May 31, 1868, exclusive of real estate, is $194,905.73 and comprizes round house, machine shop and building connected, 4 double houses, 6 cottages, aqueduct with iron pipes and reservoir holding over 70,000 gallons.

The original purchase of 334½ acres of land in Lyndon at a cost of $16,000 has furnished the corporation with all the accommodations anticipated. Of the foregoing expenditures, $10,000 has been realized from the sale of real estate, leaving about 300 acres for their own use and for sale. In addition to the above, the corporation have 2000 acres of wood and timbered land lying near their track, from which lumber, wood, and sleepers can be obtained advantageously.

The bonded debt of the Company has been reduced $20,000 leaving outstanding $533,800 of which $10,700 are in the hands of the trustees as a sinking fund.[44]

By 1868 the three major officials of the company—Superintendent Perry, Cashier Hubbard Hastings, and Master Mechanic Alden—were occupying their new homes[45] bordering the north side of the park.

Lyndonville railroad passenger station (*Harriet Fisher*)

From the very beginning the company took pride in the appearance of the village. In 1867 it planted small elms and maples along both sides of many streets; many of these died, so replanting was undertaken in 1869. In 1884 the village set out about 500 more elms and maples, and in 1886 200 balms of Gilead; in both cases Austin W. Houghton, street commissioner and village trustee, served as the impetus, as he did in many other village beautification projects. Enough survived from these various plantings so that only occasional replacements were needed for many years to assure the village of shaded streets. The trees on Depot Street were badly damaged by the 1894 fire and never were replaced, but wholesale destruction did not come until after 1950 when Dutch elm disease wreaked such havoc. The original landscape plan of the village designated several parks, and others developed as the village grew. Among the railroad shop buildings, small grass plots were created at strategic spots. These were carefully trimmed, and frequently beds of showy flowering plants were established. In 1901, for instance, the company purchased 50,000

Lyndonville railroad yards (*Leo Hebert*)

flowering plants to be set in every railroad community where the neighborhood of the depot had the needed space. Lyndonville received its full share of such benevolences. A granite curbing was placed around the plot at the center of the circular turn south of the passenger depot, and a small park was developed within the curbing; here A. W. Houghton planted an elm.[46] Some seasons attractive plants bloomed here as well as north of the freight depot.

Beginning about 1875 and continuing for ten years or more, the community agitated for something to be done to improve the square of public land lying north of the Mathewson block which the original plan designated as a park. A fund of $500 was raised by subscription to aid with the project. Finally, Austin W. Houghton, who lived on Main Street opposite the park, accepted responsibility to get the task done. The ground was plowed several times and planted successively to potatoes, oats, corn, poppies, and—finally—grass.

Not many villages can match
Nor many parks compare,
With the beauty of our "tater patch"
Upon the public square.

Before, I sang you of the tater
That grew upon the square;
But now, I am in better nature,
For oats are growing there.

We've started flax and all the rest
of ornamenting flowers,
And find that oats are suited best
To deck this park of ours.
O oats alone, or oats and rye,
It certainly must be;
For nothing else will satisfy
Aristocratic we.

The fountain lady looks around
In deep surprise and pain
Before, she never was background
To such a field of grain.

But now, economy, you know,
Is ruling for a while;
We are not going much for show
Nor very much for style.
We have no time, or taste for praising
The flowers that smell so sweet
For we must keep that park a-raising
Something that we can eat.

O my, did you spy,
As you came by,
Those poppies on the Square?
There's poppies here
And poppies there,

> And poppies everywhere.
> There's poppies on the east,
> And poppies on the west
> And poppies in the middle
> And over all the rest
> Is this Poppyville or not?
> Or has this village got
> Poppy on the brain?[47]

The plans for the park were to place a fountain in the center with a gravel walk around the fountain. Diagonal walks were to run from it to each of the park's four corners and to the center of each side, thus making eight entrances. Another walk would go around the outside of the park. The *Vermont Union* of September 3, 1880, described the fountain thus:

> . . . a fine iron fountain 11 feet high has been selected for the center of the park. The piece is surmounted by a female figure and a swan from whose mouth a stress of water will be thrown up to fall back into a dripping pan and from thence into a second and larger pan and from thence into a cement reservoir sixteen feet in diameter. . . .

The passage of many seasons and much labor were needed for the fulfillment of these plans plus the planting of the many trees and shrubs. Eventually the park became very beautiful and contributed materially to the attractiveness of the village.

Beginning in the summer of 1885, Austin Houghton, acting for the village trustees, began developing the park between the passenger station and the freight station. Subscription funds of $500 were raised to purchase a fountain for the park; Robert Pettigrew, who went to New York to buy the fountain, was rumored to have contributed generously. The base of the fountain was two feet deep and sixteen feet across. Many trees were set, and every summer so long as passenger trains passed through, there was a striking display of blooming flowers in three or four large beds. The railroad yardmen helped tend the flowers; the company often furnished plants in the spring, and often had others of the same variety set in the beds along the grass strips extending through the yards from the passenger station to the shop entrances.

Lyndonville Park from corner of Maple and Main Streets
(*Ruth McDowell Rousseau*)

The railroad company directed and financially supported all kinds of community needs and activities. By the early 1880s the original core of officers had changed.[48] Effective January 1, 1887, the Connecticut and Passumpsic Rivers Railroad was leased for ninety-nine years to the Boston and Lowell Railroad Company; in October of the same year it was re-leased for the same period of time to the Boston and Maine Railroad Company. These events marked the tangible beginning of the end of railroad company paternalism in Lyndonville. The interest of the company in the village increasingly became that of the community's contribution to the financial success of the company, rather than the company's responsibility for the community.

Gradually the business concerns at Lyndon Corner established branch shops at the railroad village for the convenience of those who were building homes nearer their work. The first grocery store was established in the basement of the Walker Hotel. Not until nearly the end of the 19th century had the mercantile life of the town really transferred from Lyndon Corner to Lyndonville. The major changes

The Dartmouth, Engine #5, George Shorey, Engineer, a Boston & Maine woodburner, built 1851, rebuilt 1879, scrapped 1899 (*Madeline Stone*)

resulted from the massive destruction of Depot Street wrought by the fire of 1894.

Lyndon's first tandem bicycle arrived in 1896, the property of S. W. Hutchins. The first auto, which arrived in June 1903, was a Stanley Steamer made in Newton, Mass., and owned by E. T. Wood. The next month E. J. Blodgett sold a "Reo Red Devil" to Dr. Aldrich at St. Johnsbury. To pick it up Blodgett went to Lowell, Mass., with the *Vermont Union* reporting that "Ed left Lowell Saturday afternoon, going to Montpelier. He left the latter place about noon on Monday, took dinner in Marshfield, stopped over an hour and a half in St. Johnsbury and arrived home at 5:00 o'clock. Fast travelling ....??" The *Vermonter* of July 1905 gave a list of all the automobiles registered in the state;[49] Lyndon had two—namely no., 117, owned by E. T. Wood, and no. 239, by Harry V. Wakefield. The first public garage was maintained on South Street by E. J. Blodgett.

The Christmas season of 1916 marked the beginning of community observance of the season by a "community Christmas tree" in the

Lyndon's first auto, a Stanley Steamer, owned by E. T. Wood
(*Mrs. Ray Sherman*)

Main Street park. The tree was furnished by C. M. Darling and set up by A. A. Barber, with electrical work by George Goodrow; arrangements for the occasion were made by the civics committee of the Community League, with G. M. Campbell as chairman. Under the leadership of H. C. Wilson a chorus of about seventy-five presented a program of familiar seasonal songs on Christmas Eve. They were assisted by Heman Burpee and Harry Doe on cornets and Alphonse Aubin on trombone. Editor Chase in the *Union-Journal* reported that "The lights were turned on and the tree stood revealed in all its beauty with a large cross at its top and above this was the star so suspended or secured that it appears to be entirely by itself." A few years later a large illuminated star covered with evergreen branches was placed annually on the roof of the Mathewson block (Main Street at the west end of Depot Street).[50]

By 1940 an entirely different town was taking shape. The people had changed. Many were strangers to the heritage that had been Lyndon's; they were primarily interested in neighboring communities where they were employed and which they could reach easily via auto. New businesses were taking shape which had fewer employees than had been in the railroad shops. Lyndon was joining many other Vermont and New Hampshire communities in cultivating tourists, especially through the development of outdoor winter recreation opportunities. By the 1970s, since no place remained for groups of people to congregate under cover, Lyndon had become a place for its employees and those of neighboring towns to sleep and live.

ℨ☛

The Subdivisions

LYNDON'S FIRST "SUBDIVISION," Hadleyville, was begun in September 1879, when Jethro G. Hadley bought five acres of farm land from B. F. Rollins for $350. Hadley constructed or remodelled perhaps a half dozen buildings along the highway north from the Denison railroad crossing. He also built one house and laid out several building lots on a road that he opened east from the highway.

Pinehurst, the second subdivision in the town, developed on a portion of the former John Allen Farm. When Allen died in 1898, his wife, Lydia, deeded the 200-acre farm to their son Harris O. Allen, who in turn sold it to the Taplin, Rowell, Lang, and Webster Lumber Company in 1905. In 1907 the company resold the bulk of the land to Ezra John, but retained twenty-six acres that lay within the corporation limits of Lyndonville. These twenty-six acres were divided into 115 building lots, the first of which was sold to John Norton in 1908. The streets extending east to west were Maple, Pleasant, Essex, Alpine, Auburn, and Charland; those from north to south were Highland, Riverside, Lincoln, and Fletcher. Lincoln has become West View, and Fletcher is now Pinehurst Street.

In recent times Roger Lussier has been responsible for developing three separate subdivisions: the Mobile Home Park, Lyndon Heights, and Lyn-Haven. The first two used parts of the old Charles Folsom Farm where Lussier lived.

Creation of the Mobile Home Park was set in motion on July 27, 1957, when Lussier sold about five acres off the south end of the Folsom mowing to Alcide Blair. Lussier kept a 100-foot right-of-way along the river side of the tract, but after an instance of high water when Blair needed to build a dike for protection, Lussier let Blair have this strip of land as well. Blair opened about thirty lots 40 x 80 feet each for rent. On October 7, 1967, Blair deeded the property back to Lussier, and on October 2, 1972, Lussier resold it to Edward J. Tester, having in the interim added fifteen more lots 50 x 90 feet. Tester then added five more lots for a total of fifty lots. Lussier appa rently was not altogether happy with the development, however, as its sight was not pleasing from his home. He determined that if he were to participate in any similar venture in the future, he would locate it farther from his house.

Lyndon Heights was born as a result of an appeal from the Tap and Die Company for housing space. Lussier opened about twenty acres of the Folsom pasture bordering the West Burke road and built the first house in 1965. Jack Davis of East Burke surveyed the land into 21 lots of approximately one acre each; the first lot was sold to Warren and Evelyn Smith. All roads in the subdivision were con structed according to town road specifications and were turned over to the town.

Lyn-Haven, a second mobile home park, was developed by the Lyn-Haven Corporation, formed on June 2, 1969, by Harry and Wallace Infalls, Harry Davis, and Lussier. On June 4, seventy acres of land were deeded to the corporation, and on August 26 the map of forty lots was filed in the Lyndon town clerk's office. These lots were 150 x 150 feet with one exception: that including the old Cunningham farmhouse was slightly larger. This development differed from the Mobile Home Park in that the land was sold rather than rented. The development provided water from an artesian well and access to electricity. Each landowner received a septic tank and a concrete slab 15 feet by 50 or 60 feet on which to place a mobile home or to build a house at least twelve feet wide. Lawrence Urie of Urie and Morse of Barre surveyed the land. Jacob F. and Mary H. Bryan bought the first lot on July 10, 1970. Lussier emphasized that lot purchasers were under no obligation to buy their mobile homes from him, although many did so. In this subdivision, like Lyndon Heights, roads were laid out in compliance with town specifications and so became town maintained.

Robert Lawson developed the Speedwell Estates subdivision beginning in 1965. In 1922 his father, E. A. Lawson,[51] had bought the Speedwell Farms land and buildings after the death of Theodore N. Vail. Lawson successfully operated the farm until 1939, when seven of the buildings burned; he immediately rebuilt and continued farming until his death in 1953. Returning from military service the following year, Robert Lawson purchased the property and continued the farming operation until 1959, when another, more destructive fire occurred.

In 1964–65 Lawson divided the 500-acre farm into lots varying in size from one to five acres. To perpetuate the Vail farm name, he dubbed the subdivision "Speedwell Estates" and the main road therein "Speedwell Drive"; the other two original roads were Mountain View Drive, which faces Burke Mountain, and Calista Drive, honoring his wife. Lawson built the first house and lived there for a time before selling to Richard and Patricia Wagner on September 6, 1968. He then built another house for himself on top of the hill farther west. In 1973 rising taxes motivated sale by auction of the few remaining lots that had not been put on the market in the beginning.

Finney Hill (from Wm. H. Finney, a late 19th-century landowner on the hill) had its beginnings in 1968, when Howard Little and his wife Isabella F. sold two parcels of land to the Finney Hill Development Corporation, consisting of Sidney Nurenberg, Calvin C. Chester, Eric L. Chester, Fenton W. Chester (all of Lyndon), and Leon E. Hopkins, Jr. (Burke). The parcels contained approximately 100 acres each and were separated by a brook. The Littles reserved saleable timber and pulpwood, as well as the water rights previously pledged to Earl G. Bishop and James W. Emery. It is on this land that the springs are located that were originally used by the Connecticut and Passumpsic Rivers Railroad Company to provide the "company water system" for the village of Lyndonville.

The eastern parcel developed first, was divided into forty-four lots of about one acre in size. Leon E. Hopkins, Jr., built the first house for sale.

IV

Town Government

ON THE FLYLEAF OF THE FIRST BOOK of records of the town of Lyndon is the title "Records of the Doings and Proceedings of the Town of Lyndon from the first Organizing being July 4, 1791." The first entry is the following:

> State of Vermont, Orange County,[1] Whereas application hath been made to me the Subscriber and by Sufficient Number of the Inhabitants of the Town of Lyndon in the County of Orange and State aforesaid to warn a Meeting of said Inhabitants for the Purpose of Organizing themselves as the Law Directs.
>
> The Inhabitants and Freeholders of the Town of Lyndon are hereby Notifyed and Warned to meet at the Dwelling House of Mr. Daniel Reniff in said Lyndon on Monday the Fourth Day of July Next at twelve O'clock and Said Day.[2]
>
> 1st to Choose a Moderator to Govern Said Meeting
> 2nd to Choose a Town Clerk for the Present year
> 3rd to Choose a Constable Selectmen Grandjuremen
> Tracingman and all other Town officers as the Law Directs and to act on any other matters that Shall be thought Necessary when met.
>
> Dated at Wheelock this twenty-fifth day of June 1791
> /S/ Abraham Morrill J. P.

The officers elected at this first town meeting were Elder Philemon Hines, moderator, and Daniel Cahoon, town clerk.[3] It was resolved that there should be three selectmen, who should also serve as listers; elected to fill these offices were Lt. James Spooner, Daniel Reniff, and Daniel Cahoon. Also elected were Nehemiah Tucker, treasurer; Nathan Hines, constable and collector; and Daniel Cahoon, sealer of weights and measures. To facilitate the work on the highways, it was voted to divide the town into six districts, boundaries of which

Town Hall [Meeting House] with Cemetery Shed [Graded School]
(*Garnetta Wood*)

were to be set by the selectmen. Six surveyors were elected: Jonathan Davis (1st district), Jonas Sprague (2d), Andrew McGaffey (3d), Daniel Reniff (4th), Daniel Harvey (5th), and Zebina Wilder (6th). The meeting was then adjourned until the first Monday in August. At this second meeting, the clerk was instructed to petition the General Assembly to grant to the town the benefit of the tax of twopence per acre on land in the town "belonging to Non-residents and Residents Proprietors and Land Owners" for use in building roads and bridges.

Town meetings continued to be held at the home of Daniel Reniff through March 7, 1796. In some records Reniff is referred to as "innkeeper," which might imply that his house was more commodious than others. Subsequent meetings were held at the "dwelling house" of Nathaniel Jenks through March 7, 1800, when that gathering was "by vote moved immediately to the dwelling house of Joel Fletcher, innholder." At this meeting it was voted to hold future meetings at the same place. This was done until April 24, 1802, when the meeting was held at Jesse Ide's. This continued to be the place in which meetings were held through 1809, although by March 26, 1806, the building had become the "dwelling of Alpheus Fletcher". In 1810 the meeting was held in the new Meeting House.

In 1792, the year of the third town meeting, it was voted that the selectmen should be paid four shillings for each day's actual service. At the same meeting Asa Kimball was elected collector of taxes and agreed to pay eleven shillings and six pence ($1.90) for the privilege of making the collections.

Representing Lyndon in the Constitutional Convention at Windsor in July 1793 was Capt. Josias Arnold. This is the only recorded time a member of the Arnold family assumed any official obligation in the town of Lyndon.

During the town's first years, many "special" meetings were called to consider matters essential to the organization and administration of the new town. By 1800 a well-established pattern had developed for the conduct of town meetings in Lyndon. The meeting in early March, known as the "annual meeting," was called to order by the first selectman. The first order of business was election of a moderator, who presided over the remainder of the meeting, but whose authority terminated at its close. In the case of a special meeting this procedure was repeated. Reports of officers who had served during the preceding year were presented and acted upon at this March meeting, and officers were elected for the following year. In later years, the man chosen as moderator at the March meeting was the presiding officer at all town meetings, regular or special, until a successor was elected. In many instances he was reelected; W. Arthur Simpson established a record when he served as moderator for forty-three consecutive years (1926–69). For many years custom dictated that if a moderator were absent from a town meeting, a "moderator pro-tem" would be elected to serve only for that specific meeting. The freeman's meeting occurring in early September was called to order and conducted by the constable. This was the time when the freeman's oath was taken and names were added to the town's checklist of voters; also at this meeting votes were cast for state and federal officials.

In the case of urgent business a special meeting often was called to follow the freeman's meeting, and a midsummer meeting was not infrequent. For some years (1867 to 1876, at least) town meetings were regularly held in early January; in 1876 the time for this meeting was moved to December. From the minutes, it appears that the major business transacted at these January or December meetings was the establishment of the tax rate for the following year. Apparently this was not a set rule, however; in 1884 the tax rate was set at a special meeting held after the freeman's meeting.

During the first quarter century of the existence of the Town of Lyndon, the Cahoons (Daniel Jr., Daniel Sr., and William), Isaac and Joel Fletcher, Jude Kimball, Job Randall, Abel Edgell, Isaiah Fisk, and Abel Carpenter served most frequently in positions of authority and influence. In the second quarter century the Bemisses (Elias, Welcome, Amasa, Alonzo, and Elias Jr.), Epaphras B. Chase, the McGaffeys (Stephen, John, and William H.), Thomas Bartlett, Asaph Willmarth, Philip Goss, and Paul Houghton were frequently called to public service. After the mid-century the candidates for public office became much more numerous and services more varied.

The town treasury was so limited that on several occasions citizens pledged an advance of funds for a needed town expenditure on the promise of repayment as soon as the town money was available.[4] Even so, payment to town began in 1792. At the third meeting of the voters, the selectmen were authorized to collect 4s per day for each day's actual service to the town. In 1820 collection of "townrates" was put at vendue to the person who would make collection for the least sum; Alanson Shaw bid it for $12.50. In 1833 Nathan Hubbard bid it for $10. In 1865 George B. Walker promised to pay $461 for the privilege of collecting, and the next year his bid was $475, his nearest competitor being George Quimby at $450. Although Walker was elected constable and collector in 1867, the selectmen had to declare the office vacant because he was unable to find men willing to sign his bond[5] for the faithful performance of his duties. Charles Ingalls was finally appointed to fill the Walker vacancy.

In 1883, by vote at town meeting, the practice of paying taxes to the town treasurer was begun, and the collector's pay was set at 2%

of the delinquent taxes collected. Voters also approved paying the town officers $1.50 per day for the time they worked for the town; in 1889 this was increased to $2 per day, but with no pay allotted for their teams. In 1897 the school directors were added to the list of town officers "so that they would be eligible for this pay." In 1924 the selectmen received $100 a year, the overseer of the poor $200, the listers $3 per day, and the town clerk and treasurer $300 per year; in 1935 the overseer's pay was raised to $500.

At the town meeting of March 12, 1804, the selectmen were instructed to "lease-out" on long term leases the lands reserved in the town charter for public purposes (church and schools). The usual statement governing duration in such leases was "as long as wood grows or water runs." The original leases have never been changed, though the land has been bought and sold many times. The rates still vary from seven to twenty cents an acre, and payment of these fees have exempted the holder from any taxes levied by the town. The lease fees on the minister and public school lands through the years have been payable to the town clerk, whose responsibility it has been to divide the minister land fees ($79.81) between the town's churches on the basis of the number of their members. The lease payments on school lands ($54.11) were put in the general school funds. The lands reserved for the college and the county grammar school were leased by them and the fees paid to them directly. The rates were comparable with other town lease lands.

An act of the 1968 legislature somewhat changed the status of the lease lands. It authorized towns to levy taxes on lease lands at the same rates as on similar lands in the town, provided the lease fees were recognized as paying a part of the taxes. This law immediately led to the levy of taxes, payment of them to the town treasurer, and his payment of the lease fees to the various designated recipients.

From the beginning of the town its officers, as well as the voters, have been conscientious about preserving records. At the first adjourned town meeting (August 1, 1791), the clerk was empowered "to procure all Necessary Books for the Town Viz one Book for the Town Records one Ditto to Record Deeds one Ditto to Record Births Marriages Deaths Markes &c and one Ditto Containing the Statutes Laws of Vermont." To implement this vote twelve men pledged contributions to be paid within two months,[6] with the understanding that their contributions would be refunded when there was sufficient money in the town treasury. The total subscribed was 1£ 16s 6d.

In 1855 the selectmen were instructed to secure a suitable safe. Apparently the selectmen did not realize how town records would multiply, for at the March 1868 meeting "the selectmen were authorized to procure a good fireproof safe for the use of the town—of sufficient capacity to hold the town records for years to come, and to dispose of the old safe at best advantage."

The administration of the affairs of the town from its beginning have centered in the office of the town clerk. The first three town clerks (1791–1829) were Cahoons (Daniel, Daniel Sr., and William); during much of this period the office was in the second floor hall of the Cahoon house. No record has been found of the site used by the next five incumbents in the office (1829–58), but for many of the forty-four years of service of Isaac W. Sanborn[7] (1858–1902) a small building constructed near the southeast corner of his South Street home adequately housed the safe as well as the books of land and other records of the town.

After Sanborn's death, the town clerk's office was in the Lyndonville National Bank building for a year or two, then was moved into the Mathewson Block.[8] It remained here for sixty years, the annual rent rising from $150 to $1205. In 1963 the town and village purchased the two-tenement house at 24 Main Street that had recently been the residence and office of Dr. W. T. Elliott. Architectural plans were drawn by Gordon Wood of St. Johnsbury for the changes necessary to adapt it for efficient office use; these included a room-sized two-story vault in the northwest corner of the building. The second-floor apartment was maintained, thus providing a continuing source of income.

During the last months of 1866 and the first of 1867 there was much discussion, some vehement, concerning the route to be followed by the new road to be built between Lyndon Corner and the "Railroad Village"; several committees were appointed, and numerous special town meetings were held to consider the matter. Measurements were taken of the three possibilities[9] for the route from the guideboard south to the General Chase House to the site established for the depot in the new village:

> by the northern route which turns into the meadow at John Clements and crosses the Sanborn bridge, the distance was 489 rods, via the middle route which enters the meadow at Mr. Paine's it was 391 rods, via the southern route which crosses the river south of General Chase's and connects with the old road near Mr. Colton's 398 rods; the cost of the various route were estimated as $1600, $9007, and $4,431, respectively; all the road beds were planned at 20 feet wide and 3 feet above water . . . the Southern route was almost unanimously adopted.

This is the roadbed still in use, although over the years there have been minor changes in the road, especially as it becomes Broad Street near the eastern end of South Street.

In 1885 the voters instructed the auditors to print their annual report in season to be distributed at the annual town meeting the following March and to continue the process until stopped by action of the voters. Once before (1882) the auditors had been authorized to have their report printed, but it was not until 1886 that annual printings became continuous. Lyndon has been honored on several occasions because of the excellence of its town reports.

For the first time, at the 1890 March meeting, the town participated in what was to become known as "stabilization of taxes" when it voted to levy taxes on the grand list of $8000 for the next five years for the Wilder Pulp Mill and its holdings. In 1903 a similar courtesy was voted to Lucius H. & Iphus H. Gordon's Novelty Works for ten years; in 1914 the Wetherbee Woodworking Plant was declared exempt from taxes for ten years; in 1920 taxes were abated on the J. W. Copeland house, which had been willed to Cobleigh Public Library; and at a special meeting (April 19, 1924) the town voted to exempt from taxation for a period of five years any new permanent buildings to be erected in the burned district on Depot Street. In the succeeding years many favorable or unfavorable actions were taken on similar requests. By the 1960s a blanket exemption from taxation for one year was voted covering all homes and farm buildings provided the value did not exceed $15,000.

One of the largest and liveliest town meetings in many years was the special meeting held in July 1934 to consider two proposals: (1) conversion of the town house into a schoolhouse, thus avoiding otherwise necessary construction at Lyndon Center, and (2) the permission already granted by the selectmen for Lyndon Institute to enclose the Common with an ornamental wire fence. There was strong opposition to both projects, which provided impetus for heated and extended discussion, followed by negative action on the two proposals.

In the early years of the town, the voters elected each year a first, second, and third selectman, with the first to preside at meetings and exercise general leadership. Soon after the middle of the 19th century the practice developed of electing one selectman each year to a three-year term; at their first succeeding meeting the selectmen chose their own chairman for the ensuing year. A few years later it became the custom for the selectmen in the last year of his term to be named chairman.

In the last decade of the 19th century the incorporated village of Lyndonville assumed responsibility for developing two aspects of public utilities, a central system of water supply and electrical system—services that expanded to the major part of the town within a few years. To develop these services, the articles of village incorporation had to be modified to permit (1) issuing municipal bonds in larger quantities and (2) holding title to real estate. The administration of each was entrusted to a commission of three members. The electric plant proved the more profitable of the two enterprises, and its profits gave the village the courage—and money—to undertake many construction projects that otherwise would have waited long. The income from this community service was contributed annually to the general treasury for several years; in at least two separate years these funds were sufficent to allow the town to forego levying taxes. By 1974 the costs of maintenance had grown to the extent that further contribution to the village treasury was impossible.

Many elective or appointive offices of the early town no longer exist, because time has rendered their functions obsolete. The duties of hay wards and hog-reeves were related largely to weighing hay and impounding animals running at large; for instance, an 1806 law forbade rams from running at large between August 10 and November 15, and an 1838 vote excluded cattle and sheep from the cemetery. Highway surveyors had charge of the town road districts, including collection of road taxes and expenditure of money and labor in maintenance of the roads; when this activity was centralized and came under the authority of the selectmen or a road commissioner, the district surveyors were no longer needed. The inspector of leather, or "leather scaler," was often a shoemaker. He was expected to stamp "G" on any leather fit for market, and "B" on that which should not be sold; his normal pay was 2¢ for each hide inspected. No tanner or dealer was allowed to sell any unstamped leather.

The sealer of weights and measures had responsibility for maintaining standard accuracy of weights and measures throughout the town. All millers were required to use "sealed measures" and might take "one sixteenth part and no more" for grinding, and "one sixty-fourth part more" if the grain were to be "boulted" (sifted); the measure was to be "stricken" with a straight edge for exactness. Surveyors of lumber also measured wood. Fence viewers, often the selectmen, provided binding arbitration of controversies involving boundary disagreements and fence maintenance.

Until the 1920s the town rented any machinery it required. During this decade, however, quite a machinery account came into being. The 1928 town report listed two Ford trucks, a Wehr grader, a Sargent plow, a Fordson tractor, a power conveyor, a cement mixer, a team roller (two-thirds ownership), and a stone crusher. This implies a change of procedures from men with horses to men using town-owned or rented machinery. Another evidence of changing times was the vote in 1925 to place a town directional signal for aviators on the south roof of the Lyndonville Creamery garage.

At the 1922 March town meeting voters authorized appointment of a committee—Mrs. G. P. Ide, O. D. Mathewson, and Dr. F. E. Dwinell—to study the wisdom of adopting the town manager system of government. In the ensuing months many public meetings were held, and much discussion, both formal and informal, took place. At the next annual meeting O. D. Mathewson submitted a full report on the pros and cons of installing the system in the town of Lyndon, but the committee made no recommendations and so no action was taken.

Especially in early village administration, standing committees or commissions exercised major influence. As a result of a 1953 legislative enabling act, Lyndonville voters enlarged (1955) the board of trustees to five and so transferred the functions of the two major boards of commissioners (water and electricity) to the board of trustees.

In both the news media and the official records of town meetings, one finds extensive comment on the participation of women in the affairs of Lyndon town government. The first woman to cast a ballot for a town officer was Constance Gerry Blodgett (Mrs. E. J.) on March 5, 1918; at the same meeting Mrs. Melissa Stevens was the oldest woman to vote, being then seventy-eight years old. Reports from succeeding years frequently note the large proportion of women constituting the audience at town meetings.

Examining the pattern of government that developed in the town of Lyndon, several trends appear. (1) Many of the major officers have served for a long time: Isaac Sanborn was town clerk forty-four years; Arthur Simpson was moderator forty-three years; Howard Shonyo was selectman for thirty-six years; Leon Hopkins was a school director thirty-nine years; George Whipple served as school director twenty-eight years, W. H. Lyster as auditor twenty-seven years. (2) The lesser offices and boards were filled by the same men through frequent reelections. (3) These continuances in office led to much administration of the town's business by "gentlemen's agreements" rather than by vote at either village or town meeting. (4) The strong community sensitivity of the citizens in the later years of the 19th century that led to the incorporation of all three of the major villages in the town has ebbed. The last forty years have seen a steady drift toward holding the town responsible for functions that used to be zealously administered by each village in the interest of its own residents. This drift has seemed to contribute to the tacit acceptance of the acts of town or village officers. (5) The early pride in pay-as-you-go administration has given way to heavy bonding and indebtedness, and thus costs of debt service.

ॐ

Warning out of Town

THE NEW ENGLAND COLONISTS brought many customs with them from England; one of these was the "warning out" laws which appeared quite uniformly in the basic law of most colonies.[10] There are different theories about the purpose of these laws. One writer is of the opinion that "warning out" did not imply any undesirability of the person, but merely was giving public notice that there was a stranger in town. Another writer believes that this was a way of getting rid of undesirable people before they had established themselves in the community. Still another writer thinks it was to protect the town from any responsibility to provide support in case the person or family became indigent.

The first authorization of the General Assembly of Vermont for such action was in 1787. This law provided authority and permission for the selectmen to warn anyone who is "not of a quiet and peaceable behavior or is, in their opinion, like to be chargeable to such town," unless that person should obtain "a vote of the inhabitants of such town, in legal town meeting, to remain in such town." The law further provided that if the person did not leave within twenty days after such warning a warrant might be issued to a sheriff or constable to take the person out of town or to the place where he last lived, with the expense thereof to be paid by the person so warned. No person could be subject to such "warning out" after having lived in the town for a year.

In an act of November 16, 1801, provision was made that every person whose ratiable estate, other than poll, should be entered in the grand list at $60 or more for five years in succession would gain the right of legal settlement even though he had been warned to depart; also, any person who was sworn into a town office for two years gained the right of legal settlement. A person who acquired legal settlement in one town and moved to another where he supported himself and his family for seven years gained legal settlement in the town to which he moved.

The last action of the Lyndon March meeting in 1808 directed the selectmen "to warn All People that may hereafter move into the Town of Lyndon to depart said Town."[11] This appears to have been authorization for what was already a well-established custom.

The first such action recorded was the order of the selectmen (Daniel Cahoon, Nathaniel Jenks, and Isaiah Fisk) dated May 2, 1803, issued to William W. McGaffey, constable, "to summon Josiah J. Allen now residing in the Town of Lyndon to Depart said Town with his wife and all his children." The writ was served May 30, 1803. Evidence of the serving of many such writs is found in the official records of Lyndon. The results of their being served are not fully known, but apparently the order was ignored by the great majority of people concerned. Some of the names that appear in these lists are those of people who later became not only holders of town offices but also influential citizens in the activities of the community.

The Settlement Act of November 4, 1817, put an end to the system of "warning out" and provided that any person might be admitted to legal settlement by vote of a town meeting.

Lyndon Corner

THE POLITICAL ORGANIZATION of Lyndon Corner appears to have been different from that of Lyndon's other two villages. Sources of information are limited, but the following gives a sketchy idea of the village's political development.

Late in 1867 agitation began for the formation of a fire district for the purpose of protecting the property in the district from fire. Ten years later the selectmen, in response to a petition of people living in the community, constituted "Lyndon Fire District #1" as follows:

> so much of Lyndon Academy and graded school districts as is em-braced within the following boundaries, viz: on the south by the south line of Herman French's and estate of E. B. Chase, land on the east by east line of said Chase Estate land, and the whole of said Estate Land, Otis Lawrence land across the Passumpsic River, Con-necticut and Passumpsic R. R. R. land where depot is, and also where E. L. Wells lives, also land of B. F. Rollins, A. E. Jones, Simon Colton, A. J. Goodell, Rufus Young and wife, F. W. Root, Gratis T. Spencer, Mrs. Louisa Locke or Joel Locke's Estate, Mrs. Hersey Green, W. C. Wing and John A. Wing, F. J. Bundy, Mrs. C. D. Hoyt and daughter, E. H. and C. D. Hoyt, James G. Drown, Hiram Streeter, and Geo. Ide, and all lands and buildings within said bounds aforesaid. . . .

At a meeting on November 6, 1877, the voters of Fire District 1 adopted a code of bylaws, elected officers and appointed a committee consisting of D. N. Trull, J. M. Weeks, and Henry Chase to investigate the feasibility of supplying the village with water and to initiate action for protection against fire. J. C. Ide and S. S. Mattocks were named assistants to G. P. Spencer—appointed first engineer at a previous meeting—and the three were instructed to inspect all buildings in the district before November 12.

Existing records are silent until May 1896, when the selectmen es-tablished Fire District 2 in the village of Lyndon "as a result of a petition of freeholders in the village." The boundaries were the same as those of 1867, with the names of contemporary landowners appro-priately substituted. Again, a newspaper story reports a meeting (June 10, 1896) at which an organization was formed and officers elected.

The next notation found is an item in the *Vermont Union* of June 27, 1899, reporting a meeting held at the school house on January 24 "for the purpose of organizing the village"; the usual village officers had been elected at this meeting. About two weeks later (Feb-ruary 14) the voters met again, adopted bylaws, and voted a tax of 10¢ on the grand list dollar to pay rent on electric power for lights from July 1, 1898, to July 1, 1899. An article accompanying the report of the meeting states the purpose of incorporation:

> . . . the efforts to secure street lights by subscription had not been successful. Lyndon became a regularly incorporated village on January 24, but without a charter, which means that the village merely has all corporeal rights but its relation to the rest of the town is unchanged, that is, it may tax itself for any desired improvement; it does not lose its claim upon the rest of the town, neither does it escape the town's claims. The main object of incorporation was to pay for the lights by taxation; the main value to the village will be that as needed improvements appear they may be supplied by a fair means.[12]

By the annual meeting of the next year (1900) the trustees had purchased, among other things, a hose cart ($327.60). Soon the citizens of Lyndon began agitating for a change of charter that would place the maintenance of roads and sidewalks in the control of the village. In 1917 the General Assembly enacted such a change, but the document was not satisfactory to the majority, so it was laid on the table. Again in 1919 an act of the General Assembly proved unsatisfactory and was rejected.

When the Village Improvement Society had purchased S. S. Mattocks' building where they developed the Olde Bricke Tea Shoppe, the deed had provided that nonuse would cause ownership to revert to the village. In 1927 the question rose whether the village would accept ownership. A committee was appointed to investigate. At the 1928 March meeting, acceptance was voted, and at the 1930 village meeting it was voted to hold future meetings there rather than at the schoolhouse.

At the meeting of Lyndon village voters on June 17, ,1951, favorable action was taken to make use of a bill passed at the preceding meeting of the General Assembly whereby the legal voters were authorized to change the local government from a village to a fire district. Thus, the village of Lyndon formed on January 12, 1899, ceased to exist as a governing unit on June 20, 1951, and was officially designated as Lyndon Fire District 1. As a result of this new designation, three elected members forming a Prudential Committee assumed functions previously exercised by the trustees. In 1974 Lyndon (Corner) voters surrendered all rights of incorporation as either a village or fire district.

୨◖

Lyndon Center

LITTLE IS KNOWN ABOUT the exact beginning of Lyndon Center. In the early 1800s a few buildings were located in this area on the road from Lyndon to Burke. Early records tell of Job Sheldon giving six acres to the town of Lyndon to be used for a meetinghouse, a cemetery, and a common. The meetinghouse, now known as the town hall, was to be located near the center of town; it was built in 1809. A *Vermont Union* article dated May 23, 1890, speaks of Lyndon Center as being eighty years old, thus indicating that a village had existed in 1810. The Post Office was established in 1829. In 1835 seven of the freeholders petitioned the selectmen of Lyndon to "establish and lay out the Village of Lyndon Centre, (so-called) agreeable to an act of the Legislature of the State of Vermont, passed November 11, 1819, to restrain certain animals from running at large in said Village. . . .[13]

Most of the information concerning the early days of the village has been gleaned from local papers. Apparently the citizens themselves, under the leadership of the public-spirited, such as L. B. Harris and Theodore N. Vail, raised money for the needs of the village, built sidewalks, plowed roads and sidewalks, and beautified their village. The first mention of sidewalks is in 1857, when a plank sidewalk was built from the north end of the village to the Lyndonville bridge. In 1884 the village trustees planned to put a new sidewalk in the southern part of the village. When residents objected to the location, all work was suspended on the sidewalk until the residents settled on the location by themselves; the final decision was to put the sidewalk on the east side of the street as originally planned. In 1891 a plank walk was laid on Main Street and West (now Church) Street in front of Sanborn Hall. By 1892 concrete sidewalks had been installed, and many of the residents had cement sidewalks leading to their homes. In 1914 the wooden railing was placed along the walk to the Lyndonville bridge. New cement sidewalks were installed in 1915. At this time a walk and steps were placed in front to the Baptist Church.

A *Vermont Union* article of October 31, 1890, reported that the question of water rights between Lyndon Institute and the cemetery was being reconsidered, and that the original contract was to be overhauled and determined for all time. In 1891 the problem of water for the village arose. A spring on the Harris farm about ¾ mile from and 50 feet higher than the village was chosen. Pipes were laid from the spring to the reservoir above the cemetery. Later, water was secured from the Lyndonville waterworks.

Lyndon Center became an incorporated village in 1896 by act and resolve of the General Assembly of Vermont at the 14th biennial session of 1896.[14] Its boundaries were defined as "that part of the town of Lyndon known as 'fire district no. 3,' in said town." Lyndon Fire District 3 was abolished by the act, and the district's duties, property, and obligations were taken over by the newly incorporated village of Lyndon Center. From this time on more detailed records are available. The annual meeting was set for the first Saturday after January 1 each year. This was later changed twice by act of the General Assembly: once in 1900[15] to the first Saturday in March, effective at passage; and in 1935[16] to the first Saturday after the town meeting.

Under the village charter trustees were to be chosen for three-year terms, except at the first meeting, when one was elected to serve for one year, one for two years, and one for three, with the retiring trustee to be the chairman and serve as moderator at village meetings.[17] Other charter provisions of special interest were that no officer was to receive compensation for his services as an officer (Section 6); the village could use its credit only to the extent of the grand list, for current expenses and improvements (Section 10) and authority for the fire department was vested in a board of fire wardens composed of the trustees and two engineers (Section 13). The remainder of the charter provisions dealt with the routine matters of running a village.

By June 1, 1896, at the request of freeholders in the village, the selectmen had designated Lyndon Center as Fire District 3.[18] Preparatory to this action, the district had purchased "500 feet of hose, a hose cart, and full equipment at a cost of $350." There were six hydrants in the district. Hydrants were offered free to the district for a guarantee of twenty families to take water.[19] The trustees for the new village soon arranged a contract with the village of Lyndonville for the use of hydrants and for street lighting. The *Vermont Union* of December 6, 1896, reported "that the recently incorporated village had a grand list of $1000 and only a mile of streets and highways to look after."

A bill to make the village pay half the amount of the tax rate for town road purposes was killed in the legislature in 1898.[20] L. B. Harris, C. K. Hubbard, and E. M. Campbell appeared before the legislative committee for the village. As early as 1898 the need for a new school was being discussed. It was suggested that it be located between Sanborn Boarding House and the Baptist Church; and eventually a school was built there. A telegraph wire was soon strung from E. M. Campbell's home to Hines' store to Lyndonville. There it reached to the homes of J. L. Hume and Jasper Guild, and to the railroad shops and the telegraph office.

From 1898 until 1928 an annual vote at village meeting was passed which abated the village tax for not more than twelve firemen. When this policy was discontinued, it was voted to pay 50¢ per meeting. By 1933 it was voted to call in the fire chief, two firemen, and a truck from Lyndonville to help the chief and three firemen from Lyndon Center.

Until 1899, when a contract for electric lights was secured, any streetlights in the village had been put in place by individual citizens. In 1909 street lighting in the village came under the supervision of the street commissioner. By 1919 the village had given permission to erect telephone poles on streets and to string wire on them.

The charter was revised in 1920 relative to the remuneration for officers. The following year 3 percent was paid to the tax collector on collection of village taxes. Payments to a district nurse were begun

Lyndon Center Park with Wild Boar Fountain (*Bessie Harris Brown*)

in 1931. By 1934 the job of hard-surfacing Lyndon Center roads was begun by paving Main Street from the north end of the village to the Lyndonville bridge. Also paved were the Lyndon Institute road, Carpenter Road, and Vail Hill.

The stone water trough located at the intersection southeast of the Common was given to the village by L. B. Harris on January 1, 1900. Working several hours each day, Harris cut the watering trough from a huge granite block. When completed, it was said to be the most expensive water trough in this part of the state. It was five feet square, held a barrel of water, and was set in a foundation with cast bronze feet on each corner. The gift was given to the village to be used until the village ceased to exist, and the occasional efforts to remove it were voted down at village meetings. The Florentine Boar in the park was also a gift from Harris. Both he and Theodore N. Vail were benefactors of the village many times.

Over the years the village citizens demonstrated their spirit through donations from time and money for beautification projects, for the fire company, and for other worthwhile endeavors. This spirit is best stated in a *Vermont Union* article of May 27, 1892:

The old village is setting an example of public spirit and improvement which large places might imitate with profit. The common, the old June training ground, which for three-quarters of a century has remained as the forest left it, has been plowed, graded, smoothed, and rolled down, the improvement including all of the open, rough space in front of the town house. The highway has been refined by a double row of trees on its east side. The new boarding house grounds have been put in order, supplied with trees and well marked walks. The west side of the street as soon as the leaves and grass start will present a model appearance. The east side should be put in condition to match it. The street is still broad enough to allow the side walk to be set out its full width from the present position, thus making it straight from lower to upper end of the street and giving space between walk and residences for a nice strip of lawn. . . . What has thus far been done had been done not by a village improvement society, but by the public spirit of individual citizens who deserve the highest credit for their effort.

During its last few years as an incorporated village, Lyndon Center's actions evinced the trend toward consolidation. In 1949 village residents were requested to use the dump on Pudding Hill and to call the Lyndonville Fire Department in case of fire. The year 1950 was marked by the through highway being changed to Star Route 122. The name of River Street was officially changed to Center Street in 1951. In 1953 the village trustees were instructed to study having Main Street declared a state highway from bridge to bridge. The town clerk in 1955 was authorized to send out tax notices and collect the taxes.

Road construction funds were authorized in 1960 to pay for the Lyndonville bridge construction for four years. A representative was appointed to the Town Planning Commission, and the Village Planning Commission was instructed to work with the town and Lyndonville planning commissions.

The last record of the village as a separate tax unit appears in the Lyndon Town Report of 1962. The last time that the Village was mentioned as a separate highway district is in the Lyndon Town Report of 1963. The village of Lyndon Center is now consolidated under the government of the town of Lyndon.

?⬤

Lyndonville

LYNDONVILLE WAS INCORPORATED by an act of the legislature dated December 24, 1880. The organizational meeting was held in Hoyt's Hall on March 17, 1881, and the meeting was called to order by Isaac W. Sanborn, a justice of the peace. The officers elected were W. H. Fletcher, moderator; I. W. Sanborn, clerk and treasurer; W. H. Hoyt, collector; Abram Hicks, chief engineer of the fire department; and Jeremy Pearl, J. W. Copeland, and J. C. Jones, trustees. The moderator appointed a committee of L. C. Grandy, Geo. H. Smalley, and H. L. Parker to draft bylaws; the result of their labors was adopted May 16, 1881. As early as 1882 W. H. Fletcher, A. W. Houghton, and J. C. Jones were appointed water commissioners.

By the middle of the century's last decade numerous events were taking place in the life of the village. The act of incorporation of Lyndonville had been amended to authorize the village waterworks and the floating of bonds not exceeding $40,000 for their construction. There was agitation for leasing the Wilder Water Power to provide needed power to run an electric railway between St. Johnsbury and Lyndonville. The legislature permitted the further amendment of the village charter to allow ownership of an electric light plant and to issue bonds necessary for its construction. Concrete sidewalks were constructed on Depot and Broad streets, and a hose cart and 500 feet of hose were purchased.

In 1922 the village trustees—E. C. Graves, H. H. Butterfield, and Elisha Bigelow—banned the use of firecrackers, fireworks, and explosives of all kinds in the celebration of the Fourth of July. This applied to "streets and sidewalks of the Village as well as back of the blocks along Depot Street or adjacent to it." Junior traffic officers first appeared on the streets of Lyndonville in 1932. Sponsored by H. C. Wilson, officers Robert Dresser and Claude Wheeler wore silver badges marked "Special Officer." They served at the beginning and close of school, morning and afternoon, to assist the children in crossing streets.

The local newspaper proudly reported in November 1937 that the village had expended $25,000 in the following improvements: building an addition to the water system, paving Center, South, and Hill streets, painting Music Hall, constructing a half mile of sewage lines below the lower railroad crossing, creating sidewalks, pruning the park trees, and installing a new heating and air-conditioning plant in the graded school.

The village charter was repealed on March 20, 1940, and rewritten in forty-two sections. In 1953 the legislature passed an act enabling the village to combine its various boards and commissions under a five-man board of trustees. This distinct change in the machinery of government was finally accomplished in 1956.

In the fall of 1955 construction of the armory was begun on land acquired the previous year by the town for that purpose. It cost approximately $138,000, of which the state paid 25 percent and the federal government 75 percent. The building's 14,000 square feet were divided into an orderly room, three offices, a rifle range with moving target carrier, security rooms for the storage of valuable items, two classrooms, a supply room, a kitchen, and showers. The main floor is 60 x 90 feet and is used for drilling as well as the storage of trucks. In mid-December 1955 this became the home of Company H, 172 Infantry Regiment, Heavy Weapons Company, with Capt. Robert Hudson the commanding officer of 125 men and 5 officers. The company had organized in April 1953 with 14 men and 1 officer. Since neither the National Guard nor the 461st Fire Fighting Reserve were using the Gem Theatre Building, the trustees sold it for $18,500 in 1959 and the next year sold for $5000 the lot on which Music Hall had stood.

V

Public Services

The Poor

Eₐʀʟʏ ɪɴ ᴛʜᴇ ʟɪꜰᴇ ᴏꜰ ᴛʜᴇ ᴛᴏᴡɴ of Lyndon, the records show acceptance of responsibility by the town, through its selectmen, for the support of its poor and indigent residents. As early as 1801 the selectmen were appointed guardians for the wife and children of Ithamar Healy, who had deserted them.

At the town meeting in 1805 it was voted that ". . . the Selectmen Put out the Poor Children that are now Chargeable to the Town or that may Hereafter become chargeable & seize them Plased in some Respectable Familys where they may be well used respectably brought up, to the best advantage they Can for the Town."[1] Three years later the same procedure was authorized for both adults and children in slightly different words when it was voted at the March meeting that ". . . the Oversears of the Poor be Directed to Dispose of the Poor at Vandue or to them who will take the Poor on the best conditions for the Town and use them well. . . ." Throughout the years the responsibility of providing for the care of the town's poor has fallen to the selectmen if no one was voted those specific duties at the town meeting. In 1810 the first overseers of the poor were elected: John Calhoun, Job Randall, and Caleb Sanborn.

In 1814–15 the cost of caring for the town's poor—namely the Daniel Walter family and Widow Griffin and her children—was $216.05; this was itemized and consisted mainly of supplies, though there were a few doctors' bills. The following year, with Bela Shaw, Jr., as the overseer, the total expense was $16.07 for the families of James Walter and Daniel Walter.[2] The charges at the store include pipes, tobacco, tea, molasses, wheat, and fish costing a total of $7.51, and at the mill $8.46 covering corn, wheat, and rye (perhaps the grinding of them). Also approved by the auditors was this item: paid William Scannel for helping build Walter's house $2.15"; the order for payment is dated April 2, 1816.[3]

Another aspect of this care is shown by Francis Field's promissory note of $34 dated March 20, 1820, drawn to Abel Carpenter, Isaiah Fisk, and Alpheus Houghton, overseers, and witnessed by Ephraim Chamberlin, "it being for the support of an illigitimate child charge on me by Widow Polly Foster."[4] One learns of the charges made for a dependent child in the October 4, 1820, bill of Ira Wilmarth and approved by the auditors, Abel Carpenter and Alpheus Houghton:

> for keeping Jacob Foster, son of Polly Foster from the 7th of December 1819 to the 6th of June 1820, at the rate of 75¢ per week as agreed with the selectmen of the town $19.50. To making a coat and pantaloons found buttons and thread $1.00, to two flannel shirts, found all $2.00, to leather and tapping a pair of shoes 25¢, to one pair of tow pantaloons or trousers 58¢, to tow or cotton shirt 42¢, making a total of $23.75.[5]

In 1824 Joel Fletcher and Alpheus Houghton (first selectman) presented a bill (approved by the auditors) for $157.47 as the expense for the care of the town's poor. Five families were covered, with the expense varying from 62¢ to $52.04 per family.[6]

These instances show the variations in the expenditures by the town in the care of its dependents, and justify the item in the warning for the 1826 annual town meeting, calling for consideration of a proposal to build a house for the poor. At the meeting, the article was dismissed without action. At the 1827 town meeting, Benjamin Walker, overseer of the poor, was authorized to "sell the poor at vendue to such person or persons as will support them for the least sum or sums."

In 1832 overseers Joel Fletcher and Benjamin Walker indentured[7] an eleven-year-old girl, Orra Fisher, to William Pierce until she should reach the age of eighteen on February 29, 1839. The terms of the indenture provided that she receive food, clothing, and instruction in reading and writing, as well as two months schooling each year at a common district school. At the end of the indenture, she was to be provided with suitable and decent clothing. The document was signed by all three of the above-named men. In a similar situation in 1860, when S. S. Thompson was overseer of the poor, the terms were somewhat different. "James Connell, a poor boy" aged fourteen was indentured to Nathan Gilbert.[11] "at the end of his term which would be at the age of 21, James Connell shall receive $100 in money and be provided with two suits of clothes, both new, one for holiday use and the other for everyday wear, both of quality and value suited for the purposes named."

The following year the annual town meeting enacted a new type of provision for the care of the poor:

> . . . the expense of doctoring the town poor in said Lyndon shall be put up at Auction to the lowest bidder by said person so bidding off the same shall procure suitable Physicians and medicines such as shall be necessary for said poor—and that the Selectmen of said Lyndon shall attend to putting up same at Samuel Hoyt's in said Lyndon on the first Monday in April next at one o'clock p.m.[8]

This plan apparently proved satisfactory, for a similar action was taken at the annual town meeting in 1834. In 1836 the overseer was authorized to hire a sum not exceeding $200 for support of the poor for the ensuing year. At the same meeting a committee consisting of Joseph Ingalls, Epaphras Smith, and Jude Kimball was appointed "to make enquiry and ascertain what can be done with regard to purchasing a farm for the support of the Towns Poor and report to an adjourned meeting." The record fails to indicate when the report was made; apparently it did not result in a purchase, for committees with similar obligations were appointed at the March meetings of 1837 and 1838. This latter committee, consisting of Otis Evans, Joseph Ingalls, and Ephraim Fisher, was actually instructed to purchase a farm,[9] but the members were given discretionary power as to the price to be paid and the quality and size of the farm to be purchased. At the same time the selectmen were instructed to hire the necessary money to cover the purchase. As a result, the town bought the William McKoy farm on March 16, 1839, for $2000.

In 1841 at a special town meeting,[10] Job Randall and Epaphras

Chase were appointed to act with the selectmen (Otis Evans, Stephen McGaffey, and Walter Hoyt) in examining the state of affairs at the poor farm. Such an appraising committee was appointed nearly every year, but unfortunately the reports, probably given at March meetings, have not survived except for the one of 1847, when the committee consisted of Job Randall, E. W. Carpenter, and Paul Houghton. The grandson of the latter, also named Paul Houghton, inherited and saved the manuscript. It contains 121 items listing animals, equipment of both barn and house, and food supplies for both man and beast, all of which were valued by them at $1204.62.

In the 1868 town meeting an appropriation of $1000 was made for repairs on the house at the town farm. As reported in the *Vermont Union*, the main task was to remove the whole lower story and reset the second story on the ground; other minor repairs were also expected.

The value of the poor farm and its equipment had increased significantly by 1875, when the manager reported

> Overseer W. A. Bemis' report of the town farm business here shows receipts from the farm of $2460.11, expenditures (including $360.00 interest on the value of the farm, appraised for $6000.00) $1966.45, leaving a balance in favor of the receipts of $493.66. The total cost of supporting the poor for the year amounts to $1690.23. The personal property on the farm was appraised in 1873 as $2239.60, in 1874 at $2737.16, in 1875 at $3302.[12]

In 1882 a new barn 26 x 34 feet was built at the town farm; ten years later an ell 43 x 20 feet was added to the house to provide a new kitchen and woodshed, and a barn 44 x 20 feet was built. In 1898 an important improvement was accomplished in bringing a generous supply of water from the C. E. Harris place two miles away in Burke.

Through the years, the overseer or the selectmen endeavored to concentrate the expenditure of all funds for the care of the poor at the town farm, moving almost all persons there who were dependent on the town for their maintenance. By that means, all who were physically able to contribute to the care and maintenance of all, and since the farm had good land, it was possible to provide for the needs of the inhabitants as well as produce a surplus for sale.

When the town farm was sold to Fred Hutchinson in 1921, it brought $5500. The personal property consisted of twenty-seven cows, one bull, eight yearling heifers, a pair of work horses, four shoats, and twenty-five tons of hay, plus the farming tools. The 1922 town report states that this personal property was sold at auction for $2591.65.

Roads and Bridges

As NOTED EARLIER, the building of roads and bridges was forced on the town of Lyndon from its very beginning because of the charter requirement of early occupancy of the right of every grantee. The early town meeting minutes and land record books contain surveys of many roads and records of actions concerning many others, indicating the creation of an extensive network of roads. The location of a road, or part of one, was frequently changed, and land released by the abandonment of a road was frequently given to the owner of adjoining land. On many occasions, too, damages were paid as a result of the changed location of a road. Routes followed by early roads cannot be precisely identified because in so many instances the recorded points marking their boundaries were the corner of a building, a fence, a tree, or even a stump—points long since removed by the passage of time.

From various sources it appears that different types of roads were built: the bridle road and the pent road differed in width, being 1½ and 2 rods wide, respectively. Reference is also made to the post road, which appears to have been wider, perhaps 2½ and 3 rods. By 1825, a road 3 rods wide is referred to as being of a "standard width." Many references from the first two decades of the 19th century mention the "turnpike" intended to extend north to Lake Memphremagog and Canada; this seems to be the same road as that sometimes called the "County Road," but no statement has been found giving distinguishing characteristics. This County Road was surveyed, finally, in 1814 by Abner Allyn, Esq., of Barton, and appears to have followed Lyndon's so-called Middle Road.

Special taxes on the grandlist were often voted for road work. Especially in the early years of the town, appeal was made several times to the General Assembly for the assessment of a tax of ½¢ to 3¢ per acre of all the lands in the town. These levies could almost always be paid in cash, labor,[13] or grain to be delivered before the following January 1. If the tax was not paid, the constable held a vendue and sold the land involved for the amount of the tax due, thus making it possible for a purchaser to acquire a good quantity and quality of land for a small outlay of money. Usually the selectmen were automatically the supervisors of all road repair work or construction, even though there might be a road commissioner on the spot directing the activity. The repair and building of roads and bridges were often put up at vendue for the lowest price.

Due to the large number of brooks and streams in the town, an unusually large number of bridges was required. In the early years, especially, many pole bridges were constructed. Because the poles sometimes rolled when loaded teams crossed them, injuries to horses—and resultant lawsuits—were frequent. No positive evidence has been found to show when covered bridges began to be built.[14]

More information has survived about the Schoolhouse Bridge than any other. The construction of the "new" brick schoolhouse occurred in 1871–72. Access to it was provided by a new road starting from York Street, and crossing the Branch between the Congregational Church and the Geo. Cahoon place. Because this required children from the eastern end of Chapel Street to go a long distance, another road (School Street) was built from the junction of the road to South Wheelock and the so-called Middle Road past the schoolhouse to Chapel Street. The first Schoolhouse Bridge provided a crossing of the South Branch for this road. This bridge was described in the *Vermont Union* of October 4, 1872, as follows:

> The most extravagant piece of work we have seen in a long time is the new bridge over the branch, where Wilmarth is building the schoolhouse road. If the penny wise and pound foolish policy is not in that job illustrated to the satisfaction of all beholders, it never will

be. Look at it. If it cost *anything* the town would be cheated. When
the town of Lyndon learns that public improvement work doing at
all, is worth doing *well*, it will be one good step in the direction of
economy. The motive in putting in such an apology for a bridge
was good, for the intention, of course, was to save money for the
town, but in the end, like all other poor jobs, it will prove a piece
of extravagance. To save money, too, the road bed through the
meadow is stuck up from below high water mark, instead of being
filled in two feet higher than it is, as it should have been to secure
a permanent benefit. Public improvements should be permanent if
profitable.

The next week (October 11, 1872) Editor Chase added this comment
about the new bridge:

The next first class photographer who comes this way is requested
to aim his camera at the new bridge (if that is what you call it) east
of the school house. Barnum wants it as a specimen of the architecture
of the dark ages. A second class Hottentot couldn't cross it without
blushing. A few of our citizens having attempted it lost the points
of the compass and had to go back home to find out where they were.

During the succeeding years there were many similarly disapprov-
ing criticisms of this bridge. Finally the December 12, 1879, issue of
the *Union* provides Editor Chase's approval:

The new bridge on School Street is completed and is a job well
done. John Clement laid the abutments which is a guarantee that
the work will stand. J. C. Jones drew the plan of the woodwork and
Lee Goodell framed it and superintended the building.

Editor Chase's son, John B., wrote in 1931 in the *Vermont Union-Journal*, successor to the *Vermont Union*, that:

The bridge had its hardest test in the 1927 flood when it was tipped
up till the chances looked about 100 to 1 that it was going out but
it stood the onslaught of the rushing water and debris piled against
it. As the water went down the bridge gradually settled back into
place, little if any damaged.

Proof exists that bridges were in existence in the following places
and many others before the stated dates, but often we can be positive
that they were covered bridges only from the reports of repairs:

Schoolhouse Bridge (*Fenton Chester*)

Little York Bridge near Paris Mill

1867   The "new" General Chase Bridge, framed by Woodward of
       Bradford, cost $3598.

1868   The Creamery Bridge.

1873   The Chamberlin Bridge was repaired. In 1881 the *Union*
       reported "it is receiving an abutment and is to be built over into
       a covered bridge." Selectman W. W. Heath was superintendent.
       This was also known as the "Sawmill Bridge" and, for a time in
       the 20th century, as the "Whitcomb Bridge."

Covered Bridge East; E. B. Chase Home (*Mrs. Milton Kerr*)

Ruggles Bridge, East Burke Road, Lyndon

1878 The "new covered bridge" at the mouth of Miller's Run, in the north end of Lyndon Center. E. H. Stone (St. Johnsbury Center) drew the plans.

1879 The Schoolhouse Bridge. J. C. Jones drew the bridge plans, John Clement built the abutments, and Lee Goodell framed the bridge and served as building superintendent.

1880 The Root's Crossing Bridge.

1885 The Folsom's Crossing Bridge. Chandler Bullock was in charge.

Randall Bridge, East Burke Road, Lyndon

Sanborn Bridge, Lyndon Center-Lyndonville (*Gordon Amadon*)

1896   In the July 31 *Vermont Union*, Editor Chase stated that John
   Clement laid the foundation of thirty Lyndon bridges.

Lyndon's roads and bridges have suffered severely from high water,
freshets, and floods. The first serious damage of which we find report
was in 1804, which necessitated appeal to the Assembly for authority
to levy a special tax to accomplish the needed repair. Probably the
most severe damage occurred in 1869 and in 1927. In the first instance
water was fourteen feet above normal; twenty-seven public bridges,

Miller's Run Bridge, looking south toward Lyndon Center. (*Frank Forward*)

Creamery Bridge, N. Main Street, Lyndonville (*Pauline Conners*)

ten private bridges, and two railroad bridges were carried away. In the second instance the water was eighteen feet above normal; sixteen bridges were washed away, and eight others were badly damaged.[15]

The road and bridge work of the town continued to be administered by the selectmen until 1894, when Elden Hovey became the first road commissioner. During the years since, this official has either been elected at the town meeting or appointed by the selectmen,

Snow roller (*H. Graves*)

but in either case has been the person directly responsible for maintaining and repairing roads and opening new ones.

In 1887 Horace Miller made the first snow roller for the town to break out its roads. Made of hard wood, it was twelve feet wide, eight feet in diameter, and weighed about two tons; four horses were needed to draw it. At the 1888 town meeting the voters gave sanction for the construction of five snow rollers, and in 1894 two more were authorized.[16] The purpose of the roller was to pack the snow in the road, making a smooth, hard roadbed that would remain throughout the spring as long as snow stayed along the sides of the road. Later models of snow rollers were made of two rollers that, when assembled, left a space between them, thereby creating tracks for travel in opposite directions: often six or eight draft horses were used to pull these. The town roads were rolled regularly, and "snowing bridges"[17] was a sizable part of the cost of winter road maintenance through the first quarter of the 20th century. The 1924 town report notes the rebuilding of six snow rollers. Motorized traffic necessitated the use of plows having motor power. The use of horses, even for summer road work, had to be abandoned, and the town purchased its first trucks.

In 1891 Lyndon acquired its first road machine. It proved as great a boon in keeping summer gravel roads as had the roller for the winter roads. In 1909 the town of Lyndon had 87 miles plus 81 rods of road, plus 5 miles in Lyndonville and 1⅔ in Lyndon Center. No village or town in the state had a smaller mileage total than Lyndon Center.

The first efforts to control the dust on the roads was made in Lyndonville in 1886, when by private subscription the money was raised to build a sprinkler. It was christened August 24, when Austin W. Houghton used Will Webb's four black horses to draw it. Its wooden tank held 720 gallons of water.

A new sprinkler was put into use in 1909 as a result of Village Improvement Society expenditure of purchase funds. In 1911–12, again by private subscription, money was raised to spread oil on some of the Lyndonville streets; C. M. Darling was the moving spirit and collector in this project, and for the next decade money was taken from the village treasury to pay for oil to continue the project each summer. By 1927 the purchase of 23 tons of chloride installed it as a substitute for oil, and extended the practice to many roads outside the village, especially those that experienced heavy traffic.

Until the first decade of the 20th century roads were usually surfaced with well-rolled gravel. Rotten stone was also used frequently; with the assistance of a stone crusher and roller, the road could be made almost as smooth and permanent as the blacktop of later years. During the 1920s the town reports show sizeable expenditures related to the use of calcium chloride and oil, and charges increased for road machinery while decreasing for hay and grain for horses—evidence of a changed pattern of motive power for road work. During the same period, the bills for cement also increased, and funds were spent for road building further and further from the population centers of the town.

≀⊂

The Cemetery

IN 1801, WHEN JOB SHELDON deeded to the town six acres of land
on which to build a meetinghouse, he also stipulated that a part of
the land should be used for a burying ground and for a parade ground.
This was to become the present town cemetery.[18]

The first death in town was that of Daniel Cahoon, Jr., on June 11,
1793; of course, this was soon followed by others. The first burial
ground has been described as being "the flat half acre south of the
Cahoon cabin site." No positive record has been found of the remains
being moved to the cemetery at Lyndon Center, nor do we know the
identity of the persons who may have been interred in this first cemetery.[19]

Graves in early American cemeteries were usually marked with
fieldstones without inscriptions, or with only initials rather crudely
cut with a hand chisel. Somewhat later, headstones made of slate or
soapstone were used, and as time passed such stones were frequently
ornamented with carving; the willow tree, symbol of lasting grief,
was the device most often seen. At first stones were set into the ground,
but they did not retain their perpendicular position too well, so granite sockets were made and the headstone held in place by molten
brimstone; later, cement provided the adhesive material. The Lyndon
cemetery seems to have fewer of these earliest types of stones than
do most cemeteries of equal size and age. There is one marker made
of metal, and several have a photograph embedded above the lettering.

The initial burial made in the Lyndon Center Cemetery was Lucy
Fletcher, the ten-year-old daughter of Mr. and Mrs. Joel Fletcher,
who died May 15, 1803. At the 1809 town meeting the selectmen were
"authorized and directed to fence the Burying Ground as soon as
convenient with a good handsome bord fence."[20] The first sexton
was Abner Eldridge, who served 1814–16. During many years the
care of the cemetery was combined with the maintenance of the
pound. In 1858 the town meeting authorized the selectmen "to build

or cause to be built a good through picket fence to be painted white around the burying ground"; in 1874 John Noyes was voted "$100 in addition to what he has been paid for building the cemetery fence"; in 1901 a new wire fence was built around the cemetery—this was the last one!

At the 1828 town meeting it was voted that "the sexton be Paid by the town for his services." At the same meeting the "selectmen were authorized to procure two palls, one suitable for adults, the other for children, and that they be at such expense in laying out and arranging the graveyard as may be necessary for the convenience of the inhabitants in burying their dead." Ten years later action was taken to keep cattle and sheep out of the burying ground.

In 1842 Daniel Quimby was authorized to build a tomb in the burying ground at a site to be designated by the selectmen. One wonders if this authorization was used, since in 1868 the selectmen were "authorized and instructed to construct or cause to be constructed within the burial ground a tomb of sufficient size and dimension for the use of the town." Again in 1872 the selectmen were instructed to construct a suitable tomb. In 1873 the *Vermont Union* reported that Welcome Fisher had been the successful bidder for the construction of the tomb, having bid $497.20 ($2.50 less than his nearest competitor). "He was assisted by Hubbard," probably C. K. In September 1874 the *Union* reported that the tomb built the preceding year at a cost of $360.00 had not fulfilled its specifications, so had just been pulled down and was in the process of being rebuilt by John Clement with the help of Moses Miles; G. P. Spencer, the story said, was building the granite front ($600). In November the tomb was reported finished at a cost of $1200. The room was said to be 10 x 14 feet and 8 feet high. In 1936 the town report included the expenditure of $900 to provide materials for Works Progress Administration workers to enlarge the capacity of the tomb from eighteen to forty-two. In 1973–74 repairs were necessary, with the result that some "revenue sharing funds" were assigned to this task; some of the repair was accomplished in the spring of 1974 by the Northeast Construction Company ($1876), but in the very late fall Douglas Townsend was the low bidder at $891 for work on the tomb.

Early in the 19th century, horse sheds were constructed near many public buildings in town, and town meetinghouse was no exception. Its sheds extended from the schoolhouse on the north side of the town house to the cemetery, and along the cemetery line south to the parade ground. No record has been found of their construction, but they appear to have been removed in late 1874. However, the two sheds between the hearse house and the cemetery have been kept in repair through the years for the storage of town equipment such as the snow rollers and road working machines; later the sheds were inherited by the cemetery maintenance crew.

In 1853 a committee of E. A. Cahoon, Silas Houghton, and Charles Roberts was appointed to obtain subscriptions to furnish a suitable monument to commemorate the service of Lyndon men who had died in the Revolutionary War. Houghton died and Roberts moved out of town, so that at the 1855 town meeting Dr. C. B. Darling, Charles W. McKoy, E. W. Carpenter, and George C. Peck were added to the committee; their task was accomplished in 1858. The monument was set in the west end of the old part of the cemetery on a terrace above the other stones. According to the contract, the cost of the monument was $125.69, raised by private subscriptions varying in amount from 25¢ to $5.[21] The contract to furnish, deliver, and set the monument was awarded to S. C. Otis, Havaland Hoyt, and Aola Sprague; Samuel and Calvin Bigelow drew the granite base to the cemetery, donating their services (worth $5.50) to the committee.

For several years the town meeting minutes indicate discussion about acquiring a hearse. Apparently one had been secured by 1847 when William Locke was chosen a committee to "procure suitable runners for the hearse and a suitable building for to keep said hearse in."[22] It was not until 1874 that the hearse house was constructed.[23] We have no direct proof that the hearse was acquired, but it seems likely, since repairs on "the old hearse" were authorized in 1878, and in 1880 the selectmen were instructed to purchase a new hearse — obtained for $700 from the factory of Brownell and Company, New Bedford, Mass. From later town reports it appears that at least two hearses were purchased by the town, and as late as the 1920s the town was paying someone, perhaps the undertaker, to drive the hearse. At some point use of the hearse became one of the tasks included in the fees paid to the undertaker by the family of the deceased.

The size of the cemetery has been increased many times from the original Job Sheldon boundaries. Small pieces of land were acquired in 1846, 1848, 1858, 1868, 1872, and 1898 from village residents living near the cemetery; in 1899 T. M. Vail donated six acres. Subsequent purchases were made in 1936, 1951, 1954, 1963, and 1974, for the most part from Lyndon Institute; the land was taken from the school's pine plantings. Throughout the years the purchases have been of lands lying on the north and west of the original site; though all the units have been small, they have brought the total size of the cemetery to nearly twenty-five acres.

The process of arranging an orderly division of the cemetery into lots, and keeping records of ownership, burials made, and other vital facts, was a problem of long standing. At several successive town meetings the selectmen or special committees[24] were directed to perform these tasks, and the frequency with which these instructions were issued lead one to think the assignments were not fulfilled promptly. The record of burials begins in 1851.[25] An examination of these records shows that in certain periods of time there must have been near-epidemics: for instance, in 1852, out of 45 burials, 18 died of consumption; between October 1861 and December 1862 there were over 100 burials, with 67 of these deaths being from diphtheria.

Running water was brought into the cemetery in the summer of 1883. Water was piped from a spring on the L. B. Harris farm to a reservoir built on the top of the hill north of Thompson Hall;[26] this came to be known locally as "Reservoir Hill." It furnished water well into the 20th century, not only to the cemetery but also to Thompson and Sanborn halls and the village schoolhouse. This source of water was not immediately abandoned when pipes brought running water to Lyndon Center. In fact, it was not until 1902 that the selectmen and the Lyndonville water commissioners arrived at an agreement in the matter of water rates for the cemetery.

The cemetery's appearance has varied greatly over the years. Some superintendents have made it attractive through care of the individual lots and stones; others have made it a "garden of the dead" through creating of flower beds at strategic spots and changing the flowers with the seasons; others have been content to level the ground and mow the grass.

At a special town meeting[27] on August 25, 1891, the selectmen were "authorized and instructed to purchase a lot of land easterly of the Catholic Church not to exceed $200 in cost and appropriate the same to the Catholic Society in town for a cemetery." Though this was placed in the warning for the 1892 annual meeting, it was passed over without action, perhaps because favorable action would have been contrary to state law. On April 9, 1892, Daniel Smith and his wife, Caroline, deeded to J. Paquet a two-acre tract of land to be used as a cemetery for the Catholic parish at a cost of $200. This came to be St. Elizabeth's Cemetery.

ℰ•

The Pound

IN THE EARLY DAYS of any community some time usually elapses before fences can be built to limit the travels of domestic animals. Frequently, too, animals travel far enough so they are truly "astray." Lyndon was no exception. At the 1802 town meeting, it was voted that "a part of Joel Fletcher's barn be made use of as a pound for impounding all cattle that may be taken in damage fee sent till a pound can be built." At the same meeting four hog reeves were elected to enforce action taken to keep hogs penned.

On September 2, 1806, the matter of a pound was considered at town meeting, and a committee—Capt. Joel Fletcher, Nathaniel Jenks, Esq., and Leonard Watson—was appointed to choose a place and "see to the completion of the same." Apparently this committee did not act, for the minutes of the June 4, 1810, town meeting include the appointment of Nathaniel Jenks, Esq., Joel Fletcher, and Job Randall as a committee to build a pound.[28]

If the pound were constructed by the common rule of "Hoss high, bull stout, and hog tight," it was not so administered as to make an end of the problem of wandering animals, for in the report of the March meeting of 1811 this entry appears: "Voted that rams shall be restrained from going at large on the common and highways in the town from the first day of September to the 20th day of November. Any rams found at large shall become the property of the town after having been taken to the pound treasurer for disposition."

If the vote of the town meeting was fulfilled, it would appear that replacement of the pound was necessary rather frequently, for at the special town meeting of April 26, 1823, it was voted to build "a pound of wood in the form of the last one built."

Though the construction of a fence around the cemetery was authorized in 1809, it would appear that local livestock continued to find it a satisfactory place to browse, for as late as the 1838 town meeting action was taken to exclude cattle and sheep from its bounds.

The first pound keeper was Daniel Reniff, elected in 1793 and reelected each of the next three years. He was followed by Joel Fletcher, who served for ten years. The last pound keeper recorded in town meeting minutes was Philo B. Graves in 1887.

The location of the public pound has not been positively established, but it has been assumed to have been near the meetinghouse. For many years in the mid-19th century the office of pound keeper was combined with that of sexton, and perhaps this fact has contributed to the supposition concerning the pound's location.

Fire Companies

INFORMATION ABOUT THE MEANS USED by Lyndon for protection from fire is conspicuous by its absence. Minutes of the March 1847 town meeting show that a committee consisting of Silas Houghton, Joel Fletcher, Jr., and Albert W. Winsor was chosen to buy a fire engine. No further mention has been found of a townwide system. In later years three fire districts were formed, their boundaries coinciding with village political boundaries.

The first information about a fire company at Lyndonville appeared in an 1883 newspaper report, which stated that "Trustees Fletcher and Eastman went to Franklin, N.H. and purchased a Hannaman hand fire engine which arrived Wednesday, July 18th, with 150 feet of hose, a hose carrier, nozzles and everything that goes with the machine." It was later reported that this equipment had been purchased for $225, in spite of an original cost of $1500. The first exhibition of its capacity was proudly reported, when it sent a stream of water over the Mathewson block. In 1885 when the International Mill burned in Newport, the Lyndonville fire engine was reported as having thrown "a third more water than any other hand machine there," a fact that elicited considerable pride in the village.

No further report of any activity related to fire protection is found until March 1889, when we learn that Tiger Fire Company No. 1 had just elected the following officers: foreman Charles E. Bullis, first assistant Thomas Hazel, second assistant Harrison Wilmarth, third assistant Albert LaBay, secretary-treasurer J. S. Butler, Charles Blake and W. E. Lynch assistant on leading hose, J. S. Butler assistant on suction hose, standing committee Charles Blake, Harrison Wilmarth, and Albert LaBay. By fall money had been raised to purchase uniforms, described by Editor Chase as made by Simonds and Company of Boston and being of material "all of good quality, very neat and attractive." They consisted of "dark blue pants, white flannel shirt with blue shield on the bosom with white buttons and the words *Tiger No. 1* in white letters on the shield; black leather belt with white trimmings, dark blue cap, straight visor and brass badge with embossed steam fire engine on it on the front."

In 1890 the membership for the company was reported as George W. Knight, chief engineer; Harrison Wilmarth, foreman; Parker P. Ball, first assistant; Charles F. Blake, second assistant; J. S. Butler, secretary-treasurer; and Ed. Bonner, Thomas Hazel, Ned Aulif, Herbert Powers, O. M. Badger, Arthur Smith, John W. McClure, F. W. Camp, Frank Willey, E. E. Cole, Jerry Canty, Melvin Rexford, Charles Lewsey, and Charles Jenniss.

In 1891 the company began raising money for a hook-and-ladder truck. Various activities contributed to the fund, including the play *Millie the Quadroon*, successful not only here but also at St. Johnsbury and Newport; a promenade; and a Thanksgiving Ball. The truck was acquired in the spring of 1896 at a cost of $650.

In 1892 chief engineer Parker Ball and his assistants Stephen Eastman, Fred Bullock, and Harrison Hunter inspected residences in the village for their safety from fire hazards. They reported 40 as being unsafe among the 235 inspected. In the same year the first system of fire alarm signals was developed. The alarms were to be given by the railroad shops' steam whistle or by a locomotive in the yard. The system was as follows: one long whistle would be blown to announce a fire, and immediately following it the number indicating the locality of the fire:

#68   Main Street north of Grove Street.
67   Main Street between Grove and Park streets.
66   Main Street between Park and Depot streets.
65   West side of Main Street between School and Centre streets.
79   Between Depot and Centre streets.
78   Between Centre and South streets.
87   East of the railroad track between Depot and Hill streets.
86   East of the railroad track between Raymond Street and Tub Shop.

Three whistles repeated once would indicate that the fire had been put out or was under control.

The files of newspapers are incomplete for 1894, but the little information available implies "tension in the ranks." An item in the *Lyndonville Journal* of January 24 stated that "the firemen have recently notified the village trustees that unless they are paid $100 [per year] and 25 cents an hour when on duty, hereafter, they will not serve." A special village meeting was called for Monday evening, February 5, "to take action upon the matter." The *Vermont Union* of February 16 announced that "a new fire company was organized last Thursday evening with Tip (W. H.) Wilmarth foreman, Henry Watson assistant, A. A. Rand secretary and treasurer, A. Ruggles janitor, Harrison Hunter foreman of hose." In the summer of 1895 the fire department purchased a new hose cart and 500 feet of 2½ inch hose; and in late December the breach had evidently been closed, for we find listed the members of two fire companies organized December 23—Tiger

No. 1 and Enterprize No. 2—though the personnel is somewhat changed from earlier lists.[29] Tiger No. 1 comprised W. H. Wilmarth, H. Hunter, B. H. Pierce, F. W. Camp, A. E. Stevens, Fred Pound, R. Kennerson, T. H. Leland, F. G. Francis, and A. E. Ruggles. Enterprize No. 2 claimed as members Chauncey Sargent, J. Connoway, E. L. Watt (Wells? Watson?), E. D. Brown, C. R. Jenness, Rob McCullough, John Gilvray, A. E. Brown, G. G. Wheeler, and J. W. Lowrey.

The *Vermont Union* of December 24, 1897, reported that the fire department consisted of two fire hose companies of ten men each and a hook-and-ladder company of eight men.

> They have two fire hose carts with a long string of new hose, with a full assortment of nozzles, axes and small tools which go with them, and a brand new hook and ladder cart, carrying from 20-foot to 55-foot extension ladders. One hose cart and engine and the hook and ladder cart is kept in the basement of Village Hall where there is rigged a place for drying hose, reaching behind the stage from the basement to the roof of the building. Another firemen's room is in the building near the brass foundry at the upper end of Main Street.

Not until 1899 did the firemen receive their rubber suits—coats, helmets, and boots. In 1907 Gardner Menut, who had worked for the light plant, installed fire alarm call bells in the homes of the members of the fire company so that the bells would ring simultaneously. In the same year a new district and signal system was adopted: the alarms were to be blown by the railroad shop whistle or yard locomotive, the general alarm being one long or a succession of long and short whistles followed by the signal showing the location as follows:

District No.   1 B & M shops—continuation of general alarm
                   2 Church Street—two short whistles
                   3 Depot Street—three short whistles
                   4 Broad and Williams streets—four short whistles
                   5 Elm, South Center to Main—five short whistles
                   6 Park Avenue and Center to Main—six short whistles
                   7 North Main Street from Grove Street to
                         Creamery—one long and one short
                   8 Central Main Street from Grove Street to Park
                         Street—one long and two short

9 South Main Street from Park Street to Center Street
—one long and three short
10 Raymond and East streets Novelty Works—two
long and one short
11 Hill Street to Raymond—two long and two short
12 Charles and Prospect streets—two long and three
short

In 1909 the department acquired a large life net of especially strong material, and in 1917 a pulmotor that was kept in Hotel Lyndon in order to have it centrally located for emergency use; it was rescued unharmed from the ashes of the 1924 fire. Modernization continued with the purchase of a motor fire engine in 1926, and late in the season a new siren was installed on Music Hall. It was tested each day at 12:15 p.m., incidentally providing an accurate standard time.

Lyndonville has enjoyed extended continuity of service from the members of its fire department. Good illustrations of this are the men who have been chiefs in the last half century. Perley Baraw joined hook-and-ladder company no. 3 in 1906 and served as its captain from 1916 to 1926, when he was elected chief; he was reelected sixteen times. He was succeeded in 1943 by E. L. Kelley, who had joined the fire company in 1921.

Raymond Brown became chief in 1946 and served twenty-one years, retiring in 1967. William H. Davis, the first assistant engineer, followed him but served less than a year before his death; he was succeeded by Wendell Cassady, who had already seen sixteen years in the ranks.

The relationship of these volunteer fire companies to the governmental organization of Lyndonville appears to be unique. Throughout the years the village government bore the full costs of companies' equipment, insurance, etc, while the companies chose their complete slate of officers. By 1900 the "chief engineer of the fire department" was chosen by popular election at the annual village meeting; by 1956 the position was listed in the annual report as being appointed by the village trustees.

Chief Steve Eastman drew a salary of $10 a year. In 1947, when Ray Brown became chief, the rate had risen to $200 a year, and the secretary began to be paid $15 a year. Through the years at the annual meeting, the village consistently authorized abatement of the poll taxes of firemen. The rate of pay for firemen has been impossible to determine, however. Whether they were paid the same when helping a neighboring community is likewise uncertain, but for many years item credits were recorded for charges to those communities as well as to the village; these came to an end in 1954. From some entries it appears that the fire victims were responsible for paying the firemen. During many of the years the financial reports noted payments to firemen for practice sessions. The annual village reports for many years included a report from the chief engineer recording the number of fires attended in the village, in the town, and in neighboring towns; these came to an end soon after 1900. Since 1925 a constantly decreasing amount of space has been given to the report of fire department expenditures in the annual village report.

It appears that since 1974 the village of Lyndonville and the town of Lyndon have shared the fire department costs equally.

Chief Engineers — Lyndonville Volunteer Fire Department

1889	Charles E. Bullis
1890	George W. Knight
1892	Parker P. Ball
1894	W. H. Wilmarth
1901–07	Steve Eastman
1907–18	F. E. Dwinell
1918–22	Ronald Bell
1923–25	Fred T. Pound
1926–42	P. F. Baraw
1943–46	E. L. Kelley
1947–66	W. Raymond Brown
1967–68	Wm. H. Davis
1968–	Wendell P. Cassady

The central water supply was made available to Lyndon Center in the late fall of 1895, and in early April 1896 the men of the community began arrangements for organizing a volunteer fire company. Twenty-five of them signed a note of $450 for purchasing the necessary equipment: 500 or 600 feet of hose, a hose carriage, and various pieces of small equipment. E. H. Hinds was elected president and G. F. Ferguson secretary; the executive committee consisted of Hinds, W. F. Stoddard, and C. K. Hubbard. The first chief engineer (1896) was Hinds; his assistant was J. I. Welch.

Soon after the village was incorporated in 1896, Lyndon Center Fire District 3 came into being, taking the place of Lyndon District 3. The Lyndon Center district assumed the boundaries, equipment, and debts of the old district. Although those who advanced the money for the fire equipment could have been reimbursed through village taxes, the people preferred to raise the money through other means. During the next few years the members of the community were drawn more closely together by their efforts to repay this debt through promenades, box parties, numerous dramatic programs, and parties observing various holidays. In addition to the original $450, money was also raised to provide a coat, helmet, and boots for each fireman.

During the succeeding years a chief engineer and an assistant were elected at each annual village meeting, and the poll taxes of a 12-man volunteer company were abated. Activities of the district were supervised by two engineers and three village trustees, who together made up the Board of Fire Wardens. At irregular intervals the company exercised the hose cart by flushing the hydrants to keep them in prime condition for an emergency, and the cesspools to assure they would carry off the surface water from the streets. When a neighboring community needed assistance, the fire company was always on hand.

The village policy of abating the poll taxes of firemen came to an end in 1928, when that item in the warning was "passed over." In its place, the village voted to pay up to ten firemen 50¢ per meeting whenever present. This policy was continued for the next three years, though the limit on the number to be so paid was omitted. In 1933 George McLeod was reelected chief engineer, and it was voted that in case of fire the Lyndonville fire chief, two firemen, and the truck should be requested to cooperate with Chief McLeod and three firemen from the Center. Though a chief engineer and assistant continued to be elected annually—the last being Chief Clinton Adams and his assistant Stanley Amadon—a volunteer fire company in its original sense ceased to exist even before the surrender of the village charter in 1962.

In the first week of January 1900 a fire company was organized in Lyndon Corner with the following personnel: chief engineer James Lamond, assistant W. N. Hubbard; first hydrant man Wm. J. Pope, assistant E. E. Bailey; first hose man Daniel Paris, assistant Murray Paris; first nozzle man James MacFarland, assistant A. T. Hoyt; cart man C. L. Welch; first fireman Chas. Bradshaw, second fireman Richard Little, and third fireman U. S. Grant. Equipment included 600 feet of hose and the cart. As was the case at Lyndon Center, various means were used to pay for the equipment, including parties and private donations. By 1903 the fire company had adopted the name "Green Mountain Hose Company #1."

ॐ

Water

DURING THE EARLY YEARS OF THE TOWN each family assumed responsibility for supplying its own needs for water. Many brought water to their homes through pump logs from neighboring springs, and others used wells. Both methods supplied adequate water of excellent quality.

In the early 1880s the lack of available water in the town cemetery, at Lyndon Institute, and at the village school motivated discussion of the possibility of a central source of water in Lyndon Center. As previously noted, a reservoir was built on the top point of the hill back of the cemetery and north of Thompson Hall, and water was piped into it from a spring on the farm of L. B. Harris, three-fourths of a mile west and about fifty feet higher than the reservoir. An earlier plan to bring water from a source on the Whipple farm was abandoned.

Concurrently with constructing the new railroad shops in Lyndonville, a crew of about forty men was assigned to build a reservoir on a hill about 200 feet above and east of the shops to provide an adequate source of water for the shops and the community. Ready for use January 16, 1867, this reservoir, 50 x 80 feet and 7 feet deep, was capable of holding 200,000 to 300,000 gallons of water. The plan was to convey the water in iron pipes through the various streets and install hydrants at convenient distances to provide adequate fire protection.

In 1870 the railroad company purchased an additional spring from Cyrus Newcomb and added it to the reservoir; two years later the two-inch iron pipes were replaced with four-inch-bore pump logs. In 1880 the locomotive Union was converted into a stationary engine in the roundhouse and assigned the task of pumping water from the river to the reservoir. In 1881 the village trustees were instructed to investigate the possibility of acquiring the water privilege of the old Whipple Starch Factory—the price set was $250. During the next few years this waterpower was purchased by Dr. J. W. Copeland, Robert Pettigrew, Jeremy Pearl, and Isaac W. Sanborn; it has since been known as "Copeland water." By the fall of 1885 these men had incorporated as the Lyndonville Water Company with a capital stock of $3000 and the right to raise to $10,000. Contracts had been let for the necessary pipe (Hopkins and Thompson) and for digging the ditch (A. W. Houghton) to bring this water to the village.

At the annual meeting of the village on January 1, 1892, a committee of C. P. Chase, J. T. Gleason, and Jeremy Pearl was appointed to investigate the possibility of securing additional water supplies, especially needed in case of fire. A few days later Pearl refused to serve, so Milo L. Stearns was appointed in his place. This committee employed S. A. Elsworth a hydraulic engineer of Holyoke, Mass. to make a survey of the needs and the available sources of water for the town of Lyndon. During the next three years several special village meetings were held to address the problem, and the annual sessions were practically dominated by the consideration of some of the aspects of the problem of an adequate water supply. One practical action taken during this time was to secure legislative authorization for the village to bond itself for $40,000.

John W. Burk, a civil engineer from New York City (formerly with Chappell & Burk of Rutland), and Joel Foster, superintendent of the Montpelier Water Works, were engaged to review all aspects of the situation. With the village committee they carefully examined

The dam of the Lyndonville Water Works Reservoir (*Mrs. Milton Kerr*)

Quimby Brook, Burke Mt. Brook, Fall Brook, and Hines Brook as the available sources for a water system. They made extensive reports that were fully considered at a special village meeting on February 28, 1895. Though no action was taken, the board of commissioners was instructed and empowered to issue water-bonds and to construct a new water system incorporating the water from Hines Brook and to add Fall Brook if that seemed wise. This system was to be centered from a reservoir built on the Ed. Mathewson Farm.[30]

The contract for installation of the waterworks was awarded to Flood and Sherrill of Sandy Hill, N.Y. A crew of forty Italians began work near the Union House on Friday morning, May 10, 1895, digging the ditch for laying the pipe.[31] The task presented many difficulties. For example, in Squabble Hollow the ditch had to be dug nineteen feet deep through a hill of solid clay, and when that was conquered an equal depth had to be blasted through a ledge. The work was finished September 28, 1895, at a total cost of $39,888.76.

There was real satisfaction with the establishment of this central water system providing service for both Lyndon Center and Lyndonville.[32] The system was expected to provide daily domestic consumption of sixty gallons per person for a population of 4000, and fire protection sufficient to supply eight hydrant streams working in unison at sixty pounds pressure.

However, in less than ten years—many of them having below normal rainfall—the village was again forced to conserve water in spite of using both the Copeland and the railroad company reservoir supplies. In 1909 two springs were purchased from George Ingalls, one from Ed. Mathewson, and one from D. M. Silsby, all of which were piped into the Mathewson Reservoir.

The year 1913 was one of drought, and the search for additional sources of water was renewed. During the next two years the water supply was extended to Pinehurst, thereby increasing the urgency of the search. Serious consideration was given to the Shonyo Brook and the Dishmill Brook in East Burke. Finally the Copeland water supply was purchased, and a new reservoir having a capacity of 700,000 gallons was built near the icehouse on the road to West Burke. A pumphouse was built just north of the entrance to the campground to shelter the 50-horsepower electric motor used to operate the pumping plant, which had a capacity of 300 gallons per minute. The complete cost of this auxiliary system, including land damage, was $7,225.69.

The flood of 1927 damaged the water reservoirs, and in repairing the cement roads, further damage was done to the water pipes, thereby necessitating many replacements. According to the annual reports of the village officers, there were constant repairs and extensions to provide further service. In 1930 the Mathewson Dam had to be rebuilt and its walls repaired, and the bottom of the reservoir was scraped and repaired. As a result, the capacity of the reservoir was significantly increased.

The dry summer of 1936 placed a serious drain on the village water system and motivated a new quest for an increased supply of water. This time the solution was an artesian well drilled on land at the north end of East Street. It was fifty-two feet deep and capable of furnishing nearly 1.5 million gallons of water per day. A 75-horsepower electric motor costing about $10,000 was installed to operate the well pump.

The originally established water rates were $10 per year for the first family in a building, $5 for the second family. At first these charges were adequate not only to cover the costs of maintenance but also to put a creditable balance in the village treasury. At the 1952 village meeting the water rates were increased to $12 per single family, plus $7.50 for the second family and $6 for the third family in any single dwelling. At the same meeting by a vote of 36 to 12, the village voters approved the recommendation of Water Commissioner Warren Schribner to chlorinate the village water and authorized the borrowing of $10,000 to accomplish the task.

In 1964 the village water commissioners[33] and trustees began negotiations with the board of trustees of the Vermont State College for acquisition of the Chandler Pond water system. This seventy-nine-acre tract of land in South Wheelock was considered a most desirable addition to the town's fire protection complex. Vail had created the system many years before to supplement his spring-water fire-protection system and to create ornamental ponds on the Speedwell Farms Estate. The state health department decreed that if the water were to be used for domestic purposes it would have to be treated through a chlorinating plant, the cost of which was estimated at $7500. As a condition of the purchase of the system for $1, the village pledged to furnish the college with water without charge for twenty-five years, and further promised that this agreement would be automatically renewed until canceled by the College.[34] The deal was finally consummated and the connection made to the Mathewson Reservoir system on the meadow near the Hill Manufacturing Company at a cost of $30,919.89.

The water system supplying Lyndon Corner was created by Mr. C. L. Woodbury of Burlington in 1899; he had recently completed the Chandler Pond system for Vail. The reservoir was located 1¼ miles west of the village. Woodbury continued to own the property for a short time before selling to John McLellan of Barton, who in turn sold to Scott N. Farnum and his wife in 1910 for $6500; Farnum gained a $500 commission on the trade. When the payment of the commission became public knowledge, the village refused to pay the $7000, thus leaving Farnum "holding the bag." The investment proved so profitable, however, that in twelve years its value tripled, thus motivating protests when Farnum raised the rates in 1922 and again in 1934 and 1936. During the next few years several "trades" were made, and quarrels continued. In 1948 Alan W. Woodworth purchased the water system from the Farnums, and twenty years later he sold it to the Lyndonville Water Department for $18,000; the two systems were united in Hadleyville.

The extension of the Lyndonville Water service in many directions, especially to the higher land east of the village, resulted in fluctuating water pressure and made clear the need for additional water sources before many years had passed. Dubois and King were engaged to search for such sources, a process that continued for some time. Finally in 1974 they found a possible well site near the junction of highway 114 with the road onto Bemis Hill (Darling Hill), on property belonging to Guy and Margaret Birchard; the land was purchased for $13,186.12 A 52-foot-deep gravel-packed well with a rated capacity of 750 gallons per minute was constructed, plus two covered reservoirs: the east one, on Finney Hill, had a capacity of 1.5 million gallons, and the other, on the west side of Vail Hill, had a capacity of 1 million gallons. This west reservoir is about ninety-three feet higher than the east one. The cost of the sites for these two reservoirs was reported at $15,000. The annual village meeting voted authority for a $1.7 million bond issue for the new system. The water from this well was added to the village supply late in 1975.[35] Again, as so many times in the past eighty years, the community has been assured of an adequate water supply "for years to come." This promise has a greater likelihood of fulfillment than its predecessors, for the town has installed meters and has set a minimum quarterly price of $15 for each initial 15,000 gallons used plus 70¢ per each additional thousand gallons.

୨◉

Electric Power

INTENDED TO PROVIDE POWER for electric lights in the village, Lyndonville's electric company eventually supplied power for the town and even for neighboring communities.

During the summer and fall of 1888 there was much local discussion of the desirability of electric lights in Lyndonville, especially as they would contribute to the convenience of working in the railroad shops. In the early fall of 1889 a man from the St. Johnsbury Electric Plant came to the shops to make the necessary arrangements for installation. On October 30 the lights came on for the first time, with 104 of them distributed as follows: 15 in the paint shop, 2 in the boiler shop, 4 in the blacksmith shop, 2 in the tin shop, 2 in the toolroom, 31 in the woodshop, 3 in the office, 2 in the pattern room, 1 in Woodward's office, 2 in the engine room, and 41 in the machine shop.

A meeting was held at the Union House on August 19, 1895, to discuss the matter of the community providing for electric light service. A committee consisting of T. N. Vail, M. L. Stearns, L. C. Todd, Dr. Dwinell, and J. T. Gleason was appointed to investigate all aspects of the project. The idea of forming a stock company to undertake the project appeared most probable at the time.

By early October a special village meeting had voted authority to the village trustees to pledge the credit of the village to provide an electric plant expected to cost $15,000 to $20,000. A committee of S. Stern, M. L. Stearns, and L. C. Todd reported that the Wilder Company would lease the Great Falls for five years at 6 percent of the $22,000 that they asked for their title with privilege of purchase at the end of the five years. Acceptance of the offer was authorized.

Immediate activity had to be suspended while waiting for authorization from the legislature for the village to borrow the necessary funds. Pending that authorization, M. L. Stearns, S. Stern, L. C. Todd, and J. T. Gleason formed a company to take over the property.

They gave a note for $18,000 and held it until the village could take possession.

The poles for the electric lights were set in November 1895. A quotation from the *Vermont Union* of November 26 gives us the route they followed:

> . . . from the pulp mill over the hill through the Hoffman sugar place, to the John Dickerman place, then down the hill reaching the highway west of the Hall and Lincoln bridge, cross the river, the Spencer meadow, cross the track at that point, then take the hill east of the track to the south end of the village when they cross the track again and enter town. From the village the wire will run to the Centre and up to Speedwell Farms, where wires are strung for a large number of lights. Eight men are at work at the Pulp Mill putting the building in proper condition, taking out the old wheels, putting in two new ones, having under the head a 640 horse power. The plant will require 150 horse power leaving the company 500 horse power to rent to some additional electric company or to some factory enterprise. . . .

Lights were turned on in Lyndonville for the first time on Tuesday evening, February 25, 1895. The rates as stated in the *Vermont Union* of December 5, 1895, were a marked contrast to those of the 20th century.

> . . . stores and offices, each light $3.00 cellar and back room $2.00; hotels, first light in each room except sleeping rooms $3.00, extra $2.00; first light in each sleeping room $2.00, extras $1.00, each light in bath room or water closet $3.00; barn or stable $3.00. Public halls, each light $2.00, each footlight $1.00. Churches, schools, houses and society halls each light $1.00. Private houses, first light in each living room or hall $3.00, extras $1.50, each light in barn, shed, or cellar $1.00, first in sleeping room or bathroom or pantry $1.50, extras $1.00. Meter rates: ⅔ of one cent per hour per light with minimum rate of $35.00 per year for stores, $14.00 per year for all others. Meters of ordinary size cost about $14.00, to be furnished by the owner of the house, or by the village at a rental of 10% of cost with privilege of buying.

The first electric light commissioners were M. L. Stearns, J. T. Gleason, and W. S. Jeffers. Their first report, appearing in the village report of 1897, shows bills payable of $2,139.03, cash received

$4,908.99, due the commissioners $759.48. The first manager of the electric light plant was Horace Locklin.

In the summer of 1902 an accident occurred at the plant: the driving pulley on the main shaft in the wheel pit burst, and about a quarter of the face was thrown out. This left the community without electrical power for several days and forced the Electro-plating Company and Our Husbands' Company to close until repairs were completed. This shut-down time was utilized by the commissioners to finish repairs on the flume, long delayed by excessive high water. During the year 1911 meters were installed so that all current furnished outside the village was regulated by them.

The 1913 village report proudly quoted from the biennial report of the Vermont Public Service Commission that it considered the Lyndonville Electric Plant among the first in the state, both physically and financially.

On December 11, 1914, the powerhouse at the electric plant burned; on July 2, 1915, at 8:35 in the evening the current from the hydroelectric Lyndonville Electric Light Plant came on. This was a completely new plant, with generators, waterwheels, and building of the most modern type. Due to numerous unanticipated problems the cost of the plant was higher than estimated — $45,000 instead of $33,000. The electric light commissioners were H. J. Hubbard, H. E. Graves, and H. W. Lyster. The building contract was held by the Twitchell Construction Company of Lewiston, Maine, with F. C. Keene of Groveton, New Hampshire, as superintendent. The building, three stories high, was built of brick and reinforced concrete, on a foundation of solid rock, 39 x 41 feet in size, 68 feet from foundation to roof. It was doubly reinforced with ½- to 1¼-inch iron. The machinery had been manufactured and installed by the Morgan Smith Company of York, Pa., and installed under the personal direction of Superintendent Durgan. The electrical work was made and installed by the General Electric Company, with A. E. Moores superintending. The wheels were of bronze, and all the fittings were of the best. Austin Cheney and Owen Wood were established as having operating charge of the new plant.

On July 3, 1915, power from Lyndonville's new plant reached West Burke's streets and homes. In 1921 Lyndon Institute sold its Vail Elec-

Lyndonville Electric Plant at Great Falls (*Lyndonville Electric Light Department*)

tric Plant (Cahoon Falls Plant, Hall's Mills, Little Falls) to Lyndonville for $10,000 plus electrical service to Lyndon Institute for ten years at 5¢ per kilowatt-hour. During the same year connections were made between the Lyndonville Electric Plant and the Twin State Gas and Electric Company to make possible the interchange of power between them.

Lyndonville's arc light street system was converted to twenty-four incandescent 1000-candlepower units in 1923, and the next year the street lighting equipment at the plant was changed from a direct current mercury arc rectifier system to a straight alternating current circuit at a cost of just under $500. In 1925 the legislature passed the necessary authorization for issue of bonds to "renew, enlarge, and improve" Lyndonville's electric plant. After serving since 1912 on Lyndonville's Electric Light Commission, Henry E. Graves resigned in December 1927, and W. O. Erskine was appointed to fill the office until the March meeting.

The 1928 annual town report announced the lease ($25 per year) of land at the corner of Grove and Church streets from the Canadian Pacific Railroad Company for the construction of a substation. The utility also paid $6000 for a General Electric capacitor of 300 KVA capacity with automatic control in order to maintain the necessary voltage for the village. Effective October 1, 1929, new and uniform electric rates were established, with power use recorded by meters. The change was the direct result of protests by patrons charged a meter rate in contrast to the flat rate or lower meter rate charged residents of Lyndonville.

The 1929 village report shows the cost and extent of repairs resulting from the 1927 flood, which had changed the course of the river. The new cement dam cost $91,310.26 and the new canal $20,000. Installing flood gates had to be postponed, but finally cost an additional $493.69, for a total of $111,803.95. To counteract the change of river course and restore efficiency, as well as to stop the leak that had occurred under the flood gates, required work costing $4,297.78. Larger wire on the distribution lines from the Creamery to the Lyman Brown place was necessitated to supply the Darling distribution system at East Burke, due to the flood having taken out its generating system.

Henry E. Graves was appointed manager of the electric light plant by the commissioners in 1931; he retired in 1947 after thirty-seven years of service in the plant, fifteen as commissioner. When he took office the interest-bearing debt of the plant was $126,000, a residue of the 1927 flood. Under his guidance not only was this debt paid off but as of January 1, 1947, the sum of $87,175.31 had been set aside for improving and redeveloping the plant properties. The income of the plant for 1933 was $52,161.66, and in 1946, $131,635.42. In 1931 there were 52 miles of lines in operation; by 1947 the plant owned and maintained 175 miles of lines. Graves' successor was Leland F. Gray, who served until 1974.

About 13 miles of pole line were added to the Lyndonville plant when the East Burke light line was purchased from the E. A. Darling estate in 1931; in 1932 8 miles of lines were built from the Don Easterbrooks farm to Whipple Mills in Sutton; 45 miles of distribution lines were added in 1947 when the West Burke village light system was acquired for $18,000.

John Chase proudly announced in the *Vermont Union-Journal* that:

> One of the most successful and profitable of the municipally owned electric light plants in Vermont is located in Lyndonville and on an investment of a quarter of a million dollars closed the year 1938 free of debt and with a net profit of $21,546.29. In the past eight years the Lyndonville plant paid off from its earnings interest bearing indebtedness to the amount of $126,000. In the meantime the Village treasurer has deposited in the Lyndonville Savings Bank and Trust Company $5,900 as a savings account.
>
> Forty-three years ago, February 25, 1896 the municipality started this profitable enterprize. Even in the depression year of 1933 it reported net profits of $12,697.21 which increased to $19,497.41 in 1936.
>
> The plant consists of two hydro-electric generating stations situated on the Passumpsic River at the southern end of the town of Lyndon. The upper plant was built by the late Theodore N. Vail to supply his Speedwell Farms Estate with light and power. The lower one is located at what is locally known as the Great Falls. From these two modern stations the electric energy is distributed over 92 miles of transmission wires furnishing both light and power.
>
> In addition to their net profit the plant furnished the past year without charge the current for lighting the village streets, the park, the municipal buildings and also furnished the power for the pumping of the municipally owned water supply. The free service has an estimated value of approximately $6500 a year.
>
> Henry E. Graves is superintendent of the plant; the finances are handled by P. R. Griswold as village treasurer, and the board of electric light commissioners are David R. Grapes, the garage owner, A. W. Edmunds, druggist, and Dr. A. A. Cheney. These all share in the credit of the financial success of the plant. The annual profit is used in part to reduce the village tax rate and help in making many village improvements. . . .

During the 1930s and '40s not only was the plant service sufficiently profitable to pay off its indebtedness, establish a reserve fund for development of the Vail plant, and rebuild the Great Falls plant when needed; it also contributed to the village general funds so that for a few years no taxes were levied.

In April 1948 one of the first major acts of the new manager was presenting to a special village meeting the proposal for a $200,000 bond issue to cover cost of constructing a new hydroelectric generating plant to replace the existing one. As a result of this work the Vail station was closed for several months in mid-1949, and two 12,000-volt substations were constructed, one adjacent to the Great Falls, the other in the village; when they were put in operation (October 23, 1949), they reduced the voltage drop in transmission of power by 30 percent. Because of increased costs of operating expenses, a petition was made to the Public Service Commission for a rate increase, which became effective September 1, 1949.

For the months of May and June 1950 the Great Falls station was shut down for repairs, work being done by the O. W. Miller Company of Ludlow, Mass. (the same company as had constructed the new Vail station), at a cost of $29,177.18.

On August 1, 1951, Lyndonville became the first community in the country to have its main street lighted with a flourescent system—one only recently developed to the point where it had been offered for commercial use. A number of officers of the General Electric Corporation, manufacturers of the system, were present to witness the event. The new system consisted of ten of the largest street lighting fixtures in the world. Thirty-foot high tubular aluminum poles supported by aluminum alloy cast bases were staggered at 65-foot intervals along both sides of Depot Street. The actual lights suspended from the poles were 8-foot-long fluorescent luminaries, each equipped with four slimline lamps putting out a total of 21,000 lumens. The cost of the system was estimated at $6000.

On January 24, 1954, Music Hall burned, resulting in destruction of many of the records of the Lyndonville Electric Plant and the loss of much equipment. Through quick and effective action of employees, however, much was saved and the disruption in service was minimal. On the last night of January 1957 twenty-one fluorescent lights were placed along Main Street, making it as bright as Depot Street had been for the last few years.

From 1955 to its closing in 1963 the North Concord Air Force Station on East Mountain in East Haven was a major user of Lyndonville electric power, with its use increasing each year. The bill for 1962 was $43,468.17, and for 1963, $56,842.79. The 1957 town report announced the capital investment of the light plant at year's end as $1,339,073.57, a net valuation of $882,932.87. In mid-1961 the office staff of the Lyndonville Electric Plant, after several years in more or less temporary places, opened new quarters in the Norris block at the northwest corner of Church and Depot streets in space occupied for many years by the post office.

Manager Gray reported in December 1961 the necessity of replacing the then-existing power rate (established in 1949), with a higher rate, due to the increased cost of power purchased by the plant. This cost had risen from $1.65 per kilowatt per month (1949) to $2.35 (1961) and to $2.50 as of the beginning of the new year (1962). This new rate schedule did not change the rates for residential, rural, farm, commercial, water heating, or street lighting.

In 1968 the voters of Lyndonville at a special meeting authorized (174 to 10) a $300,000 bond issue for the purchase of 3000 shares of Vermont Yankee Nuclear Power Corporation stock. The apparent justification of the action resulted from expectation of lower power costs over a twenty-five-year period by $11,000 a year, and retirement of the bond issue without increase of village tax rate, no rise in power charges, and no drop in the utility's annual appropriation to the village.

Membership in the New England Power Pool the following May at a cost of $1000 made reserve electrical power available to the plant at a lower rate.

Village Hall

THIS BUILDING, located at the northwest corner of Broad and Center streets in Lyndonville, probably provided the most diverse services of any building in town—a fact that justifies the different names applied to it: the Opera House, Village Hall, Music Hall, the Armory.

In the summer of 1883 two trustees, W. H. Fletcher and Stephen Eastman, purchased a secondhand fire engine for the village. No place existed to store it, however; several village meetings had authorized construction of an engine house, but none had been built. Therefore, at the annual village meeting in 1884, the trustees were "instructed to build an engine house and in connection therewith a village hall, at an expense not to exceed $4000." This hall was to accommodate 1000 people. Although voters authorized the trustees to use their discretion in the choice of the site, their choice was not universally approved, and in fact the entire project remained the subject of controversy and even ridicule. The lot was provided by subscription.[36]

Editor Charles Chase provided posterity with this description of the new building on the eve of its dedication:

> The Village Hall which has occasioned the creations of so many rhymers, pro and con, will be completed next week, and the public will be very much surprised, when they step into it, to see so fine an opera house in a village no larger than Lyndonville. They will also be surprised to see that so good a building has cost the Village so little money. The building stands on a firm foundation 50 x 90 in size. The basement is 8 feet high and is divided as follows: kitchen 19 feet square, dining room 30 x 50, police room 10 feet square, two lock-ups 5 x 8, a wood room 10 x 50, a furnace room 10 x 50, water closets 10 x 20, an engine room on the east end under the stage 11½ feet high and 20 x 50 in size. Entering the main hall you step up a half dozen steps into the ante-room 21 x 21 with two doors leading into the concert room and two into the gallery. The main audience room is 50 x 60 and 25 feet high. At the west end is a stage, 3 feet above the floor, 20 x 50 in size with the opening arch for the drop curtains 17 x 28. On each side of the stage is a dressing room 7 x 8, in the rear of which space is left for the sliding of stage scenes. . . . The gallery, self supporting and sustained by 4-inch iron rods is built on two sides and the east end. The floor of the gallery is 9 feet above the main floor and 15 feet under the top ceiling. The side galleries are 9 feet wide and are supplied with two rows of seats, and the east end gallery which extends, by a series of rising steps, back over the entry is 21 feet wide and supplied with 10 rows of seats. The entire gallery is supplied with 348 individual chairs fixed to the floor, and every

chair gives a perfect view of the whole stage. . . . On the lower floor
there will be 652 chairs. The seats were built in the building according
to a plan invented by Trustee W. H. Fletcher, and are very neatly
contrived and very comfortable. They are built in rows of six and
nine, fastened together, with bottoms so contrived that they can be
turned up and packed away with great economy of space. . . . The
cost of the chairs was only 40¢ each, about half as much as the same
space (1½ feet per person) costs in the ordinary settee. The front of
the gallery is of open iron work . . . nicely ornamented. The audience
room floor is of hard wood and laid in a manner to accommodate
the roller skaters. The Main hall will be lighted by a 24-light chandelier costing $125 and 20 side lamps . . . the cost of scenery ordered
will amount to $325, the cost of the chairs $400. . . . The work has
been performed wholly by the day under the direction of the trustees
W. H. Fletcher, Steve Eastman, and A. W. Houghton, with Fletcher
as chief designer and Houghton as boss of workmen. . . .

The dedication of the New Hall . . . will be with an entertainment
Thursday evening August 7 by the Boston Opera and Concert Company. The first part, grand concert, second part the second act of the
opera "Martha" in splendid costumes; Miss Louise Baldwin, so-
prano, Miss Alta Pease contralto, Mr. Harry G. Snow tenor, Mr.
Henry L. Caswell basso, Mrs. M. G. Shepard pianist. . . .

From Chase's description it is evident that there was adequate provision for storing the village fire apparatus. Throughout its existence
the hall also provided the village lockup, whose first occupants were
two young men from St. Johnsbury: J. J. Walker and Charles Hendricks in August 1884.

In 1891 the Village sold the west part of the Village Hall lot to
J. C. Eaton for $300, reserving 25 feet for a driveway back of the hall.
Eaton had purchased the Judge Baxter house[37] on Depot Street and
wished to move it so as to use its space for the construction of a
business block, to which he planned to move his hardware store from
Lyndon Corner.

The hall was wired for electric lights in 1895, and two furnaces were
installed in 1897. In the same year the building was painted on the
outside and wholly redecorated inside, and dressing rooms were
added at the basement level. Not until 1908 were fire escapes added

Music Hall [Village Hall, Opera House] and Lyndonville Savings Bank &
Trust Company & Depot Park, Broad Street, Lyndonville
(*Cobleigh Public Library*)

to the building. In 1910 an Ivers and Pond grand piano was purchased,
to be replaced in 1916 by a Merrill piano. In 1914 the lighting system
was changed:

> . . . the central chandelier being replaced by five 200-candle pendant
> lights, one in the center and four on the sides of the ceiling. These
> are covered with Alba-glass globes making a soft light. On the walls
> of the balcony are two-light-bracket-fixtures with roughed glass
> globes, while beneath the balcony are ten ceiling lights 32-candle
> power in similar globes. Red lights are placed over the exit doors by
> the fire escapes. The lights of the stage 135 in all, are red, white, and
> blue, located in sunken footlights and sky borders. The lighting also
> includes a new switch board, three dimmers, and two outside lights
> with large round globes of rough glass.

> The decorating done by U. S. Grant is soft and harmonious. The
> ceiling and balcony are done in old ivory with a bit of gold, which
> lights up very attractively in the evening. The tint of the ceiling drops
> into the border and blends gradually with the steel-gray of the walls,
> the woodwork being of a deeper warmer gray. The halls are done in

green and the three new dressing rooms downstairs are practically completed. The outside of the building is done in two shades of olive green. . . .

Throughout the years Village Hall was the most popular place in town for entertainments, especially those which might appeal to a sizable audience.[38] In fact, it was the center of the social life of the town. It was here that Memorial Day programs were held; here diplomas were given to the graduates of the Graded School and Lyndon Institute; in the balcony the Village meeting was usually held; here the Washington Ball was held for fifty years, and a host of other balls were sponsored for various holidays; bazaars and flower shows were held here in an annual procession. During the winter season all kinds of dramatic programs and concerts were presented to the public; few weeks passed without at least one such program, and some weeks they occurred every evening. Basketball games, roller skating, dancing schools, and the Village Improvement Society's Lecture Course programs were among the kaleidoscope of events. Here the community celebrated its triumphs and mourned its defeats. It was the village policy to waive the charge for renting the building when the sponsoring organization used its funds primarily for charitable purposes.

In early 1923 the village rented the hall to the state for $240 a year for the use of Company C of the National Guard; management of the building was vested in Capt. Herman L. Carter. One of the conditions of the lease was that existing agreements giving special privileges to local organizations such as V.I.S. and American Legion should be honored, but this proved not easily done. The village reserved the basement rooms for the continued use of Lyndonville Electric staff. The state could rent the building for local purposes, with the receipts to be used toward defraying the cost of heating and lighting as well as of repairing damages caused by the guard. Exterior repairs, however, remained the responsibility of the village. In 1927 the village trustees and the Improvement Society again joined forces to repair and renovate the hall. They put up a new steel ceiling, painted the building inside and out, put new shades on all the windows, and installed a new toilet on the first floor. The V.I.S. had a portico built over the steps, to which the electric plant contributed wiring for a new light and its globe; U. S. Grant painted the portico. In celebration of these accomplishments, there was a dance on October 14 with Dunbar's Orchestra supplying the music.

In 1929 the hall's furnace exploded, causing serious damage to the interior. Pieces of the boiler tore through two floors, cut off a large beam, and stuck in the balcony ceiling. Fortunately, V.I.S. women who had been arranging decorations for the Washington's Birthday Ball had just left the building.

When Company C was called to service in 1941, the Armory was unused for a short time, but before the end of the year the State Guard had been organized, so military use continued. Such use ended in 1954 when the village purchased the Gem Theatre and converted it into an armory.

The trustees' report in the village report for 1953 has this closing paragraph:

> In the fall of 1953 the Village voted to remodel the hall (Music Hall) and add a floor to the balcony height so that the two upper floors could be leased and bring in revenue. This remodelling had been completed, but before much benefit could be realized, fire on January 24th (1954) destroyed the old landmark—just 30 years to the day after the "big fire" in 1924.

In November 1953 the village leased the building to the Vermont Shoe Company, which immediately converted it into a shoe factory employing about thirty people. On Sunday, October 23, 1954, a fire of undetermined origin broke out on the second floor and had a vigorous start before it was discovered, and the building was completely destroyed.

The Public Library

THE FIRST LIBRARY IN THE TOWN had come into existence by 1865 as the "Agricultural Library"; on November 21 of that year its members met in the Lyndon Corner jewelry store of Cephas Appleby and elected him treasurer and librarian in place of L. R. Brown, "who has removed to St. Johnsbury." The *Vermont Union* carried infrequent references to this library, sometimes calling it the "village library" or "The Lyndon Agricultural Library," as in a final reference in 1896 when a call was issued for a meeting of its stockholders on June 31. At this meeting the major matter for consideration was apparently whether or not to give the "50–60 volumes of books and fair bookcase . . . to the town library about to be started."

During this period various groups attempted to establish a library. In June 1869 the employees of the railroad met to form a library association. They completed its organization the following month and elected officers: Hubbard Hastings, superintendent; A. H. Perry, treasurer; T. A. McKinnon, first librarian and clerk; I. W. Cunningham, second librarian; Geo. Magoon, third librarian; and J. C. Manser, H. A. Allen, W. W. Mack, J. R. Baldwin, N. P. Lovering, G. W. Newell, and H. P. Alden, directors. This association has been called "The Mechanical Employees Association." In December 1871 a group interested in forming a reading association met in the Mathewson block. After subscribing $40, they proposed to raise $200 and to secure the use of the room then known as the Thomas Bartlett office. According to the *Union*, "the Railroad folks proposed to place their library in the room when the organization is perfected."

Early in 1873 a club of ten members formed in the village of Lyndon. Each paid $5 toward the club's subscription to several "leading magazines" that circulated among the members. The headquarters of the club was in the store of L. K. Quimby & Company. In 1875 W. H. Fletcher and his wife established a lending library in his drugstore in the Mathewson block. Their charge was a penny a day; in 1880 the library had 300 volumes.

At the town meeting in March 1895 townspeople voted "to accept the provision in the law regarding free public libraries."[39] About a month later the trustees held their first meeting in the office of the Campbell and Blodgett Insurance Company. Rev. John Nason was elected chairman, E. M. Campbell was elected secretary and treasurer, and Professor Walter E. Ranger was made a committee to prepare "rules and bylaws to govern the distribution of books, and to report at the next meeting." E. M. Campbell was elected librarian and authorized to select the location for the library for one year; he chose the new Campbell and Blodgett office in the Ide block. By Christmas 1895 the books given by the state to start the public library had arrived and been unpacked.

The "Lyndon Free Library" was formally opened on February 29, 1896. On March 5, 1897, the *Vermont Union* reported:

> There are now 522 volumes in the library, in the 1st year there were 2544 takes from the library by 270 different persons. . . . During the year 203 books were purchased, 103 rec'd from the state, 104 from Lyndon Agricultural Library, 82 from Mr. Vail, 34 from other parties. The library has received $197, of which $100 came from the town, and the rest from the proceeds of entertainments contributed, with a few dollars from fines for keeping books beyond the allotted time. The receipts for the year were $196.89 and the expenditures $184.22 leaving a balance in the treasury of $12.67.

The original rules governing the use of the library's books, drawn up by Professor W. E. Ranger and adopted by the trustees, were as follows:[40]

1. Librarian has charge under the trustees and is responsible for the safety of the books.
2. Library open from 9 to 12, and from 2 to 6, Sunday and holidays excepted.
3. Entitled to books: any Lyndon inhabitant over 21, certified by trustees in writing to be a proper person; any inhabitant under 21 whose parent or guardian signs a certificate that they will be responsible for the observance of the rules by the minor, and for the loss or injury of books. Any person may read books in the library rooms.
4. The librarian furnishes record cards to each taker, who must always return it with the books and pay 2¢ for a new one if lost, and the taker must return it if he moves out of town.
5. Only one book at a time to be taken, kept a week only, but the permit to keep it a week may be renewed twice. Books restricted from circulation may be taken out only order from two trustees.

6. A fine of 2¢ a day on a book kept over time. Pencil marks, leaves turned down, or other injury subject to fine. No book to be loaned by the borrower.

7. A book kept two weeks over time shall be sent for by the librarian at the expense of the borrower, and a book retained a week after demand for it if made shall be considered lost and librarian shall collect its value with costs from the borrower. If the book belongs to a set the full value of the set shall be so collected. A book injured and in the opinion of the librarian rendered unfit for circulation shall be replaced by the borrower, and if it belongs to a set he shall replace the set or pay the value.

8. If a person violates the rules he may be suspended from the privileges of the library by the trustees. The librarian has power to suspend for two weeks in cases of emergency.

If the above rules are strictly adhered to, Lyndon will soon have a fine town library and one which will become popular and productive of much good.

After a year Campbell resigned as librarian, and Mrs. Rowena Duston was elected in his place at a salary of $25 a year; Miss Annie Houghton was elected as her assistant. On March 1, 1897, the library was moved from the insurance company office to Mrs. Duston's millinery store in the Cass block, where it was open three afternoons and two evenings each week. The next year Mrs. Duston asked that her salary be increased to $5 per month, and she agreed to furnish a room for the exclusive use of the library patrons.

After the death of Isaac W. Sanborn in 1902, it was found that his will gave to the town the knoll opposite the Folsom house on Center Street (opposite the end of Park Street) plus enough adjoining land to make two acres, providing the town built a free public library within five years. The town could erect other buildings on the land, but the library had to be built first. The will further provided a gift of $5000 for the benefit of the library if this site were used, and $3000 if it were not. In either case the library had to be owned by the town. After considerable quibbling, voters declined the Sanborn land gift at a special town meeting on May 28, 1904. At another special town meeting on December 14, 1904, voters authorized the trustees of the Lyndon Free Library to accept the monetary gift and invest it by

Cobleigh Public Library (*Harriet Fisher*)

purchasing the late Sanborn residence to be used as a library, provided it could be gotten for $3000.

Before the trustees had acted, Eber W. Cobleigh offered on January 9, 1905, to give the town $15,000 to erect a public library building. The conditions of the gift were few: (1) the building must be erected within the village limits of Lyndonville; (2) it must be known as the "Cobleigh Public Library"; (3) the name must be properly inscribed on the front of the building; (4) the building construction must be directed by a committee of three Lyndon residents elected at town meeting; and (5) if the building were not constructed by the end of 1906, the money must be returned to the donor or his estate. On the following Saturday evening the Women's Club arranged a reception for Cobleigh in Odd Fellows Hall, so the townspeople could express their appreciation for the gift. On January 21 a special town meeting accepted the Cobleigh gift, appointed the necessary building committee (G. M. Campbell, L. B. Harris, and N. B. Harvey), and authorized it to secure a site.

In late February the building committee reported six available sites for the library: (1) the corner of Main and Depot streets occupied by

D. M. Silsby's livery stable ($7000); (2) the Sanborn residence ($3000) and vacant lot ($1000) on South Street; (3) the Cheney lot ($1000) on Church Street north of the post office; (4) land on Center Street south of the C. L. Stuart residence, offered as a gift by C. M. Darling; (5) land on South Street east of J. T. Gleason's residence, offered by Gleason; and (6) land on Broad Street between the Lyndonville National Bank and Music Hall, offered by the bank. The Silsby lot was preferred, but its price looked prohibitive. However, T. N. Vail offered to pay one-third of the amount and townspeople donated an additional $3456.67.[41] At the annual meeting on March 7, 1905, the voters unanimously authorized the selectmen to purchase the Silsby lot and appropriated $1150 for that purpose.

The plans for the library building were drawn by a native Vermonter, William J. Sayward, an architect in the employ of McKim, Mead and White of New York City, a well-known firm that had designed the Boston Public Library and the Congressional Library in Washington, D.C. Dr. Edward T. Fairbanks of St. Johnsbury rendered invaluable assistance. The plans provided for a brick building with granite foundations and trimmings and a copper roof. The frontage was to be 53 feet on Depot Street and 51 feet on Main Street. The contract for construction—covering everything but electrical wiring, which was done by C. G. Norris—was let to C. W. Spear of Burlington at a cost of $15,500, with the building to be completed by July, 1906. Spear began work on September 4, 1905, and was later granted a three-month extension to allow the walls to dry completely. The brick came from Woodsville, N.H., and the granite from Hardwick, Vt. The entire finish of the ground floor is quartered oak rubbed to a dull luster.

The Women's Club furnished the northeast corner room at a cost of $446.08; it was intended to serve as a natural history room and a trustees' room. The club committee in charge was Mrs. W. S. Jeffers, Mrs. C. C. Trull, F. H. Davis, and Mrs. E. A. Shorey. On the outside of the building near the entrance was placed a bronze plaque bearing the inscription "This building was given to the Town of Lyndon by Eber W. Cobleigh, A.D. MCMV." Wood's Brass Foundry in Lyndon made the plaque: Charles Ladd carved the pattern by hand using a pocket knife and chisel, E. T. Wood cast the plaque, and H. F. Stahler put on the bronze finish. T. N. Vail donated one piece of sculpture (a Winged Victory of Samothrace) and twelve distinguished paint-ings,[42] all of which were advantageously placed in the Library.

The dedication of the Cobleigh Library took place in Music Hall on January 29, 1907. Seated on the platform were Cobleigh; members of the building committee; the board of library trustees; Mrs. Walter P. Smith of St. Johnsbury, chairman of the State Library Commis-sion; and officers of the Women's Club and its library committee. Dr. J. W. Copeland, chairman of the board of library trustees, served as presiding officer. Rev. William Shaw, pastor of the Methodist Church, offered a prayer; Mrs. C. G. Norris played a piano solo; Rev. I. W. McLaughlin read Cobleigh's remarks in presenting the gift, and Mrs. E. J. Blodgett graciously accepted for the town; Rev. W. C. Clark of Lyndon gave the dedication address; and Miss Alice Hutchinson sang. In closing Dr. Copeland read a telegram of congratulations from E. T. Fairbanks of the St. Johnsbury Athenaeum, and Mrs. A. L. Finney, president of the Women's Club presented the furnish-ings of the trustees' room as a gift to the library. After Rev. E. G. French of the Congregational Church pronounced the benediction, the library was opened to the public, and many visited it.

In 1907 the library made plans to open a branch in the Swett Store at Lyndon Corner, but they did not develop. However, in 1910 the library succeeded in establishing a branch in the south room of the E. C. Morse store building. The books were changed each month, and the library was open from 2 to 4 each Saturday afternoon. In the fall of 1907, in behalf of the heirs of the longtime *Vermont Union* editor Charles M. Chase, his executor, E. B. Chase, "offered to place in the Cobleigh Public Library the full bound files of the Union, the same to remain the property of the said heirs." The trustees accepted the offer.[43]

On April 1, 1908, Mrs. Duston resigned. The trustees asked Mrs. T. N. Vail, Mrs. E. J. Blodgett, and Mrs. W. S. Jeffers to serve as a committee to find a successor and then serve as an advisory committee to the trustees. Mrs. Flora J. (Campbell) Watson and Mrs. E. J. Blodgett served as interim librarians until March 4, 1909, when Miss

Elizabeth C. Hills was named to the position. She served until her death on November 2, 1920. Succeeding Miss Hills as librarian on November 15, 1920, was Miss Angie Hunter (Mrs. Frank B. Carr, 1936). She served faithfully in this capacity until the end of 1938, when she was succeeded by Mrs. Dora Forrest.

During World War I, in the interest of fuel conservation, the library was closed except for one afternoon each week. During part of 1918 it was completely closed by the quarantine of the State Board of Health because of the flu epidemic. During the war and again after the 1924 fire, a room in the library basement provided a central location for the thrift shop that local relief agencies and the Red Cross maintained. The "work room" on the main floor opposite the charge-out desk was converted into a children's room in 1926. During the latter years of the depression the Free Public Library Commission in Montpelier helped Cobleigh Library repair and catalog its books; the library modernized its methods of charging out books and installed the Dewey system of cataloging.

Hortense (Mrs. C. R.) Hoffman, succeeding Mrs. Forrest as librarian in 1954, instituted a program for high school students, in addition to the "story hour" for preschool children long sponsored by the Mothers' Circle of the Women's Club. Classes in the use of the library were given for high school freshmen; these met four days a week following a week's preparation at school. Lyndon Teachers College freshmen enrolled in the class in Children's Literature conducted the Story Hour during the first semester, and the Mothers' Circle handled the project from February to May 1. The library also borrowed films of children's literature from the Vermont Free Public Library Commission in Montpelier and showed them at the Lyndonville Graded School. At the end of 1962 Mrs. Hoffman resigned as librarian and was succeeded by Elizabeth Wyllie (Mrs. Douglas), who had been working part-time as an assistant since the preceding May.

The bimonthly film program instituted in 1968 at Darling Inn Convalescent Home had to be abandoned after a couple of years due to the lack of availability of a projector. In 1969 the library developed a similar program for senior citizens.

From its beginning Cobleigh Library has been a community endeavor, and many organizations have held benefits to raise money for it. The Women's Club has been the library's most faithful supporter, consistently contributing amounts—albeit small amounts during the first years—that have aided the growth of the institution. During its early period the library received many small gifts and bequests that were quickly used to meet urgent needs. Some of those funds that maintained their identity were the Copeland, Isaac Sanborn, Jennie Darling Folsom, Elizabeth C. Hills, Lyndon Women's Club, Mechanical Employees Association, and Cora B. (Mrs. M. E.) Daniels. In 1956 the "Tribute for Remembrance Fund" from the Universalist Church ($195.26) was added to the Elizabeth Hills Fund. This was appropriate, since she had helped to raise it, and the last of the women who had been responsible for the fund for many years—Mrs. G. F. Ferguson, Mrs. Albert Ruggles, and Mrs. G. A. Whipple—had recently died. From these various endowed funds the library received about $7500 in 1975—a welcome addition to the appropriations received from the town and village.

In 1896, when the public library began, the town appropriated $100; over the years it gradually increased the grants, to $4000 in 1975. The village did not begin financially supporting the library until 1917, when it donated $100. For nine years after 1947 the village donated the library's light bill in addition to its other grant; it then began to gradually increase the appropriation until 1975, when it reached $2700. In recent years the library has received federal and state grants. There follows a list of major grants from various sources, including in some cases the use to which the grant was put. (1) The initial renovation of the library basement in 1956–60 was made possible by a $1600 grant of the Lyndon Women's Club in cooperation with Sears and Roebuck. This provided a place for many small groups to meet and work: Lyndonville Band, Girl Scouts, Brownies, Boy Scouts, Lyndonville Fair Association, Lyndon Planning Board, Northeastern Vermont Development Association, Vermont Unemployment Service, Society for Prevention of Cruelty to Animals, Democratic Town Committee, Junior Democratic Town Committee, Republican Town Committee, Yankee Watters, OCCSA. (2) At the same time this renovation was taking place, the children's room opposite the charge-out desk was benefiting from investment of the $150 memorial Martin E. Daniels flower fund. (3) In 1972 the library was honored by a so-called incentive grant of $1000 from the Vermont Department of State Libraries. (4) In 1974 from the same source came a grant of $2000 in acknowledgment of the library having met state standards. (5) In 1974, $5000 became available—$2750 from a federal grant and $2250 from local funds—to reconstruct the basement into a library for juveniles and young adults, thus adding 1350 square feet. Thanks to Mr. and Mrs. Dean Parker, it was possible to incorporate in this reconstruction several pieces removed from the library of the Vail Mansion when it was razed. The total cost of these renovations, which extended from 1974 to 1976, was $6231.77. (6) In 1975 a special purpose grant provided $2500 to establish audiovisual facilities in the new youth library.

Lyndon has been privileged to have citizens willing to serve long terms as trustees of the Cobleigh Library; that continuity of service has been a major factor in the steady growth of the institution. The first chairman of its board of trustees, Dr. J. W. Copeland, served twenty-two years in that capacity. Not only did he give in unlimited measure of himself, but at his death he left a generous bequest of money to the library ($16,335.85), and at the termination of the life lease of his widow, their home[44] on Main Street and the "rest and residue of his estate" was "given to the town for the benefit of Cobleigh Library." He specified that "the income only shall be used . . ." ($35,193.30). Martin E. Daniels served as a member of the board of trustees for nearly fifty years; he was its secretary for forty-five years and treasurer for thirty-seven years. Perhaps his long years as superintendent of the town's public schools explains his constant interest in cultivating the enthusiasm of youth for the library. E. M. Campbell was secretary-treasurer for eighteen years. Other trustees who performed lengthy service were John King, nineteen years; Mrs. A. L. Leonard, eighteen; W. Edward Wilson, seventeen; Willis C. Conner, fifteen; and Walter L. Hughes, thirteen.

Notable among nontrustees was Constance Blodgett, who rendered long, tedious, and faithful service: cataloging and ordering books, substituting as librarian on a moment's notice, searching for new librarians—in short, doing anything that needed to be done.

Cobleigh Library has received many nonmonetary gifts. In 1907 Dr. A. A. Cheney gave a beautifully mounted blue heron for the natural history room; in 1911 Luther B. Harris presented two Indian jars, and Governor Proctor donated a case of different kinds of Vermont marbles; and in 1922 Henry E. Wilkie gave the library a case of nicely mounted birds.[45] In October 1924 the library received a real heirloom: Miss Jennie Trefren's gift of a grandfather's clock, in memory of Jude Kimball. Miss Trefren's father, James, had been an employee of Kimball and at the latter's death in 1851 had purchased his farm on the west part of Right 11 (the Barton right;) this clock was in the house at that time. Kimball had come to Lyndon in 1798 and had held many offices in the early years of the town.

In 1962 Wilfred Elliott gave the picture of Lake Louise for the children's room. Many citizens have bequeathed their libraries to Cobleigh.

VI

Village Improvement Societies

❧

Lyndonville

So MUCH HAD BEEN DONE by the railroad company in laying out the village of Lyndonville that beautification did not become a community concern for some years. Not until April 1891 did community interest in the subject prompt a meeting. Rev. J. C. Bodwell was chosen chairman, and a committee of Dr. J. W. Copeland, J. T. Gleason, Dr. F. E. Dwinell, Mrs. C. P. Chase, and Miss Nellie Davis was appointed to draft a constitution and bylaws.[1] Dues were set at $1 per year.

The bylaws provided that the name of the organization would be "The Rural Improvement Society of Lyndon." At the first formal meeting on May 9, 1891, officers were elected: Rev. J. C. Bodwell, president; Mrs. Allen Twombly, vice-president; H. B. Davis, secretary; Miss Ida S. Pearl, treasurer; and C. P. Chase, F. W. Silsby, L. S. Edgerton, W. A. Densmore, Mrs. C. P. Chase, Miss Nellie Davis, and Mrs. H. F. Balch, executive committee. The newspaper report of the meeting closed by noting that "the new organization starts off swimmingly with over $100 in the treasury and the promise of more, plus 60 members."[2]

Before its first summer had passed, the society had put name markers on the streets[3] throughout the village and had set some shrubbery. They had also appointed committees to consider other tasks. In 1893 new officers were elected: Dr. J. W. Copeland, president; Mrs. John Murch, secretary; M. L. Stearns, treasurer; and Jennie Darling (Mrs. H. E.) Folsom, Mrs. C. P. Chase, F. W. Silsby, M. L. Stearns, and J. T. Gleason, executive committee.[4] During the following year the men withdrew. The society became the Village Improvement Society, and the women accepted the responsibility of leadership with the 1894 election of officers: Mrs. H. E. Folsom, president; Mrs. E. L. Wells, secretary; and Mrs. F. W. Silsby, treasurer. The executive committee consisted of these officers plus Mrs. H. M. Pearl and Mrs. F. H. Davis. In reporting this election, the newspaper said: "Under this administration Lyndonville will get up early, comb all the snarls out of her head, wear a clean face, and file in towards the head of the procession of modern village progress. See if she doesn't!!" From this time on the society was a woman's organization, though many men, especially those in the original group, retained membership until their deaths;[5] they, and many others, gave generous moral and financial support and physical assistance whenever there was a need.

According to the by-laws, the purposes of the society were "planting and care of trees, the improving of parks and other public lands, the removal of unsightly objects, the making of needed improvements in beautifying the village of Lyndonville, and advancing its interests mentally and morally." A careful examination of the organization's activities over the years, creates a firm conviction not only of its faithfulness to these purposes but also of the diversity of ways in which it pursued them. For example, in the 1890s the society contributed both labor and money to the beautification of the Common. Throughout the nearly forty years of her service in the society, Jennie Darling Folsom was a tireless moving spirit, an inspiration to the community as well as to all who worked with her. Other members also contributed mightily; as compared with its accomplishments, the membership of the society has always been small.[6]

During the society's first years, the various presidents planned monthly meetings of members, but these were so poorly attended they were abandoned. It was found that more could be accomplished by appointing committees, each having some specific project to develop. This placed a greater responsibility on the officers and the executive committee, for they served as leaders of the various programs. The tradition began — and still continues — of holding an annual meeting, usually in April or October, at which members reported on the activities of the preceding year and elected officers and laid plans for the ensuing year.

The society obtained a charter from the state legislature in 1902 in the names of Jennie D. Folsom, Nettie L. Schofield, Alice L. Wilson, Emma B. Wells, Ida S. Pearl, Mary E. Campbell, Hattie T. Stuart, Minnie B. Wilmot, Ella S. Paige, and Mary S. Gleason. The charter granted the society many rights, including that of holding real estate and other property. Over the years the society has received the following major gifts: (1) $500 from Isaac W. Sanborn; (2) $1000 from Dr. J. W. Copeland; (3) $3000 from Jennie D. Folsom (to be used for young people); (4) $13,000 from W. I. Powers; (5) $5000 from Mr. Powers' daughter, Theia Powers Watson (Mrs. Homer); (6) $2821.91 from Mary Lincoln Lyster (Mrs. Haddon); (7) $3000 from Ida S. Pearl; (8) a gift from Miss Elizabeth Hills, apparently used in current society activity rather than becoming part of the endowment and thus of an unknown amount; and (9) the church building and grounds contiguous to the Powers Park entrance, from the Universalist Society for community use).[7]

From its beginning the society recognized that the major task in furthering its goals would be the raising of funds. The group established a policy of avoiding solicitation or subscription, and instead seeking funds by offering the community something worthy of a small charge.[8] The first such offering was the Calico Ball in 1894; attended by 25 couples, it netted the society $35.93. Many groups of citizens and organizations furthered the work of the society by contributing to its treasury the income from some specially staged entertainment.

Especially during the first quarter of the 20th century, there were many traveling entertainment companies of questionable character seeking not only monetary return but also a place like Lyndonville's Music Hall in which to perform. To counterbalance these, the society staged many dramatic programs using local talent every year: minstrels (using both men and women), concerts, operas, operettas, and plays, some directed by professionals and using casts of 100 or more characters. These events were nearly always followed by dances. In many instances these programs were repeated in Barton, Newport,

Cobleigh Public Library Benefit, "Merry Milk Maids", April 1897 at
Music Hall (*Cobleigh Public Library*)

St. Johnsbury, Wells River, or other nearby communities. The following were some of the outstanding events:

1896   Ladies Minstrel — *The Belles of Corkville*
1897   Continental Kettle Drum
1902   Hurdy Gurdy Party and Poverty Ball
1903   *Millie the Quadroon*
          Elite Lady Minstrels
1904   *The Mikado*
1907   Festival of the Nations (a bazaar)
1915   *Heir of Mt. Vernon*
          Visions of Fair Women
1921   *Eliza Comes to Stay*
          Some Girl (musical comedy, cast 125)

1922 Ladies Minstrel Show
      Forest Princess (a pageant)
1923 Minstrel Show
1924 *Some Boy*
1925 *My Mary*
1928 *My Uncle's Niece*
1929 *Marrying Marion* (musical comedy)

Other sources of revenue included the movie *Silver Dollar* (1933), a bazaar (1937), a flower show (1938), and an auto and appliance show (1939).

For many years the Village Improvement Society sponsored a school providing training in ballroom and folk dancing for children and adults. Also, the society held dances every Saturday evening in either Music Hall or Cable's Hall, events that were especially popular with the young people and that provided wholesome entertainment for them. In addition, the organization sponsored two or three "special occasion" dances each year. For instance, for thirty-six consecutive years (1899–1935) the Washington Ball was held on February 22 or thereabouts. The major social event of the winter, it was sometimes a masquerade, sometimes a white ball, or a fancy dress ball, or a poverty ball, or carried out some other distinctive characteristic. Music Hall was always lavishly and artistically decorated. Not only did people enjoy dancing to the music of a distinguished orchestra, often brought from Boston, but the balconies were filled with spectators who had paid a small fee (10¢, 25¢, 35¢, or 50¢) for the privilege of watching. The society also sponsored dances or other events on various holidays and anniversaries. Too much credit can not be given to Stella (Mrs. B. G.) Morrison for the success of these entertainments, for she was chairman of the society's entertainment committee for many, many years. During her years of service, the society invested heavily in improvements in the interior of Music Hall and in equipment to be used there. The group added dressing rooms, a kitchen, and a serving room in the basement, and bought equipment to serve 300 people; purchased new scenery and stage equipment and new lighting fixtures; and paid half the cost of a new floor in the auditorium. In fact, a large portion of the $8000 earned by Mrs. Morrison's programs was spent there.

01329 Lyndonville, Vt. Cor. South & Centre Sts.

Park at intersection of South and Center Streets, Lyndonville; Dr. Davis'
House in background (*Mrs. Milton Kerr*)

The society did not lose sight of its goal of beautifying the village.
One example involved an unsightly place in Shadeyville, just north
of the corner of Grove and Main streets. Through a series of Saturday
afternoon community "bees" in 1901, men, women, and children
cleared out the underbrush and half-rotten stumps, leveled the
ground, planted grass and flowers, and installed benches to create
the so-called North Park. The society also had a hand in developing
West Park, a triangle on the north side of the junction of West Street
(later Park Street) and Center Street; South Park, on the north side
of the junction of South Street and Broadway (later Broad Street);
Depot Park, between the passenger and freight depots; and "Park
Benjamin,"[9] at the junction of South and Center streets. These were
the larger parks; but there were many others so small that they were
little more than a flower bed protected by a granite curbing at a point
where two streets met.[10]

At its annual meeting in 1907, the society decided that the most

Ide Block, railroad passenger station, fountain, Depot Park
(*Ruth Blodgett Doolin*)

Depot Park fountain in winter (*Mrs. Harry Robie*)

urgent village improvements was the replacement of the 800-gallon street sprinkler built in 1886 by Austin Houghton. In 1911 the society had lights installed on the common at a cost of $362.09. Two years later it spent over $400 in putting the four standards—each having five ornamental lights—around the fountain. In 1912 the ladies persuaded the village trustees to provide the needed conveyances for the village "clean up day," a project repeated many times after that.

The first series of winter entertainments later known as the "Lecture Course" occurred in 1891; the program continued annually under a committee of men until 1904, when the Village Improvement Society accepted the responsibility for its administration. This series of five to eight performances provided varied programs of worthwhile entertainments: lectures, concerts, dance recitals, minstrel shows, dramatic performances, and the like. The performers, men and women of outstanding ability and training, came from all parts of the country. The series was intended not as a money-making project but as a community service, and in many years it ran a deficit, but when the course earned profits they were usually spent to add one or more programs to the series. The reserved-seat season tickets sold for $1.50 each, and usually about 300 were sold. Tickets for individual programs were also available at the door; when a program seemed likely to have special interest for children, tickets were made available to them for 10¢ or 15¢ each. These programs were brought to an end in 1930, after several years of losing money.

In the summer of 1914 the Village Improvement Society developed a new source of revenue by transforming E. A. Darling's cottage at Willoughby Lake into the Boulders Tea House, which soon became a popular social center. Mr. and Mrs. E. L. Wells were in charge a couple of years before the business was leased, with the society receiving three-fifths of the season income and the lessees receiving at least $75 for the season. In 1917 the "good will and equipment" of the Boulders was turned over to the Lyndon Red Cross, which netted $200 that year and more than $300 the next. In 1921 Darling graciously added a casino; at its formal opening on August 3, 1921, 220 couples were on its floor—a foretaste of the patronage of the next years. From the available annual reports, 1925 was apparently the last year of real profit ($1123.28 from the casino and $132.72 from the Boulders). The society leased the teahouse and casino to nonmembers for a few more years, but 1929 appears to be the last year it contributed to the society's income.

The society's special interest in providing recreation for the young people of the community apparently dates to 1903. At its annual meeting that year the group set aside $125 to equip a gymnasium for boys and also voted to build a tennis court. In succeeding years the society added money to the gymnasium fund and ultimately maintained such a recreation room for some years in a building belonging to the Episcopal Church; the first tennis court was created in North Park. The organization also was the moving spirit in forming the Snow Shoe Club, which prospered for several winters. In addition, the Society provided a skating rink on the Darling Meadow—the south side of Center Street between Main and Park streets—for several winters, but lost money each year.

The acquisition of a tract of twenty to twenty-five acres off north Main Street—the Grove—in 1915 further influenced the activities of the society. Before his death in 1915, W. I. Powers had nearly completed negotiations with the railroad company for the purchase of the Grove, intending that it should become a community playground. Under the terms of his will, the Village Improvement Society received $13,000; $3000 for the purchase of the property and $10,000 to become a trust fund for the maintenance of the grounds. At its annual meeting in 1916 the Society voted to name this area Powers Park in honor of its donor and of his daughter, Theia Powers Watson, who was the first Society chairman of the project. From this time on the Society gradually abandoned its other community activities and concentrated its efforts on developing this recreation center for the children of the community.

During the war years of 1916–18, the land near the Main Street entrance to Powers Park was loaned to members of the community for use as "war gardens." In the years after the war, community "work bees" concentrated on the park. They removed cottages and other remnants of the fifty years' use of the land by the district campmeeting of the Methodist Church; cleared underbrush and removed dead wood; leveled areas for immediate recreational use; cleared a road from the Main Street entrance to the athletic field at the back of the tract, at a cost of $1204.59; built tennis, archery, volleyball, and basketball courts; created croquet grounds; installed swings of various sizes; and leveled, graded, and seeded the area immediately west of Main Street. In 1923 the park employed its first trained supervisor for the playground.

The plans of the architect—Larson and Wells of Hanover, N.H.— for a memorial entrance from Main Street took shape in 1925, when the Rowe Construction Company of Woodsville, N.H., put in a granite coping and brickwork on which ornamental lights and a bronze memorial tablet[11] were set. The inscription on this tablet was as follows:

Powers Park
Given to the
Village Improvement Society
and generously endowed
By
Washington Irving Powers
1915

The cost of installing this memorial entrance was $1677.11.

The swimming pool was built in 1939. Prior to that time local children had swum in four different places: two spots in the Passumpsic River—one west of Powers Park, the other at Folsom's Crossing—the "ice pond" on Whipple's Brook, and Vail Pond. None of these had been entirely satisfactory, so the new pool had been a much wanted addition to the equipment of the park. In anticipation of its construction Theia Powers Watson, for the Village Improvement Society, deeded on August 5, 1938, a tract 70 x 180 feet and a right of way to it to the village, thereby making the project eligible for a federal grant. Assistance in construction and maintenance of the pool has been periodically sought from various civic organizations, especially Rotary and Jaycees. This assistance has sometimes been urgently needed because of vandalism.

It is very doubtful if the parents of the growing children of Lyndon and neighboring towns in the last half century have been conscious of their debt to the Lyndonville Village Improvement Society. In Powers Park their children have been professionally supervised and entertained, rain or shine, daily from 9:00 in the morning to 5:00 in the afternoon, for eight weeks every summer, without a penny's cost to them.

In 1971, due to the increasing costs of replacing and repairing equipment damaged by vandalism, the park instituted a seasonal charge of $5 for children six and over and $3 for those under six. These funds plus the income from the society endowments from a limited number of money-raising projects have made it possible for the society to break even.

When the Bemis Memorial Church (Universalist) disbanded in 1930, it offered its building to the Village Improvement Society for use as a community house. The Society made some immediate repairs and formally opened the house with a "community chicken pie supper" serving 280 people on July 31, 1930. The supper committee was Mrs. P. R. Griswold, chairman, Theia Powers Watson, and Mrs. Wesley Emerson; the kitchen committee was Mrs. P. P. Greenslade and Mrs. Clayton Libbey; decorations were managed by Mrs. B. G. Morrison, Mr. and Mrs. Greenslade, and Mr. and Mrs. W. N. Perkins. In the following decades the building served some of the needs resulting from the loss of Music Hall. However, the building was neglected and abused, with the result that in 1975 the society sought to sell it for commercial use and, failing that, closed it.

Lyndon Center

ON MAY 15, 1893, ACCORDING TO THE *Vermont Union*, a Village Improvement Society was formed in Lyndon Center, and the following officers were elected: Professor W. E. Ranger, president; E. M. Campbell, secretary; Mrs. Emma Miller, treasurer; and E. M. Campbell, Professor Ranger, R. E. Rice, E. H. Hinds, George Hubbard, and Mrs. C. S. Cahoon, executive committee. Membership fees were set at $2 for gentlemen and $1 for ladies, with dues to be half that amount. The first project was the removal of dooryard fences, which had been a necessity when the law had forced a resident to fence out his neighbor's livestock. The society next turned to cleaning up rubbish and planting trees. The members of this group also helped raise funds to equip the Lyndon Center firemen.

No reference to the society between 1896 and 1914 has survived. In the latter year a *Union Journal* article called for a May 23 meeting of interested persons. At that meeting officers were elected: Mrs. A. R. Merrill, president; Mrs. H. W. Atwood, vice-president; Mrs. W. E. Campbell, secretary; Mrs. S. G. Collison, treasurer; and Mrs. F. A. Dresser and Mrs. Lewis Lapoint, executive committee. The first project of this new group—to place rubbish cans at strategic points—was followed by several projects aimed at developing community spirit. In 1917 it united with the Ladies Aid of the Baptist Church to assist in Red Cross work. The last mention found in the press was in the issue of February 1, 1928, announcing a meeting on February 7.

ℨ❧

Lyndon Corner

A VILLAGE IMPROVEMENT SOCIETY formed at Lyndon Corner in 1905, a few years later than in the other two Lyndon villages. About thirty men and women met at the Academy building in May to elect officers: Rev. W. C. Clark, chairman; Miss Rose Brown, secretary; Mrs. J. S. Thompson, treasurer; and Rev. Clark, Rev. William Shaw, and Wells Quimby, executive committee. In August the group adopted bylaws and elected permanent officers: Rev. W. C. Clark, president; Rev. William Shaw and Mrs. W. T. McGovern, vice-presidents; Mrs. M. K. Paris, secretary; Mrs. J. S. Thompson, treasurer; and W. L. Newell, auditor. Miss Hattie Colby was elected to serve as head of the three departments under which the society's activity would be conducted. The first purposes of the society were to beautify the village, and to foster cooperation with the law by preventing the post-ing of advertisements on bridges, fences, trees, posts, poles, etc. The group carried out several programs to raise money for these projects. Soon interest developed in building sidewalks in the community.

By 1909 the society had three vice-presidents, each with a separate responsibility. The first vice-president was working on community morals and education, motivating, among other things, a public read-ing room. The second vice-president was also chairman of the "De-partment of Good Taste," directing work on the grounds of the rail-road station, on the schoolhouse, around the bridges, and at the in-tersections of roads. The third vice-president was directing her efforts toward motivating social activities in the community. During July and August the society conducted a "recreation school" at which twenty-eight children participated in classes in carpentry with George R. Winslow of the Billings School (Woodstock), Rev. E. G. French, and William Bailey; cooking with Mrs. John B. Chase; and sewing with Miss Ella Wilmarth of St. Johnsbury. In mid-December the so-ciety received a granite watering trough, to be substituted for the wooden one on Main Street near the site of the former Lyndon House. The gift of L. B. Harris, who made it and put it in place, was inscribed "July 4, 1908."

The Lyndon Village Improvement Society formally drew up articles of association in October 1910, with Mrs. Estella Quimby, Mrs. John B. Chase, and Mrs. May Morse as incorporators.

In August 1910 the unused building of the Lyndon Carriage Com-pany burned, leaving standing only the brick building that had been the company's blacksmith shop. In October S. S. Mattocks sold the building to the society for $200, with the stipulation that if the society became inactive the title to the property would revert to the Village. (The property is now Mattocks Park.)

In November 1910 the women began a Saturday "food exchange" that provided a regular exchange of home-cooked food, with the so-ciety administering the sale and receiving the profit. The following summer the group sponsored a baby show involving thirteen babies under two years of age and twenty-one over two years. A Halloween party added $27.25 to the society's treasury.

In 1912 a fourth vice-president, Mrs. George Ide, was added; her special responsibility was the teahouse. In this project the dreams of some of the society members came to fruition when they opened the Lyndon Carriage Company's former blacksmith shop as a social center under the name of the Olde Bricke Tea Shoppe. During the two years since its purchase the women had collected some antiques for furnishings and cleaned up the grounds and the inside of the building. The *Vermont Union Journal* of June 26, 1902, made this report of the site and the proposed plans:

> The grounds include about ¾ acre of land, a small pond, several springs, and a little hill at the east side. . . . S. S. Mattocks who owned the property at the time the carriage shop burned, sold it to the Village Improvement Society two years ago. It has been the object of the society to drain and clean up the land and convert it into a village green, with trees and paths, seats about the pond, a small summer house at the top of the hill from which there is a fine view, and on the whole, to make it a pleasant, useable place where anyone might like to go to sew, or read, or visit, or just rest on a warm summer day. . . .
>
> The old Bricke Shoppe . . . is over 40 feet long . . . built by the old time brick mason, Carl Blanchard. . . . We have heard of the time when six forges were kept busy there. . . . The Village Hose Company occupies now a quarter of the building the remainder being furnished with antique furniture and curios. It is to be used this summer as a tea shop and will be open to the public on July 4th. It is a unique interior . . . old ladies will be there spinning, weaving, making rugs, carding wool, dipping candles etc., and other old time ladies will serve you with many good things to eat . . . it is to be open every week day from 10:00 A.M. to 9:00 P.M. Miss Mead of St. Johnsbury is to have charge of the Shoppe and will serve among other things at any time, tea, coffee, chocolate, iced tea, lemonade, iced milk, a variety of dainty sandwiches, eggs, biscuits with marmalade, ice cream and small cakes, home made candies, salted nuts, etc. . . .
>
> A reading table with magazine and books from the Cobleigh Library occupies one corner, and also a children's table with books and quiet games. The green is not to be a play ground for children, but as long as the children wish to come there to play with the games and to read quietly they will be as welcome as the grown-ups. . . .

This first season proved very successful, and the project continued for a number of summers. Not only was management vested in local committees, but local young women and students in various New England colleges spent their summers there gaining valuable experience. Among summer managers were Miss Caroline Bowen, Miss Mollie Martin, Miss Amelia Lee, Miss Maud Wetherbee, Mrs. Allen and daughter Grace of East Orange, N.J., Miss Madeline Kennedy, Miss Bernice Trefren, Miss Mildred Grady, Mrs. Adeline Brownell, and Miss Elizabeth Hubbard of Schenectady, N.Y.

Through the years the Tea Shoppe became a popular place for informal gatherings of people from all around town. In some years the shop served regular meals one or two nights a week, and also frequently served meals on special occasions. Light refreshments were also available, especially when social functions were held there. The shop sometimes maintained a well-stocked gift shop, and older women there plied industries long unused, such as spinning, weaving, and drawing and braiding rugs; many of their creations were sold to visitors.

The "Garden Club" work of Mrs. John B. Chase and Miss Gertrude Newton among rural school children of the town radiated from the Bricke Tea Shoppe. The purpose of their work was to motivate the children between the ages of five and seventeen to participate in the work of the rural home, hoping to encourage them to remain in Vermont. This work enjoyed encouragement not only from the Village Improvement Society, but also from the State Extension Division, the Vail Agricultural School, and Vail himself. Apparently, it was a forerunner of the National 4-H Club work. Each year's work culminated in a "Fair" held on the grounds of the Tea Shoppe, where there was ample exhibition space. As many as 300 children may have been involved in this work. The *Vermont Union Journal* of September 9 and 16, 1914, included a report on one such fair:

> 171 children out of the Club exhibited, during the past summer 239 children out of 270 in the 11 rural schools of this town have done the work of the class, maintaining an interest in the majority of cases to a remarkable degree.
>
> The main object of the class is not to encourage children to work

for the fair or to work for a prize, but to acquire an interest in the activities of the home, to employ their waste time for the help of the family. . . .

There were displayed canned fruits, vegetables, pickles, jellies, 300 cans displayed; maple products; carpentry; lambs; pigs; an excellent display of cooked foods; poultry; arrangements of flowers; the effort to encourage calves, ponies, horses, met with a fine response, there being some 30 or more fine specimens shown. Sewing developed a much larger response than last year. . . .

Violet Parker exhibited 28 varieties of canned goods, Mildred Grady 25, Helen Gilmore 23, Hazel Willey 19, Alice Hoyt 19. . . .

The members of the Lyndon Garden Club went on each year to exhibit at the Caledonia County Fair (St. Johnsbury) and the Eastern States Exposition in Springfield, Mass., and in both places they won recognition and prizes each year.

The women of the Village Improvement Society continued for some years with their sewing, quilt making, and other handicrafts, applying the revenue received to community improvement projects, although no one knows exactly how long these activities continued. Unused for several years, the building was finally pulled down by E. E. Bailey and his son, Delwyn, and Jim Smith in the late fall of 1942; Smith disposed of the bricks.

VII

Religion

ੋ✆

The Meeting House

A T A S P E C I A L T O W N M E E T I N G held December 23, 1800, fifty-one men signed the list as members of the organization named the "Religious Society in the Town of Lyndon for the Purpose of Promoting Public Preaching of the Gospel in the said Town."[1] William Winsor was chosen moderator and treasurer; Daniel Cahoon, Sr., clerk; John Johnson, collector; and Isaiah Fisk, Abner Jones, and Job Olney, assessors. After choosing a committee of William Winsor, Daniel Cahoon, and Elijah Ross, the meeting was adjourned to the first Monday in January 1801. At this meeting it was voted unanimously "that the Meeting House be set as near to the centre of Town as convenant [*sic*] Place can be Procured to set it on,"[2] and the society's committee was instructed to search for such a piece of land. The quest must have been successful, for the town land books contain a deed dated May 30, 1801, from Job Sheldon to the selectmen

> . . . for the Purpose of Promoting the Preaching of the Gospel in the said Town—Have given, granted . . . For the Use and purpose of Seting and Building a Meeting House on, and for a Burying ground, Common and Parade, to be appropriated for the aforesaid purposes and no other forever, Six acres of Land with allowance for a Road through the same on Right Number Thirty.[3]

On the same day at a special town meeting the selectmen were directed to employ someone to fell the trees on the meetinghouse lot in June, and to get the land "Cleared off and Seeded on such Tearms as they shall think most advantagious to the Town so as to produce a Crop next spring."[4] It is unclear whether this task extended over a period of time or whether the workers were not paid promptly, but not until 1804 does an entry in the Town Records show the total cost—$57.55.[5] At the following town meeting (March 12, 1804), it was voted that the selectmen lease the use of the meetinghouse lot "in the situation it is now in[,] on the best terms that can[,] in their definition[,] be gotten for the benefit of the town." The warnings for succeeding town meetings indicate that some consideration was given to the town for the use of this land.

Apparently no action was taken toward creating a meetinghouse until 1809,[6] when Alpheus Houghton, Isaiah Fisk, Bela Shaw, Jr., Gideon Brown, and Noah Cushing were chosen as a committee to "draw a Plan of a Suitable Town House, Estimate the cost, and make a report accordingly"; later in the meeting Benjamin Walker and Elias Bemis were added to the committee. At the adjourned meeting, this committee estimated the cost of a one-story building 40 x 45 feet as $1249.30. They also presented an estimate for a two-story building, size 45 x 50, to be finished on the outside, at $1035.66. The estimate for this latter building was itemized into its various parts and the specific kinds and sizes of lumber to be used, bricks, nails, and the cost of labor. The plan and estimates for the two-story building were adopted, and a committee of Isaiah Fisk, Joel Fletcher, and Bela Shaw, Jr., was chosen to superintend the construction. Also, it was voted to levy a tax of 7½¢ on the dollar on the grand list as taken June 20, 1808, to defray the expense of building. Those taxed should have the privilege of "paying the tax in materials if they will furnish them on as reasonable terms as the Committee can purchase them of Others . . . in Neat Stock in the month of October . . . or in grain in January following . . . or to be paid in money after the first day of February."

Apparently, progress was made during the summer of 1809. On September 30 the freeman's meeting was held at Capt. Alpheus Fletcher's house, but as soon as Nathaniel Jenks was chosen moderator it was voted "to adjourn this meeting to the Town House." At this meeting[7] a committee of "Isaiah Fisk Esq., Nathaniel Jenks Esq. and Mr. Bela Shaw" was chosen to "lay out the Pew ground and sell the same at auction," with the returns from the sale to be used in "Compleating the House." At the town meeting of March 9, 1810, a committee of Abel Brown, William Winsor Esq., and Abel Carpenter Esq. was selected to settle with the committee that had been in charge of building the town house.[8]

The town house continued to be a subject of concern. In March 1811 a committee of Abel Carpenter, John Cahoon, and William W. McGaffey was chosen to "devise means to finish the town house"; only $1200 was reported raised, however. Discussions continued at meetings held in November 30, 1811, and March 23, April 25, and June 6, 1812, when the following action was taken:

> Whereas much difficulty and misunderstanding had arisen respecting the finishing of the Townhouse, and to effect an object so desirable to the Christian Moralist and to add to our respectability and union—It is motioned and voted that the Town relinquish the Pew Ground in their Town house on condition that the purchasers of the Pews will fully compleat and finish the house. — Yet the Town reserves to themselves the right of occupying the house for all Town business, and that the doors of the house shall be open for the reception of a Preacher of Religion and Morality at all times unless the house is occupied by a Preacher settled and supported by a Majority of the Pew Owners—and that a Committee to be appointed to sell the Pews and report to the Town on the second Wednesday in January next, without expense to the Town.
>
> Committee chosen Messrs Isaiah Fisk, Bela Shaw, Jr., and Abraham Smith.

One wonders what was the result of this action, for a similar and, apparently, more desperate vote occurred at the town meeting in 1815 as follows:

> Voted that if any number of persons will associate raise money sufficient and finish and complete the Townhouse in a workmanlike manner, they shall have and hold the pews or pew ground in said house, or may sell dispose of and convey the same in such manner as shall be agreed on by the association, to repay them the expenses of completing said house, and the whole sum raised by the sale of the pews or pew ground shall belong to the association to be by them apportioned to each individual according to his subscription.
>
> Provided allways that the town shall have, and do reserve, the right and use of said house for all town business, at all times when needed.
>
> Provided, the outside of the said Town house be completed within one year from the first day of December next, and the inside within two years from the time last mentioned.[10]

			Pulpit			
No. 41	No. 42	No. 43		No. 44	No. 45	No. 46

No. 40						No. 47
	No. 25	No. 24	No. 9	No. 8		
No. 39	No. 26	No. 23	No. 10	No. 7		No. 48
No. 38	No. 27	No. 22	No. 11	No. 6		No. 49
No. 37	No. 28	No. 21	No. 12	No. 5		No. 50
No. 36	No. 29	No. 20	No. 13	No. 4		No. 51
No. 35	No. 30	No. 19	No. 14	No. 3		No. 52
No. 34	No. 31	No. 18	No. 15	No. 2		No. 53
No. 33	No. 32	No. 17	No. 16	No. 1		No. 54

Diagram of pews in Meeting House—First Floor

No.

No.		No.		No.	
1		16		31	M. Sheldon
2	Jonᵃ Park	17	John Meigs		Benj. Powers
3	Samˡ Park	18	Wm. Ruggles	32	Wm. Fairbrother
4	Elijah Bundy	19		33	Josiah Rawson
5	Nathan Weeks	20	Abel Edgell	34	Abel Carpenter
6	James Sherman	21	S. W. Winsor	35	A. Houghton
7	Eliphas Graves		B. Walker	36	Danˡ Kathan
8/9	Abram Smith	22	Isaac Fletcher	37	Ish Fisk
10	M. Haskell	23	J. Kimball	38	S. A. Willard
11	Hubbard Field	24/25	Wm. Cahoon	39	Joel Fletcher
12	Wm. W. McGaffey	26	B. S. Deming	40	Oliver Chaffee—½
	Stephen McGaffey	27	James Knapp	41	Samuel A. Willard
	Philip McGaffey	28	Danˡ Harvey	42	Gaius Peck
13	H. Hoffman, Jr.		Asa Smith	43	Minister
	Caleb Parker	29	Asa Goodwin	44	Betsey Hubbard—½
14	Abel Wilmarth		Herman Meigs	45	
15	Samˡ Hoyt	30	Nathan Hubbard	46	

No. 69	No. 68			No. 67	No. 66
No. 70					No. 65
No. 71					No. 64
No. 72					No. 63
No. 73					No. 62
No. 74					No. 61
No. 75					No. 60
No. 76		GALLERY			No. 59
No. 77	No. 78	No. 79	No. 80	No. 55	No. 56	No. 57	No. 58

Diagram of pews in Meeting House—Gallery

47	Joseph Lawrence—¾	49		52	Job Randall
	Otis Lawrence—¼	50		53	
48	Wm. Way	51		54	

GALLERY

55		65	Ira Sprague	74	P. Houghton
56		66		75	Wm. W. McGaffey
57	Sam¹ Orcutt	67	Wm. Fairbrother		S. McGaffey
58		68	Alanson Shaw		P. McGaffey
59	Jonas Allen	69	S. A. Willard	76	Ebnʳ Peck, 2nd
60	H. B. Williams	70	B. H. Sherman	77	
61	Joel Fletcher	71	Otis Evans	78	Joshua Lockling
62	John Gates	72	D. McGaffey	79	Ira Evans
63	Jonᵃ Blanchard		J. E. Stowell	80	Wm. Fisher, Jr.
64	Elijah Ross	73	J. Lockling Jr.		Nath¹ Barron

This vote, too, failed to achieve the desired results, and in 1817 another committee—Bela Shaw, Jr., Joel Fletcher, and Benjamin F. Deming—was charged with selling the pew ground in the town house, and instructed to "immediately proceed" to use the funds received in finishing the town house.

Inserted among the town deeds is a diagram showing the placement and ownership of the eighty pews.[11] It does not bear a date, but from its location in the deeds it appears to be from about 1821. The top of the page bears the heading: "The following is a Plan of the Lyndon Town House, presenting a view of the Pew Ground, and the No. of each Pew and by whom owned." At the bottom of the two pages containing the diagram is this notation:

> We the undersigned, having been appointed a Committee by the Town of Lyndon to sell the pew ground in the Town House, and to finish said House, by applying the avails of such sales to said purpose—do hereby certify, that the foregoing plan exhibits a correct view of the Pews in said House, as numbered and sold, by the Committee—that the several Pews as numbered, were sold to, and purchased by, the persons whose names they are respectively entered to each number on said plan—and that they, by virtue of the power vested in us, by a vote of the Town the 17 September 1817, to make such sales as become the lawful owners of the respective Pews by them purchased, as is made to appear by this record
> /S/Joel Fletcher
> Committee
> Isaiah Fisk

A loose sheet inserted at this point in the book of deeds is apparently the first page of a report signed by the initials "A. B., C. D., E. F." It states that attached is a list of the persons who purchased the pews "at the prices stated," but the attachment is now missing; nowhere has a statement been found of the prices paid for the pews, either singly or collectively.

Whenever a speaker was available on Sunday, the meetinghouse was opened, and a majority of the townspeople attended the service. Methodists, Congregationalists, Baptists, and Universalists shared use of the building and participated in any service without denominational concern. Town records provide no information about the combination meetinghouse–town house between 1821 and 1840. Apparently by this time the old meetinghouse was in need of repair, for each succeeding warning for a town meeting contains some article proposing repairs or alterations.

At the annual meeting on March 5, 1850, a committee of Job Randall, J. T. G. Cunningham, and Silas Houghton was appointed to arrange for removal of some pews and make "alterations as in their judgement may seem best, not exceeding $100." On January 7, 1851, the committee reported[12] the removal of fourteen pews, to whose owners[13] the town was obligated to pay $1 each. However, the report said nothing about any other repairs being made. On November 21, 1859, Selectmen Charles Folsom, and N. Baker contracted with John McGaffey for extensive repairs. The "Memorandum of bargain to repair the Townhouse in Lyndon," found among the Sanborn Papers and bearing this date, is worth copying here, for through the changes McGaffey agreed to make, we acquire a better picture of the original meetinghouse.

This certifies that I, John McGaffey agreed to make the following repairs to wit to put new sills on each side and confine them to the cross sills with iron rods sufficient to hold the same in place & level up the sides & fit up all the underpinings take off the Belfry & projection of the roof now on the East End & finish a Projection of the Rafters of the Main Building to correspond with the Eve Projection Board & clapboard the space where the Belfry now stands except putting a window in the centre of the 2nd story Build a Piaza across the East end 7 ft. wide 4 posts in front 10 feet high set on Stone 4 inches above the floor of the same which is to be made with suitable timbers covered with round spruce or hemlock plank 2 inch thick to finish 20 inch double frieze with 8 inch plain cornice roof Boarded with inch Boards covered with good pine or cedar Shingles to take out two windows in the East End of 2nd Story & all the windows of the 1st Story & two nearest the corners of the 2nd Story of the West End & take out the alternate windows on the sides nearest the East corners & every alternate window in Both Stories that is 20 in all & Board & clapboard the same on the outside & lathe & plaster on the inside & put one window in the centre of the 1st Story at the west End repair up the rest of the windows by putting in whole round sash painted over & fill the same with whole Glass & put Board shutters of suitable Pine Painted Green or Blue hung with good substantial hinges & suitable fastenings take out the double doors in the centre & put one of the side doors leading into the Belfry & Paint the outside with two coats of white lead & Oil take out the Pulpit & remove the desk for receiving Votes Back where that now stands with a shelf on the Backside for counting Votes put suitable timbers over the open space Betwixt the 1st & 2nd Storys on the inside & lathe & Plaster the same level the floor in front of the centre Pews down with the Isles & fit up the floor & Pews on the sides of the 1st Story as they formerly were case the Posts with clean spruce or Pine & repair up the Base round of the outside where needed all to be done in good workmanlike manner by the 15th day of May 1860 for the sum of three hundred and Eighty dollars which we the undersigned Selectmen of Lyndon agree to pay the said John McGaffey for all repairs done Before the next January Meeting for raising money to pay the expenses of the said town when that money is raised & the remainder in one year from that time.

Dated at Lyndon this 21st day of November A.D. 1859

| John McGaffey | /S/ | Charles Folsom) | Selectmen |
| Contractor | | N. Baker   ) | of Lyndon |

During the 1860s consideration was given to finishing off the second floor of the town hall for public purposes, but no evidence has been found of any action. In 1872 a change was authorized in the seating arrangements. Two years later the selectmen were "authorized and instructed to remove the old town horse-sheds, or cause them to be removed and build a good substantial fence on the line on which they stand."[14] At the same meeting the selectmen were instructed to build a hearse house and store room for the cart and tools belonging to the town, and "to purchase land of School District No. 6 for the same if it can be done at a reasonable rate.

Article 5 of the warning for the 1884 town meeting proposed that the town consider uniting with the village of Lyndonville in the construction of a building to be used jointly for public meetings.[15] This was the first of a long, long list of unsuccessful proposals aimed at the removal of the town house to Lyndonville. It was not the fault of the editor of the *Vermont Union* that the town house was not abandoned; periodically he wrote sarcastically of its need for work, especially painting. In 1888 enough repairs were made to quiet those attacks. In the early 1890s a new town house was proposed as a memorial honoring the soldiers of the Civil War, but no action followed.

In September 1909 the townspeople observed the 100th anniversary of the town house with a daylong program, including a morning spent in the cemetery with guides to point out the location of the last resting place of some of the distinguished citizens; a picnic lunch on the Common at noon; and an afternoon of historical papers, reminiscences, original poems, and music. Mrs. C. T. Walter was in charge of the centennial program with Rev. J. W. Burgin being the presiding officer.

During succeeding years many suggestions have been offered for the use of the town hall, most being to remodel it in some way for school purposes. At various times it has been used as a community center for the PTA, the Village Improvement Society, and the Lyndon Center Fire Company. Minor interior changes have resulted, including the laying of a hardwood floor in 1945. Many attempts have also been made to abandon the building and move the town meetings to Lyndonville, most vehemently in 1884, 1896, 1897, 1899, 1909, and 1940, but invariably this article has been dismissed. In 1971 the meeting voted to adjourn to the auditorium of Lyndon Institute because of the crowded condition of the town hall. At the 1974 town meeting, the voters accepted the selectmen's recommendation that part of the town's revenue sharing funds be used to repair and repaint the town hall, and this was done.

ᣅᑅ

Baptists

THE FIRST DENOMINATIONAL GROUP to form in Lyndon was Free Baptist, organized[16] May 30, 1802, at a conference held at the home of Luther Holton. Elder Peleg Hicks was chosen moderator and Caleb Fisk clerk. Those who signed the church covenant were Samuel Winslow, Benjamin Esterbrooks, Isaiah Fisk, Caleb Fisk, Luther Holton, William Harvey, Anna Winslow, Hannah Fisk, Phebe Fisk, Anna Holton, and Abagail Windsor. Information on the further existence or activity of this group is completely lost.

Sometime after 1810 Daniel Quimby moved from Sandwich, N.H., to Lyndon and settled on Pudding Hill, where he was ordained in 1816.[17] Soon after his arrival he built a small church from logs felled on his farm.[18] No records of this "Quimby church" have been found, although reports of itinerant ministers of the first half of the 19th century contain several fragments referring to the energy and enthusiasm of "Brother Quimby's church. Reference has been made that he

> succeeded in collecting a large church, while continuing to worship there until 1840, when the Methodists having vacated the meeting house at Lyndon Centre, and some of the Freewill denomination residing in that vicinity, it was deemed good church tactics to remove their place of worship to the Centre, which was done, consolidating the different memberships in one communion at that place.

On May 27, 1843, Rev. T. P. Moulton organized a church in Lyndon Center. Its original members were Anson Meigs, William Frasier, James Briant, Joel Fletcher, Elisha Sanborn, T. P. Moulton, Betsey Frasier, and Louisa Moulton. It appears that the meetinghouse was used for some years as a gathering place. Finally seven men of the church assumed the monetary obligation for constructing a building: Benjamin Sanborn assumed 3/10 of the cost, A. J. Willard 2/10, and Jonathan Woodman, George Paine, Charles Lougee, Isaac Denison, and Daniel Quimby each 1/10.[19] Smith Folsom and John McGaffey took the contract to build the church for $1400. The foundation was laid in the spring of 1848 and the building completed in August of the same year at a cost of $1710.73. The church was located[20] on Main Street facing east on a tract 44 x 60 feet in size, purchased for $100 in 1849 from the Andrew J. Willard estate; the church building completely covered the land owned.

On February 16, 1853, the Free Will Baptist Parsonage Committee—

Lyndon Center Baptist Church with horse sheds (*Fenton Chester*)

Benjamin Sanborn, Elisha Sanborn, Jeremy Pearl, A. D. Smith, Alpheus Quimby, Thomas Quimby, Daniel Quimby, A. Meigs, J. Brunson, C. Aldrich, P. P. Houghton, John Park, and H. M. Nichols—purchased three acres of land and "buildings thereon" from Hiram and Susan Bemis for $1500. This land was identified as the Bemis' homestead and was located west of the Common, north of the S. S. Thompson property, and south of the cemetery. When the site of the Lyndon Literary and Biblical Institution was selected, this tract of land was needed to complete its normal land boundaries. Therefore in 1867 Jeremy Pearl sold the Baptist Church a building lot on Main Street, to which the parsonage was moved and where it has remained through the years.

In 1872 the church building was moved to its present location, the lot being six rods facing the street by ten rods deep and its price $500.

This larger lot made it possible to turn the building halfway around so that it faced north instead of east. A vestry was put under the church, the vestibule section was added in front, the whole upper part of the building was remodeled, a 90-foot belfry was added to house the bell from the earlier church, and fourteen horse sheds were built at the back of the church. The alterations and repairs were so extensive that they were not finished until the next year, the first services being held on January 11, 1874.

In preparation for the observance of the 50th anniversary of the founding of the church, numerous repairs were made on the church. This may have been when an addition was made to the rear of the church building, of sufficient size to provide the choir and pulpit spaces of the present church building. No specific information has been found.

In the spring of 1892 a Christian Endeavor Society was organized; no information has been found about its activities or the length of its existence.

The year of 1898 was significant in the history of the internal organization of the Baptist Church. Some twenty or thirty members and people who regularly attended the church withdrew and formed the First Baptist Church in Lyndonville because of a disagreement over church administrative policies. As a result the original church revised its bylaws, materially changing some of its governmental practices, and also secured incorporation by the state legislature.[21] The church at Lyndonville continued to function for about five years, performing the religious, financial, and social functions common to churches of the period. At the end of this time some of the bitterness had abated. It was recognized that a second Baptist Church in the town was not justified, so the church disbanded, its members scattering to the other existing churches and three returning to the church at Lyndon Center.

In 1902, in anticipation of entertaining the Wheelock Association of Free Baptists on its 100th anniversary, the church was renovated: the roof was reshingled, and the ceiling of the audience room was frescoed, and its walls redecorated. The wall at the south end behind the speaker's desk received an artistic scroll with the inscription "Peace on Earth, Good will toward Men." On the side of it was a design of a cross and crown, and on the other, back of the choir, appeared a neatly worked lyre; both designs were enclosed in a wreath. The Wheelock Association meeting was an important occasion, as sixteen churches held membership; they sent forty delegates and fourteen ministers. The South Wheelock church had been the "mother church," the association having been formed there in the barn of Gideon Leavitt. The Wheelock Association disbanded in 1917 and joined the Danville Association.

In 1906 an indoor baptistry was installed in the front of the auditorium under the speaker's platform. Not until 1913, after many years of agitation, were electric lights finally installed in the church.

October 7, 1928, provided an occasion for rededication of the church following the installation of the pipe organ, a gift from the disbanding Bemis Memorial Church (Universalist) at Lyndonville. The Baptist Church held morning and afternoon services in which other churches and their parishioners participated; the musical events appear to have been of exceptional quality and to have elicited marked appreciation.

In 1939 the Lyndon Center church joined with those of South Wheelock, Wheelock, and Sheffield (the Federated Church) to form the "Larger Parish of Northern Vermont"—the first "Larger Parish" to be created by the New England Baptists. This was later named the "Hilda Ives Larger Parish"[22] in honor of Mrs. Hilda L. Ives, president of the New England Town and Country Church Commission. The pastor serving the Larger Parish lived in the parsonage at Lyndon Center, and his associate pastor lived at Sheffield. This association came to an end in 1970.

The 100th anniversary of the founding of the church was properly observed in August 1943, with morning and afternoon services providing especially effective musical programs. Principal O. D. Mathewson of Lyndon Institute and Editor John B. Chase of the *Vermont Union Journal* participated.

Over the years repairs and renovations have been financed by generous donations and through the work of various groups within the church. The Ladies Aid Society for many years raised money from its monthly dinners and suppers and from various annual events such as the town meeting day dinner, the chicken pie supper, the election day dinner, and the Easter dinner. Men's clubs and youth clubs over the years also made their contributions to the welfare of the church.

During the 1960s many changes were made in the church's facilities and trappings: the building was extensively repaired and renovated, the church bought robes for the choir, and parishioners gave new sanctuary furnishings. Among these were a new dossal, given by Mr. and Mrs. Gordon Smith and Mr. and Mrs. Leon Hopkins; a cross from the Senior Youth Group; a portable lectern from Mrs. Roland Greenwood; a communion table, a pulpit appendium, a table scarf, a maroon rug to cover the pulpit and altar area, and vases, donated by Mrs. Smith; offering plates from Howard and Leah Smith and Armand and Priscilla Hebert; candlesticks from Robert and Beverly Simblest; a lectern from Samuel and Margaret Simblest; 34 new hymnals, given as memorial gifts by various people; new tables and chairs in memory of loved ones; and new drapes, given by the United Women. Also, the Eastman Room was added. Later, in memory of Clinton Adams, his wife, Marion, donated a Yamaha piano for the sanctuary.

No history of this church would be complete without mention of its close ties with Lyndon Institute during the school's early days. The founding of the Lyndon Literary and Biblical Institution (now Lyndon Institute) here in 1867 was made possible by the Baptist Church, whose pastors and members made large contributions of energy, time, and money. The Baptists remained a dominant influence in the school's administration until 1882, when its serious financial problems forced it to close. One of the conditions of its release by its creditors, and its reopening two years later, was that it be non-denominational.

≥€

Congregationalists

F OUNDED WITH TEN MEMBERS on November 30, 1817, the Lyndon Congregational Society was the first formally organized in Lyndon. The members struggled along without a minister until 1828 and without a church building until 1829. Early gatherings, including Sunday school, were held wherever room could be found, such as the top floor of the Dana block.

Evidently the church building was raised before the land was purchased.[23] Pews, or "slips," were sold for $30 to help defray the cost of construction. The result was the Lyndon Congregational Church,[24] the oldest denominational church still standing in the town.

The committee in charge of building the new church consisted of Deacon Halsey Riley, Deacon Richard Stone, and Dr. Phinneas Spaulding. They were temperance men, who were few and far between in those days. Much was made of the fact that when the building was raised no rum would be used, in contradiction of the common practice of drinking at "building raisings."[25] Before the roof was completely on, however, someone was seen "tipping up the bottle" on the roof, thus spoiling the committee's plans.

In 1846 a pipe organ built for the North Church in St. Johnsbury was purchased for $300. In 1854 the pulpit was installed. This had a reading desk of mahogany veneer and was oblong in shape; the top was covered with red plaid. The desk stood on a high platform enclosed with side pieces like a reading desk and was reached by three steep stairs. The whole structure rested on a step-high platform with a rounded front. The desk was furnished with a massive copy of the Bible. Sister Mrs. Swan and Grandma Goss made a bookmark of bird's-egg blue ribbon in three sections, each tipped with a cross. In the center of the church was a chandelier of exquisite design and workmanship with cut glass prisms that tinkled musically when the

Lyndon Congregational Church (*Harriet Fisher*)

windows were open in the summer. A small diamond-shaped window was built over the reading desk.

Horsesheds were built in back of the church in 1846.

In 1870 the Lyndon church members voted to share a minister with the Lyndonville church. The following year they appointed a committee of three—J. N. Bartlett, L. K. Quimby, and B. F. Lincoln—to work with a committee of the same size from the Lyndonville church in selecting a minister. This led to a period during which the Lyndon church was yoked successively with the Lyndonville church in 1875, Kirby in 1879, and St. Johnsbury in 1890.

Repairs accomplished in 1873 included painting the church with two coats of white paint and gilding the weathervane, ball, etc. on the steeple.

Extensive repairs were undertaken in 1882: the inside was painted and frescoed, the old gallery over the entry was removed, pews were put in, a one-story porch with stairs to the audience room was added, a rear platform 1½ feet high was built across the south end for the pulpit and pipe organ, a cellar was excavated, and a new furnace was purchased.

According to the *Vermont Union* of December 10, 1875, Dudley P. Hall put a new Estey organ in the church, a superior instrument with twelve stops that he purchased from Shorey and Bailey in St. Johnsbury. In 1920 Ray Newell of Duluth, Minn., donated a new Estey organ in memory of his father, Oliver Newell.

On September 22, 1905, a hymn board of black walnut, made by Bigelow and Cunard of Boston, was installed. The plaque read: "In Loving Memory of Mrs. Theodore N. Vail, 1844–1905."

From time to time over the years the Methodists joined with the Congregationalists in the use of facilities. On July 16, 1924, the two churches agreed to use the Methodist Church in cold weather and the Congregational Church during the summer months. This alliance continued until 1967–68, when it was abruptly terminated by the Congregational Society.

The society filed for Articles of Association as the First Congregational Church of Lyndon on September 21, 1927. Today the church is used for a few meetings during the summer season.

The first meeting of Congregational parishioners in Lyndonville was held in the schoolhouse in 1869, with about 100 people attending. For a time evening meetings were held there on Sundays. By 1870 the meetings were being held at Mathewson Hall at the head of Depot Street. After the February 6, 1870, service, the Sunday school was organized with 50 members.

In March 1870 about 187 people met at Mathewson Hall to found a Congregational society. They adopted the bylaws of the Lyndon Corner church and chose officers: Hubbard Hastings, moderator; A. H. Perry, vice-moderator; W. H. Fletcher, clerk and treasurer; G. H. Weeks, A. H. Perry, and J. C. Morrison, the executive and financial committee. Members united to form the First Congregational Church of Lyndonville,[26] stating that 125 people in the village needed a church. The Council of Congregational Churches granted approval on December 6, 1870.

In 1871 the society chose a church building site on the newly formed Church Street at an angle facing east. The building was to be 50 x 70 feet in size with a tower on the right; a vestry was planned in the rear, with a kitchen and study so arranged that they could be made into one room. The sanctuary would seat 350, the vestry 100. The total cost was to be $7500. The building committee of G. H. Weeks, H. P. Alden, and W. W. Mack, were to proceed as soon as $5000 was raised by subscription. The railroad was to be asked to donate the land. The cornerstone for the new building was laid September 6, 1871. Beneath it was placed a box with the church history and architectural plans. The building was to be of a dark straw color with brown trim and a slate roof.

In 1872 a 1000-pound bell keyed to B flat was purchased, and stained-glass windows were installed. The first services were held in September 1872, the dedication following on October 29, 1872. Gifts received included a generous share of the pulpit costs from T. B. Wentworth of Boston; a center pulpit chair from Mrs. Joseph Mathewson; a communion table from Mr. Miner of Boston; chandelier and double lights from Mr. and Mrs. Fisk of Trenton, N.J.; a flower stand from Mose Reed & Company of Boston, discounts on carpet by a Boston dealer, and lumber from Lyndon Mill Company; a sash from Dubois of Peacham; various cash gifts; and about $1200 worth of transportation and shop work by the railroad.

Church parishioners put on many programs. The ladies were famed for their May dinners.

On August 27, 1967, fire destroyed the Congregational Church in Lyndonville. The only articles saved were a pulpit Bible, a baptismal font, and gold crosses and candlesticks. However, the catastrophe

Lyndonville Congregational Church (*Harriet Fisher*)

brought the parishioners closer together as they discussed ways and means of rebuilding. Architect Ralph A. Branon of Burlington was chosen to design the new church. Plans called for a sanctuary with vaulted Gothic ceiling, a choir balcony, an organ at the rear, a dining room and kitchen, classrooms, and a furnace room in the basement. The contractor was to be Dan Bovert, Inc. The old bell, cracked by the fire, was to be set on the lawn. A tower amplifier which would play organ chimes or records was to take its place in the steeple. About two years after the fire the new church was ready for services.

ᘒ☛

Universalists

LITTLE IS KNOWN OF THE EARLY DAYS of the Universalist Church in Lyndon. In 1828 Ezekiel Vose and Isaiah Boynton are mentioned as being church leaders. During its early days the church evidently met at the meetinghouse. This is confirmed in the minutes of the annual town meeting adjourned to meet March 29, when a committee for the town was empowered "to make such arrangements with the 1st Universalist society of Lyndon as to so alter or make over the town house as to best promote the interest of said town & said society."[27]

The first Universalist Chapel was located north of the town house. On March 19, 1849, Welcome, Amasa, and Alonzo Bemis deeded land for the chapel—which was apparently already constructed—plus six feet more on each side of the Chapel.[28] The building was well known for a beautiful decoration—the golden "Angel Gabriel"—placed on its roof. A description of the angel has survived in a document dated July 7, 1848:[29]

> This certifies that I Moody Heath of Marshfield agree to carve & gilt with pure gold leaf an image in imitation of a Seraph blowing a trumpet as represented in a universalist paper called the trumpet to be full size about six feet in length fitted in all respects suitable for a fane to a Meetinghouse with an inch & ¼ hole for the rod to pass through to be delivered to them designed by the last of this month at Lyndon Centre for which we agree to pay the s^d Moody Heath the sum of twenty five dollars & one dollar as expenses at the tavern at Lyndon Centre now due.
>
> /s/ Moody Heath   /s/ Welcome Bemiss
>   John W. Evans
>   Charles Randall

Many stories are told of attempts to take Gabriel off the roof. It is said that in 1872 five people engaged in this task were frightened

Angel Gabriel (*Lyndon Historical Society*)

away, leaving ropes hanging from the angel's neck, arm, and feet. On the night of July 3, 1883, the rod was cut through and the angel stolen.[30]

According to Isaac Sanborn's diary, services were held in the chapel as late as 1859. However, within a decade the building had become a bone of contention because of its state of disrepair. It was sold in 1887, after which it had a succession of commercial and private uses before burning in 1938.[31]

In 1881 the Universalist Church became active again when the First Universalist Parish of Lyndonville was organized. Meetings were held at Mathewson Hall for a while and were later moved to a small hall in the third story of the Eaton block.

On his death in 1892, Emory Bemis willed that all his property—worth some $6000 to $8000—go to the Universalists for a building fund upon the death of his wife. She died in 1896, and the following year the society acquired a lot near the entrance to the campground. By March 24, 1899, the Bemis Memorial Universalist Church was ready for dedication. With its stained glass memorial windows, it was one of the finest church buildings in the area. The Universalist Society contracted with the Rider Organ Company of Boston to build a $1200

Bemis Community House, formerly Universalist Church (*Harriet Fisher*)

organ for the church; this was the first fine organ ever built for a church in Lyndonville. By 1900 the church was financially the best heeled in town. In 1902 a parsonage was built on a lot in back of the church; this had been purchased from the railroad company. In 1903 the Reverend and Mrs. Kimball moved into the new Universalist parsonage. The Northern Association of Universalists of Vermont held its 104th annual session at Lyndonville in 1907.

Available records suggest that from time to time the Lyndon church shared its minister with nearby towns.

In 1930 the church trustees—G. A. Whipple, H. C. Hovey, Mrs. Edith M. McDowell, H. E. Colby, Mrs. G. F. Ferguson, A. E. Ruggles, and O. J. Leonard—turned over the property to the Village Improvement Society of Lyndonville. They reserved the right to drive across the southerly side of the lot to the parsonage at the rear of the church. The following restrictions were also placed on the sale.

> Upon condition that it shall at all times be kept in a good state of repair and shall not be used or sold for any purpose that would be

objectionable to the Village. The Universalist people shall have the privilege of using it at any time, if they so wish. The pictures of Mr. and Mrs. Emery Bemis suitably marked shall be hung somewhere in the building as a memorial.[32]

On the sale of the church the congregation became affiliated with the St. Johnsbury church. During the tenure of the Village Improvement Society the building became known as the Bemis Community Center.

ॐ

Methodists

IN 1812 ELDER PHINEAS PECK, a Methodist circuit rider, received a part of Ministerial Right 1 located on the east side of the hill known as Minister Hill.[33] He lived there until 1819, when his health failed. The stewards of the Lyndon Corner Methodists leased the land in 1825 for use as a parsonage; the rent was $2 a year, payable each January 1. This arrangement continued until 1855, when Ruth C. Houghton (Mrs. Silas) sold her home beside the Methodist Church to the Stewards for a parsonage. In turn, this was used until there was no longer a Methodist minister resident in Lyndon. It was then sold in 1930 to Murray and Bertha Paris. Finally, it was one of the victims of Interstate Highway 91 in 1972.

Though Bishop Asbury appointed Benjamin Hoyt an elder in the Lyndon community in 1811 and Daniel Fillmore an elder in 1815, the Methodists continued to share worship at the "Meeting House" until near midcentury.

The "Lyndon Wesleyan Centenary Association" was formed in Lyndon Corner in 1835. At a meeting held December 24, 1839, it was voted to build a house "to be located on some suitable spot between Lyndon Corner and Bucklin Corner," to be paid for by subscribing for slips at $34 each plus whatever additional might be obtained for choice, when sold at auction. Forty-nine slips were immediately subscribed

Lyndon Methodist Church and Parsonage, destroyed in 1973 for
Interstate 91 (*Col. and Mrs. Karl Davis*)

for, providing $1677.33. The choice of slips was sold at auction and
brought from 5¢ to $10 each. In 1840 when the "Centenary Chapel"
was built, the church boasted 140 members, making it the largest
church in town.

The church was first remodeled in 1867. In 1879 E. H. Stone of St.
Johnsbury Center was in charge of "lowering" the church building
and making some changes in the interior, so that for a time it was
necessary to borrow the Congregational Church in order to conduct
the normal services. In 1898 even more extensive repairs and alterations
were made: electric lights were installed, new windows were added
throughout the building, and a dining room and kitchen were created
in a portion of the building at the back of the audience room. The
church was reoccupied on August 21, 1898.

During World War II, the Methodist and Congregational churches
developed a pattern of cooperation in the interest of saving fuel by
holding services for six months in each church. In 1944 major repairs

Original Lyndonville Methodist Church before additions (*P. R. Griswold*)

were found to be necessary at the Methodist Church, and its use was limited to twice a month. In one week the schedule combined the activities of the church women and the Women's Farm Bureau, and in the other week the Juvenile Grange shared the church with the subordinate Grange. The preaching services were transferred completely to the Congregational Church. On August 29, 1949, the trustees sold the vacant church building to Paul and Merrium Aiken, who developed a furniture store there. Ten years later the Aikens sold to Robert Clark, who in turn sold to J. W. Barber, Sr. He owned the property until it was taken by the state for destruction to make way for I-91.

The Congregational Church terminated the merger in 1968, and the Methodists used the Grange Hall for a time. Finally, the Lyndon Methodists became a part of the United Methodist Church in 1969, using the church building in Lyndonville.

The Methodist Church in Lyndonville dates from 1867, when Rev. George W. Bickford, the resident pastor at Lyndon, first conducted services over the wood shops of the railroad company. After a time services were held in the village schoolhouse, and then for a time in Brown's wholesale store.

In 1878 Rev. W. R. Davenport came to Lyndonville as the first resident pastor. The same year the railroad company sold to the Methodists a lot of land on Church Street, on which they built a chapel that was dedicated in late December 1878. The building committee for the Chapel was D. H. Smalley, Jeremy Pearl, Aaron Twombly, and T. E. Parker. The chapel was 30 x 40 feet in size with a 12 x 6 foot vestibule in front. The choir occupied a recess in the east end of the auditorium with the pulpit in front. It was a pleasant room that seated about 200 people. It was heated by a homemade furnace. There was no steeple.

During the succeeding years the conference made many changes in the combinations of pastoral responsibilities. Lyndon was linked with Lyndonville in numerous pastorates. Lyndon and St. Johnsbury Center were combined on occasion; Lyndonville was with East Burke. East Lyndon was usually combined with Lyndon or Lyndonville or St. Johnsbury Center. It has been impossible to find any explanation of the combinations or their frequent changes.

In 1897–98 the church was enlarged. The *Lyndonville Journal* of February 2, 1898, described the results as follows:

> The committee in charge was Rev. W. C. Johnson, C. G. Morrison, J. S. Butler, G. G. Morrison, Thomas Bean, Joseph W. Spencer, H. L. Parker, and A. H. Hicks. The architect was F. M. Davidson of Newport. The contract for the building above the underpinning was let to W. K. Annis of Albany. The digging of the cellar and the laying of the wall was done by day labor. An addition of nine feet was put on the east end of the chapel to enlarge the audience room and an ell 27 feet long by 23 feet wide was built on to the south side of the lecture room and kitchen. A new and higher roof to correspond with the new dimensions was put on. In the intersection formed by the ell and the main part on the street side, a belfry tower was erected. Through this tower is the main entrance and vestibule opening into

the audience room on the left hand and the lecture room on the right. A rearrangement of the audience room was effected by building an alcove on the north side for the preacher's stand, the seats being arranged in a semi-circle lengthwise of the building, affording a seating capacity of 200. These seats are regular opera chairs each being separated from another by arm rests, the seats tipping with a place for a hat underneath, they are made of veneered elm and are very handsome. A raised platform was provided for the choir in the northeast corner. Around this platform and around the altar is a brass railing with draperies. . . .

The most noticeable feature of the new church are the memorial windows of which there are five, one large one in each end of the church, and three smaller ones, two on the north side and one on the south side. The west window is in memory of Rev. H. P. Cushing, the east window Mrs. J. W. Nelson, the two north Mrs. Aaron Twombly and Carlos Parker, the south one George Smalley. . . . Through the generosity of H. L. Parker the church is wired for electricity, four four-light chandeliers will illuminate the audience room, one chandelier and two wall brackets will light the lecture room. The audience and lecture rooms can be made one by opening the six large folding doors between them. The kitchen is in the south end of the ell and is well-fitted . . . so that the Society is proud of their new quarters. . . .

A great deal of credit was given to Rev. and Mrs. W. C. Johnson in raising the money needed to accomplish this renovation.

From 1883 to 1910 the Lyndonville and Lyndon Methodist churches were under one pastor, who lived in the parsonage at the Corner. In 1910 the Lyndonville pastor was made responsible for East Lyndon also; Lyndon was put with St. Johnsbury Center. This made more urgent the wish to raise the needed funds so that there could be a parsonage in Lyndonville.

Early in the term of Rev. F. A. Woodworth's pastorate a house was purchased on Prospect Street; it was sold in June 1916 to Maurice Seligman, the merchant tailor. Immediately Fred D. Smith, Enoch F. Smith, R. J. McDowell, and J. S. Butler proposed plans for a new parsonage on a large lot that had recently been purchased adjoining the church property. The cottage of Mrs. Elvira Gray at the Campground was purchased, moved to the lot, and made into a barn.

Camp meeting at The Grove (*Ruth E. Croft*)

Melvin Davis of East Lyndon was engaged to build the house. Early in February 1917, Rev. and Mrs. R. H. Moore took possession of the new parsonage.[34] The first board of parsonage trustees comprised J. S. Butler, Fred D. Smith, A. R. Smith, W. W. Eastman, and R. J. McDowell. The committee on parsonage furniture consisted of the Ladies Aid officers: Mrs. Iphus Gordon, Mrs. A.I. Beane, Mrs. Daisy Batchelder, Mrs. J. S. Butler, Mrs. Enoch Smith, and Mrs. Fred Smith.

In 1930 the basement of the church was converted into a 24 x 30 foot kitchen and a 50 x 30 foot dining room, with much of the work being performed by the congregation members. These rooms were dedicated March 17, 1931, with a banquet serving 150 members and a short program commemorating the dedication of the first church. Several former pastors participated: Rev. Alba H. Markey, Rev. W. J. McFarlane, Rev. Howard White, and Rev. W. R. Davenport.

In 1962 the church began its most ambitious renovation under plans made by architect Gordon Woods. This was heralded in the newspapers as a "$30,000 Improvement Job". Changes called for a new entrance, four additional rooms at the rear, and a 26-foot steeple. The first stage of these plans was consummated and dedicated on June 2, 1963.

On October 5, 1969 the members of the People's Methodist Church of Lyndonville, the Lyndon Methodist Church, and the East Lyndon Methodist Church met in a special conference and voted to merge their churches into the "United Methodist Church." The union became effective November 12, 1969. The membership at the time was 424: 63 people from the East Lyndon church, 104 from Lyndon, and 257 from People's Methodist. The church building and facilities of the Lyndonville unit were adopted as the center of the United Church.

In the summer of 1972 the provisions of the will of Mrs. Jessie Folsom were finally fulfilled by the installation of the steeple. Her will had provided not only for the steeple but also for a set of computer-controlled bells that can be programmed to play hymns or to chime every half hour. A picture of Mrs. Folsom and a bronze plaque have been hung just inside the main entrance to the sanctuary, with this inscription: "Our carillon and steeple given to the glory of God by Jessie Folsom 1875–1970 and dedicated to her memory by the congregation June 25, 1972." Mrs. Vanessa Brown had lights put on the steeple in memory of her son, who was a victim of multiple sclerosis.

The formation of the church at East Lyndon was the result of the revival led by Rev. F. S. Brigham, pastor of the Union Church in Kirby, during the winter of 1876–77. A church was constructed on land given by Amasa Knapp using funds locally subscribed. On the day of its dedication—July 15, 1877—the remaining debt was raised from the audience present for the occasion. The first pastor was W. J. Johnson.

For fifty years (1867–1916) the Lyndon Methodist community—in fact, the entire town—was enlivened by the St. Johnsbury district camp meetings, held anually over a period of five to fifteen days in the Grove,[35] a tract of about twenty acres owned by the railroad company that lay west of its shops, extending from Main Street to the Passumpsic River. (Before 1867 this site had been Deacon Benjamin Sanborn's sugarplace.) It was a popular place for all kinds of public meetings and summer recreational activities, and the railroad company often arranged special train schedules and rates for patrons of the Grove. The railroad customarily issued round-trip tickets on the payment of one-way fare for those attending camp meeting.

Of the first "Monster Camp-meeting," held September 9–15, 1867, the *Vermont Union* reported in its issue of September 20:

> The camp meeting held last week in the Railroad Grove in this town, was the largest meeting ever held in northern Vermont. . . . Ten cars

Camp meeting stage viewed from rear of congregation (*Ruth E. Croft*)

all crowded, came in the morning [Sunday] from the North and ten from the South. These, with the thousand teams entering from every direction added to those already in the camp grounds, swelled the number in the tents to about 7000 people. Some set the number as high as 10,000, a gentleman in this village [Lyndon] counted over 400 teams, averaging three in a wagon, between 3:00 and 6:00 o'clock, passed through our street Chapel toward South Wheelock, Danville, and St. Johnsbury, returning home. . . . We give the names of the tents, beginning on the right of the pulpit and going around the circle in the order of their location. Kirby and West Concord (in one tent), Irasburg, Barton, Barton Landing, Craftsbury, Landaff, N.H., Hardwick, Derby, Danville Green, North Danville, East St. Johnsbury, Lyndon, St. Johnsbury Centre, Brownington, Newbury, St. Johnsbury, Lunenburg, Peacham, North Concord, Victory and Granby (one tent), East Burke, Troy, Newark, and Eden (one tent),

Sheffield and Sutton (one tent). . . . About 50 conversions were made during the week. . . .

The facilities available to the campers were primitive and meager even by the living standards of the time. The grounds were fenced on all but the river side. The fence along the Main Street side was placed about 250 feet west of the street; it had two gates, one across the pedestrian path and one across the driveway. About ⅛ mile back from the entrance was a two-story central building, the front of which provided a speaker's platform as well as room for the volunteer choir. Back of the platform were several conference rooms. The platform, about 5 to 7 feet above the ground, could be reached by a flight of steps at either end as well as from a door at the back, which opened into the conference rooms. The location of this building had been chosen to take advantage of the slight rise in front of it for audience seating, and the railroad company had graded the rise so as to make it even more pronounced. Facing the platform were wooden frames; when planks were placed across them, they provided seating for some 4000 to 5000 persons. About half these seats were sheltered by a large canvas attached to the roof over the platform and securely lashed by ropes to a wooden frame. Nature provided the shelter for the rest by the overhanging branches of the trees.

Each day, at least three general religious programs were held; in many seasons, a "sunrise service" was rotated from cottage to cottage, and sometimes the midmorning program developed in the same way; the afternoon and evening programs were uniformly directed from the main platform. The speakers were ministers from nearby communities, missionaries recently returned from foreign service, biblical scholars, or outstanding denominational leaders; sometimes these programs were developed as a series extending over a number of days. Especially important to those people who attended the evening programs were the smoke smudges—metal frames, set at intervals of 25 feet, on which damp wood was kept burning to discourage the mosquitoes.

In a half circle about 150 feet distant from the audience space, tents or cottages provided shelter for the many people attending the meetings. In some instances these were erected at private expense, but for the most part they were the property of the Methodist Church in some neighboring town. The cottages provided little in the way of physical comfort except protection from the rain. Usually the beds were wooden frames on which were placed straw ticks; for tables and chairs, boards were set on crossed boards; partitions were created by hanging sheets from the rafters. Such cooking as was done was over a fire outside the cottage or, in later years, over an oil stove brought by some camper. The railroad company provided water from its water system at three or four strategic locations.

Before the 1868 camp meeting, the railroad company built what was known as "THE Boarding House," a single-boarded building 72 x 22 feet. The first story provided a place to set up two long tables for serving meals and in one corner a wood cook stove. The second story held twelve bedrooms, the partitions of which — like the rooms in the cottages — were created by cloth hangings; the necessary equipment for these bedrooms was provided each year by families in the local congregation. Not all transients attending the camp meeting stayed in the cottages or the boarding house. Rooms were rented in private homes, and the hotels in Lyndon, Lyndon Center, and Lyndonville offered special rates and sent teams at regular intervals to carry passengers to or from the grounds. Furthermore, many who wished to attend the programs renewed friendships with kinsfolk or even casual acquaintances in order to have a convenient stopping place.

Rev. P. N. Granger, chief of the eighteen-man police force, stated in the September 3, 1869, *Vermont Union* that:

> The meeting of last year considering the number of people present was remarkably orderly, and furnished a pleasing contrast to the old fashioned camp meetings where cider barrels, apple, and gingerbread carts formed the attractive side shows. The temporal wants of those in attendance at the campmeeting are well supplied as the Twombly Brothers merchants of Barton, who keep the victualling saloon in the Grove, have erected a refreshment stand adjoining it. They furnish board at $1.00 per day, dinners for 50¢ and breakfasts or suppers for 35¢. They pay $50.00 for this privilege during the meetings. They are giving excellent satisfaction, by keeping every thing

to be obtained in the best hotels, and bringing it on the table in the shape to please the daintiest appetites.

It was also possible to purchase individual items of food at reasonable prices. Through the years various schemes were tried for handling the problems of meals. These responsibilities were rotated among the churches for a time, but customarily the women of the local Methodist Church prepared the food, with many of the staple items being purchased from the local bakery. In later years a small building was constructed near the gate at which fruit, candy, and nuts were sold except during services at the platform.

In the space between Main Street and the fence, long hitch rails were set up to accommodate the teams of the many who did not come by train or stay in the cottages. Especially on a sunny Sunday the attendance was large, frequently estimated by the newspapers as being 7000 to 10,000. Friends and relatives pooled their picnic lunches and renewed friendships, while 600 to 800 teams stood hitched at the rails and many more horses were tied at trees inside the fence. Attendance during the week frequently totaled 3000 to 5000 a day for the three programs. From 30 to 50 ministers would be present, and services in the local protestant churches were canceled for the duration. Special programs were always planned for children during the week days; frequently these combined some kind of Bible study with handicrafts and games.

For the later years of the camp meetings, no records are available to indicate how much the railroad was used to attend. The *Vermont Union* of October 4, 1867, carried this statement: "tickets sold north of Lyndon 945 ($860.75), sold south of Lyndon 1427 ($670.70), the largest number sold in any one place was at St. Johnsbury 821." In 1868 the sales for one Sunday were from the north 1200, and from the south 1893, for a total value of $2240. The *Vermont Union* of September 1871 reported the railroad ticket sales for the first five years as follows: 1867—$1531; 1868—$2240; 1869—$1320; 1870—$1586; 1871—$1361.

For many years the Woman's Christian Temperance Union held an annual state convention lasting for several days either just before or just after the Methodist camp meeting. Participating in this conven-

Teams hitched east of camp meeting at Grove (*Ruth E. Croft*)

tion were local, state, regional, and national officials. Addresses provided information about the use and abuse of liquor, and plans were
laid for combatting the extension of that use.

The camp meeting had a significant effect on local businesses, as
shown in this August 25, 1871, article in the *Vermont Union*:

> The business people in the village are making some preparation to
> accommodate an extra trade next week. A. G. Tolman, who keeps
> one of the best groceries in the county, has built on a back room and
> fitted it up with dining tables, where meals can be obtained at all
> hours. Walker's Hotel is prepared for the rush. F. W. Silsby has marked
> down his clothing goods and has a stock from which any one can
> be accommodated. Dodge & Quimby expect to fill orders for furni-
> ture, and while they hope no one will ever need a coffin or casket,
> they are quite willing to supply any demand in that direction if neces-
> sary. Fletcher, however, has a full stock of patent medicines, drugs,
> &c., designed to destroy any such demand. G. P. Smith, at the post
> office, who has a new advertisement in this week's *Union* has a good
> stock of groceries, and a large and choice assortment of boots and
> shoes. Quimby and Co. are ready to furnish kitchen ware for tempo-

rary or permanent use. The Weekses are ready as usual, to buy or sell anything from a plug of tobacco to a $3,000 acre farm. Applebee, with his watches, jewelry, toys, and notions, will take in from $500 to $1000 in ready money, and call it "pesky good luck." The beauty and fashion, of course, will make headquarters at Geo. Hasting's photograph saloon, where they are sure of a picture highly flattering, and at the same time true to nature.

Catholics

ST. ELIZABETH CATHOLIC CHURCH is situated on a hillside in the eastern part of Lyndonville. The parish consists of Lyndon and the surrounding towns of Burke, East Haven, Kirby, Newark, Sheffield, Sutton, and Wheelock and is part of the diocese of Burlington, which encompasses the state of Vermont. The diocese was created in 1853 with Rt. Rev. Louis de Goesbriand consecrated as its first bishop.

The previous decades had seen numerous French-Canadian Catholics cross the border and settle in northern Vermont to work on the land, on the railroad, or in small industries. About thirty of them lived in Lyndon in 1854, among them Joseph and Charles Trudelle, Regis Lavigne, and Joseph Corbeille. Joseph (Collette) Trudelle, an illiterate man of great piety, would drive to Stanstead, Quebec, in horse and buggy to attend Mass. Undoubtedly he and other Catholics also attended Mass in St. Johnsbury, which had been visited occasionally by missionary priests as early as 1831.

After his consecration, Bishop de Goesbriand made a visitation of his diocese, which had a Catholic population of 20,000. Among his stops in 1854 was the twenty-five acre farm of Joseph Trudelle on Miller's Run north of Lyndon Center. Here he celebrated the first known Mass in the town of Lyndon, under a large hemlock tree, with the participants, who included a number of non-catholics, seated on improvised benches made of boards. Several people were baptized.[36]

The bishop now took steps to meet the spiritual needs of the Catholic population of northeastern Vermont. On September 28, 1854, he invited Rev. Francis X. Pelletier of Stanstead to take charge of several settlements of Catholics in this region including Lyndon. If he visited Lyndon is not known.[37] A Mass said by de Goesbriand on May 18, 1856, in St. Johnsbury drew 400 people, undoubtedly Catholics from Lyndon among them.[38] In July 1858, St. Johnsbury received its first resident priest, Rev. Stanislaus Danielou, who also had charge of "enjoining missions."[39] Recruited in France, he served in St. Johnsbury until 1874. Catholics from Lyndon could now travel the nine miles to St. Johnsbury on a regular basis to attend Mass.

The coming of the railroad brought an influx of Irish settlers; predominant, however, were French-Canadian Catholics, who found employment in the railroad shops in the new village of Lyndonville. In 1866 Rev. Charles P. Beaubien from Quebec preached a mission to them in the old wholesale store,[40] while Bishop de Goesbriand visited in 1872 and noted in his diary: "A good many Catholic families around this place, owing to the Rail Road shops. Most are apt to go away at any day."[41]

Recognition of their permanence was taken by Rev. Jean Antoine Boissonnault, who became pastor of the church in St. Johnsbury on August 2, 1874, with Lyndon also under his care.[42] Recruited in Quebec by Bishop de Goesbriand, he served at Rutland and Fair Haven before coming to St. Johnsbury. Father Boissonnault was a builder. In St. Johnsbury, where he served until his death in 1909, he constructed the former Notre Dame des Victoires church, a hospital, a convent, and a school. In Lyndonville he took steps to build a church. On August 5, 1875, he purchased two lots at the northeast corner of East and Hill streets from Louis Doucett of St. Johnsbury for $200.[43] The building of the church by Cleophas Coté under Father Boissonnault's supervision proceeded rapidly, and early in November it was ready for use. A white, wooden frame building, 60 feet long and 38 feet wide with a peaked roof, it stood on the site where St. Elizabeth Church stands today.[44]

On Sunday, November 14, 1875, the Church of St. Martin was dedicated by the pastor, three days after the feast day of St. Martin of

Former St. Martin's School, now Dawson House (*Harriet Fisher*)

Tours, a 4th-century French monk and bishop. Between 500 and 600 persons, Catholic and non-Catholic, attended the service, with 300 taking a special train from St. Johnsbury. The seats were temporary and the interior of the church was still unpainted.[45] According to Father Boissonnault's first report to the bishop at the end of 1875, construction had cost $1842.96, of which $589.75 had been raised through subscriptions, and $1076.21 had been borrowed. The excursion train brought in $75, while the collection at the Mass of dedication was $102.[46]

In this same report the pastor stated that there were thirty-nine

Catholic families in Lyndonville, and that he visited others in Burke, East Haven, Kirby, Wheelock, and Westmore. "Probably I shall find more," he wrote. "They use[d] to come to Lyndonville."[47] Two years later he would write, "All come to Lyndonville."[48] At first Mass, vespers, and benediction were held one Sunday every month, and later Mass was said on the second and fourth Sundays of the month.[49] The first baptism in the parish records was that of A. Napoleon Berube, the son of Joseph and Marcelline (Blanchet) Berube, performed by Father Boissonnault on September 14, 1874. The first marriage recorded, with Father Boissonnault officiating, was on November 20, 1874, between Thomas Cahill and Margaret Rice.[50] Between twenty and twenty-five persons made their first communion in 1875.[51]

Priests would occasionally come from Canada to conduct special services. On December 12, 1875, a week-long mission began with Father Simons of Montreal assisting the pastor. A high Mass was also celebrated at midnight on that first Christmas in the Church of St. Martin.[52] In the fall of 1876, Bishop Louis A. Rappe, the former bishop of Cleveland, preached a mission.[53] Bishop de Goesbriand confirmed 28 young people and adults on Saturday, May 22, 1880, in what was the first recorded confirmation in the parish.[54] On his next visit in 1882 he described Lyndonville as "a growing place."[55] By that year the number of parishioners from Lyndon attending St. Martin Church was estimated at seventy-five families and fifteen single persons. Two hundred people received communion at Easter time.[56]

Meanwhile, the inside of the church was completed. Pews were installed in 1881 and an organ was purchased the following year.[57] On June 16, 1881, Father Boissonnault personally purchased the Henry Charland house, the barn, and a lot immediately north of the church property from the Lyndon Bank for $900.[58] It was later sold by Father Boissonnault to the bishop for $600 and became the property of the diocese.[59] The house became the rectory. A school was constructed by Cleophas Coté south of the church at a cost of $586 and opened in the fall of 1881 with an enrollment of approximately fifty children.[60] Mrs. Harney from Montreal was the first teacher. Other teachers were Mary McNamara in 1889 and Louise M. Weber of St. Johnsbury in

1891.[61] Enrollment, which was limited to the lower grades, reached seventy in 1882, declined to thirty-two in 1885, and increased steadily to sixty in 1891 and 1892.[62]

The fluctuations in school enrollment were reflected in the parish census. Father Boissonnault wrote, "This congregation has not so many people, as before. Good many have left since they have shut the boxes factory."[63] The number dropped to sixty families and twelve single persons in 1885. Thereafter a gradual annual increase occurred.[64] The 1889 report distinguished for the first time between English- and French-speaking families with ten of the former and fifty-seven of the latter, an indication of the overwhelmingly French-Canadian makeup of the parish.[65]

In 1889 the Passumpsic Railroad Company instituted a regulation requiring all men from Canada working in the shops and on certain types of train service to bring their families to reside in Lyndonville. The intention was to keep money from wages circulating in the community.[66] The ensuing influx of French-Canadian Catholic families prompted the building of a gallery in the church in April 1890, with a capacity of forty to fifty persons.[67] Rev. Ludger Z. Marceau, also from Quebec, was appointed in 1889 to assist Father Boissonnault.[68] The continued growth of the parish convinced the bishop to give Lyndonville its first resident pastor. Rev. Joseph L. Paquet was appointed on August 3, 1891, and said his first Mass in Lyndonville six days later.[69] Born in 1863 in St. Albans and ordained in Montreal, he served in Brandon, Rutland, Burlington, and Winooski before coming to Lyndonville. A slight, bespectacled man, youthful and energetic, Father Paquet was immediately accepted by the community. He also had missions in Wells River and Ely Mines under his care, and periodically visited Catholic settlements in Bradford, Groton, and South Ryegate.[70] Mass was said at St. Martin Church at least two Sundays per month. In his first annual report to the bishop, Father Paquet stated that his congregation in Lyndonville consisted of 10 English-speaking and 115 French-speaking families plus 7 single individuals, a remarkable increase over the last figures reported by Father Boissonnault.[71] On April 19, 1892, Father Paquet purchased land for a cemetery east of the church from Daniel and Caroline F. Smith for $200, with frontage of 231 feet on Hill Street and a depth of 379½ feet.[72] The first burial, on April 28, 1892, was of Mrs. Peter Gaudette.[73]

Developing a cemetery, however, was the least of Father Paquet's concerns. On Wednesday, February 3, 1892, at 4:45 a.m., the interior of the church was discovered to be on fire, and by 5:00 a.m. the flames had burst through the roof and were illuminating the sky for miles around. Firemen and volunteers saved the school and rectory, but the church was a total loss. The origin of the fire, which started near the altar, perhaps from a candle, was never determined. Total damages were estimated at $4000, while insurance covered only $1020.[74]

Father Paquet immediately went to Burlington with plans to build a new church. By April the parishioners had already raised $1150 toward the construction of the new building, while Dr. J. W. Copeland had raised nearly $600 from non-Catholics in the community. Work began in April. The level of the church site was lowered while the rectory was raised five feet. Hector Guyer of St. Johnsbury did the stone work for the foundation, while the granite base from Groton was furnished by A. Mulliken of South Ryegate. The construction of the church was under the supervision of James Dalton of Wells River and Thomas Ranné. Fairs and other fund-raising activities produced over $1150 in 1893. Mass was said in the schoolhouse while the new church was under construction.[75]

The cornerstone was laid in an impressive ceremony on Tuesday, May 30, 1893, at 11:30 a.m. Inscribed with the words, "Presented by the Ryegate Granite Works Co., South Ryegate, Vermont," the year 1893, and a cross, it was blessed by the Very Reverend Thomas Lynch, vicar general of the diocese. Father Paquet acted as master of ceremonies, and sermons were delivered by Rev. Joseph Brelivet and Rev. Daniel J. O'Sullivan. The High Mass at 9:30 a.m. that preceded the groundlaying was celebrated by Rev. Edward R. Moloney.[76] According to the *Vermont Union*, the cornerstone was to contain "the local papers, coins, and other things to indicate to people of different generations what is doing today and how they do it."[77] The wooden steeple with a seven-foot-tall cross at its apex was added in July. The interior was completed in the fall and the statues arrived in December.

St. Elizabeth's Catholic Church (*Col. and Mrs. Karl Davis*)

Meanwhile the bell was raised into the belfry on the evening of Tuesday, November 14, with help from the railroad repair shop workers. It weighed over 2000 pounds—3000 with the oaken yoke and trimmings. The bell was blessed the following Sunday at 2:30 p.m. with a special train bringing people from St. Johnsbury for the occasion.[78]

This red brick church, built in Romanesque style, was 93 feet long and 40 feet wide, with a seating capacity of 350. The interior walls were frescoed in water colors with stained glass windows donated by various parishioners. The building was heated by steam from a coal-fired furnace in the basement and illuminated by thirty-four electric lights. The total cost of construction was $13,000.[79] The church was named St. Elizabeth in honor of the mother of St. John the Baptist. Mass was said on every Sunday of the month but the first, when Father Paquet visited his missions.[80]

The 1893 depression brought hard times to the parish. The school, whose expenses were high, did not open for the fall term in 1893 and remained permanently closed. The building was eventually sold to William Edward Riley, a parishioner, who moved it partway up Hill Street. It is now the home of Mr. and Mrs. Rufus Dawson.[81] The parish possessed a debt totaling $6,500 in 1894. Father Paquet did not take his salary for several years.[82]

While the church was under construction, a drive had been started by the Village Improvement Society to raise funds for a town clock that would be placed in the belfry of St. Elizabeth Church. When the drive lagged, Theodore N. Vail made a significant contribution, and a $600 Seth Thomas clock was purchased and installed in November 1894.[83] The clock is the property of the village, but according to an agreement signed between Father Paquet and the trustees, the village would pay for any repairs, while the church was obligated to keep the clock running.[84] A member of the Aubin family has wound it weekly for many years.

Numerous parish organizations were formed during Father Paquet's ministry. The most significant was a chapter, Caledonia Court No. 428, of the Catholic Order of Foresters, an insurance organization that paid sick, disability, old age, and death benefits. The order had started in Chicago in 1883, and the first court in Vermont was organized in St. Johnsbury in 1892. Caledonia Court was established on April 13, 1894, with twenty-three charter members. They finished an area in the church basement for a meeting place, which was called Forester's Hall. The chapter continued to grow, and in April 1897 the group, now numbering fifty-four members, rented the hall in Ide's block. The chapter continued in existence until 1943, when it was disbanded and the members who remained were transferred to St. Johnsbury Court No. 300.[85]

Other organizations were St. Cecilia's Choral Union, formed shortly before Christmas 1894; St. Aloysius Club, organized in March 1895 "to promote good reading and general intellectual culture" for boys between the ages of ten and seventeen; and the League of the Sacred Heart, organized in November 1898. The 1896 report lists a donation from the Altar Society, the first time a group of that name is mentioned in any documents.[86]

In September 1899, Father Paquet received word that he was being transferred to Richmond, Vt. Termed "a faithful worker and successful pastor, . . . [who] leaves many friends in church and society," he was honored at a farewell reception on September 26.[87] He was to continue to serve the church in a number of parishes and died on February 17, 1940, at the age of 77.[88]

The new pastor was Rev. Theodule E. Blais, who left no lasting impact on the parish. He was pastor from October 1, 1899, to May 14, 1900, when he left the diocese for reasons of health.[89] His successor, Rev. Charles L. Pontbriand, arrived on June 16, 1900, and was to serve the parish for over thirty-three years. Born in Vergennes in 1870, he attended St. Joseph's College in Burlington and the Grand Seminary in Montreal. Ordained in 1894, he served as Bishop de Goesbriand's secretary for eight months. He received his first pastoral experience in Highgate and its missions in Hyde Park, Bakersfield, and Hardwick before coming to Lyndonville.[90]

Missions as far apart as Westmore, Wells River, Groton, Copperfield, Bradford, and Fairlee were under his care until 1906, when those in the south were placed under the jurisdiction of St. Johnsbury. Thereafter Mass was said every Sunday in St. Elizabeth Church. That year the remaining debt on the church was paid.[91] In 1910 the basement was further dug out and converted into an improved parish hall. A donation of $775 from Theodore N. Vail covered the cost of the concrete work, while volunteers from the railroad shops did the actual digging.[92] The great pipe organ, which carried a plate, "Rebuilt by James P. Bartholomay Co., Dorchester, Mass.," was purchased in April 1914, after a fund-raising drive which netted $742.58, and inaugurated with a recital. The church was now basically complete.[93]

During World War I a number of young men from the parish

donned the uniform and served the country on the battlefields of France. Father Pontbriand was active in raising money for the Red Cross, Liberty Bonds, servicemen's recreation centers, Belgian and Polish relief, and other endeavors.[94] Parish life ran smoothly under his care. Entertainments and suppers raised funds for the church. New societies made their appearance. Chief among them was *L'Union St. Jean Baptiste d'Amerique*, a fraternal group of men and women that soon surpassed the Foresters in number of members and was active throughout the 1920s. Others that appeared early in the century but lasted only a few years were St. Veronica's League, the Holy Name Society for boys, and the Altar Society.[95]

A saintly man, active in community affairs, Father Pontbriand was an avid sportsman who loved to hunt and fish. A member of the town baseball team in his younger years who later served as umpire, he was also the state skeet-shooting champion at one time. He played a piano and had a fine singing voice. In the evenings he could often be found in the Lyndon Men's Club playing cards or billiards.[96]

Parish life was not without its sorrows. The parish census figures, which reached a new high of 770 in 1915 and then diminished slowly to 716 in 1921, took a precipitous drop. The railroad shopmen's strike of 1922 prompted the closing of the shops in Lyndonville and the transfer of the operation to Billerica, Mass. Families were split by the strike, and many French-speaking parishioners left. The census revealed only 333 parishioners remaining in 1926, of whom 228 were French-speaking.[97] Father Pontbriand showed his courage during the flood of 1927, when, with the aid of a neighbor and a collapsible canvas boat, he rescued eighteen people whose three homes were surrounded by the rising flood waters.[98] The advent of the depression in 1929 brought additional hardships upon the parish. Father Pontbriand rarely took his entire salary and used his own funds to assist the poor. His health suffered, and he was transferred by Bishop Joseph J. Rice to Holy Family Church in Essex Junction as pastor in December 1933. During his thirty-three years in Lyndonville he had baptized nearly 1000 persons, officiated at 138 weddings, and buried 288 persons.[99] On December 13, 1933, a crowd numbering in the hundreds overflowed the Lyndon Community House—now the Breslin

Center—to wish him well. Many parishioners traveled to Essex Junction for the celebrations of the fortieth and fiftieth anniversaries of his ordination. He was named a monsignor in 1945, resigned as pastor of Holy Family Parish in February 1947, and died at Fanny Allen Hospital in Winooski on November 19, 1950.[100]

Rev. Louis I. Sevigny now became pastor of St. Elizabeth Church and was to remain for almost nineteen years. He saw the parish through the economic problems of the depression and the turmoil of World War II. Born in West Rutland in 1894 and ordained in 1922, he served in Burlington and St. Johnsbury and as pastor in Sheldon and Franklin before coming to Lyndonville.[101] Father Sevigny kept the property in good repair. Despite the depression, parish financial contributions increased, and by 1936, $2600 was on hand to renovate the interior of the church. The walls and ceiling received a new coat of paint, the woodwork and statues were cleaned, and the pews varnished. The work was done by Perley E. Grant in the fall of that year.[102] The hurricane of 1938 damaged the rectory, which necessitated repairs and painting. In the fall of 1941 a metal-bronzed crucifix on a new cement base was installed in the cemetery.[103] During World War II seventy-seven young men from the parish entered military service.[104] The Foresters officially transferred to St. Johnsbury, but efforts were made to establish other parish organizations. In 1946 a short-lived parish unit of the Diocesan Council of Catholic Women was attempted, and in 1948 forty-three men formed a Holy Name Society, whose members received communion as a group one Sunday a month.[105]

The summer of 1952 saw the beginning of a new era in the history of St. Elizabeth Church. Ill health forced the retirement of Father Sevigny, who died on July 9, 1974, and Bishop Edward F. Ryan appointed Rev. Aime J. Trahan, S.S.E., as pastor. A twenty-four year association between St. Elizabeth Parish and the Society of St. Edmund now began. Founded in 1843 in Pontigny, France, the society came to Vermont in 1892 and subsequently founded St. Michael's College in Winooski in 1904. The society recruited priests and religious in Vermont and spread out to serve the church in England, France, Canada, and South America, and missions in the south. Father Trahan was born in 1909 in Highgate Center and was ordained to the priesthood in St. Jean, Quebec, on June 11, 1938. He served in France during the German invasion and occupation. Linked to the resistance, he fled in disguise to the United States. He spent ten years in Greenfield Park, Quebec, and a year in Selma, Ala., before being appointed pastor of St. Elizabeth Parish.[106]

Father Trahan was an exuberant individual with an impish sense of humor, outgoing and well-liked by Catholics and non-Catholics alike. He loved to fish and to play golf. He took an active interest in the young people of the parish, rejuvenating the Confraternity of Christian Doctrine, or catechism program, for elementary school students and the Catholic Youth Organization for high school students. In 1955 a Newman Club was founded at Lyndon Teachers College with Father Trahan serving as chaplain. Subsequent pastors continued to serve as chaplains to the Catholic college students.[107] Beginning in 1961 he was also chaplain to the Air Force radar base in East Haven.[108] The Holy Name Society continued, and a new Altar Society was started and soon became an active force in parish affairs. Meeting monthly, it organized the annual Christmas Bazaar and other parish functions.[109]

The number of parishioners increased from over 500 to 800 during the next two decades as the entire town experienced a population growth. The cemetery was expanded in 1956 with the purchase of a plot of land from Shonyo's, Inc., with an additional frontage of 82½ feet on Hill Street west of the cemetery.[110] Six years later property on the west side of East Street opposite the rectory was purchased for $200 from the estate of Wilmer A. Lyon. With a frontage of 74¼ feet and extending 66 feet to the rear, it became a parking lot.[111]

Beginning in 1957 the interior of the church underwent extensive renovation. Two years earlier the pews had been raised and new kneelers with cushions installed.[112] In December 1957 the communion rail was brought down to the first step, thus enlarging the sanctuary. Three new altars of Italian marble were installed, the main altar raised on marble steps, and all three supported on a cement foundation with steel beams. The Doig-Bernardini Studios of New York were responsible for the design and execution of the changes. Above the main altar was placed a hand-carved, gilded, burnished wood canopy, or tester, supported by four cast bronze pillars. The long, dark red and gold drapes served as a background to the large hanging crucifix above the altar. The crucifix was made of hand-carved lindenwood, as were the statues of St. Joseph and the Virgin Mary above the side altars. The front of the main altar was decorated with a carved marble pelican. New tabernacles were added on the three altars, and the stations of the cross on the side walls were recessed. The walls and ceiling of the church were painted in subdued color tones to emphasize the beauty of the main altar. The cost of the alterations was $16,900. A building fund drive raised $5500, parish savings yielded $4400 and $7000 was borrowed from the Lyndonville Savings Bank. The altars, which contain relics of the martyred saints Felix, Zeno, and Donatus, were consecrated and the stations of the cross blessed by Rt. Rev. Damase Carrieres of Newport on March 17, 1958. On Sunday, May 11, 1958, Bishop Robert F. Joyce blessed the renovated church at a solemn High Mass celebrated by Father Trahan at 10:00 a.m. Rev. Gerard P. Duford, S.S.E., of St. Michael's College, delivered the sermon. Nine additional priests were present at the ceremonies, and dinner was served in the parish hall by members of the C.Y.O. and the Newman Club.[113]

The parish hall also underwent extensive changes. The kitchen was enlarged and equipped in 1955, and in 1961 the hall was transformed into an effective teaching facility with the addition of folding walls, a new soundproof ceiling, and fluorescent light fixtures. The cost was $4903.65. Folding desk chairs were purchased the following year.[114]

Access to St. Elizabeth Church was improved. Since the Church of St. Martin was constructed, parishioners could attend services by entering from Hill Street or climbing the long wooden stairs from East Street. The latter were occasionally replaced. In 1960 they were replaced with a cement stairway of twenty-eight steps containing an electric cable to melt ice and snow. Parking was also improved with the removal of a bank of soil behind the church and the purchase of the Lyon lot on East Street. The old barn behind the rectory was town down, and an attached garage with an apartment above for the housekeeper was constructed in 1962. The costs of $10,900 were partially met by a $3500 loan from the diocese.[115] With the parish increasing in size, Father Trahan was granted a young assistant pastor in March 1966, Rev. James T. Holden, S.S.E. He took an active role in the spiritual guidance of the youth of the community and of the college, but was transferred to Selma, Ala., in the summer.[116]

The Second Vatican Council, which met from 1962 to 1965, brought great changes to the Catholic Church. English replaced Latin as the language of the Mass. In May 1965 a new altar designed by Father Trahan and Paul Aubin and constructed by Gerald Aubin of oak with a blond finish was placed at the front of the sanctuary, enabling the priest to say Mass facing the congregation.[117] Later the altar rail was removed and the main tabernacle moved to St. Joseph's altar. The concept of church as community was fostered, and the laity began to take a more active role in parish life. Laypersons served as lectors during services. Adult discussion groups were formed. As early as 1959 an executive committee for the C.C.D. program was formed.[118] Later a parish pastoral council with twelve laypersons elected by the parish was created to advise the pastor. Committees for religious education, social concerns, liturgy, and stewardship were established. The elimination of fasting since midnight before the reception of communion increased the number of communicants at Sunday Masses. Consequently, the Holy Name Society disappeared by 1967. A Saturday evening Mass at 7:00 p.m. was added to the Sunday Masses at 8:00 and 10:00 a.m.[119] In 1984 the Saturday Mass was changed to 4:30 p.m.

The ecumenical spirit had always been present in Lyndon. The priests were often praised for the contributions to good relations among the different religious denominations in town and participated in many community functions. The Second Vatican Council lifted restrictions on participation in joint religious services. St. Elizabeth Parish became a member of the Lyndon Area Council of Churches, now the Lyndon Area Ecumenical Council, and joined with other churches and their clergy in religious services and social concerns.

In the fall of 1966 Father Trahan was transferred to Putney, Vt. At a farewell party held on September 8, Lyndon Institute Alumni Auditorium was filled to capacity as numerous representatives of church and community lavished praise on the dear friend who was departing. He retired on September 7, 1979, and lived at St. Michael's College until his death on August 14, 1984.[120]

Edmundite priests continued to staff St. Elizabeth Parish for ten years. Rev. Leo Martel, S.S.E., was pastor from September 1966 to February 1968, when illness caused him to leave.[121] Rev. Anthony M. Larkin, S.S.E., arrived in the fall of 1967 as assistant pastor and was temporarily left in charge of the parish. A man of great faith, friendly to all, and an accomplished golfer, he remained until a stroke incapacitated him in late November 1975. He lived in retirement at St. Michael's College until his death six years later.[122] Rev. Maurice J. Bouffard, S.S.E., was pastor from April 1968 until September, 1971. He kept the church in good repair and the parish running smoothly until he left for the southern missions.[123] Another familiar figure in the parish was J. Lawrence Ouimet, S.S.E., who spent the summers of 1970 through 1973 in Lyndonville as a seminarian and deacon while preparing for the priesthood.[124]

Rev. Francis A. Donnellan, S.S.E., was appointed pastor in September 1971.[125] Quiet and unassuming, yet filled with a deep spirituality, he was faced with a serious practical problem in July 1973. The slippage of one or two roof beams caused the side walls of the church to buckle and parts of the ceiling to fall. The church was rendered structurally unsafe. The views of the parishioners were solicited through a questionnaire and several public meetings, and the parish decided to maintain the foundation, tear down the side walls, and reconstruct the church as similar to the original structure as possible. A building committee chaired by Robert Michaud and finance committee chaired by William McCormack were established and a building fund drive began. A second collection was instituted at weekend Masses, bingo was held in the parish hall and later at the Grange Hall in Lyndon Corner and at the Bemis Community House, pledges were made, and bazaars, rummage sales, food sales, raffles, and an auction was held. Ed Hahr Construction Company of Kirby was awarded the contract for the reconstruction project.[126]

Other churches and the Lyndon community assisted in maintaining the spiritual life of the parish. Saturday evening and Sunday morning

Masses were held in the Lyndonville Graded School Auditorium. The First Congregational Church was made available for Masses on Holy Days and on special occasions as well as for religious education classes on Saturday morning. The United Methodist Church and St. Peter's Episcopal Mission were also placed at the disposal of the parish. Weekday Masses were held in the rectory while the C.Y.O. and adult discussion groups met in private homes.

The actual work of repair on the church began on Thursday, March 7, 1974. The pews, windows, wainscotting, and stations of the cross were removed and stored. The roof and side walls were torn down and the basement covered and secured from weather damage. New walls of cement block and brick veneer construction were erected by May. Approximately fifty scissor-type trusses for the roof were installed and covered with shingles. Interior work was begun in July with the application of sheetrock ceiling and walls. In August new heating units were installed, the wainscotting restored, and the electrical work finished. New lights were installed in the ceiling, which was altered from an arched to a peaked style with beams breaking up the monotony of the light yellow paint. The stations of the cross, freshly painted by Bertha Koury, were placed in their new recesses, and the pews, cleaned and varnished, were again installed on new wall-to-wall carpeting. In the parish hall a fire exit was built in the southwest corner of the church, and the floor and ceiling were painted. The steeple, which had remained standing, was repaired, painted, and newly shingled thanks to a bequest in memory of Alan Leach. The rectory underwent some interior alterations, the outside was covered with vinyl siding, and new storm windows and aluminum shutters were added.[127]

On Saturday morning, October 12, catechism classes were again held in the parish hall, and services resumed in the church on the following weekend. The annual Thanksgiving service of the Lyndon Area Ecumenical Council was held in the newly refurbished church at 7:00 p.m. on Sunday, November 24, and served as an open house for the general public. Father Ouimet returned to conduct the service, which was followed by refreshments in the parish hall.[128]

The total cost of the repairs on the church and rectory was

$87,138.74. In 1974 a ten-year loan for $50,000 at 5½% interest was taken out at the Lyndonville Savings Bank. The debt was paid in full on November 9, 1976! An industrial appraisal company hired by the diocese evaluated the property at $520,112.[129]

In November 1975 the Catholic Church in Lyndonville celebrated its centennial. On Friday, November 24, 1975, at 7:30 p.m. on a snowy evening, a special Mass marked the 100th anniversary of the dedication of the Church of St. Martin. The main celebrant was Father Trahan. Concelebrating with him were Fathers Donnellan and Larkin, Father Duford, a native of Lyndonville, Revs. Peter A. Rousseau and Michael Madden of St. Johnsbury, Rev. Julien LaFlamme of Hardwick, Rev. William Gallagher of Island Pond, and Rev. Armand P. Fortin, retired priest of St. Johnsbury. Also present were Sister Theresa Duford, R.S.M., and Brother Thomas Berube, S.S.E., both natives of the parish. The organist was Leo Hebert, who had played the organ since 1922 and continued to do so until his death in 1984. Dr. Alfred Toborg, professor of history at Lyndon State College and a parishioner, presented an address on the history of the parish entitled "One hundred Years of Service to God." After the Mass a reception hosted by the Parish Council was held in the parish hall, at which a pictorial and historical exhibit was on display. About 200 persons were in attendance. Bishop John A. Marshall joined in the celebration with a visit to the parish on December 12 and 13.[130]

A great change occurred in July 1976, when the Society of St. Edmund turned the administration of the parish back to the diocese. Father Donnellan and Rev. Robert J. Sheehey, S.S.E., who assisted him in the early part of 1976, received other assignments.[131] Rev. Paul A. Citti became pastor on July 23, 1976. Born in Niagara Falls, N.Y., on March 18, 1926, and educated at Niagara University, he had been a public high school teacher and administrator before entering the priesthood. Ordained in Buffalo, N.Y., on May 22, 1965, he had assignments in St. Albans, Montpelier, Newport, and Rutland as Catholic school administrator and parish priest before coming to Lyndonville. Active in community affairs, Father Citti is a trustee of Lyndon Institute, a member of Rotary, a member of the Facility Committee of the Lyndon Graded Schools, and chaplain of the Lyndonville Fire

Department. He was named dean of Caledonia County by Bishop Marshall in 1984. An able administrator, he has kept the church property in good repair. In 1977 lights were added in the parking lot, and a drainage system to prevent leakage into the parish hall during spring thaws was installed by Hahr Construction Company. Insulation was added to the church and rectory in 1980. Inside the church a public address system in memory of Elizabeth Charron was installed, and a new confessional room, in keeping with changes in the rite of penance, was constructed in the rear of the church. The C.C.D. program was coordinated for several years by sisters from St. Johnsbury. Upon their departure in 1979 Father Citti assumed the administration of the program, ably assisted by volunteer lay teachers. About 165 elementary school students and 30 high school students attend religious education classes.[132]

Parish life has been complemented by the addition of an adult choir, a children's choir that sings at the ecumenical choir festival, family communion Sundays, parish coffees, breakfasts, suppers, and other programs. On Sunday, May 19, 1985, the parish honored Father Citti with a reception celebrating the twentieth anniversary of his ordination.[133]

Masses are held on Saturday evenings at 4:30 p.m. and on Sundays at 8:00 and 10:00 a.m. with a 7:00 p.m. Mass added on Saturdays during the summer months. Weekday Masses are said at 8:45 a.m. The parish currently contains approximately 300 families, and the annual budget is about $30,000. Although a number of families still are French-speaking, virtually all parishioners understand English.

A number of parishioners have entered the religious life. Gerard Peter Duford and his brother Leo both entered the Society of Saint Edmund, the former as a priest and the latter as a brother. Their sister, Theresa, joined the Sisters of Mercy. Richard N. Berube became a priest in the Society of St. Edmund, while his brother, Robert, joined the society as Brother Thomas. Priscilla Cristill Morse became Sister Mary Stella, and Sister Lucille Belval is a member of the Sisters of Providence.[134]

From its humble beginnings at that first Mass at the home of Joseph Trudelle in Lyndon Center, the Catholic community in Lyndon has

grown to become a major religious force in the lives of the townspeople.

✌

Episcopalians

LITTLE IS KNOWN OF THE EARLY DAYS of the Episcopal Church
in Lyndonville. Early newspapers contain a few items regarding visiting Episcopal churchmen. For example, on June 18, 1869, it was
reported that Bishop Bissell would soon visit Caledonia County, and
Lyndonville was mentioned as a favorable site for a church. In its
beginning years, the church held meetings in the Universalist Hall
in the Eaton block; by 1895 church meetings were being held in the
Methodist Chapel. The first service in town was said to have been
conducted by the "Wild Englishman," Edward Boulter. Evidence indicates that the first regular church services were in 1892, when Rev.
Stephen H. Alling, assistant rector of St. Andrews Church in St.
Johnsbury, began services in Lyndonville, along with those in North
Concord and Victory. The first Episcopal burial was that of Jane Ayer
on April 15, 1896 (the church's baptismal font was a memorial gift).

The first tangible move to establish a church in Lyndonville occurred on August 6, 1897, when the Episcopal Society purchased from
Elisha Bigelow a lot 90 x 86½ feet on Elm Street for $1000.[135] Mrs.
J. B. Van Wagner of West Orange, New Jersey, represented the Episcopal Diocese of Vermont. By the next June bids for a building were
being received. The original specifications called for a brick building
24 x 58 feet, with a steeple of the old style, six windows on each side,
one window in front, and one window in the rear. The interior was
to be of hard pine polished to the ridgepole, with stress beams ex-
posed. The cost was to be $4000.

St. Peter's Mission was designed by Henry Vaughan, also the architect of the Church of the Holy Cross, the Chapel of the Incarna-
tion, three chapels of St. John the Divine in New York, the Cathedral

St. Peter's Episcopal Church (*Harriet Fisher*)

of St. Paul in Washington, D.C. (in collaboration with the English architect George Frederick Bodley), the Chapel of St. Paul's School in Concord, N.H., and Christ Church, New Haven, Conn. The architect's preference for the Gothic style is shown in the tracery of the windows at the ends of the church.

George Edward Gookin of Maine built the church, and W. K. Annis of Albany did the woodwork in the main church. On September 11, 1898, the cornerstone was laid, with Reverend Alling conducting the services. Bishop Hall conducted consecration services on January 8, 1899, pews arrived later that year, and the Boys' Choir gave its first performance in 1900.

Rev. F. W. Burge, the rector in 1925, gave the church reredos for the altar and choir stalls. Made from the communion rail of Trinity Church in Brooklyn, N.Y., they were dedicated on October 9. On June 2, 1928, Ronald Bell and Tinal Elizabeth Little became the first couple to be married at St. Peter's Mission.

Over the years a vicarage, which was built about 1900, was secured, and repairs were made to the church as needed.

In the summer of 1930 two statues were secured from the Daprato Statuary Company of Chicago, New York, Montreal, and Pictrasanto, Italy. These were placed on either side of the chancel. A window depicting the Transfiguration of Christ was set upon the chancel wall in May 1931. This was a gift from Mrs. Homer Watson in memory of her parents, W. Irving and Emma H. Powers, and her godmother, Mrs. Mary A. Vail. The window, made by J. & R. Lamb of New York, represents the scene of the Transfiguration on the mountain before Moses and Elijah appeared, with three apostles, Sts. Peter, James, and John, kneeling in the foreground.

In March 1984 a group of parishioners voiced the wish that the church have a bell. On July 28, Glenn and Gwen Jacques, representing the Canadian Pacific Railroad, arrived from Newport to select and prepare a bell for St. Peter's. The bell selected used to top Diesel Engine 8402, which had been built in 1949 and retired in July 1983. It had operated in the Newport and Lyndonville subdivision. Glenn Jacques and Philippe Grenier painted the bell's inside the traditional red and polished the brass, then mounted it on a bracket that enabled it to swing freely. The bell is about 12 inches in diameter and weighs about 100 pounds.

ॐ

Christian Scientists

IN 1906, WHEN TOLD THAT HER CASE of consumption was hopeless, Mrs. E. G. Parker consulted a Christian Science practitioner in Littleton, N.H., and was healed. On hearing of the healing, her doctor told her that she had never had lung trouble. Soon healing services began to be held in the Main Street apartment of Albert Goss, which was located near the Creamery. The first Christian Science Society of Lyndonville was formally organized on January 27, 1907, with 11 charter members: P. F. Parker, Irene E. Parker, Jennie D. Folsom, Emma B. Wells, Edna M. Hill, Cora W. Fraser, Emma M. Ide, Albert A. Goss, Mrs. A. A. Goss, M. M. Keough, and F. E. Simpson. The mother church in Boston approved the Lyndonville society on September 10, 1907, and its name appeared in the October journal.

Meetings were based on the text "Science and Health with Key to the Scriptures" by Mary Baker Eddy, read by the first reader, and passages from the Bible, read by the second reader. These passages were then correlated. At first only Sunday morning services were held, but soon added were Wednesday evening meetings, a Reading Room, and a Sunday School. Two registered healing practitioners carried on the healing work.

The Church prospered financially and gave of its bounty to individuals, churches, and charitable projects such as war and flood relief, CARE, the mother church, and publishing house funds. The church received generous bequests from friends and members. For many years its $10 a month rent check was returned, and it received a yearly donation from the lease land rent from the town.

In 1921 the society moved to the Universalist Church (now the Tom Breslin Community Center), where it held services until 1925, when it moved to the more centrally located G.A.R. Hall. In 1933 the society began to look for a lot on which to build a church. In 1941 a 55 x 186 foot lot was purchased for $1000 from P. S. Lang Livestock, Inc. On January 29, 1942.[136] The Society incorporated for the purpose of buying the land, as required by Vermont state laws.[137] When the G.A.R. Hall was sold in 1947, meetings for a time were held in various places. In 1949 the society for the first time had a room entirely its own, which it rented in the John Norris building on Broad Street. Here the Society grew in numbers and prospered in its program. The room was previously committed to another renter, however, and the Society was again forced to move in November 1950, this time to "The Chapel in the Meadow" on Center Street opposite the foot of Main Street, where it remained until its new church was ready.

In May 1955 ground was broken for the new church on Center Street. Constructed by Carlton Basner at a cost of $16,500, the building was a simple, white frame structure 23 x 44 feet that seated sixty people—

Christian Science Society of Lyndonville (*Marion Sutton*)

five people to each of the twelve pews. There were two private reading rooms, another large room at the right of the entrance, and a cloak and storage room on the left. The news and readers' desks were built of Philippine mahogany with hangings of old gold, and the walls were delicately tinted with green.

From its dedication on June 10, 1956, the church was in use until May 30, 1976, when the last service was held. The building was sold on August 11, 1977, to Earl F. Daniels, Jr., of Lyndonville.[138] From funds received as a result of the sale, donations were made to the First Church of Christ, Scientist, St. Johnsbury, the Christian Science Society of Newport, and the mother church in Boston. The pews were given to the Christian Science Society in Middlebury. The remaining members of the Lyndonville society joined with the St. Johnsbury church.[139]

VIII

Education

꒰◐

Common Schools

VERMONT'S FIRST CONSTITUTION, adopted by the Windsor
Convention in 1777, was borrowed almost completely from the
Pennsylvania constitution of 1776. It provided that "a school or
schools shall be established in each town . . . by the legislature . . .
making proper use of school lands in each town . . . one grammar
school in each county and one university in each state ought to be
established by direction of the General Assembly."

As explained in "The Lyndon Grant," the town's charter (1780)
provided for the division of Lyndon's 23,040 acres into seventy rights,
six of which were reserved for public use. Three of these reserved
rights were for schools, namely: (1) the seminary or college, (2) the
county grammar school, and (3) the English or common schools in
town. The charter authorized the proprietors to designate the location
of all six public rights. They chose to assign the rights of the church,
minister, and common schools so that they shared a right or lot in
each of three places, rather than each holding a single whole right.
Lot 1 was bounded by the mill right and rights number 14, 12, and
2; lot 2 was bounded by rights number 32, 34, 31, and 21; lot 3 was
bounded by rights number 49, 55, 50, and 43.

The first school law passed in Vermont, on October 22, 1782, established the district school system. In 1787 the legislative council authorized any town, at any town meeting, to establish as many districts
as necessary to accommodate all the town's children. By this act, too,
town trustees received power to appoint and remove schoolmasters.
As a result of legislative action, in 1795, schools had to be in session

two months out of the year in order to receive support from the state; not until after the Civil War was this two months changed to three. The state revenues were divided, at first, among the districts in proportion to the town grand lists; in 1795 the division was made by population and, later, by pupil attendance.

At the Lyndon town meeting of September 5, 1797, a committee consisting of Daniel Cahoon, Capt. W. W. McGaffey, Nathaniel Jenks, Nathan Hines, Samuel Winslow, and Welcome Jenks was elected to divide the town into six school districts. Their report was to be given at a meeting set for October 2, to which this September meeting was adjourned. The report was adopted as follows, listing residents of each district:[1]

I

Daniel Cahoon	Ely Dickerman	Wm. Blake
William Cahoon	Benjamin Bucklin	Job Olney
John Evans	Joel Bemis	Noah Taylor
John Johnson	John Brown	Timothy Ide
Gaius Peck	Joseph Coburn	Elijah Ross
Simeon Smith	Joel Ross	

II

John McGaffey	Daniel Houghton	Roswell Johnson
Andrew McGaffey	Benj. Easterbrooks, Jr.	Stilson Hacket
Jude Conver	Zibia Tute	Nicholas Tucker
Stephen Walker	Wm. W. McGaffey	
Reuben Healy	Jacob Houghton	

III

Thomas Peck	Daniel Reniff	Jeremiah Fisher
Abel Carpenter	Jonathan Park	James Fisher
Nath'l Jenks	Ephraim Hubbard	Samuel Leach
Joel Fletcher	Levi Locklin	

IV

David Harris	James McGaffey	Wm. Ruggles
Samuel Winslow	Daniel Garritt	Benj. Easterbrooks
Amasa Hutchins	Caleb Parker	John Hutchins

V

Joseph Harris	Nathan Hines	Jonas Sprague
Samuel Frye	Stephen Sly	Wm. Harvey
Peter Tibbets	Nehemiah Tucker	Luther Houghton

VI

Wait Bemis	Jesse Doolittle	Nehemiah Jenks
Elias Bemis	Daniel Hall	Jeremiah Jones
Welcome Jenks	Moses Evans	
Thomas Thurston	Dan Harvey	

Under the 1787 rule of the legislative council, three or more inhabitants of any neighborhood could petition the selectmen to warn a meeting of the voters of that region. When the meeting occurred, if the voters approved a proposal to establish a school, they elected a moderator, a district clerk, a collector of rates (taxes), and a committee of one or more persons to take care of the business affairs of the district; thereby a new school district had been born.

All affairs related to the school were settled by each district school meeting, with no apparent consistency among districts: the building, its furnishings, and its maintenance; employment of the teacher; the length and number of school terms in the year; the subjects to be taught and books to be used. All expenses of the district school were raised within the district. Usually one of two methods of assessment were used, or a combination of the two. One was based on the grand list of the taxpayer, and the other on the number of children in his family to be served by the school. The need of families to have their children help with family work appears to have been a factor in determining the number of terms and the seasons in which school was in session. A three-month winter term appears to have been most common; fall and summer terms were more varied in occurrence and in length. Each term was a unit, and the teacher was hired for a single term, though sometimes reemployed. The only permanent feature of these school districts was change. Scarcely a town meeting passed without some family being added to, or subtracted from, some district. The number of districts also increased with amazing rapidity, the original six having become as many as seventeen before the district system was abandoned in 1893.

The first element of unity among the town's schools resulted from action taken at the April 24, 1802 town meeting, whereby a school trustee was elected from each district. With the selectmen, these trustees were to "superintend and take care of the several schools in the town." The first trustees so charged were Abraham Smith (District 1), William W. McGaffey (2), Joel Fletcher (3), Wm. Winsor (4), Isaiah Fisk (5), Jeremiah Jenks (6), Henry Watson (7), and Pardon Sheldon (8). At the same town meeting a committee report was adopted establishing eight school districts; the number of children (ages four to eighteen) concerned were reported as follows: District 1, 46 children; 2, 32; 3, 42; 4, 40; 5, 16; 6, 29; 7, 17; and 8, 11, for a total of 233.

During the early 1800s, under the district system, it was common to hold school for three months in the winter, the teacher being a man; if a summer or fall term were held, a woman was usually the teacher.[2] Wood for heating the schoolhouse was usually supplied in two-foot lengths, each family being obligated to provide ½ cord or its equivalent in money per scholar. The families of the district boarded the teacher, with the length of time dependent on the number of family children attending the school. About the middle of the century, the task of furnishing the wood was sold at auction to the lowest bidder. The contract included delivery of the wood and piling it in the school woodshed not later than the end of June so that it would be dry for winter use. Frequently it was specified that the wood must be "good maple, beech, or birch suitably prepared for the stove." Though "boarding around" was not entirely abandoned, sometimes the boarding of the teacher was sold at auction, as were the fuel and the building repairs. In 1854 the teacher's board sold for $1.24 per week, in 1858 it was 95¢ per week, and in 1865 it was $1.50 per week in summer and $1.75 in winter. The teacher's pay early in the 19th century was often not more than 50¢ per week for a woman and twice that for a man; later salaries of $10 and $15 per term were common.

During the 19th century the legislative assembly passed many laws that exerted major influence on the character of public education. In 1823–24 Governor Van Ness urged that the state provide additional schooling for Vermont children and additional taxation to pay for it. Because of his influence, the legislature enacted laws giving the common school the funds accrued to the state from (1) the late Vermont

State Bank and (2) the fees received from licenses issued "to Peddlars." In 1826 selectmen of any town were authorized to levy up to a 3% tax on the town's grand list for school purposes; this and the school land revenue were to be divided among the town's districts on the basis of district population. By 1884 this 3% tax had increased to 12%. In 1827 provision for town supervision came into existence as well as examination and certification of teachers. In the same year the legislature elected a "Board of Commissioners of Common Schools"; abolished in 1833, it was revived in 1856.

In 1845 the offices of town, county, and state school superintendents were created. The office of town superintendent existed continuously until 1915, except for a brief period from July 1889 to March 1891, when the county superintendent was tried. Also in 1845, an act of the legislature provided for teaching orthography, reading, writing, English grammar, arithmetic, history of the United States, and good behavior.

In 1864 provision was made for free, entirely tax-supported common schools. Under the 1889 county supervisory system, each town elected a member of the county board of education, and this board in turn elected a county superintendent. W. H. Taylor of Hardwick was the Caledonia County superintendent.

From the beginning the school at Lyndon Corner has been "Lyndon District No. 1." In the early years it had the largest enrollment in the town.[3] Greenleaf says that the first school in the town was taught by Abel Carpenter in the Widow Jenks' log cabin. Others have said that Dr. Abner Jones was the first teacher; though there is agreement about the site, opinions about the time vary widely. The first school building of which this writer has found positive identity was the Chamberlin School located on the rise of ground south of the Branch at the west end of York Street. This building burned in 1837.

Nowhere has any information been found regarding the location of school buildings in the years immediately following this fire. But by the 1850s there were two school buildings, known as the East School and the West School.[4] Apparently, each served the needs of the children resident in its immediate environs until 1866, when at a school meeting it was voted "to send the larger scholars in this district to a male teacher, who will keep the school near the ledge, while the smaller scholars will go to a female teacher who will teach in the house near the church. . . . It is the first step toward grading the scholars."

By 1869 agitation had begun for the construction of a new "union" schoolhouse, and for geographical enlargement of District 1. The building was begun in 1871 and occupied the following year.[5] The building committee consisted of L. K. Quimby, J. M. Weeks, and M. D. Miller; the location committee was Dr. C. W. Scott. The bricks for the building's construction were fired at a kiln built by T. A. Ceyr of St. Johnsbury on the road to South Wheelock. The stone for the foundation came from the ledge on the parsonage lot opposite Galusha Bundy's. Reuben Goodale did the woodwork, the lumber was processed at the Chamberlin Mill, and C. B. Fisk of Littleton did the brick work. The building was dedicated in formal ceremonies on February 23, 1872;[6] its cost was $12,126.99, and payment of the debt was completed in 1875.

Apparently to increase the number of people who could be taxed to help pay for the new school, some townspeople proposed that District 1 be expanded to include the Cahoon District, part of Red Village, and part of Cold Hill District. This proposal was the subject of heated discussion in and out of both regular and special town meetings over a period of several years. This expansion project was generously supported by Editor Chase in many issues of the *Vermont Union*. Finally in the November 29, 1872, issue he announced, apparently with great satisfaction:

> The bill to incorporate the Lyndon Academy and Graded School with the enlarged dist., passed the house on Monday evening, and will easily go through the other steps to the governor's signature. The dist. now contains territory from Hall's Mills on the east to Razee Right on the west, south to St. Johnsbury line and north including the farms of W. E. Pierce and Mrs. Locke. . . .

On November 12, 1831, "Caledonia County Grammar School at Lyndon" was chartered and authorized to use funds from the grammar school lands of the towns in the county. The corporators were Wm. Cahoon, Benjamin Walker, Daniel Dathan, Epaphras B. Chase, Halsey Riley, Charles Roberts, and Philip Goss. At the first meeting

Lyndon Academy and graded school (*Vermont Historical Society*)

of the corporators five trustees were chosen: Phineas Spaulding, Esq. (Lyndon), Joel Trull (Burke), John Beckwith, Esq. (Sutton), Job Randall (Danville), and Deacon Richard Stone (Lyndon). Construction of a building begun that year was completed in time for the fall session of 1832. The school was located halfway between the stores on Main Street and the Bucklin turn, 15 rods back from the street on a rise of ground that necessitated a double half-circle of terraces in front with five steps leading up each terrace to the front door. The first preceptor (principal), Cyrus Lancaster, oversaw two assistants—Mary E. and Abigail J. Whiting—and ninety-four pupils. Tuition was $3 per term, or $3.60 with languages, higher mathematics, drawing, and the like.

A committee of the trustees, E. B. Chase, Otis Evans, and Phineas Spaulding, petitioned the General Assembly in 1836 for passage of a

Lyndon Academy, original location (*Dorothy Walter and Elizabeth Nelson*)

Lyndon Academy as modern residence (*Harriet Fisher*)

law permitting the Caledonia County Grammar School at Lyndon to take possession of and lease grammar school lands in the county. The law was passed but was immediately challenged by Peacham Academy, which claimed that its 1795 charter from the legislative council entitled it to the fees from the grammar school lands of the county. There followed years of legal charges and countercharges in the county courts, with the schools being represented by the ablest lawyers in the state; finally the supreme court handed down a decision favorable to Peacham. This left Lyndon Academy—as it was now known—financially dependent on private contributions and tuition fees. These proved inadequate, and the school was forced to close in 1866. During these few years of operation, from 1832 to 1866, Lyndon Academy enjoyed a reputation as the most outstanding school in the northeastern part of the state. Its students came from the neighboring towns as well as from New Hampshire, Massachusetts, Connecticut, and New York. They boarded in the private homes of the community, and when they left they acquitted themselves well in academic, professional, and business activities.

In 1872 the classes which had been taught at the academy on Chapel Street were moved to the new brick building on School Street when its doors opened to the pupils from the Ledge School and the West School. Editor Chase applauded the school—in adopting a course of study in twelve units divided into three departments of four years each—as being the beginning of a graded school.

On March 25, 1873, the voters of Lyndon Corner held their first school meeting under the new charter ("Lyndon Academy and Graded School"). At this meeting it was voted to assume up to $500 of the debts of the old academy, and a committee was appointed to dispose of the academy's property . In 1874 Reuben Goodell removed the cupola from the old academy and installed the bell in the new brick schoolhouse, where it still rings (1975). The same year Editor Charles Chase purchased the academy building at auction for $525. He sold it later in the year for the same price to D. P. Hall, who converted it into a boarding house—ideal, he thought, for teachers and boarding students of the "Lyndon Academy and Graded School." The building was used for this purpose for a number of years and under a number of landlords. Finally in 1885 Dr. W. C. Blake rented

School on Vail Hill (*Rose Skinner via Grace Mathewson*)

it from the D. P. Hall estate, and eventually he bought it and converted it to a private home, which it has continued to be ever since.

Though Lyndon Academy, after 1872, was unable to maintain the outstanding academic stature of the preceding years, and lacked accreditation for college admission, until 1909 it continued to offer many courses equivalent to those in neighboring high schools. The legislature agreed to change the school's incorporation name to "Lyndon Incorporated School District No. 1" in 1910.

By petition of I. W. Sanborn, W. W. Mack, H. A. Alden, J. R. Baldwin, J. C. Morrison, and L. C. Brown to the selectmen, a meeting was called for April 4, 1868, to organize school district 7 (Lyndonville). As reported many years later by one of the original pupils, Homer C. Wilson, school began December 28, 1868, in the preacher's stand at the Grove, with the teacher, Miss Ranney, overseeing ten students.

In the meantime, a committee of H. A. Alden, F. Randall, and W.

Mosquito School (*Garnetta Wood*)

W. Mack were authorized to pay $200 for an acre of land located on West Street at the end of Maple Street. The construction of a building 38 x 58 feet, the intended cost of which was to be $6000 to $8000, was begun immediately. The building committee was J. C. Morrison, H. A. Alden, and Chandler Bullock.

At the 1893 town meeting the voters approved the town public schools being united into the "Lyndon Town School District" under authority of the legislative act of 1892. By this action the district system in use since 1797 was abandoned. As noted earlier, the six districts established in 1797 had expanded to an upper limit of seventeen, and contraction was already underway before 1893: Bemis Hill had been

Squabble Hollow School, 1881 (*Karl Davis*)

West Street looking north, first Lyndonville Graded School, last building
(*Mr. and Mrs. C. M. Spencer*)

Lyndonville graded school (*Harriet Fisher*)

abandoned, Cahoon (District 3) had been absorbed by Lyndon Corner (1), and both were covered by the new act of incorporation ("Lyndon Incorporated School District #1"), but there remained Cold Hill, East Lyndon, Hog Street (Fletcher, Shonyo), Lyndon Center, Lyndonville, Harris Hill (Sanborn, Vail Hill), Squabble Hollow, Pudding Hill, Egypt, Mt. Hunger, Red Village, and Mosquito (Gilbert). Responsibility for administration of the district schools was vested in the town school directors. The first elected (1893) to assume that responsibility were I. W. Sanborn, L. B. Harris, and Mrs. H. E. Folsom; Mrs. Folsom soon resigned, and S. G. Collison was appointed to fill the vacancy.

By 1900 various problems had developed in District 6, not the least of which was the overcrowding at Lyndonville. Agitation for construction of a new building did not bring adequate cooperation from the town, so Lyndonville withdrew from the town school district and petitioned the legislature for the incorporation of all of the old District 6 that lay east of the Passumpsic River. This request was granted, and it became "Lyndonville Graded School Inc." Thus, at the beginning

Cold Hill School, Pearl Kent standing (*Dennis Locklin; Grace Mathewson*)

of the century, there were three incorporations among the schools of town: (1) Lyndon Incorporated School District No. 1, which included Lyndon Corner, the section of Red Village District near Hall's Mills (the old Cahoon District 3 and part of 13), plus parts of Districts 2 (Cold Hill) and 14 (the Sanborn or Harris District); (2) Lyndon Town School District, including thirteen of the districts scattered over various parts of the town; and (3) Lyndonville Graded School Inc. All three were completely independent of one another.

The building committee for the construction of Lyndonville's new brick schoolhouse, finished in 1905, was Dr. J. W. Copeland, F. W. Silsby, and O. G. Chase. The architect was William Butterfield of Manchester, N.H.; the contractor was J. H. Smith of Lancaster, N.H. The old schoolhouse was moved slightly toward the street to provide additional space to use during construction. When the new building was completed, the old one was sold at auction December 24, 1904, to L. B. Harris for $125. He moved it to Lyndon Center, placing it beside his sheep cote in the sidehill pasture at the south end of Main Street. It was incorporated into the building that has been the home of the family of his son, Theodore, ever since.

Fletcher School (*Harriet Fisher*)

Slowly but surely a drift toward school consolidation manifested itself, as many came to see consolidation as bringing the greatest good to the greatest number of children. The school director's report of 1898 stated that "We believe in combining small schools so far as is practicable, but find great objection being made to this plan."

In 1903 the Harris Hill School[7] was closed, as only the Ed Randall children were using it.[8] In succeeding years several of the rural schools closed for a time but later reopened, and various schemes were utilized to avoid a final closing, because the state board of education strongly opposed maintaining a school for eight or fewer pupils. In 1937 the Egypt schoolhouse, after suffering neglect and vandalism for several years, was sold for $100. Cold Hill School was closed, reopened, closed for several years, and finally sold (1946) for $25. From 1944 to 1949 the East Lyndon and Red Village schools combined, first under teacher Elizabeth Garfield and then under Marguerite

Pudding Hill School after being moved to airport (*Harriet Fisher*)

Blakeslee; the children were transported so that school sessions were held in one place, though registers were maintained as if separate sessions had been conducted.[9] By this ruse the town received full "state aid allowances" without the expense of two schools.

The Hog Street School (Fletcher, Allen, Shonyo) was no longer used as a schoolhouse after 1949–50; it was rented to Jehovah's Witnesses (1951) and others off and on until 1959, when it was sold to Earl Bishop. The East Lyndon schoolhouse was sold in 1958 for $800 after the town meeting voted to dispose of all schoolhouses not in use. The Mosquito District schoolhouse burned in 1951. The Pudding Hill schoolhouse was sold in 1968 for $4500 to become a part of the Caledonia Airport facility.[10] Mt. Hunger School was the last to be sold, at an auction in 1973 for $7100, after being vacant as a school for at least three years.

By action of the General Assembly in 1906 the county supervisory system was made available to towns in the state. It provided that any two or more schools could form a union, and employ a superintendent at a salary of not less than $1250; the state would make a rebate of $1000 to the towns in such combinations. In 1907 Lyndon joined such a union with Burke, Newark, Sheffield, and Sutton. In 1908 the law was modified to reduce the minimum number of schools to twenty-five and the maximum to fifty; it also provided for a rebate of one-half the salary of the superintendent above $1200, with the state's contribution not to exceed $1800. During the next fifty years the town schools of Caledonia County formed many different groups with a variety of district names. The first superintendent was Martin E. Daniels. He resigned in 1915 and was replaced for a year by H. G. Leavens of Cambridge, Mass. Daniels was then reappointed and continued service until 1941. He was succeeded by Merwin B. Forbes, who was soon called to military service. Irwin Hoxie served as acting superintendent from 1941 to 1945, when Forbes returned for a short time. He was succeeded by Urban Wakefield, who held the office from 1946 to 1973.

Decades of discussion resulted in mid-1964 in the union of the town's three school incorporations: the Lyndon Incorporated School District No. 1, the Lyndon Town School District, and Lyndonville Graded School District Inc. Probably one of the major factors contributing to the final union was the action of the General Assembly in adopting the Simpson Aid Formula for distributing state funds to education. It was believed that all the districts would receive a larger share of state aid if they surrendered their individuality and accepted the share that would come to them as a part of a single town district. Also, savings in costs of local administration would undoubtedly result. The unification created the need to transport all the children in town for a portion of their elementary school attendance.

Over the years the town's educational facilities underwent repeated changes, including repairs and remodeling. The Lyndonville school building was renovated at the end of the 19th century, and the Red Village schoolhouse was rebuilt in 1899. The one-room red schoolhouse in District 6 (Lyndon Center), located beside the town house and Moulton's Training Stable, was vacated December 17, 1900, and the school moved to its new building (constructed at a cost of $1441.08) between the Sanborn Student Home (later known as Sanborn Hall) and the Baptist Church. No town school changed as much

Lyndon Center graded school built 1900

as the one at Lyndon Center, built in 1900 on a tiny 50 x 50 lot. The roof was raised and another room added in 1903. In the early 1930s, after more land was acquired, the building was moved back from the street southwestward about a hundred feet and materially enlarged at a cost of $9132.96. The school building was enlarged again in 1956 at an expenditure of $34,526.59. In 1969, to complement the work of the Education Department at Lyndon State College, as made possible by the use of rural town schools, portable classrooms were installed in the playground area of the Center School. Becoming virtually an addition to the school, these rooms were used for grades one and five.

During the 1920s a Parent Teacher Association was organized in practically every school in the town. The longevity of these groups has varied. In a few places they have been continuous and consistent in their contributions to the school of which they are a part. In most cases, however, their activity has been sporadic. The PTA in District I, which changed its name in 1939 to Lyndon School Aid, has been perhaps the most consistently active. Its most notable activity has been in raising funds for items to improve the work of the school—items that could not otherwise have been obtained.

Campus School, formerly Lyndon Center graded school with additions
after being moved (*Harriet Fisher*)

Lyndon schools were affected by the development of the teacher
training program at Lyndon Institute that expanded into Lyndon
Normal School and later Lyndon State Teachers College. The
privilege of being designated a "demonstration school" fostered a
keen competition among the schools. The children and parents considered it an honor offering some special opportunities; for the
teacher, it meant a small monetary bonus. The school in Lyndon
Center was designated "Campus School." The Pudding Hill, Mosquito District, and Hog Street (Fletcher District) schools were demonstration schools for different periods of time. The designation
seemed to provide a special motivation to both parents and children
to cooperate in effecting improvements in furnishings and equipment, and in developing the school as a community center.

ꝫ☛

Lyndon Institute

REV. MOSES C. HENDERSON'S *Historical Sketch of Vermont Yearly Meeting of the Free Will Baptists* provides now-obscure information about the beginnings of Lyndon Institute: [12]

> The importance of an institution of learning in the Yearly Meeting was first considered by the Conference in 1840. The Conference then resolved to establish a Seminary of learning in some central location, that would best accommodate the churches. The friends in Corinth . . . received a large number of pledges upon condition that the sum of eight or ten thousand dollars be secured, that the location be within one-half-mile of the meeting house, and the building be erected within three years. The necessary amount was not pledged and the enterprize was abandoned.
>
> From this time no action was taken until 1853 when Rev. R. D. Richardson was appointed an agent to solicit funds for the establishment of a school, and in 1854 reported $3000 pledged. Rev. J. Woodman was appointed to continue the agency. The year following (1855) a special committee consisting of Revs. J. Woodman, G. Sanborn, M. C. Henderson, A. Moulton, A. D. Smith, M. Atwood, and J. W. Lewis, was appointed to locate the contemplated institution. The committee received requests from several towns for the school, but after careful consideration, decided to locate at Lyndon Centre. From a misapprehension of the action of the committee, exceptions were taken and notice was given by parties in Sutton and Wheelock that a remonstrance from each . . . would be presented at the first opportunity. In order to consider the action of the committee, and give an opportunity for the remonstrance to be presented, an extra session of the Yearly Meeting was called in February 1858. The Conference, when met, considered objections presented as to the location, recommended and finally voted to set aside the decision of the committee and give the location to Barton. . . . The reason given by the Conference for not sustaining the committee was ". . . the location selected

was not the most eligible." *From this time on Yearly Meeting as such, ceased to be a party to the enterprize of founding a school* [italics added].

Reverend Henderson continued:

> A few years later some felt that an institution was a necessity, and must be had. In order to accomplish their purpose certain brethren applied for and obtained, in 1862, an act of incorporation for an institution, known as "The Green Mountain Seminary." The trustees named (not the Yearly Meeting) now had the matter in charge. They first decided to locate in Sutton, then East Orange, but finally at Waterbury Centre. Immediate steps were taken for the erection of a suitable building for the school. . . . In the fall of 1869 the school opened with a large number of students, and the prospect was most favorable. But the auspicious beginning was soon followed by disagreement in the management and by financial embarrassment. . . .
>
> Our friends in Lyndon had hoped for the school, but their waiting ended in disappointment. The trustees of the Green Mountain Seminary were not disposed to give them the school and the Yearly Meeting was powerless to grant them the desired favor . . . some of the leading men of the town (Lyndon) applied and obtained a charter from the State Legislature for a school which came to be Lyndon Institute.

The charter for the Lyndon Literary and Biblical Institution was granted November 20, 1867, and listed the following as corporators (most of them were residents of Lyndon): L. B. Tasker, S. S. Thompson, S. B. Mattocks, D. P. Hall, I. W. Sanborn, Jeremy Pearl, F. Randall, William F. Ruggles, William H. McGaffey, T. P. Moulton, J. Coffrin, D. H. Adams, C. H. Smith, Thomas Spooner, Calvin Morrill, Henry Keyes, Charles Rogers, Jr., Moulton A. Taft, Thomas Randall, Elijah Guilford, F. H. Lyford, and J. M. Nelson. The act of incorporation made these individuals the first trustees, and authorized them to increase their number to twenty-seven. The charter created a corporation with a capital stock of 2000 shares valued at $24 each. The trustees were forbidden to contract debts exceeding one-third of the capital stock actually paid in, and no part of the capital stock could be diverted from the objects of the corporation. Even though the Baptist Quarterly Meeting did not sponsor the establishment of the seminary, the church's clergy and lay members did not waiver in their support of the project. All the corporators were Baptists, and their denominational loyalty was evidenced in the charter requirement that two-thirds of all trustees must be members of the Freewill Baptist denomination.

The people of Lyndon pledged to raise $20,000 if $5000 were raised elsewhere. The raising of these funds was a slow and tedious process. An examination of the list of contributors (279 names) shows that the amounts given varied from $10 to $3100, but by far the most were of the first class. All who contributed $25 or more were made associate corporators. Probably those who served most loyally were Rev. L. B. Tasker, Rev. D. H. Adams, Rev. Jonathan Woodman, Rev. M. C. Henderson, Rev. R. H. Richardson, S. S. Thompson, D. P. Hall, I. W. Sanborn, and Hon. Calvin Morrill.

The organization of the trustees was completed on March 5, 1868. Officers elected were as follows: president, Rev. T. P. Moulton; secretary, Rev. L. B. Tasker; treasurer, S. S. Thompson; auditors, I. W. Sanborn and W. F. Ruggles; and the executive committee, L. B. Tasker, Calvin Morrill, S. S. Thompson, C . H. Smith, and Thomas Spooner. The committee to determine the site of the building, subject to the approval of the executive committee, was Hon. Calvin Morrill, Rev. C. D. Peckham, and Rev. T. P. Moulton. The building committee was S. S. Thompson, Jeremy Pearl, and D. P. Hall. In direct charge of building was Amasa Harris, Calvin Bigelow, and Sewell Bradley. L. K. Quimby was authorized to employ an architect; he chose George Ropes of Boston, at a fee of 2 percent of the cost of the building. The site chosen for the seminary was the hill back of the S. S. Thompson residence, west of the Common.[13] It was planned to move the Thompson house and barn as well as the Baptist parsonage, thus providing about ten acres of land for the seminary grounds. The committee to appraise the Thompson property was William F. Ruggles, Sewell Bradley, and I. W. Sanborn, who reported at the November 12, 1869, meeting of the executive committee that the value of the whole property was $3200, and of the northerly lot without the buildings, $850. Thompson chose to retain the lot lying on the road and all the buildings, and sell the remainder to the Institution at the appraised value of $850.

At a meeting on July 30, 1869, of the trustees and friends of the proposed seminary, it was reported that the last dollar of the $20,000 pledge of Lyndon people had been raised, thus assuring construction. Jeremy Pearl and Alpha Quimby were appointed the committee to secure the cornerstone. The ceremony placing it was held August 27, 1869. At nine o'clock in the morning a procession consisting of the officers of the Institution, clergymen, and citizens formed at the Freewill Baptist Church and marched to the site, where prayer was offered, and addresses were made by Judge Morrill of St. Johnsbury and others. Music for the occasion was furnished by the local band. At an August 25 meeting, the trustees passed a vote of thanks to P. B. Laird and Company of St. Johnsbury "for their timely and beautiful present of the corner stone," and to C. L. Ingalls for transporting it without charge. This was a block of Newport granite 2 feet by 3 feet 10 inches thick with a 2-inch wash. In the upper edge was a chest for deposits.

Some preliminary work was done in the fall of 1869 to facilitate the work of the following spring. The plans for the structure provided for a main building 50 x 50 with an ell on each side 25 x 25, thus providing a 100-foot frontage. The whole building was to be built of brick, three stories high, on a granite base 5 feet high. Attached to the rear of the main building would be a second structure of wood, 40 x 40 feet. The basement was to be a finished 9-foot-high room, to be used as an apartment.[14]

Spaulding Fisher received the contract for the granite stonework; stone for the foundation, to come from the Charles Sanborn Bridge, was to be "got out at once." The 200,000 bricks were engaged in Newbury, and C. B. Fisk of Littleton did the brick work.

Water from a spring on the Charles Sanborn farm (later Speedwell Farms) was piped to a reservoir on the top of the hill to the north of the new building. It provided water for the masons' use during construction, and continued for more than thirty years to supply running water for the school. For many years the cemetery and public school as well as Thompson and Sanborn halls received water from this reservoir. This hill was known locally as "reservoir hill" until the pine seedlings hid its cupola.

At a November 22, 1869, meeting the executive committee voted to "secure a board of Instruction and the school be opened the coming fall." At the January 4, 1870, meeting, the committee reported that it had endeavored

> to secure Rev. DeWitt Clinton Durgin for principal, but failing in this we soon after engaged Mr. George W. Worthen for principal at a salary of $500 per year and board. Miss Sarah E. Mason as preceptress at a salary of $250 a year and board. And Mr. H. M. Pearl as teacher of the Commercial Department teaching one hour each day in some other branches under the direction of the Principal at a salary of $300 a year. Mr. Pearl in addition has the privilege of instructing in Plain and Ornamental writing and the tuition of that department for his service. Miss L. L. Meigs was employed as Music Teacher with such compensation as the tuition may afford. S. R. Foss has been engaged to keep books and stationery etc. for the school.

In September 1870 the *Vermont Union* reported that "the Baptist High School is flourishing well and as a beginning of the Seminary enterprize more than meets expectations."

Early in the fall of the 1871 school year, $300 was subscribed for the purchase of a bell for the seminary. In November of the same year, one Saturday was declared a "help day" for planting trees. Editor Chase reported that "by ten o'clock the ground was covered with men, boys, and teams." About seventy trees were brought, of which fifty-two were set before dark. The task was completed the next Saturday, when the walk from the building was graveled also.

New faculty were in charge in the fall of 1871. John C. Hopkins was principal, Miss Mary C. Bradford was preceptress, and Miss Ella L. Nye taught music. The following spring J. S. Brown, a senior at Bates College, accepted the position of principal for the remainder of the year due to the resignation and departure of Hopkins.[15] After graduating from Bates, Brown returned and remained principal until 1881, when the school closed due to financial problems.

The 1874 catalogue of the Lyndon Literary and Biblical Institution had an interesting entry—sixteen regulations governing the student body, among them the following:

Every departure from gentlemanly or ladylike deportment by any of the Students will be subject to discipline.

Students are subject to the rules of the school so long as they remain in town, during vacation as well as term time.

The first bequest to the school was $100 under the will of Mrs. Polly Quimby, who died in November 1877.

In the late 1870s the trustees tried to secure an endowment for the Institution. Although many dollars were raised, the trustees decided in August 1881 to suspend activity of the school until the necessary funds were in hand. Even though the school had been relatively prosperous, it had never paid its operating expenses and was then in debt by $13,000. S. S. Thompson had made good the previous annual deficits and so had retained a lien on the real estate. When the school closed, he foreclosed on his claim of about $15,000. Various trustees, including Thompson and D. P. Hall, proposed to pay the outstanding bills. Hall offered $10,000 as a conditional pledge, provided an equal amount plus $5000 could be raised; this would provide a start of $25,000 as an endowment fund.

At a meeting of the friends of the Lyndon Literary and Biblical Institution in early June 1883, a favorable financial report was made. The funds raised almost matched Hall's offer, and met Thompson's financial conditions for releasing the building, grounds, and apparatus. At this meeting it was agreed that if the Baptists were unable to raise the needed pledges of funds, S. S. Thompson, D. P. Hall, Robert Pettigrew, L. B. Harris, and T. N. Vail would assume financial responsibility for the Institution. Among Thompson's conditions for releasing the property was a requirement that the Free Baptist denomination have at least a one-third role in control and management of the Institution, but that the school not be sectarian.

At the regular meeting of the corporators on July 2, 1883, it was reported that the conditions of the Thompson gift and the Hall endowment had been met, that needed repairs would be made at the expense of Vail and Harris, and that the school would open August 23 with Walter E. Ranger as principal. Also, it was announced that a boarding hall to accommodate forty to fifty students would be ready for occupancy by that time. To fulfill this promise, ten rooms, each to accommodate four persons, were finished on the third floor of "Thompson Hall,"[16] and a dining room and kitchen were constructed in the basement.

Thompson Hall [Lyndon Literary and Biblical Institution]
(*Kevin and John Calkins*)

During the school year of 1883–84 a school paper, "The Institute Chimes," began publication.[17] It continued intermittently through the years, normally having six issues annually. In the December 1884 issue one finds:

> The Commercial Department has been granted a charter under the name Lyndon Commercial College.[18] Hardwood tables and desks with drawers have been placed in No. 3 also a Bank and Post-office front have been made. All the offices bank, postoffice, express, freight, and merchants' emporium are furnished with drawers, pigeonholes, etc. . . . There are twenty-seven pupils who do work in this department this term.

During the summer of 1885 about thirty-five students from the Boston Conservatory of Music, under the leadership of Mr. and Mrs. Eben Tourgee, occupied Thompson Hall. They seem to have been greatly appreciated by the people in town and St. Johnsbury, as they not only presented numerous musical programs but also participated regularly in various church activities. They returned the following two summers.

Graduation exercises were held in the school chapel through 1887, after which inadequate seating prompted a move to Music Hall.

In May 1889 the alumni elected a committee—O. D. Mathewson '86, Forrest Brown '88, and Alice Hall '87—to arrange an organizational meeting to be held June 12, 1889, for the purpose of forming an alumni association. At this meeting Charles T. Walter was elected president, Hattie T. Allen vice-president, and Alice Hall secretary-treasurer.

By 1889 the seminary building had a chemical laboratory, a large and valuable cabinet of minerals, and fossils, philosophical apparatus, a fine reading room, a library of 750 volumes, and many comfortably furnished rooms. The school had steam heat, spring water, large grounds, and a boarding department. In 1889 a new art studio was fitted up through the generosity of Theodore N. Vail. The walls of the studio were a sage green tint. Around the edge of the ceiling a heavy frieze hung just below a cherry molding. Numerous cherry easels were placed about the room, works of art were displayed in a case of dark wood, and the room was furnished with two large tables. Paintings, landscapes, portraits, pieces of still lifes, masks, and plates were shown to advantage with the cherry color of the furniture contrasting with the tint of the walls.

At a meeting in the summer of 1890, the trustees allocated up to $7000 to build a two-and-one-half story boarding hall 32 x 100 with an ell 39 x 25. The structure was to include a dining room capable of seating 100 pupils, a kitchen, 48 sleeping rooms, reception rooms, a parlor, and so forth. The site chosen was the vacant corner where the Baptist Church had previously stood. Arthur Lambert Packard of St. Johnsbury was chosen as the architect, and the building contract was awarded in October to Bragg and Morris of St. Johnsbury, the work to be completed by December at a cost of $8400. Mr. Guyer of St. Johnsbury quarried the stone for the foundation on the farm of L. B. Harris in Sutton, and Mark Russell, also of St. Johnsbury, received the contract for excavating the cellar and laying the foundation. The new building was finished[19] in time for the opening of the spring term on March 17, 1891. Both students and teachers lived in the "Sanborn Student Home,"[20] named in honor of Isaac W. Sanborn, who had been secretary-treasurer of the institution since 1870, and a corporator and trustee from its beginning. Rooms, furnished or unfurnished, were available to students with or without board.

In June 1896 Principal Ranger resigned after thirteen years of service to accept the principalship of the State Normal School at Johnson. His administration had been a successful one: the enrollment had nearly tripled, and the services rendered to both students and community had been broadened. His successor was F. L. Pugsley, also a graduate of Bates College.

During the summer of 1896, Sanborn Hall was remodeled into two six-room tenements in addition to the one on the ell. This was a result of a dearth of demands for student rooms, and was intended to be a temporary arrangement. At the same time the trustees were faced with the need for major repairs on Thompson Hall, especially new heating equipment. This was installed by Bagley of White River Junction at a cost of about $2000, of which T. N. Vail paid about half.

State law required every community of 2500 or more inhabitants to provide adequate opportunity for its children to prepare for college admission if they so desired. Rather than construct and maintain a public high school for fifty to seventy-five pupils, Lyndon sent its students to the Institution which in 1898 charged the town $445 tuition per pupil.

At the annual meeting of the trustees in 1899, Vail, president of the board, offered to pay half the $5000 debt of the Institution provided the other half could be raised among other friends; agreed to pay the deficit in the operating expenses of the preceding year, whatever it might be; provided $300 to $500 for inside repairs of Thompson Hall; and promised to make a personal effort to raise the permanent endowment fund from $20,000 to $50,000.

In 1903 the graduating class donated new furniture for the platform of the chapel. The same year Principal Pugsley resigned and was succeeded by Merritt M. Harris. In 1904 the alumni began raising money to acquire portraits of the former principals (Worthen, Hopkins, Brown, Ranger, and Pugsley) to be hung in the chapel. Also in 1904, the school received the silver trophy cup from the Northern Interscholastic League for success in football. The class of 1905 was the first to acquire class rings. The same year an athletic association was organized to take charge of the school athletics.

In 1904–5 Thompson Hall underwent another major renovation: the museum was moved from the second to the third floor into a room made by combining three rooms, thus releasing the old museum for use as a large classroom. The room formerly used by the commercial college was converted into a study hall and library. Electric lights were also installed, the class of 1905 contributing materially to the project. In 1909 another renovation was necessary at a cost of $3600. To cover this bill, Vail offered to match any funds that could be raised from other sources; one of these "other sources" was the sale of the Lyndon Women's Club Cookbook, which produced about $600.

From the very first year, the faculty was so chosen as to provide for teaching music, art, and elocution. Especially during the first twenty-five or thirty years of the school's existence, the recitals and public speaking programs were well attended community entertainments; frequently every seat was occupied. Many of these programs were enlivened by a monetary prize. An announcement of an 1894 musical program stated that there would be "pianos, harmonicas, castinets, tambourines, triangles, duets, quartets, and one piece would be two persons playing at each of two pianos plus Mrs. Ranger at the organ." Until about the end of the century no charge was made for admittance to such programs.

At the end of the school year a full week was devoted to the commencement activities. These always began with a Sunday morning baccalaureate program in the Baptist Church, during which all Protestant churches in town cancelled their usual services. At least one evening featured a competitive public speaking contest, and often another evening was given over to a musical program at which students displayed skills acquired during the year. The week ended with a very full day, beginning with the morning graduation exercises in Music Hall, at which every member of the class participated by reciting his or her essay giving the class history or prophecy (often containing some humor and usually much absurdity). Graduation was followed by the alumni banquet at noon, with the new graduates being guests of the alumni; this was often served by the women of the Congregational Church in their dining room. Usually there was some afternoon activity, often of an athletic nature. In the evening there was a concert, sometimes by an out-of-town group, and the day ended with a promenade or dance in Music Hall after the concert.

Even though it had been necessary to close the Institution only once, every board of trustees was troubled by the school's persistent inability to meet its annual obligations. S. S. Thompson, the second president of the corporation, contributed more than $20,000 in covering annual deficits; D. P. Hall, his successor, fully equaled the Thompson gifts, ending with a $10,000 gift to help establish an endowment fund. No record exists of the gifts of the next president of the corporation, L. B. Harris, but it is logical to assume that they were generous since he made large contributions both before and after his term as president. From the time Theodore N. Vail became a citizen of the town in 1883, he evidenced a marked interest in the school and gave most generously on many occasions, especially during his quarter-century term as board of trustees president. Changes of administration brought no reduction in financial problems. Merritt M. Harris resigned as principal in 1907, to be succeeded by Cardinal L. Goodwin (1907–10) and Harry L. Bradford (1910–12).

In 1912, Vail entered into a contract with the trustees to assume full responsibility for the school's operation; the tuition receipts were to be turned over to him, to be applied to the maintenance expenses of the school. He immediately expended about $60,000 in purchasing property and equipment and making repairs. In addition he met the operating deficit of $8000 to $12,000 from that time until his death in 1920. It was during these years that Vail founded the Lyndon School of Agriculture, also known as the Vail Agricultural School. Under the terms of his will, Vail not only gave a generous bequest to the Institution, but also provided that the Agricultural School should revert to the Institution if not retained by the State of Vermont, which had accepted it as a gift on March 31, 1915.

A significant step in the development of the school under Vail's contract with the trustees was his hiring of Ozias D. Mathewson as principal. Mathewson brought to the office longer and more successful experience than any of his predecessors, including twenty-two years at Barre's Spaulding High. Under the joint motivation of these two men, the appearance of the central part of Lyndon Center was materially changed.

A building was purchased that had been a general store from the very beginning of the community, operated in succession by Marsh & Co., The Bemisses, J. M. & W. H. Hoyt, Foss & Denison, and H. M. Nichols. The latter had converted it into a residence, which was owned in 1912 by E. L. Clement. The barn and shed were removed, as were most of the partitions on the first floor, which was then remodeled into a general store and post office; the second floor's two tenements were reduced to one. The large and very old pine trees in the building's southwest yard were cut down.

Next to this structure on the south was a small building that for years had been the general store and village post office; this building was removed to Hadleyville. The next building on the south was "May Sherburne's tenement house," built early in the life of Lyndon Center. During most of its existence it had been a tavern, its landlords having included N. W. Ruggles, W. F. Ruggles, H. M. Nichols, James R. Hoffman, Caleb Garfield, L. M. Hall, Luke Farley, and A. D. Massey. In 1879 it had come into the possession of Mrs. Betsey Sherburne, and at her death her daughter, May, had inherited it. Under Vail's plan, the property's barn—entrance to which had been a driveway close to the store—was destroyed, and the ell part of the house was moved to the south end of Main Street beside Fanny Pickle's house, and made into two tenements. The main part of the house was moved in back of the newly created store–post office, remodeled into a dormitory for boys, and named the Tavern.

About 1900, May Sherburne had sold off from the south side of her property enough space for a street—"Eastern Avenue"—and a building lot. The buyer, S. G. Collison, had built a house here, which he now sold to Vail. Not long after the Collison house had been built, Mrs. Nancy Darling had purchased a lot and had a small house constructed on the north side of this new street. At Mrs. Darling's death this house had become the property of Mrs. Kate Smith of Northampton, Mass.; Vail purchased the house and had it moved north into line with the Tavern, for rent to school faculty as "Smith Cottage." In the space remaining between the Collison house and Smith Cottage, as near as possible to the bank, a dormitory for girls was built: Mathewson House. Thus was created "the Quadrangle." Vail also purchased from Austin Bean the one-story house next south from Sanborn Student Home, a structure that had served successively as the residence of Fernando Randall, Deacon Larnard, Daniel Winter, Mrs. Sanford Gray, Will Bean, and Austin Bean. This was remodeled into a dormitory known as "Bean Cottage" and later into two tenements.

At the 1915 commencement Vail gave to the Institution the I. H. Hall property and meadowland along the Passumpsic River, the girl's dormitory, four houses on the Quadrangle, the Bean Cottage,[21] and lands in Lyndon Corner formerly belonging to the late E. B. Chase.

Vail died on April 16, 1920. That fall the controversy concerning the state maintaining the Vail Agricultural School, simmering since 1915, burst out anew in the legislature. As a result, that body reversed its action accepting the gift. Immediately the trustees of the Institution took the necessary action to secure the release of the property to the Institution. During the next two years the property was sold to various buyers.

Reporting to the trustees on July 2, 1922, Principal Mathewson stated that

> the amount received from Mr. Vail directly from his will was $122,669.38, the amount received indirectly from the sale of the Agricultural School property returned by the State was $129,161.60. These figures are approximately correct. These figures include the real estate as estimated by the finance committee in its report of even date; also the Creamery stock at its present market value of $20,000 and Lyndonville National Bank Stock of $16,500.

On April 23, 1921, at a corporator's meeting, the name "Lyndon Literary and Biblical Institution" was changed to "Lyndon Institute, Inc."[22] At the same meeting a committee consisting of Principal Mathewson, H. E. Folsom, and A. W. Edmunds was appointed to draft a revision of the corporation bylaws.[23] This was presented and adopted June 1, 1921.

During the night of January 2–3, 1922, Thompson Hall was completely destroyed by fire. While the smoke was still rising from the ashes, $20,000 was pledged to the rebuilding project. More than 600 residents of Lyndon and neighboring towns added their pledges to the insurance — $4000 on the building and $2000 on the furnishings. The trustees met the next day, voted to rebuild, and elected Elmer A. Darling, Harley E. Folsom, W. N. Hubbard, John L. Norris, and O. D. Mathewson as a building committee. Larson and Wells of Hanover, N.H., served as architects for the new building, and the contract for construction was awarded to H. P. Cummings Construction Company of Ware, Mass. Work began on March 27, and the dedication took place on December 21. The building was 100 x 68 feet; the wing on the back was 50 x 43 feet. The total cost was $200,707.93.

Soon after Thompson Hall was destroyed, Hon. Samuel W. McCall (son-in-law of S. S. Thompson, for whom the building had been named) expressed the hope that the new building would be long and low, built of red brick and white mortar, and with a cupola on it like that of Independence Hall (Philadelphia) or like the delicate belfry on old Dartmouth Hall (Hanover, N.H.)

A dignified service of dedication took place in the chapel of the new building at two o'clock on December 21. Representatives of several New England colleges and secondary schools, members of the Vermont Board of Education, and local people filled all available space. The Verde Monte trio of St. Johnsbury provided special music, Hon. Samuel Walker McCall, former governor of Massachusetts, offered the dedication address, other distinguished guests made congratulatory remarks, and a large number of letters and telegrams of a similar nature were read.

Special attention was called to numerous items in the building. Two items had been saved from old Thompson Hall, namely, bronze door plates marked "office" and "library"; these were duplicate plates that had been wrapped in paper and happened to escape the heat of the fire. The old cornerstone had been resurfaced and relettered: "Chartered November 20, 1867, Founded August 27, 1869, Rebuilt 1922." John Norris had generously given a new Meneely bell to replace the 1871 bell, too damaged in the fire for further use. The specially designed lights at the front steps were the gift of Elmer A. Darling, who had also made arrangements for and contributed the oil painting of the Parthenon in the chapel; this was painted by a Greek artist of the Sofus L. Mortenson Company in Boston. The clock was a gift of the Lyndonville Creamery Association. Near the main entrance was a bronze plaque bearing this inscription:

PER ASPERA AD ASTRA[24]

LYNDON INSTITUTE
holds in grateful
remembrance
SUMNER SHAW THOMPSON
zealous promoter and
liberal benefactor
DUDLEY PETTINGILL HALL
staunch friend, donor of
The Hall Fund
THEODORE NEWTON VAIL
faithful supporter and
munificent endower
ELMER ALFRED DARLING
sincere friend and generous
contributor

During the dedication program, Elmer A. Darling presented Mathewson with a gold watch and fob, engraved with his initials and the school motto, plus a memorial signed by every member of the board—symbols of the trustees' appreciation for his services in the work of rebuilding.

In November 1922 the school purchased the old home of S. S. Thompson from his daughter, Mrs. Ella Thompson McCall, for $3500, with $1000 of this being a gift from Mrs. McCall. In 1932 the two houses next south of the southern line of Eastern Avenue were acquired from the George Willey estate. Mr. and Mrs. Willey had been living in the one nearest the street; the other had been the home of Mr. Willey's late father, David, and at the time of sale it was rented

Lyndon Institute (*Lyndon Institute Alumni Association*)

to the Cutting family.[25] The major portion of the land between these houses and the bank (about six rods) had been purchased by Vail and formed part of his 1915 gift to the school.

The first "annual track meet" between St. Johnsbury Academy and Lyndon Institute occurred in 1919; L. I. won in 1921. Over the years the teams have been so well-matched that the title has changed hands frequently, and so the rivalry has remained keen. From the early 1920s, athletic activity has flourished at Lyndon Institute. In 1921 the team claimed the baseball championship of northern Vermont by winning nine of ten games; the loss was suffered at the hands of an out-of-state team. However, by 1926 student interest had shifted to track, so baseball was dropped in favor of that sport. Robert K. Lewis came to the school in 1924 to teach history and serve as coach of football and track as well as supervisor of the boy's dormitory. He introduced competitive skiing and for the next twenty years aided and abetted the various disciplines within that sport. Largely, as a result of his motivation, the town selectmen in 1929 leased the Common.[26] for twenty years to the Institute, and the cinder track was laid in 1934 with the assistance of the Civil Works Authority at a cost of $1551.51. As athletic director for many years, and later as principal, he was at the forefront in expanding athletic programs for both boys and girls. This expansion has continued through the years, so that by 1974 the opportunities available for boys included football, basketball, ice hockey, indoor and outdoor track, cross-country, skiing, and gymnastics. Available for girls were basketball, field hockey, track, cross-country, skiing, and softball. In 1973–74 the Nordic Training Center was established for training potential Olympic contestants. The record of championships that the school has amassed in various sports is an enviable one:

> New England Ski Champions: 1947, 1960, 1963, 1975
> Boy's State Ski Champions: 1944, 1945, 1946, 1947, 1949, 1950, 1951, 1952, 1955, 1956, 1959, 1960, 1961, 1962, 1963, 1966, 1970, 1975
> Boy's State Track Champions: 1927, 1929, 1931, 1945, 1956, 1957, 1958
> Boy's State Cross-Country Champions: 1969, 1974, 1975
> State Football Champions: 1933, Co-Champions 1966
> Girl's State Basketball Champions: 1954
> Girl's State Track Champions:1974
> Girl's State Cross-Country Champions: 1974, 1975

In 1971 work was begun on an athletic practice field on the Pearl meadow, and the next year it was named "Forrest Field" in recognition of the long and faithful service of Albert Forrest.

In October 1933 the school recognized academic accomplishment by awarding forty-seven scholastic letters: fifteen to students who had graduated in 1933, eight to seniors, twelve to juniors, and twelve to sophomores.

Although Dr. Mathewson resigned as principal of Lyndon Institute at the close of the 1942–43 school after thirty-one years of service, he continued as president of its board of trustees. He was succeeded as principal by Walter F. True, who had begun his teaching career in 1919 at Lyndon Institute, after three years had gone to the principalship of Wilmington High School, and then for twenty years had been at Randolph High.

During World War II, the Institute students participated in many

home-front activities. October 6, 1944, marked an alumni day observance in honor of its members who served in the military forces (360
is the estimated number). Special honor was given to the five who
had made the supreme sacrifice. Memorial tribute was also paid to
Dr. Mathewson, who had died in mid-August. As a part of the alumni
day observance of 1948 Governor Ernest Gibson dedicated a shaft of
Vermont granite as a war service memorial. Located in front of the
main entrance to the building at the junction of the two paths, it has
a bronze plaque on one side and the names of those for whom it is
a memorial on the other.

Expansion of the school's vocational program began in the 1940s,
when the auto mechanics and building trades fields were added to
existing programs in vocational agriculture and home economics. In
September 1947 mechanical drawing, shop mechanics, and aeronau-
tics were offered. The building trades courses started in 1955. First,
existing buildings were remodeled to provide facilities for the courses.
Then the old auto mechanics building was razed and a new one constructed on the same general site. Orcutt and Marston were the architects, and the construction contract was awarded to Carlton Bas-
nar. The cost was $24,898.52, plus $3,152.36 for equipment. The building was ready for occupancy at the opening of school in 1955.

Over the years, the school outgrew the once-generous facilities of
Thompson Hall, so plans were developed for a new wing to provide
a 550-seat gymnasium and a 650-seat auditorium. Robert K. Lewis
headed the building fund drive and was very successful. Arthur Lord
was chairman of the faculty committee making plans for the building.
Norris Edmunds, the first chairman of the building committee, was
succeeded by Maurice Hill, president of Hill Manufacturing Company; also on the committee were Hazen Russell, Dr. Ralph Jardine,
Curtis Sargent, and Everett King. The architects were Freeman,
French, and Freeman of Burlington. The general contractor was the
Leo Spear Construction Company of Springfield, Mass. John Gilman
did the brickwork on the main building in 1922, and he also did it
on this addition. Ground-breaking ceremonies took place on April
15, 1964, and on June 12, 1965, John Norris, Jr., president of the board
of trustees, dedicated the new addition as the Alumni Auditorium

and Alumni Gymnasium. It was accepted by Donald Beattie, president of the alumni association.

At the death of Principal True in 1957, he was succeeded by then-assistant headmaster Robert Lewis; Albert Forrest became assistant headmaster. In 1963 Lewis resigned and was succeeded by Archie P. Mallon, with Forrest continuing as his assistant until poor health made his retirement necessary; he was followed by Gerald Dennis. In 1973 Mallon resigned and was followed for a year by David C. Leavitt. After a year as "acting headmaster" Dennis was given the full title in January 1976.

The building trades program has developed practical application of its training in the construction of buildings, including the following: 1961–62, a house on Skyline Terrace purchased by Mr. and Mrs. Robert K. Lewis; 1966, a house in Speedwell Estates purchased by Mr. and Mrs. Ralph Devereaux; 1968, a house in Speedwell Estates purchased by Mr. and Mrs. R. P. Semones; 1970–71, the fieldhouse for the athletic teams of Lyndon Institute, located southwest of Sanborn House; 1972, a residence on Calista Avenue in Speedwell Estates purchased by Mr. and Mrs. Melvin Lane; 1973–75, a duplex on Eastern Avenue named in honor of Miss May Campbell that provides housing for L. I. faculty. The next construction project, begun in late 1975, will also be a building for the school; it will house the building trades courses and perhaps some vocational agricultural classes.

The academic year 1966–67 was important in the life of Lyndon Institute. The graduation weekend of June 9–12, 1967, was the culmination of the year's work and planning to observe the 100th anniversary of the issue of the school's charter. John Norris, Jr., the chairman of the board of trustees, was general chairman of the planning committee; he was assisted by Clair Holbrook as chairman and W. Arthur Simpson as honorary chairman. There were ten committees[27] totaling fifty-six members. The *Caledonian-record* published a supplement on Friday, June 8, containing an extensive history of the school, which had been compiled by Mrs. Catherine Mallon with the assistance of Mrs. Winifred King and Albert Forrest — the result of nearly two years of research. This supplement also contained many pictures from the school archives, including eleven of the twelve headmasters, successful athletic teams, and groups of distinguished graduates, plus the congratulatory advertisements of many local merchants.

The mammoth parade of June 9 was described in the press:

> Thirteen gigantic tri-colored floats, distinguished personalities, four bands and a score of other units comprised a mile-long parade here Saturday afternoon, witnessed by an estimated 3000 persons that highlighted the Lyndon Institute centennial celebration. The parade wound from the park off Main Street down Depot Street, off Broad Street, and the length of Center Street to Lyndon Center where the units passed a reviewing stand and then dispersed around the athletic field for further benefit of viewers and camera fans.
>
> Miss Bertha Koury, instructor in Art at Lyndon Institute, was chairman of the parade committee and deserves much credit for its success.

Each of the thirteen floats represented an era in the history of Lyndon Institute, and each float had a local sponsor; thirteen other local businesses sponsored the program, which described the significance of each float.

About 700 persons attended the alumni association barbecue and meeting Saturday evening. This was followed by the annual alumni association dance in the Alumni Gymnasium. Rev. Arlington Wry was the speaker at the Sunday afternoon baccalaureate service. At the Monday morning graduation program, Dr. Lyman S. Rowell, president of the University of Vermont, was the speaker.

Lyndon State College

IN 1910 THE VERMONT GENERAL ASSEMBLY passed an "enabling act" authorizing establishment of a one-year teacher-training course in some of the state's high schools.[28] The Lyndon Literary and Biblical Institution (Lyndon Institute) was one of the twelve high schools designated by the commissioner of education to have this privilege the following year, and to receive state aid for the course. Harry Bradford, who was principal at the time, had worked very hard to bring this distinction to the school. Only seniors and graduates of four-year high school programs were eligible to register. Miss L. Eleanor Cloudman of Gorham, Maine, was selected as the first instructor. Her extensive experience included ten years as a teacher in rural schools, ten years as a critic teacher at Maine Western Normal School (Gorham), nine years as principal of a primary training school in Bangor, Maine, one year as an instructor at Wellesley College, and one as principal of the Essex Grammar School, Essex, Conn.

The physical plant of this new department was one room on the third floor of Thompson Hall. Nine women enrolled for training as elementary teachers. Eight weeks of the training were spent in actual teaching. The program utilized the nearby village and rural schools for observation and practice teaching. Eliza Allen succeeded Miss Cloudman in 1914. The Vermont Board of Education in 1922 approved the establishment of one- and two-year courses in teacher training in Burlington, Castleton, and Lyndon.

In 1927 Rita Bole, a 1916 graduate of Lyndon Institute's teacher-training program and later a graduate of Middlebury College, was placed in charge of Lyndon Institute's normal program. By 1928–29 enrollment in the teacher-training program had reached sixty-nine, and a fifth teacher was added. Squabble Hollow School became the rural practice school. The state paid Lyndon Institute $4000 a year for use of its facilities. Sanborn House was inhabited exclusively by normal students; Bean Cottage was added the following year, and Willey House—under the name Bole Hall—in 1932. In 1933 the Vermont Board of Education limited the enrollment in the Lyndon Institute program to 100 students and added a third year of training. The state increased its pay for use of Institute facilities to $6000. For the first time the graduation program of the teacher-training students was separate from that of the Institute.

The facilities of the teacher-training program were materially enhanced in 1938 with the addition of a 60 x 40 foot brick library featuring a three-room basement. This was built on the east side of Lyndon Center's main street between the village post office and the Pearl place.

By 1942 the "Lyndon State Normal School" employed ten instructors and offered a lecture course with Louis Fischer, Col. Carlos P. Romulo, and Norman Thomas as the speakers. In 1943 there were twenty-nine graduates, the last under the two-year and three-year system.

The 1944 graduation exercises of Lyndon State Normal School marked a milestone in its development; the graduates numbered forty-five, and had finished either two-, three-, or four-year courses. In his brief address Dr. Ralph E. Noble, state commissioner of education, called attention to the fact that Miss Rita L. Bole, principal, was that day, by authority of the state legislature, conferring the first Bachelor of Education degrees permitted by any normal school in the state. That summer, for the second year in a row, the school's workshop for experienced teachers—with a corps of seven instructors and five visiting consultants in residence—proved most successful.

By legislative action in 1947 Lyndon State Normal School was designated a "Teachers College"; Miss Rita L. Bole was named its president. In June of the same year a two-year contract with Lyndon Institute trustees was signed, establishing payment of $12,000 per year for the use of four rooms in the main building and other facilities. The contract contained no provision for renewal, so termination of the teachers college in Lyndon appeared even more likely than before. The years immediately following were ones of great tension and uncertainty; rumors were rife, especially that the teachers college in Lyndon was to be abolished and its work transferred to Johnson. In mid-summer 1951 the state effected a twelve-year lease of the Vail Mansion. This had provisions for automatic renewals for two additional terms of four years each and an option for the state to purchase the property, with the rental price being applicable to the cost of purchase.

In mid-summer 1955 Miss Rita L. Bole retired, to be succeeded as president of Lyndon Teachers College by Arthur B. Elliott. He was succeeded in 1959 by Dr. Robert E. Long.

In July 1957 the state purchased the Vail Mansion for Lyndon State Teachers College use. The purchase price was reported as $150,400 in exchange for the annual rent of $17,900 plus taxes. A month later Vermont Tap and Die offered to give its Darling property to the Teachers College.

Lyndon State College located on former Vail estate (*Lyndon State College*)

In 1961 the Vermont General Assembly authorized the "Lyndon College Corporation" to take over the operation of Lyndon Teachers College. This body was charged with developing the college into a private, liberal arts school; according to report, sale or lease of the institution to a private company was expected by 1965. Among the twenty-four corporators were former U.S. Senator Ralph Flanders, who was to head the organization; William Lockwood, president of Burlington's Howard Bank and head of Vermont Building Authority; John Hooper, editor of the *Brattleboro Reformer*; and Dr. Robert Long, Lyndon Teachers College president.

In the spring of 1964 new constructin began on the campus, with Bean Construction Company of Keene, N.H., receiving the contract for a new dormitory and dining room with a bid of $831,392. Ground-breaking exercises took place May 2, and completion was expected by the fall of 1965.

The year 1965 was important for the College: (1) it received accreditation from the New England Association of Colleges and Secondary Schools for its B.S. in Education; (2) it received $1,130.10 as part of a federal grant applied to construction of the new Samuel Read Hall Library; (3) the Thaddeus Stevens dining hall and the Eleazar

Wheelock dormitory for girls were completed; (4) four more new dormitories, Jonathan Arnold, Jacob Bailey, Robert Rogers, and Luke Poland, soon followed. Three years later Thaddeus Fairbanks Science Hall, the Alexander Twilight Theatre, and General George Stannard Gymnasium were added to the buildings of the college.

In the spring of 1973 Lyndon State College received full accreditation from the New England Association of Colleges and Secondary Schools for all its ongoing programs in all its departments.

Also in early 1973, after inspection by many committees of the legislature, various state boards, and other interested officials, the Vail Mansion—used up to this time for classrooms and offices—was declared unsafe as a public building. Temporary reinforcements were made to permit partial use of it, and the next year it was demolished.[29] The following year construction of a new building on the site was begun.

ૢ❧

The Vail Agricultural School

This is a school to teach boys the lessons of life. It is not a charity school. The chief lesson of life is, that industry, application, and intelligence combined are necessary to success, and that some sacrifice of our natural inclination to take things easy is necessary if we want to accomplish anything. Those who wish to take things easy do not need any education to do it.

T.N.V.

THE LYNDON SCHOOL OF AGRICULTURE was organized in 1910 at the direction of Theodore N. Vail as a private school to make available training in farming for all Vermont boys. It was not intended to prepare students for college, but rather for the immediate use of the skills of farming and such allied industries—carpentry, blacksmithing, masonry, and cement work—as they would use to maintain farm buildings and equipment without the aid of outside skilled labor. It was expected that the program could be completed in two school years of nine months each. The faculty of Lyndon Institute would provide the theoretical work, and the faculty of the agricultural school would direct the practical work in the shops and on the school farm. Admission was not to be denied any student who was eligible to attend an approved high school. However, he must have reached the age of sixteen years and possess a certificate of grammar school completion. The catalog added that "It may be possible to accept a few young men who have not had this amount of schooling, providing they can personally satisfy the Director that the work of the school can be profitably followed."

The first class had 31 members. Initially, the working spaces available to the students were limited to the former I. H. Hall (Jeremy Pearl) farm in Lyndon Center, which provided the residence of the director. The 1918 catalog fully described the school's facilities and equipment:

> Probably no secondary school of agriculture in this country excels the T. N. Vail School in its plant and equipment. It consists of approximately 1800 acres of land, about 700 of which are suitable for tillage. The rest of the property is in pasture and woodland. There are about 10,000 sugar trees on the farm.
>
> The property is made up of a Main Farm known as the Speedwell Farm and eight outlying contiguous farms. The school is located on the Main Farm. This farm is extensively equipped with buildings. The dairy barn is built in the form of a Greek Cross, each arm of which is 38 x 100 feet. The cow stable on the ground level has cement floors, gutters, platforms, and mangers, and is fitted out with Louden stalls and stanchions for 136 cows and 12 calves. It is well lighted, ventilated, and convenient. The second floor is used for hay storage, having a capacity for over 200 tons of hay. A complete hay unloading equipment consisting of an electric hoist, slings, carriers, etc., is installed.
>
> The horse barn is 45 x 105 feet. The basement is used in connection with the dairy barn, and is divided into pens for calves. The second floor is arranged into 25 horse stalls, 4 box stalls, and harness room.
>
> The sheep barn is 30 x 180 feet, with suitable pens for sheep and livestock.

Vail Agricultural School model barn under construction (*B. M. Cheney*)

The piggery is 26 x 120 feet, and is separated into pens with a total capacity for 125 hogs. The floor and troughs are of cement. A complete slaughter room is attached.

The carpenter and blacksmith shops are equipped for doing the repairs and blacksmithing on the farm, and are arranged to provide instruction in handwork. This building contains a power planer, power saws, and wood working machinery of various kinds.

On the farm there are large machinery, fertilizer, and grain storage sheds.

Six cottages conveniently located on the Main Farm are occupied by members of the faculty and the farm foreman.

The inventory of stock on July 1, 1918 was:

     cattle 222   horses 35   swine 70   sheep 161   poultry 300

The eight outlying farms are equipped with buildings such as are found on the typical Vermont farm. Four of them are stocked and it is the policy of the school to develop these into farms where different types of Vermont farming can be demonstrated. . . .

Vail Agricultural School Dormitory created out of The Speedwell Farms
Overseer residence (*B. M. Cheney*)

The school owns its electric lighting plant which is located on the
Passumpsic River. . . . It comprises a water privilege with land adjoining both sides of the river, a cement dam for impounding the water,
a power house equipped with two Holyoke turbine water wheels
which develop about 100 horse power, two dynamos and other equipment. Near the power house is a cottage for the use of the superintendent of lights. The value of the plant and equipment is about
$28,000. The water system includes Chandler Pond water right,
about 65 acres in area. From this pond water is brought about four
miles in an 8-inch main pipe, from this pipe it is distributed in 6-inch
pipes to all the buildings. This system furnishes an abundant supply
of water for the school and farm, giving excellent protection from
fire, and water for irrigation if needed. The system is valued at
$50,000. . . .

A modern creamery . . . is equipped with a steam boiler, hand
and power separators, hand and power Babcock testers, hand and
power churns, and other necessary apparatus.

The section of the dairy barn assigned to the school herd . . . is
equipped with a Sharples milking machine. . . .

During its first five years of existence, the school was maintained tuition-free to Vermont boys at Vail's expense. The annual expenses of each student were tuition, $36; board and room, $120; and books and laboratory fees, $19, for a total of $175. These could be met either by cash payment or by work. Under the cash payment system, a third of the yearly tuition was payable at the beginning of each term, and charges for board and room were due each week. The cash-paying students were not required to remain at the school during vacation periods, but during term time they were assigned practical field and barn work. Each student was required to do 400 hours of such work in order to graduate.

Under the work payment system, which was open only to Vermont boys, students financially unable to pay their way were permitted to meet their expenses by manual labor. This required that they reside at school during the summer vacation period as well as during term time. They were paid by the hour during the school year, and by the month during the summer vacation, with the rate of payment to be determined by the quantity and quality of work done and by the method of application. The maximum pay was 15¢ an hour during term time, and $25 a month plus board, room, and washing during the summer vacation.

Sanborn Hall was renovated in the summer of 1910 to serve as a dormitory accommodating seventy-five students electing the agricultural courses. In the summer of 1914 the "farm house"[30] on Speedwell Farms was remodeled into a dormitory for those students who worked on the main farm. Rooms for thirty-five students were fitted up as a result of partition changes and of adding a second story to the ell part of the house.

Vail was as concerned about providing training for girls as for boys, feeling that both sexes should be prepared for effective, efficient lives on the farm. Therefore, intensive, up-to-date courses were established in homemaking, cooking, canning, sewing, and millinery. These were not part of the agricultural school, however, and so have continued within the home economics program of Lyndon Institute.

An adjunct to the agricultural program grew out of the work of Elizabeth Chase (Mrs. John B.), who about 1908 began an elementary department in home extension work in Lyndon that involved cultivating young children's interest in home gardening and related activities. It developed under various names—"Boys and Girls Home Project Club," "Home Garden Class," etc.—and was initially sponsored by the Lyndon Village Improvement Society. Its members ranged in age from five to nineteen, and the projects undertaken varied to some extent according to the age predominating in any year.

A few years after its start Mr. and Mrs. Vail became interested in the program, which was joined by Miss Gertrude Newton, a field expert of the General Extension Division. By 1915, under Mr. Vail's encouragement, the Home Project Club had grown to comprise several elementary and high school groups in different parts of town, and in 1916 it was added to the Institute plan of extension work with the assistance of the district superintendent and a field expert. For some years the club had sponsored an annual fair, and this event continued to provide competition and prizes for excellence in many practical activities. Among these were vegetable gardening, including the canning and marketing of fruits and vegetables raised; flower gardening and arrangement; maple syrup production; forestry; sewing; raising farm animals of all kinds; using milk in various products; and carpentry. In short, the whole program anticipated the "4-H clubs" of a generation later.

The first twenty-five students to complete the program of agricultural studies were recognized by a week's activities, beginning with a baccalaureate service in the Baptist Church on June 23, 1912, and ending with graduation on Friday, June 28, in the Lyndon Institute chapel.

In 1915 Mr. Vail offered the school plus his estate, Speedwell Farms, as a gift to the state of Vermont. The legislature accepted the gift—popularly valued at $150,000 to $200,000—by the passage of Act 16 on March 31, 1915, establishing a state agricultural school at Lyndon to be known as the Theodore N. Vail Agricultural School and Farms. The management of the school was placed in the hands of a board of trustees appointed by the governor. Two years later the legislature placed the control and management in the hands of the Vermont Board of Education.

During the summer of 1918 special efforts were made to recruit farm laborers because of the shortage caused by the war. The state commissioner of education placed the Vail Agricultural School at the disposal of the state department of agriculture. This was designated Camp Vail, a training camp for boys enlisting in the service of the state. The state planned to secure recruits through appeals in the state's high schools, and believed that training received in the two-week camps would make these boys more helpful to the farmers in need of assistance. Three camps, each to accommodate fifty boys, were planned for May 20–June 1, June 3–15, and June 17–29. The first group arrived at Camp Vail by May 19th. The only cost to the boys was to be transportation to the school. The state labor agent, with the assistance of the county agents, planned to place the boys in farm homes where they could be most helpful in the production of the food so essential in the wartime year.

During its years of prosperity, the agricultural school's graduations were separate from those of the Institute. Vail always participated and gave out the diplomas, and the speakers were distinguished educators or men in public life drawn from his wide circle of friends: in 1914, A. Lawrence Lowell, president of Harvard, Ernest Fox Nichols, president of Smith College, and Col. Henry Lee Higginson, chairman of Harvard's trustees; in 1915, John Hibben, president of Princeton, John Finley, president of New York University, and Howard Elliott, president of the board of directors of the New York and New Haven Railroad; in 1918, Vermont Governor Horace Graham and Vermont Commissioner of Education Milo B. Hillegas.

From 1915 to 1920 the school continued to function, subsidized by the state to the extent of some $22,000 a year. It quickly depreciated due to neglect and careless use, however; depreciation by 1921 was estimated at between $38,000 and $45,000. Frequently committees of the legislature inspected the school, and some of them reported enthusiastically. Meanwhile, the friends of the school at Randolph continuously urged the abandonment of the Vail school. Finally in the fall of 1920, following Vail's death in April, a committee of the Board of Education recommended to the legislature that the state abandon the property—a recommendation the state accepted. Under the terms of Vail's will, Lyndon Institute then became the sole heir to the property.

Thus ended the Vail Agricultural School, after ten years of existence and the graduation of many young men.[31] During the next few years Lyndon Institute liquidated the extensive land holdings Vail had collected since 1883. "The Mansion" and its related facilities had been excluded consistently from the holdings of the agricultural school, however, and its disposition was thus a matter of family concern.

The graduates of the agricultural school formed an alumni association soon after the first graduation; the initial reunion was held in 1914. Soon the third Sunday in August was established as the day of the annual meeting, and for more than sixty years this tradition has continued. The location of these meetings has moved from place to place in the state: the homes of various members have been used, as have the graded school building and the vestry of the Baptist Church in Lyndon Center.

At the 1972 annual meeting the president of the association, Bunal Cheney, brought up for discussion the desirability of placing some sort of marker to commemorate the Vail Agricultural School, and to honor both its founder, Theodore N. Vail, and its first director, Arthur R. Merrill, who had the major responsibility for the effectiveness and success of the school. The committee appointed to gather information consisted of Howard Merrill (son of the director), George Cate (from Calais), and Leonard Goss (St. Johnsbury Center). Discussion continued at the next two annual meetings and at the third—on August 18, 1974—a shaft of granite 6 feet x 2 feet 8 inches and a cedar tree from the farm of Bunal Cheney in Barnet were dedicated. Cheney had made the major arrangements. The stone and tree were his gifts, and at his direction Anair Memorials, Inc. had secured and set the bronze plaque with the following inscription:

Vail
Agricultural School
1910–1920
Theodore N. Vail, Founder
Arthur R. Merrill, Director

Before the annual luncheon, the members of the association assembled at the southeast corner of the Common, where the marker had been set, and held a short program of dedication. This included brief remarks by Maurice Hill, president of the board of trustees of Lyndon Institute, and Mr. Howard Merrill, son of Director Merrill.

IX

Lyndon and the Military

Many of the earliest settlers in Vermont are said to have become interested in the area as a result of their activities in the Indian wars. However, Lyndon was not settled until after both the Indian wars and the Revolutionary War had become history. Nineteen of the original grantees of Lyndon had participated in the Revolution, but none of these ever lived within the limits of the town. How many veterans did live here we have no way of knowing. In the mid-19th century funds were raised by private subscription to erect a monument in the cemetery honoring Revolutionary War veterans buried here.

Probably some Lyndon residents participated in the War of 1812, but if so, their identity is unknown.[1]

The only town residents known to have taken part in the Mexican War (1846–48) were Joseph C. Mathewson and Delmar M. Miller, two privates who enlisted for "Frontier Service."[2]

২৫

Militia

According to William Slade, who compiled the first collection of Vermont laws, the first act related to militia was passed in February 1779, but a law compelling militia service was not passed until March 10, 1797. It provided for the enrollment of every free, able-bodied, white male citizen in the state who was between the ages of eighteen and forty-five. Certain persons were exempt, including those having conscientious scruples against bearing arms, provided they paid, before the first of May, the sum fixed by the legislature. This fee—originally $2, and later raised to $3—was applied to the support of the schools in the town in which the exempt person resided. The act provided for organizing the militia into divisions, brigades, regiments, and companies, each with a specified list of officers. The company membership was limited to a given community. Its officers were "one captain, two lieutenants, one ensign, four sergeants, four corporals, six gunners, six bombardiers, one drummer, one fifer, and not less than twenty-four, nor more than thirty, privates or matrosses." The company's officers were chosen by the members of the company.

Every citizen enrolled in the militia and providing himself with a uniform, arms, ammunition, and accoutrements was exempt from poll taxes. About 1825 the law required as "full equipment a good musket with an iron or steel rod, a sufficient bayonet and belt, a priming wire and brush, two spare flints, a cartridge box, and pouch with a box therein sufficient at least to contain twenty-four cartridges suited to the bore of his musket, a canteen, and a knapsack." Each militiaman was responsible for keeping his equipment in suitable condition. Many men who enlisted in the militia were unable to find a sponsor to furnish their equipment and were too poor to buy it themselves. As a result the men used anything from a stick to a pitchfork or hoe as a substitute for a musket. This apparently explains why the Lyndon group's contemporaries so often called it "The Flood-Wood Militia."

Every captain or commanding officer was required to call his company together each year on the first Tuesday in June to examine and take an exact account of every man's arms and equipment, and also to drill and establish discipline. The law required that the men be called to meet at 9 a.m. and be kept through the day in military exercise. The strictness with which these requirements were fulfilled depended largely on the discipline of the officers in charge. The law also required the militia to assemble once in two years between September 20 and October 15 for review, inspection, and discipline, by regiments or by separate battalions, as the commandant of the brigade directed. These biennial reviews provided an excellent opportunity for comparing the merits of the rival companies, and so fostered the development of well-equipped and well-drilled companies in rival communities, as well as fife-and-drum corps.

From surviving legends the "June training day" must have been a gala holiday, and far too often an occasion for drunkenness and rowdyism. The system came into marked disfavor in the late 1830s, perhaps because of the rising temperance sentiment in the state. Apparently, June training was conducted in at least three different locations in Lyndon. Unfortunately, no evidence exists to prove when these sites were used. One location was the "parade ground" that was a part of the Job Sheldon six acres at Lyndon Center; another was the level field south of the Cahoon house near the Little Falls; and third was the Gen. E. B. Chase meadow (destroyed for Interstate 91) west of Chase's residence.[3]

Among those who served as Lyndon captains of militia were Daniel Quimby (1832), Church Meigs (1833–35) with some sixty men, Samuel A. Clogston (1833) with thirty-two men forming the "Lyndon Rifle Co.," Daniel Randall (1833–40) with thirty-two to thirty-four men forming the "Independent Company of Washington Guards," David M. Hoit (1834–35), Stephen Crain with thirty-four men forming the "Lyndon Rifle Company," Leonard Wilmarth (1835), Samuel Bemis (1835), Ephraim B. Ryan (1837), Henry Houghton (1838, 1840), Loved Porter (1844), and Joel and Welcome Fletcher (dates unknown). In 1835 Epaphras B. Chase was brigadier general, Second Brigade, Fourth Division of Vermont Militia.

The earliest militia list found was that of Capt. Darius Williams' company, Lyndon, June 4, 1822.

ᘛᐡ

The Civil War

THE CIVIL WAR (1861–65), longer in duration than its predecessors, affected the community much more directly. Early in 1861 the town voted to abate the taxes of all men in the town who volunteered for military service.

At the freeman's meeting of September 2, 1862, Hon. Thomas Bartlett presented two resolutions that were unanimously adopted, with copies to be forwarded to the senators and representatives elect:

> Resolved—That our Senators are hereby requested and our Representative hereby instructed, to use their best efforts, to procure the passage of a law authorizing the several towns in the State, by vote, to raise money upon the Grand List, to pay bounties to volunteers.

> Resolved—That our Senators from this County are hereby requested, and our Representative is hereby instructed, to use their influence to procure the passage of a law, organizing the militia of this State into companies, regiments, and brigades, and to arm and equip them at the expense of the State.[4]

By March 1, 1864, the nation faced increasing difficulty in enlisting men for service, so the selectmen were authorized to pay a bounty not exceeding $345 to each volunteer who enlisted during the next three months. At the end of that period a special town meeting (June 27, 1864) voted to empower the selectmen to pay a bounty not exceeding $500 or, if the term of service were to be one year or less, $300. At the same time the selectmen were empowered to raise $15,000 to pay bounties or other bills related to the war.

Later that summer another special town meeting was called (August 6, 1864), at which the selectmen were 1) instructed to raise the Lyndon quota under the recent call of the president for 500,000 men, paying such sums of money as necessary to secure three-year enlistments; and 2) authorized to borrow on the credit of the town such sums of money as necessary to fill the quota, up to $25,000. A resolution to raise the enlistment bounty to $700 was eventually tabled.

Finally, a third special meeting (December 19, 1864) instructed the selectmen to raise, for one to three years, the twenty-five men necessary to fill the standing quota and to make trades for substitutes and authorized the borrowing of up to $20,000 to pay these twenty-five men for their service.

At the next annual town meeting on March 7, 1865, the town clerk was instructed

> to prepare a Soldiers Record at the expense of the town; embracing the names of the soldiers who enlisted, or may enlist or serve for the town of Lyndon; when and where mustered into service; promotions; time, place, and cause of death, if deceased; date of discharge, if discharged; together with such other facts and particulars of interest as maybe gathered by the Clerk or come to his notice, in regard to the Soldiers of Lyndon who have so noble gone forth to defend the cause of the Union.

How effectively these various resolutions were carried out is unknown. The warnings for several successive meetings after the end of the war contain entries concerning payment of the town bounty to Abram Hicks for his services. The minutes of these town meetings almost invariably refer to the payment of bounties or the money that the selectmen were authorized to borrow for that purpose. The March 3, 1868, minutes contain this entry: "The report was made by the selectmen in regard to receiving and disbursing of town bounties, George Cahoon chairman, the report was adopted, it 'gave satisfactory evidence of the faithful discharge of the duties of the said board.'"

❧

The Spanish-American War

THE EXTENT TO WHICH Lyndon citizens participated in the Spanish-American War has proved impossible to learn. The *Vermont Union* of April 24, 1898, reported the enlistment of Fred Ayer, Walter Quimby, Mike Gorham, Albert Messier, Ernest Sawyer, Bert Strong, and Charley Gleeb, and noted that S. S. Mattocks, Homer Wilson, and E. M. Campbell had been appointed recruiting officers in Lyndon. The *Vermont Union* of May 19, 1899, reported that George Gookin II, C. W. Gleeb, John A. McAuley, D. N. Martindale, George Newton, Charles G. Norris, W. H. Quimby, and W. H. Smith had received Webb medals in recognition of their service in the war.

&

The Mexican Border Dispute

EVEN LESS RECORD HAS BEEN FOUND of Lyndon participation in the Mexican border clash of 1916. Some townsmen were involved, as established by a picture taken by Harry Robie at Fort Ethan Allen on the eve of a group's departure for the border. Stories in the *Vermont Union* on October 4 and 11, 1916, stated that the men in St. Johnsbury's Company D—of which Lyndon men were a part—arrived back on October 7—and after three months on the border, the Lyndon men returned to St. Johnsbury as guests for a "Welcome Home Banquet" on October 9 that served 300 people. The Lyndon Community League provided automobiles to transport the men to and from the banquet.

&

World War I

THE VERMONT UNION-JOURNAL's first report directly associating Lyndon with World War I appeared in its issue of November 11, 1914, announcing that Mr. and Mrs. John LeBourveau would donate to the Red Cross the proceeds from the afternoon and evening performances at the Star Theatre on November 16.[5] The same issue

The Lyndon Members of Company D. St. Johnsbury, taken by Harry Robie at Fort Ethan Allen in 1916 before going to the Mexican border. *Standing (left to right)*: Harry Blake, George Murch, Ed Vignault, Earl Lang, Herbert Stahler, Walter Daigle, John McNamara. *Seated*: Ed Hazel, John Bedard, Roland Spencer, Floyd Hartwell. *In car*: Earl Peterson, A. W. Edmunds [car owner]. (*Mrs. Harry Robie*)

reported that the Lyndon Women's Club was doing work for the Red Cross.

In early March 1916, forty-three railroad cars loaded with ninety-three Buick autos bound for France went south through Lyndonville. Early the next year forty cars containing 800 mules and horses went through Lyndon en route to Boston and thence to Europe.

The winter of 1916–17 introduced Lyndon citizens to a shortage of anthracite coal, and thus to the postponement of opening schools to the closing of Cobleigh Library. H. J. M. Jones, state fuel administrator, urged lodges, clubs, amusement places, homes, and churches to minimize the use of coal and burn wood in the daytime.

As the winter of 1917–18 approached even greater emphasis was placed on conserving fuel. The shortage was said to result in large part from the government having taken over so many of the ships previously used in transporting coal to New England and from the excessive war load on the railroads.[6] As the winter wore on and the fuel shortage became more acute, churches were urged to consolidate their programs and to arrange activities in union with other denominations. Stores closed the major portion of one day a week. The fireless cooker flourished. By spring, coal dealers were permitted to fill orders for six tons or less, but no larger orders could be more than two-thirds filled until all similar orders had been proportionately met. Dealers also urged customers to order their supplies for the coming winter and to do so early, encouraging such action by offering a discount of 30¢ per ton. No one was permitted to obtain coal without certifying on a triplicate application card the number of net tons purchased the preceding year, the amount on hand, and the amount needed for the ensuing year. A fine of $5000 or imprisonment for two years was the maximum penalty for willfully making a false statement on the card. The state administrator urged careful measurement of coal on hand, allowing 36 cubic feet per net ton of egg coal, 35 cubic feet for stove coal, and 34 cubic feet for nut coal. For the early winter, the administrator asked consumers to use small quantities of buckwheat coal as a means of conserving the larger coal. The local fuel administrator was Chas. L. Stuart; the other members of his committee were H. W. Lyster and H. P. Burpee.

Even greater emphasis was placed on the conservation and increased production of food. Herbert Hoover was appointed U.S. food administrator. He appointed Governor Horace F. Graham as chairman of the Vermont committee, and Graham in turn named James P. Taylor, secretary of the Greater Vermont Association, as the organizer of the program in the state. James Hartness became the Vermont food administrator. A Council of National Defense was formed with state, county, and local divisions. H. E. Folsom and E. A. Darling were members of the Vermont Committee of Public Safety. The district division included the towns of Lyndon, Burke, Wheelock, Sheffield, Sutton, Kirby, and Newark. Its members were F. T. Porter (West Burke), chairman; H. C. Wilson (Lyndon), secretary-treasurer; and G. M. Campbell (Lyndon), H. P. Simpson

(Sheffield), and W. P. Russell (Kirby). The women's committee of the Council of National Defense had Mrs. H. E. Folsom as county chairman. Mrs. E. L. Wells was local chairman; the committee members were Mrs. Geo. F. Ferguson, Mrs. John Cleary, Mrs. Edith McDowell, Mrs. H. J. Hubbard, Mrs. W. C. Way, Mrs. D. M. Smith, Mrs. C. B. Dodge, Mrs. E. T. Wood, Mrs. Geo. Griffin, Mrs. Effie Solomon, Mrs. C. J. Buckley, Mrs. Earl Fletcher, Mrs. T. W. Blaisdell, Mrs. J. S. Buell, Miss Addie Hutchinson, Miss Susan Cunningham, Miss E. C. Allen, Miss Edith Gray, and Miss Ella Wilmarth. C. L. Stuart was Lyndon chairman of food conservation; the committee members were O. D. Mathewson, G. M. Campbell, C. M. Darling, H. C. Wilson, J. W. LeBourveau, and W. C. Conner.

From early 1917 on, these local leaders developed many projects to increase the production and preservation of food stuffs. Boys' and girls' 4-H Clubs received new incentives to plant, harvest, and can; exhibits were held, and various certificates and prizes were provided. Acres of fertile ground were offered to the public for cultivation in large or small plots, and even front lawns were converted into vegetable gardens. A pledge campaign was carried out under which every signatory household became a member of the food administration. In fulfillment of this pledge, every household abstained from using white bread on Wednesday and Thursday, with the first wheatless day being September 26, 1917. In the spring of 1918 this was extended to a limit of 1½ pounds of wheat per week per person; later every person was asked to abstain from eating any wheat until the next harvest (four months). Under the same pledge, Tuesday was made a meatless day, and one meal every day was also meatless; this was extended in early 1918 to a limit of 2 pounds of meat per week per person. The use of lamb and mutton were urged instead of exportable beef and pork.

Sugar had been in short supply for some months. Finally in midsummer 1918, retail dealers in sugar were ordered not to sell more than 2 pounds of sugar to any person living in a village or city, or more than 5 pounds to a person living in the country, and "such sales must be further limited so that the people supplied may not have for consumption more than 2 pounds per person per month." No extra sugar could be secured for use in canning, though the leaders continued to ask that foodstuffs be preserved. Later in the fall the quota was raised to 3 pounds per month.[7] During the summer of 1918 the Vail Agricultural School became Camp Vail, where a total of 125 boys were enlisted in the three camps of two weeks each, with R. G. Reynolds, the school director, in charge. The military discipline of the camps was overseen by Harvey P. Wingate of Norwich University. The staff of instructors included Carroll Pike, Jerome Fitzpatrick, Seth Wheat, George Burnham, Ray Hamlin of the Vail school faculty, and Harly Leland and G. A. Blood of the Vermont State College of Agriculture.

The record of the citizens of Lyndon in supporting the conduct of the war was most laudable. In each of the five Liberty Loan drives, Lyndon went well over its quota, with the subscriptions totaling $1,222,000. The local chairmen for these drives were Theodore N. Vail for the first, G. M. Campbell for the second, and O. D. Mathewson for numbers three, four, and five. The children in the Lyndonville Graded School bought $3500 in Liberty Bonds, mostly with money that they had earned, and they were active in selling Thrift Stamps and in soliciting for other drives. For oversubscribing the second Liberty Loan, the town received an honor flag featuring two stars representing the 200 percent oversubscription (really 278 percent); Lyndon was the leading town in New England in the amount oversubscribed ($118,000 subscribed—quota $31,200). In the third Liberty Loan, Lyndon helped the state become the first in New England to reach its quota.

In the various other calls made, Lyndon equally well fulfilled its responsibilities—to the Library War Fund ($538.25), the Red Cross drives, calls from the Y.M.C.A., and Y.W.C.A., books for hospitals, etc. Throughout the war the Women's Club assumed leadership in supporting the Red Cross: knitting sweaters, socks, and helmets, providing base-hospital surgical dressings, hospital and refugee garments, and front line packets, and offering some civilian relief. The local Red Cross chapter produced 2,000 pairs of socks, 300 sweaters, 800 mufflers, wristers, and helmets, 1162 garments, a box of hospital linen, 28 layettes, 100 Christmas packages, 140 comfort bags and kits, and 8 boxes of surgical dressings—having a total value of $4881.

In the early fall of 1918 the Red Cross issued an appeal for the salvage of nut shells and fruit pits to provide carbon for gas masks.[8] Only a few days later the War Industries Board asked that paper be salvaged because less than half the paper needed for the war industry could be acquired from the mills.

On April 2, 1917, Company D, St. Johnsbury, received the order from the War Department calling for the mobilization of the Vermont National Guard. Lyndon provided a full platoon of thirty-two men to the St. Johnsbury company as follows: C. D. Murch, Guy N. Vigneault, Herbert Stahler, Floyd Hartwell, Herman Carter, Earl Lang, John Bedard, Walter L. Daigle, Raymond Pease, Franklin Dennison, Fred Stone, Lon Hudson, Jack Johnson, Earl Bemis, Clarence Ladue, Frances Charron, H. J. Roberts, Clarence Wheelock, P. A. Jones, Ernest Norton, Harold Currier, Carroll Gleason, Raymond Harris, Clifton Day, George Paquette, Oliver Ouellette, Cecil Frappied, Alvin Dresser, Lucien Croteau, Ernest Berubee, Frank Quimby, and Lewis Mitchell. Company D, under the command of Capt. H. D. Wilcox, consisted of 3 officers and 109 men. About 2500 people gathered near the St. Johnsbury railroad station to wish the soldiers well as they entrained for Fort Ethan Allen on April 6, 1917. They were drafted into federal service on August 5.

Within a few days the War Department ordered the discharge of all married men. As a result Company D lost eleven men; twelve more were transferred, and twenty-seven were discharged because of physical disability.

The selective conscription program became effective July 20, 1917. This lottery was held in the public hearing room of the Senate Office Building, Washington, D.C., with War Department officials in charge of the actual drawing, and the members of both the Senate and House Military Committees serving as witnesses. Thereby every registered man in the country received a definite place in the liability-for-service list. The first man drawn from Lyndon was Ralph L. Prescott of Lyndon Center, who had number 9. The quota from Caledonia County was twenty men. Dean Simpson, a resident here during his boyhood, was also among the "1st 20." The first men drafted from the county left St. Johnsbury on September 17, 1917, but no Lyndon men were in the group.

The men of Vermont had hoped that when the U.S. military forces were reorganized into a unified army, they might serve as a unit bearing some insignia of the state. This hope did not materialize, for they were scattered throughout the various units of the army. However, Vermont's National Guard was the first to report, and with other groups from New England made up the first unit on the firing line in France.[9]

Saturday, August 16, 1919, was "Welcome Home Day" for those citizens of Lyndon who had served in World War I.[10] Depot Street and its stores were generously and patriotically decorated. The Community Theatre presented morning, afternoon, and evening programs with free admission for all soldiers and sailors. About 1:30 the crowd started from Music Hall to the ball games at Lyndon Center. The eighty-five soldiers and sailors commanded by Capt. Earl Lang followed the drum corps.[11] Two games were played: Lyndonville beat Woodsville 5–4 in the first and Island Pond 5–0 in the second.[12] On the return march to Lyndonville Lt. Clayton Fisher, commanded the soldiers and sailors.

At 6:00 the ladies of the Village Improvement Society served a banquet at G.A.R. Hall for ninety-eight soldiers and sailors.[13] The room was decorated with flags and patriotic bunting.

> There were two long tables at each side of the hall and two shorter tables at the ends of the hall. The tables were attractive with flowers, and at each place there was an aster. In the center of the space created by these four long tables there was a small table set with four places having a large bouquet of white flowers as a centerpiece; at this table there were four vacant places, at each of which was a flag at half mast as well as one of the town's medals. These places were a tribute to the four Lyndon boys who made the supreme sacrifice: Clinton Laducer killed in action, Howard Spaulding and Earl Johnson died of disease and Joseph Smith died of wounds. Rev. A. J. LeVeer, one of the chaplains of the 26th division, said grace before the banquet.
>
> At the close of the banquet Lieutenant Fisher announced the evening's program and then asked all to form in a line and march by the small table in the center, placing on it the asters that had been on the tables. . . . Afterward the flowers were divided and, together with a medal, sent to the mothers or nearest relatives of the four boys.

About 8:00 the Lyndon servicemen gathered at the front of the Cobleigh Library. Reverend LeVeer spoke briefly, followed by O. D. Mathewson, who in closing his remarks presented a medal to each of the servicemen.[14] These were pinned in place by the young ladies who had served as waitresses at the banquet.

Following the presentation of medals came the closing event of the day—the street carnival and dance. Depot Street was brilliantly illuminated with strings of electric lights, and above all glowed a large "WELCOME" sign in colored lights. Decorations on the buildings and in the store windows added to the gay appearance of the street. The crowd was estimated at 3000.

> A bandstand was erected in the center of the street nearly opposite the Library . . . occupied by the Lyndonville Military Band. Another band stand was erected in the center of the street about opposite the Church Street entrance, where the Newport Band had seats. A layer of sawdust had been placed between the two bandstands for easy dancing.

Early in the carnival a minstrel and chorus entertained the crowd from a large truck.[15] The bands alternated in playing. At midnight the Lyndonville Band played "The Star-Spangled Banner" as a signal for the end of "The Day."

۶✺

The National Guard: Company C

ON APRIL 18, 1921, Company C, First Infantry Vermont National Guards, was organized. The occasion was honored by the presence of H. T. Johnson, adjutant general of Vermont; Major Halliday of Boston, representing the First Army Headquarters; and Capt. Steward Cheney of Company D, St. Johnsbury. Officers elected were Capt. R. A. Eggleston, 1st Lt. C. M. Ladue, and temporary appointments of noncommissioned officers were made. Company quarters were to be established in Cable's Hall, and drills were to be held in

Music Hall every Monday evening and the last Friday of each month. Within a few months "Music Hall" became "The Armory."

At the 1922 encampment at Fort Ethan Allen, Company C—comprising men plus officers—gained the highest efficiency record and fielded the champion baseball team.

By 1923 Herman L. Carter had been elected captain, Clayton E. Fisher first lieutenant, and Robert Pierce second lieutenant, and Company C had become part of the 172d Infantry. Though the company performed well, in 1925 Adjutant General Johnson warned that the unit must, as a rifle company, maintain a membership of at least sixty-five men or the company would be transferred elsewhere.

In 1931 and 1934 Company C won the Proctor Trophy for all-around military excellence—the highest award in the 172d Infantry—at the annual encampment at Fort Ethan Allen. In 1940 the company received a citation "for especially meritorious and outstanding service during the first Army Maneuvers." The citation read as follows:

> This organization, as a reconnaissance detachment, was ordered on August 19th to seize and hold Buck's Bridge. It left its base camp at 5:00 o'clock a.m. as ordered and arrived in the vicinity of Buck's Bridge, about one hour later. It found the bridge in the possession of a strong enemy force and was unable to capture its objective. It was entirely surrounded by the enemy and there was no avenue of escape open at the moment. However, due to the marked leadership of the Commanding Officer, Battery C, 172nd Infantry, and the high state of training of his organization, they were able to avoid capture and continued to harass the enemy during the entire day.

In addition, the War Department Office of the chief of the National Guard Bureau (Washington, D.C.), the corps area commander (Boston), and the regimental commander cited Company C as the outstanding company of the regiment at the full field inspection. The field inspection report cited Capt. Robert F. Pierce "for the high standard and superior performance of Company C at all times during the exercises."

On March 3, 1941, the Lyndon community expressed its appreciation of Company C in several ways. First, the ladies of the Village Improvement Society served a banquet at the Bemis Community Houses.[16] The banquet room was decorated with flags and bunting, the tables had red, white, and blue nut cups centered with a tiny flag, and the napkins bore the nation's seal. After the meal brief talks were given by Rev. George E. Jaques of the Lyndon Center Baptist Church, Rev. N. C. Webster of the Methodist Church, and Rev. John D. Staffield of the Congregational Church, each praising Company C's record. Company C Lt. Walter Hughes presented a trophy to Robert F. Pierce in recognition of his recent promotion to the rank of Major and of the outstanding service he had rendered as captain of Company C, as well as of the affection the company felt for him.

The Lyndonville Band then continued the tribute by leading the company back to the Armory. At 8:15 the guardsmen entered the Sunset Ballroom to attend a reception and dance sponsored by the Board of Trade and townspeople. They were received by Mr. and Mrs. John B. Chase, Maj. and Mrs. Robert F. Pierce, Mr. and Mrs. Robert K. Lewis, Mr. and Mrs. Martin E. Daniels, Mr. and Mrs. W. C. Conner, and Mr. and Mrs. Perley S. Harris. During the reception and speaking program the band played several selections. John B. Chase gave the address of welcome, followed by Robert K. Lewis representing the American Legion, Trustee Willis C. Conner representing the village, and Superintendent Martin E. Daniels representing the schools. All praised the company's accomplishments and gave thanks for the honor it had brought the community. The hall was then cleared for dancing to the music of Sherrer's Orchestra. All services and materials for the occasion were gifts of the community. The committee arranging for the later part of the evening were L. D. Shonyo for the Board of Trade, W. C. Conner for the village, and Commander H. A. Berry of the Lyndon Post American Legion.

ৡ❧

World War II

ON FEBRUARY 24, 1941, ninety enlisted men and eight officers—the personnel of the National Guard unit at Lyndonville—were inducted into federal service, and on March 12 they were sent to Camp

Members of National Guard Departing for Military Service, March 1941,
Lyndonville railroad station (*Grace Mathewson*)

Blanding, Fla., for intensive training. Their commanding officer was
Lt. Walter J. Hughes, who later transferred to the Air Transport Command and became a major. All but thirty-five of these men and officers
were eventually transferred to other bases and officers candidate
schools on the outbreak of war in December of that year. The thirty-
five men who stayed with the original Company C, 172d Infantry,
were sent to the Pacific Islands on the S.S. *President Coolidge*, which
crossed the Pacific Ocean without escort but then sunk after striking
a mine 100 yards off shore on the morning of October 26, 1942. There
were only two casualties, but some 60 percent of those aboard landed
with all their clothing and other belongings ruined by oil; many
landed with no clothing at all. The resources of the island were
exhausted, and the first night ashore the men slept in the mud, with
no shelter, equipment, or supplies, and very few rifles. Other units
on the island doubled up to allow these men to have part of their
quarters.

A headline in the newspaper of January 6, 1944, reads, "Lyndonville 'Barracudas' Spearhead Landing." The landing referred to involved the storming and capture of Rendova, the largest Japanese base in the New Georgia group. Lyndon men distinguished themselves equally well in other parts of the world, on every battle front, on land and on sea and in the air. Of the 369 servicemen from Lyndon, approximately one-third were officers, including three colonels, eleven majors, and a general. Ten boys from the town lost their lives in the conflict: two in the South Pacific, three at sea, and five in Europe—France, Belgium, and Italy.

After the induction of the National Guard unit and the start of hostilities, a State Guard was organized with headquarters in the Lyndonville Armory. Robert K. Lewis, the first commandant, was later promoted to colonel and given a larger responsibility, and Maj. Ralph Hovey became commander. The purposes of the organization were stated as follows:

> to enroll, mobilize, and train the citizenry of a community for service in an emergency, for which they may be called by proper authority; to classify and index volunteers according to the type of service they are best fitted to perform; to give its members in instruction in first aid, map making and reading, signalling, aircraft spotting, guard duty, fire fighting, sanitation and other phases of preparedness and defense; to study and prepare plans for protection of public works and to devise methods for the maintenance of transportation and communication.
>
> It shall also be the object and purpose to furnish military drill and training, that the members may at all times be under proper discipline and control.

Appointed as local recruiting officers were Harry Berry, commander of Lyndon Post No. 30, American Legion, and Howard Shonyo, selectman of the town. They hoped to secure at least fifty company members. Special training was developed for these men to aid them in providing emergency protection of such vulnerable spots as the car shops, the light plant, the Mathewson Dam, the Cummerford Dam, the airport, and the Tap and Die plant. At one point the State Guard maintained a twenty-four hour watch at the pumping station on the Sutton road. The guard broke up after the end of the war, and the National Guard was reorganized for peacetime duties.

The Civilian Defense Organization was set up in the early days of the war under the efficient supervision of Ralph Hovey. The C.D.O. divided the town into sections with air raid wardens and first aid assistants for each division or street. It gave courses in first aid, stressing emergency measures in the events of bomb raids. W. H. Parker was placed in charge of the auxiliary police and Perley Baraw of the auxiliary fire crew. Blackout lights were installed on all emergency cars and trucks, and a five horsepower siren was placed on Music Hall, headquarters of the State Guard. Fire drills involving the whole community were held in alternate months; blackout curtains were installed everywhere, and blackouts were practiced until letter-perfect. Ray Brown has been credited with the successful coordination of the civil defense program. All local arrangements were closely coordinated with the state organization in Montpelier.

The C.D.O. sponsored a Tag Day to obtain funds for first aid supplies. Dr. and Mrs. Reginald Hill equipped six first aid and emergency shelters with surgical dressings, blankets, splints, and other supplies. Mrs. Hill surveyed women volunteers for various emergency services—cooking, housing, sewing, child care, nursing, canteen—and 110 signed up. Many noted lecturers explained to the public the seriousness of the situation and the need for constant alertness. One of these was Col. Carlos P. Romulo, famous not only as a writer and lecturer, but also as aide to General McArthur, and as "the last man off Bataan." During his lecture a blackout warning was sounded, and Colonel Romulo was greatly impressed with the prompt and efficient response.

A local O.P.A. Board was organized with Raymond Campbell in charge, assisted by Mrs. Beulah McDonald, Corrinne Burns, and Ruth McCann. This board continued to function until it was discontinued after the war.

Early in the war period, the federal government was concerned about the possibility of an air attack on the United States, especially from across Canada. As a result the Aircraft Warning Service was organized, and Lyndon's nearness to the Canadian border soon in-

Aircraft Warning Observation Post, Skyline Drive, Lyndonville, World War II (*Ed Houghton*)

volved it. The American Legion established three observation posts in Lyndon. Post 1, with Frank Bull in charge, was originally established on Pudding Hill but was rebuilt on the Paul Hutchings lot on Sunset Terrace; Post 2, under Leon Hopkins, was on Burke ridge just north of the Burke Green Cemetery on the west side of the road; Post 3, under Howard Wetherbee, was originally in Wheelock on Steve Cree's lawn, but was later moved to the hill behind the church and schoolhouse. A twenty-four hour watch was maintained at each of these posts; whenever a plane was sighted or heard it was reported to the regional headquarters in Albany, N.Y. People from Wheelock and Burke gave some assistance in the watch at the posts nearest them, but even so, a large number of Lyndon citizens accepted regular or substitute watch assignments in order that each post could maintain its necessary 100 to 150 observers. Frank Bull was chief observer for the area. A school with courses in airplane recognition and spotting was conducted evenings at the Armory. Over 10,000 hours were spent at the station by volunteer workers. One "spotter," Elroy Gilman, did the night watch from 10 p.m. till 8 a.m. alone for two months.

All bond drives were highly successful; many were oversubscribed by a huge margin, due to the efficient work of the chairman and to the fact that C. H. Davis, owner of the Tap and Die Corporation, always headed the list with a large purchase of bonds. From November 1943 to November 1944, townspeople invested $428,336.50 in bonds. Up until May 1943, pupils of Lyndonville Graded School had purchased bonds and stamps worth $1037.00. Lyndon Institute organized a weekly sale of war stamps and bonds, with the goal for one year being to raise enough funds for a "triple threat jeep:" a "flying jeep," an amphibious jeep, and a regular jeep at a cost of $7000.

With Mrs. Lewis Shonyo as chairman and Mr. Shonyo as fund chairman, the Red Cross in Lyndon did a remarkable job. For several years the quota was oversubscribed by a large margin, and in the drive of 1943, Lyndon was the first town in Vermont to top its quota. The Red Cross opened a surgical dressing room with Mrs. Izella Wishart in charge and Mrs. Helen Gilman assisting; branches at Lyndon Institute and Lyndon Center were under the respective supervision of Mrs. True and Mrs. Liggett. These ladies and Mrs. Shonyo attended a school and received certificates as instructors in surgical dressings. The local chapter made nearly half a million surgical dressings, filled over 500 kit bags, and knitted and sewed many hundreds of garments. Mrs. Grace Mathewson was in charge of production, and Mrs. Theia Watson supervised the kit bag program.

Emergency equipment was collected, including a fifty-bed unit complete with ether and hospital beds.

Among other successful drives carried on in the town were those of the War Chest and the U.S.O. Groups solicited phonograph records, cigarettes, and clothing, and ran a Victory Book campaign. The Boy Scouts regularly collected waste paper. Three places were opened for registering donors of blood for the Vermont Blood Plasma Bank, and people regularly donated blood at the hospital. Jean McLane, a Lyndon Institute student, recruited other coeds to form a farmerette group that volunteered to dig potatoes whenever the Farm Labor

Office urgently called for such labor. The Lions Club and businessmen also volunteered for this kind of service.

The Tap and Die Corporation devoted its entire facilities to wartime production, tripling its work force and winning the coveted "E" award of excellence for outstanding work and effort. Other smaller industries also geared their equipment to wartime needs. For its efforts in the salvage campaigns the town received a citation from the governor of Vermont.

As everywhere, there was an acute shortage of labor, especially of farm help; but as for the necessities of life, the community did not suffer the acute hardship that was the lot of larger communities in other sections of the country. Housing difficulties did not become serious until the end of the war and the return of the veterans. Fuel, gasoline, and tire shortages were the most serious, with minor hardships through the rationing of coffee, sugar, and soap. Victory gardens flourished, and all available land was used. Club agents gave instruction on planting; on the best ways to utilize available space, however small; and on the canning and care of food. A community canning center was established one summer.

Public health and religious and cultural life were not affected to any extent, and the educational systems were not impaired. Although several students left school to join the service, a large percentage resumed classes upon their return.[17]

KOREAN AND VIETNAM WARS

Although men from Lyndon served in both the above wars, few records exist telling of Lyndon's involvement.

ǝ☙

The Radar Station

AS PART OF THE NATION'S continental defense system, the federal government constructed a station in 1954–55 on East Mountain in East Haven. This is the highest peak in Vermont east of Mount

Mansfield and Jay Peak, being 3420 feet above sea level. The government acquired the first forty-four acres of land from the St. Regis Paper Company, and secured additional lands from several owners for the construction of an access road and, later, of family housing units. The property totaled 60.03 acres at a cost of $10,000 and 163.75 acres easement at a cost of $4825; buildings, structures, and utilities constructed on the site cost $3,356,000. A space near the top of the mountain was cleared of trees to provide space for the station and for other necessary facilities. Transferred on April 17, 1956, from Syracuse (N.Y.) Air Force Base, the station's unit was assigned to the Thirty-second Air Division and designated the 911th Air Control and Warning Squadron. In October 1959 it was redesignated the 911th Radar Squadron.

The nearest communities to this site on the east side of the mountain were Gallups Mills (ten miles), Granby (nearly twelve), Victory (sixteen), and North Concord (about eighteen). This last village had the nearest railway and paved roads, so the headquarters of this Air Force cantonment was designated the North Concord Air Force Station (M-103). In the early spring of 1962 a new 7½-mile access road from Route 114 to the site was completed, materially shortening the travel distance from the station to Lyndonville and St. Johnsbury. Therefore, postal service was soon moved from North Concord to Lyndonville, and the name was changed to the Lyndonville Air Force Station (Z-103). A ceremony officially marking the change was held at the station on March 1, 1962, with military and civilian dignitaries attending. The list was headed by Lt. Col. Colvin Rich, of the Air Force's Bangor Air Defense Headquarters, and Maj. Robert B. Little, commander of the 911th Radar Squadron.

The station was dependent on the Lyndonville Electric Department for its power, as were the twenty-seven houses eventually built at the foot of the mountain for the employees and their families. The first contract, negotiated in the summer of 1955, provided for the construction of a 12,000/7200 Y-volt line from East Burke to Hartwellville, a distance of approximately five miles, for which the Air Force guaranteed a monthly minimum power use for five years. To offset the electric department's cost for providing a further five miles of three-phase 12,000-volt line from Hartwellville to the base itself, the Air Force agreed to pay a connection facilities charge of $34,000, although the line would continue to be the property of the electric department. Other terms of the contract protected the electric department against possible loss in connection with supplying the electric service to the Air Force base. Authorization to start the work was received on August 11, 1955, with completion requested by October 15, 1955. Truline Surveyors of St. Johnsbury were immediately employed to set up the center line on which the power line would be run. Hodge and Pickering of Lisbon, N.H., began clearing the right-of-way—a path sixty feet wide through five miles of heavily wooded terrain. Thirty of the last forty poles were set in solid ledge, which necessitated drilling and blasting the pole holes. Meanwhile, the electric department's line crew built the five miles of line from East Burke to Hartwellville, completing that task in time to assist in finishing the line to the Air Force base. The entire system was completed on October 28, 1955.

In 1956 the station was the largest user of Lyndon's electrical power; its peak demand exceeded its original contract request of 350 KW, reaching 1,544,400 KW. Because additional energy-using equipment was to be installed, the Air Force renegotiated the contract, upping its requirements to 816 KW. By 1961 the station's needs had increased to 595 KW, and on March 14, 1962, the electric department agreed to supply 2000 KW of power to the station. The contract called for the electric department to provide nearly a quarter million dollars worth of facilities and services; the department was guaranteed against loss. It was expected that the radar equipment would be fully installed by September 1963, resulting in an energy use of 12,264,000 KW per year, or a gross anticipated annual revenue of $177,576.00.

The Lyndonville Air Force Station was inactivated on May 1, 1963, and the site was declared excess to the Air Force on January 1, 1964. The site was disposed of in two parcels: 9.83 acres fee sold to Coffey and Teachout Partnership on October 18, 1965, for $115,108, and 50.20 acres easements sold to Edward G. Sawyer Associates on November 4, 1965, for $41,500. Thus was removed the largest user of power from the Lyndonville Electric Department. The station's total bill for energy in 1962 and 1963 was $43,468.17 and $56,842.79, respectively. By 1967 much of the equipment used in carrying power to the station, especially that on the eastern end, had been removed.[18]

ع⬤

Memorial Day

LYNDON'S FIRST OBSERVANCE OF Memorial Day took place apparently in 1886, when Lyndon members of Chamberlain Post No. 1, Grand Army of the Republic (St. Johnsbury), decorated the graves of their comrades-in-arms in the Lyndon Cemetery. This was done early in the day before the members joined the post in its program scheduled in St. Johnsbury. The Lyndon Cornet Band assisted, and the people of Lyndon provided flowers.

The next year this observance was more elaborate. A program was arranged for Sunday, May 29, at 2:00 p.m. at Lyndon Center, with an address by Reverend Perkins.[19] All veterans, whether members of the G.A.R. or not, were invited to meet at Mathewson block at 1:30 and march with the others to attend the service. On Memorial Day (Monday) a special train left St. Johnsbury at 8:45, bringing members of the Chamberlain Post, its auxiliary, and the Sons of Veterans without charge to join with Lyndon veterans in observance of the day. Any others who wished to attend paid one-way fare. All formed in procession at Music Hall to march to the Lyndon Cemetery and place flowers on the graves of soldiers. Again the Lyndon Cornet Band provided music. At the close of the services the special train returned its passengers to St. Johnsbury. In 1888 both the Quimby Post (Barton) and the Chamberlain Post assisted the Lyndon veterans with the Memorial Day services.

After the founding in 1890 of the Orrin Farnsworth Post No. 106 in Lyndon, its officers or committees planned the annual observances, which over the years developed a consistent pattern. On the last Sunday in May a religious program was held in Music Hall at 2:00 p.m.

The pastors of the churches in town took turns in providing a patriotic address, Scripture reading, and prayers. Various musical selections—chorus, solo, duet, quartet, or instrumental—were offered. On Memorial Day itself, the public school children—carrying small bouquets or wreaths (usually wild flowers, and often sadly wilted)—all the patriotic organizations, perhaps the various fraternal organizations, and the Lyndonville Military Band met at Music Hall and marched to the cemetery at Lyndon Center. Often many people in teams constituted the last unit in the parade. At the cemetery the children placed at least one bouquet on every flag-marked grave. There were always washtubs full of little bouquets made by the Women's Relief Corps and other groups to supplement those the children brought. After the graves had been decorated, the children and their veteran escorts returned to the G.A.R. plot[20] in the cemetery, where a short program was held: a prayer was offered, one or more addresses were given, and taps was blown from the top of the hill.

On some occasions the G.A.R. and its auxiliaries returned from the cemetery to the G.A.R. Hall, where members served a meal. Then in the evening the G.A.R. post put on a program in Music Hall. These programs usually included music provided by local or imported performers; sometimes the students of Lyndon Institute displayed their talents. Occasionally, dramatic programs were presented as well as "Campfires"—mainly war reminiscences.

With the dissolution of Farnsworth Post No. 106 in 1923, the American Legion assumed the G.A.R.'s Memorial Day responsibilities. The placing of flags at the veterans' graves, the march to the cemetery, the short program, and taps have continued, but the other aspects of the early Memorial Day observance gradually have been lost. Throughout the years, however, the children in the public schools have continued to make the Friday afternoon before Memorial Day an occasion. So long as members of the G.A.R. were physically able to do so, at least one of their number attended these programs of patriotic music and recitations, and always contributed some personal reminiscences. In later years, frequently some adult has been invited to speak about patriotism or the significance of Memorial Day.

Now that Congress has sacrificed May 30 to the goddess of commercialism by giving Memorial Day a floating date as part of a "long weekend" and placing it on the last Monday of May, it seems probable that changes in its observance will be even more marked in the coming years.

ॐ

The G.A.R. and Sons of Veterans

THE FIRST GRAND ARMY OF THE REPUBLIC post in Vermont was organized in St. Johnsbury as Chamberlain Post No. 1 on April 10, 1868, with some Lyndon veterans as members. In 1886 Lyndon comrades from the Chamberlain Post fulfilled the functions of Memorial Day for the first time in the town.

On July 18, 1890, a Grand Army Post—the Orrin Farnsworth Post No. 106—was instituted in Lyndon, named for the first Lyndon soldier to lose his life in the Civil War. The official work of installation was performed by Assistant Adjutant General A. H. Hall and Assistant Quarter Master General E. S. Johnson (both of Island Pond), Inspector W. W. Sprague (St. Johnsbury), and Chief Mustering Officer A. W. Davis (White River Junction). The officers elected were W. A. Loomis, commander; L. B. Harris, Sr., vice-commander; Richard W. Chaplin, Jr., vice-commander; A. W. Wilson, quartermaster; Dr. J. W. Copeland, surgeon; Rev. J. C. Bodwell, chaplain; W. H. Hubbard, officer of the day; Richard Jenness, officer of the guard; S. E. Dutton, adjutant; W. H. Hunter, sergeant major; and A. W. Bean, quartermaster sergeant; other charter members were Ralph Davis, James Hubbard, and Robert McVicar. About twenty members of Chamberlain, Quimby, and Rattery posts attended.

The wives of veterans organized the Women's Relief Corps No. 67, auxiliary to the Orrin Farnsworth Post No. 106, on March 13–14, 1891. The first officers were Mrs. Julia Child, president; Mrs. Mary L. Gleason, vice-president; Mrs. Jennie A. Goss, junior vice-president; Mrs. Lucinda L. Willmarth, secretary; Mrs. Lydia Allen, treasurer; Mrs. Margaret Jenness, chaplain; Miss Edith Allen, conductress; Mrs. Huldah L. Collison, guard; and Mrs. Jennie Emerson, assistant guard. There were twenty-three charter members.

A Lyndon camp of the Sons of Veterans was mustered in on April 16, 1891, as the W. A. Loomis Camp No. 75, named in honor of the commander of the G.A.R. post at the time. In 1897 the name was changed to Lyndon Camp No. 75. The first officers, installed by past commander-in-chief Frank P. Merrill of Boston, were Robert A. Child, captain; H. S. Southworth, first lieutenant; W. H. Bean, second lieutenant; E. A. Shorey, orderly; George D. Thompson, quartermaster sergeant; Edward J. Bodwell, chaplain; H. O. Allen, sergeant of the guard; and Erton A. Shorey, Edward J. Bodell, and Charles R. Jenness, camp council.

The Sons of Veterans Auxiliary was organized on September 9, 1903, with thirteen charter members; this number grew to ninety-seven within twenty-five years. The first officers were Miss Sadie Houghton, president; Mrs. Lucy Huntley, vice-president; Miss Carrie Cannaway, treasurer; Mrs. Cora Lynch, chaplain; Mrs. Emma Simpson, guide; Miss Ethel Philbrick, assistant guide; and Mrs. Agnes Ruggles, Mrs. Margaret Ruggles, and Mrs. Lucy Huntley, trustees.

These four organizations were closely knit and complemented one another in activities; basic to membership was some relationship to service in the Civil War. Each organization generously participated in the activities of its state body, and over the years many Lyndon members served as state officers. In 1898–99 L. B. Harris was Vermont State Department commander, G.A.R., at which time there were 4111 members in the 111 posts in the state. The state convention was held in Montreal, so Harris secured a reduction of railroad mileage charge to 1½¢ per mile and obtained a special train from Brattleboro for members' transportation. In 1892 Rev. J. C. Bodwell served the state G.A.R. as its chaplain. In 1897 F. J. Willey was elected service vice-commander at the state encampment. In 1904 the Vermont State Division met in Burlington. J. B. Ripley was elected a member of the Division Council, and H. O. Allen became delegate-at-large to the national encampment. Mrs. Lucy Huntley was elected president of the state auxiliary, Mrs. J. B. Ripley became treasurer, and Emma Simpson was installed as chaplain. In 1921 L. H. Gordon was elected commander of the Vermont Sons of Veterans at the encampment held in Montpelier; Arthur Guild was appointed instructor of the Sons of Veterans of the state; and Mrs. L. H. Gordon was elected a member of the council of the state body. Harvey S. Powers, a resident of Lyndon and a member of Chamberlain Post No. 1 (St. Johnsbury), was elected deputy commander of Vermont G.A.R. in 1934.

The Lyndonville Military Band participated with the local patriotic organizations in many activities. On several occasions it accompanied the state delegates from the local G.A.R. post to national encampments.

Due to the character of the membership qualifications, these organizations inevitably came to an end. The Farnsworth Post once had sixty-two members, but in 1923 the department encampment instructed A. W. Wilson, the last charter member, to turn over the property of the post to Cobleigh Public Library and thus bring the organization to an end. Records provide little information about the demise of the other groups.

ᘒ❧

The Lyndonville Military Band

FEW COMMUNITIES HAVE BEEN PRIVILEGED to have so fine a band as Lyndon's. The date of the organization's origin is disputed. It may have been formed on August 1, 1867, under the leadership of A. G. Eastman; others say Frank Leonard founded the band in 1875 with N. P. Lovering as director. The first recorded public appearance of a Lyndonville band was on April 14, 1869, to provide music for the Calico Ball in Walker's Hotel; thirty-five couples attended. In 1877 the band was known as the Lyndonville Brass Band and had eighteen members.[21]

The first bandstand was built in the park on Broad Street between

the freight and passenger stations, using funds raised by private subscription from people who lived or conducted business near the park.
O. G. Chase was in charge of fund-raising. It was dedicated with a
concert on August 10, 1878; after the concert the band members were
entertained at the Union House. In 1888 the bandstand was moved
from the Depot park to the Main Street park, and two years later a
new bandstand was built on the Main Street park. In 1898 a bandstand
was again built on the park between the passenger and freight depots.
In 1912 the railroad company asked that the band concerts be moved
because of the potential danger posed by trains at the nearby crossing;
the company offered to give property for another site. The removal
to the Main Street park on June 12, 1912, has proved to be permanent.
The bandstand has since been rebuilt and enlarged twice, in 1953 and
1971.

In October 1879 Lyndon's band competed with five other bands
in a tournament at Newport. The resulting scores, out of a possible
240 credits, were as follows: Lyndon, 168 credits; Sherbrooke, 133;
Victoria Band, also of Sherbrooke, 132; Newport, 123; Union Village,
105; and White River, 97. The band earned $50 for its first-place finish.

Interest lagged for a couple of years but revived in 1882 under the
leadership of Henry Prouty, and during the next few years the band
gave many concerts here and in neighboring communities. The band
was known under varied names—the Brass Band, the Silver Cornet
Band, the Lyndonville Cornet Band—but eventually people would
drift back to calling it the Lyndonville Band. After the death of
Prouty, J. W. Batchelder led the band for a time, to be follwed by
Matt Robinson. There were many other directors, especially during
the group's early years, including Thomas Hanna, C. F. Berry, E. J.
Sawyer, Bowen R. Church, Edward Roche, Platt (from South Paris,
Maine), Johnson (from Barton), W. B. Best, and Will Webb. In 1888
Homer C. Wilson became director and continued, except for short
intervals, until 1937—forty-nine years. Following him were Perley
Harris (1937–1963), and then John L. Norris, Jr., and Roy Christophersen. In more recent years Gerald, Gary, and Douglas Aubin
and James Heath have taken turns with Norris and Christophersen,
thereby creating greater diversity in the concert programs.

Lyndonville Band in front of Music Hall, 1890 [St. Martin's Church right rear] (*Garnetta Wood*)

In 1889 the village trustees permitted the band to finish off a room in the basement of Music Hall to use as a practice room and for the storage of instruments, uniforms, and music. This was used for some years. The group moved to the Eaton block in 1900 and to the Stern block in 1904, where they were when the fire of 1924 destroyed everything, including uniforms and equipment. The band's next home was in the basement of the library.

From its infancy, the band has accepted many engagements to play in other communities, especially in Vermont and New Hampshire, and has appeared both indoors and out. At the same time, it has participated through the years in nearly every occasion that has occurred in its own community. Dedications, fairs, Memorial Days, and parades just could not happen without the music of the band. Whenever any local organization could take a band to a state or national convention, the Lyndonville Band not only went but won enviable acclaim. It accompanied the Masons several times. It went so many times with the Grand Army of the Republic to national encampments and performed so creditably that it became the "official" state

Lyndonville Military Band at Salt Lake City in August 1909, the last western trip of the Band. 1 Harley Johnson, 2 Peter Gaudette, 3 Ed Blodgett, 4 Frank Lanctot (St. Johnsbury), 5 Bill Cleary, 6 Frank Burns, 7 Herman Squires, 8 Charles Winter, 9 Wm. S. Harris, 10 Lute Cree, 11 Perley Harris, 12 Walter Smith (Brockton, Mass.), 13 Charles Aubin, 14 Howard Sherrer, 15 Mace Gay (Brockton, Mass.), 16 Bill Bemis, 17 Charles Fisher, 18 Clint Eastman, 19 Paul Cheney, 20 Ed Spenser, 21 Homer Wilson, 22 John Moore (St. Johnsbury), 23 Dr. Cheney, 24 Alphonse Aubin, 25 Perley Baraw, 26 F. E. Vitus (Brockton, Mass.), 27 Carl Clark, 28 Frank Willey, 29 Unknown. (*Alphonse Aubin*)

band at the encampments at Cincinnati (1898), Montreal (1899), Boston (1904), Denver (1905), Minneapolis (1906), Saratoga Springs (1907), and Salt Lake City (1909), where it received the honor of being the first band to play in the Mormon Tabernacle. It was invited to go to St. Louis in 1908 but declined. This long association resulted in "Military" being added to its title. In 1914 it was designated the Third Battalion Band of the Vermont State Guard.

Though it had given occasional concerts outdoors, it was not until 1891 that the band presented concerts at regular intervals throughout the summer — ten or twelve of them between late May and the end of August. The effectiveness of these concerts was greatly increased through the installation of an amplifier in 1949. The concert of August 4, 1949, was the first to be broadcast.

The village of Lyndonville has subsidized the band since the late 1890s, at first paying $150 a year but gradually increasing that sum to $700 by 1975. The town subsidy has remained at $200 per year since 1919.

Band members secured their first uniforms in 1897, when twenty-two cost $325. Editor Chase said of them: "They are dark green, good cloth, nicely trimmed, and look finely, they are neat rather than showy." The uniforms lost in the 1924 fire were not replaced until 1928, when they were first worn on Memorial Day.

During the late 1800s a group of band members performing as the Lyndonville Orchestra and another group as the Albino Minstrels contributed to the entertainment of the community. They were able by these means to add to their treasury, allowing them to provide for their own needs and to contribute to such projects as the library and the Village Improvement Society. During many periods the band has been forced to hire people from other parts of the state to play essential instruments. Since 1938 women have been playing in the band. Much assistance also has come from the young people in the Lyndon Institute Band.

Three families have contributed heavily to the membership of the Band. The Freeto family has provided Charles, Philip, Alva, and Roy, and the Harrises have offered Perley, Willard, and Lincoln. Most notable has been the Aubin family, including Alphonse (sixty-three years in the band) and his four sons: David (forty-five years), Paul (forty-four years), Gerald (forty-two years), and Charles (twenty years). Alphonse's grandchildren in the band have included Peter, David J., Patricia, Gary P., Ronald C., Richard D., Douglas A., and Cheryl A., and Clara M. (Mrs. Gerald) has also been a member. Many times there have been nine Aubins playing at one time.[22]

X

Businesses

ALTHOUGH A SUBSEQUENT VOLUME of this project will include a comprehensive history of businesses in the town, a few seg-
ments of the commercial scene are described here. All were central
to the life of the town and important in its development.

ॐ

Hotels

PERHAPS THE FIRST HOTEL in town was the Tavern, or Hotel
Lyndon, built in Lyndon Corner about 1807 for John Johnson by
Capt. Alfred Fletcher, who accepted a lease of the property as pay
for building it.[1] Credited with being the first framed house in town,
it was a square, two-story red building with a hip roof, and had a
swing sign at its northeast corner.[2]

Fletcher ran the Tavern for about five years until it was bought by
Ephraim Chamberlin, who kept it until 1823 or 1824. He was followed
by Isaac Cutler, landlord until 1832, when Epaphras B. Chase came
into possession of it. Chase, who also had a store across the street,
built the hotel barn in 1832. Not finding a satisfactory landlord, he
moved into the hotel for a couple of years, then hired Bunker Gay
Hubbard, who continued in charge until 1845. His successor was
T. B. Brickett for a year; then Jonathan Dow, Hubbard's longtime
clerk; and thereafter Dr. Edward Mattocks kept it for a year. A. W.
Titus was the next in line, followed by W. H. Watson (1847–52) and

Lyndon Hotel [Tavern] with stage coach (*Paul Houghton*)

the old stage driver Daniel Clough (1852–54). J. M. and W. H. Hoyt owned the building from 1854 to 1858, when John A. Darling bought it. In 1866 he sold to Curtis Stevens, who resold it a year later to J. McHubbard. After eight months he relinquished ownership to Stephen McGaffey. Harris Bemis went in with McGaffey for a year, then sold out to him. McGaffey continued as owner until 1877, when Curtis Stevens rebought the hotel, only to sell again in November 1896 to George Warner. He leased it the following May to Al Breakwood for one year; Breakwood lost heavily when the building burned on May 24, 1897.

The first major change in the physical appearance of the Tavern was made during the administration of Dow and Mattocks, who replaced the hip roof with a pitched roof, added a double piazza on the front, and built a two-story ell on the west side. John Darling built the carriage shed and the hall between the hotel and the stable.

Known to travelers far and near, the Tavern did a thriving business for most of its lifetime. From 1835 to 1850 it was a major overnight stop for the four- and six-horse stagecoaches operating between Boston and Montreal. Even after the stagecoaches were discontinued, it never failed to be profitable when well kept. The hall over the carriage shed was well known to dancers, many of whom enjoyed its springy floor.

Major Pierce kept a hotel in Red Village during the 1820s. It's major patronage consisted of farmers on the way to or from Portland or Boston with commodities for sale, such as pork, butter, or other farm products. The last proprietor of whom this writer has found record was Deacon Samuel Hoyt. Pierce's hotel was probably typical of its period. In those days taverns—usually located some five or six miles apart—provided meals for both man and beast as well as lodging, cigars, and rum and even stronger drinks. Most convenient, all these services could be had without any limitation of time schedule.

Apparently, the first hotel in Lyndon Center was built by Josiah C. Willard about 1800. It was a long low building known as the Willard Residence,[3] and Willard was referred to as *the* village landlord at the time of his death (1830). In the fall of 1839 Lewis Davis, alias George McCollister, went to the hotel for some rum, and, being refused, chopped down the signpost and was taken to jail. Soon afterward Mrs. Willard closed the house as a hotel. The building continued to exist until 1876, when C. K. Hubbard tore it down.[4]

In 1831 Stephen McGaffey and Deacon Samuel Hoyt built a hotel near the center of Lyndon Center that was called the Tavern for many generations. It was located on the east side of the road between Burke and Lyndon, on the site of the building that has been used as the village post office for many years. Hoyt kept it until 1837; he was followed by Howard Fletcher (until 1844), Erastus Woodruff (until 1850), and Nathan Ruggles (until 1854). Hiram Hill, the next owner, employed Saul Simonds as manager. After a year Lafayette Buck came in for two and a half years, followed by a Mr. Blanchard, who lasted only a few months before Ruggles returned for a couple of years. In 1865 C. Filch bought the property, but sold two years later to W. F. Ruggles, well-known as "the old drover," who kept it until the business failed in 1869. At the auction of the Ruggles property on August 2, 1869, H. M. Nichols bid off the hotel ($3125) and, according to the *Union*, "also most of the household furniture." The following November, Joshua Tripp of Cavendish bought the property from Nichols for $3300, but before he had paid more than the binder, James B. Hoffman offered Nichols a bonus of $50, so the hotel immediately belonged to Hoffman. Nichols retained the lot north of the hotel, three rods wide and thirty rods long, where the present-day Lyndon Center post office stands.[5]

Hoffman leased the hotel to his son, Charles E., in 1873 and to Alanson Fletcher in 1874. It changed hands later that year, going to Caleb Garfield, who in December leased it to Charles Hall for three years at $300 per year. In 1875 L. M. Hall of Hardwick was reported to be "opening" the hotel with a ball on March 24, 1875. In December 1876 the *Union* reported that Luke Farley and his son Oscar had "swapped their sugar place on Pudding Hill for the Lyndon Centre Hotel and furniture, the trade being even. Both pieces of property were under mortgage, $258 more on the hotel than the sugar place, the exchange was even with the mortgages allowed to remain as they were. . . ."

In December 1878 the *Union* reported that A. D. Massey was "the new landlord at the Centre," and the following April it announced that "Mr. Massey moved out of the hotel into the Harvey house last week. The hotel is now closed and will soon come into the possession of the mortgagee." The unprofitableness of the Tavern in its last years was credited at the time to the fact that in 1870 the society known as "The People's Practical Temperance Association", with I. H. Hall as president, was formed, and during the succeeding years the landlords maintained the hotel as a "temperance house." This was the end of the Tavern as a hotel. The new owner, Mary Sherburne, in 1879 converted the building into several tenements that were rarely vacant until the property was acquired in 1912 for the development of the "Lower Campus" of Lyndon Institute.

Welch's Tavern, located in Squabble Hollow near the foot of Mathewson Hill, is another contender for the title of the first tavern in Lyndon. The only tangible evidence this writer has been able to find is a paragraph in the report of its destruction by fire in 1923:

> The house, a two and a half story brick structure, had been a landmark for many years. The brick were made in the field near the house and in the place where the work was done many broken bricks are still to be found. Not far from 130 years ago the house was erected by Jacob Welch and later on his two sons Jacob and Charles, owned it and conducted a well-known wayside tavern that was very popular with coaching parties before the days of the railroad. These two brothers sold the property to Alfred Baldwin who sold it to Lang Welch. The next owner was Silas Dunton and he sold to N. G. Simpson in February 1909.
>
> Mrs. Ellen Dunton, who lives with her son, Arthur Dunton in Sheffield, is a granddaughter of Jacob Welch who lived there when the house was a wayside tavern, and the widow of Silas Dunton. The ell part of the house, of wood, was built 21 years ago. The house was constructed in very thorough manner and had been well kept up. Part of the walls, about a foot thick, are still standing.

On August 6, 1866, five days after the building of the railroad shops began, George B. Walker started constructing a hotel on the southeast corner of what was to be Main and Depot streets of the new "Railroad Village." He moved in on November 20 and by the first of the year had fifty or sixty regular boarders—men employed by the railroad company.

The building burned November 26, 1867, the ell part being completely destroyed and the main part badly damaged. Firemen from St. Johnsbury came in a train sent for them and rendered valuable assistance. Walker was reported to have lost about $20,000. Repairs were soon accomplished, and the hotel property—with its large livery stable—continued to occupy the present Depot Street between Main and Elm streets. Soon after the reconstruction a wing was added; its dedication ball was held March 16, 1868. This description of the hotel has survived the passage of time:

> The hotel was 60 feet square, 3 stories high surmounted by a cupola

12 feet square. On the west and north sides it had a two-story piazza, 13 feet wide. The first story was 11 feet 4 inches high, the second story 10 feet 4 inches high. Each story was provided with earth closets and all the large rooms had water connections. The dining room was 34 feet square and would accommodate without crowding 112 people. There were about 60 bedrooms, all large and airy and were furnished with carpets, mattresses, suitable furniture. The whole house was warmed by a furnace.

In 1871 the *Union* reported that G. H. and J. M. Weeks and L. K. Quimby had purchased Walker's Hotel and furnishings for $10,500 when Walker was overtaken by bankruptcy. They still held title to the property when it burned December 10, 1874, at a loss estimated at $25,000.

The livery stable register of Walker's Hotel has survived; the first entry is dated December 1, 1868, and the last July 3, 1872.[6] The stable rented horses for driving or for work such as drawing wood, hay, ice, or stone, or for plowing and similar tasks. Driving to St. Johnsbury was $3 for two days; to Wheelock or East St. Johnsbury, $2.50; Lyndon Corner, 75¢; and Lyndon Center, 50¢. Renting two pair of horses to draw potatoes cost $5 (no statement of time appears), and a pair to draw ice one-half day cost $4; rental "for the day" was $26 in one instance and $30 in another. Frequently, a horse was let out more than once in a given day, usually to be employed within a radius of ten or fifteen miles. One entry dated September 24, 1869, was of "Gray" to Thomas Bartlett for forty-four days at a charge of $55. The names of the horses let out were given in most instances; the stable appears to have had a total of seventeen horses during this period.

Charles Webb first occupied his new hotel on November 30, 1877. Located on Depot Street extending east from the corner of Elm Street, it contained thirty-six sleeping rooms, a first-class dining room, and other standard facilities. In December of the same year the *Union* reported that C. Cave of Barton Landing was moving into the hotel, but then ten years noted that Webb was improving the hotel barn.

The fire of November 27, 1894, started in one of the rooms on the

Webb Hotel, Lyndonville before 1900

south side of the Webb Hotel. On June 8, 1895, it became the first building to be reoccupied on Depot Street, just eight weeks after the beginning of reconstruction.

The basement of the hotel was used at various times for varied purposes. Ed McGinnis employed it for many years as a harness shop selling all kinds of equipment for horses, especially leather goods. He sold to Eli Currier, who added boot and shoe repair.

By 1910 the administration of the hotel had changed hands several times, and its name had become "Hotel Lyndon." D. I. Grapes, who owned it for several months, made more physical changes than had occurred for many years. Grapes leased (1911) to H. L. Doyle, who ran the hotel successfully until he sold his lease to Guy Harris. In 1915 J. J. Neagle, who also owned the old Union House, leased the hotel for five years. By 1919 the property had come into the possession of Mr. and Mrs. E. D. Thompson of Danville, from whom S. S. McDowell acquired it in exchange for his store, stock, and building. He began managing it the next year, and was in charge when the 1924 fire destroyed the hotel.

In 1876 L. F. Shonyo purchased from G. L. Mathewson a lot of land opposite the railroad passenger depot on which to build a hotel. First occupied on April 28, 1877, this new hotel was named the Centennial House. In October 1877 it was leased to Mr. Gilmore, who was succeeded the following March by Steven Wiggin of Coventry. In June 1879 Coventry turned the Union House, as it had become known, back over to Shonyo. In 1888 Shonyo sold to O. G. Chase, who increased the size of the house in 1891 by adding twelve sleeping rooms and enlarging the kitchen, laundry, and dining room; the work was done by Harley Butterfield.

After twenty-three years (1888–1911) a new proprietor, J. J. Neagle, acquired the property, and the Union House became the Pleasant View House. In 1915 Neagle purchased the lease of the Hotel Lyndon from Guy E. Harris, and Mr. and Mrs. Neagle moved there. The Pleasant View House was converted into a tenement and rented rooms; Dr. D. J. Sheehan rented the tenement and maintained his office there. After the death of Mr. Neagle in 1920, Mrs. Neagle sold the Pleasant View property to S. S. McDowell. He reopened the place as a hotel in 1925 and continued to operate it successfully until 1939, when he traded it to C. W. Gray for the Variety Store and the former Congregational parsonage on North Church Street.

Gray eventually sold to Henry Roy, who in turn sold (1947 to E. F. Duggan of Worcester, Mass. The next sale, in 1953, was to John Herrity of California. About five years later Mr. and Mrs. John Gracie became the owners and changed the name to "Gracie's Inn." On March 30, 1964, Mr. and Mrs. Frank Stiles of Post Mills, Vt., moved into the hotel as its new owners. Little more than a year later title to the property was transferred to Florent Parentrau of Waterbury, Conn., and Walter Parenteau of Westmore, Vt.

Throughout the last half century of its existence, the Union House changed hands often, and each new owner made alterations in both the building and its services to the community. Consistently, however, many men employed in the region who did not have families nearby found the hotel acceptable as a full-time residence. For many periods of time, luncheon clubs patronized its dining room service. The building burned on June 3, 1969.

When the ashes of the 1924 fire had cooled, the building of a modern hotel in the business district of the village seemed imperative, so the Lyndonville Hotel Company was formed and incorporated. A committee consisting of Dr. H. M. Smith, A. W. Edmunds, and H. M. Atwood was appointed to nominate officers and directors. Unanimously elected were President E. A. Darling of East Burke, Secretary W. E. Riley, and Directors O. D. Mathewson of Lyndon Center, H. E. Folsom, John L. Norris, and D. E. Grapes. Hudson of the Hanover, N.H. Firm of Wells and Hudson was chosen as architect. This firm had been the architect of the new Lyndon Institute building, the Realty Building, and the recent addition to the bank building. The Rowe Construction Company of Woodsville, N.H., who had built the Realty Building, were in charge of construction. The site chosen for the building was that which had been occupied before the fire by the Webb Hotel (Hotel Lyndon) and the Eaton block. President E. A. Darling donated the site to the Lyndonville Hotel Company, and also contributed generously to the building fund.

The first manager was William C. Roberts, then assistant manager at the Weldon House in Greenfield, Mass. The formal opening, with a series of banquets, took place during the first week of June 1928. The building was of four-story brick construction, with 115 feet of frontage on Depot Street that extended back about 75 feet at the two wings. It contained fifty-five sleeping rooms plus the necessary auxiliary rooms. The dining room was 42 x 32 feet, finished, decorated, and furnished by Darling. The Darling coat-of-arms, painted over the fireplace, contributed to the dignity of the room, as did the andirons in the fireplace—silver owls resting on bronze serpents. Throughout the house, discriminating taste and careful attention were evidenced in the details of finishing and furnishing.

During the next thirty-five years, the Darling Inn was highly esteemed among regional hotels. Many years it was closed from late fall to early spring as a means of conserving resources and because of the seasonal decline in the use of its facilities. It changed ownership several times, and the personnel of its administration changed even more often. In October 1963, Mr. and Mrs. Andrew Janis of Manchester, N.H. purchased the Darling Inn from the New England States

Corporation with reported plans for the expenditure of $25,000 to remodel it into the Darling Inn Convalescent and Retirement Home to accommodate about seventy-five residents.

Banks

DURING THE 1830S LYNDON CITIZENS made several petitions for the establishment of a bank in town. The first, in 1833, had 71 signers, and the one in 1834 had 139 signers; others followed in 1835 and 1836. Finally in 1854, the Lyndon Bank was chartered, and it began business on May 1, 1835. The originally authorized capital of $75,000 was raised to $100,000 in 1856. The first cashier was Edward A. Cahoon; because of ill health he resigned in 1856 and was succeeded by S. B. Mattocks. The first board of directors was E. B. Chase, J. M. Hoyt, Samuel W. Slade, Lucius Denison, J. M. Weeks, Joel Fletcher, and Wm. B. May. E. B. Chase was consistently reelected president until his death in September 1867, when he was succeeded by J. M. Weeks, who held the position for several years. In 1865 the Bank became the First National Bank of Lyndon.

During its years of service there were few changes in the bank's board of directors, and the semiannual dividend of 4 percent fell to 3 percent only rarely. The bank's charter was renewed in 1885 for twenty years; at the time its undivided profits totaled $27,000. The directors were D. N. Trull, Henry Chase, Charles M. Chase, L. K. Quimby, and B. F. Lincoln; at their organizational meeting D. N. Trull was elected president, Charles M. Chase vice-president, and W. J. Stanton, Jr., cashier. At their annual meeting in 1889, the stockholders voted to reduce the bank capital from $100,000 to $50,000.

In 1893 the *Vermont Union* reported that since the organization of the bank in 1854, nineteen of the men who had served on its board of directors had died: M. W. Newell, Lucius Denison of Burke, Moses Kitteredge, S. W. Slade, Joel Fletcher of St. Johnsbury, William H.

Baxter of Derby, A. C. Robinson of Barton, W. B. May of Concord, Milton Hoyt, E. A. Cahoon, E. B. Chase, C. S. Cahoon, L. R. Brown, S. B. Mattocks, Sewell Bradley, C. W. McCoy, S. S. Thompson, D. P. Hall, and D. N. Trull.

At a meeting on September 27, 1904, 428 of 500 stockholders either present or represented by proxy voted to go into voluntary liquidation. The stockholders received little more than 100 cents on the dollar of investment. The directors sold the bank safe and banking room fixtures at auction on February 9, 1905. The bank block was sold to E. E. Gage for $2300; the Marvin safe, weighing about seven tons, was sold for $350 to Mr. Dow for the Woodsville National Bank. The auctioneer was W. G. Hanscom.

The books of the National Bank of Lyndonville were opened for subscription on March 1, 1883. Capital of $100,000 was authorized, with the stipulation that it could be increased to $150,000. The bank was located in the southeast corner of the Fletcher block, and its safe vault was constructed in the cellar. The first directors were L. B. Harris, H. F. Pillsbury, David Trull, J. W. Copeland, and C. D. Bigelow; Sewall Bradley was president and H. M. Pearl cashier. In 1888 Bradley resigned as president and became cashier, an office he filled until his death in 1913.

The fire of 1894 destroyed the Fletcher (Ide) block, so the bank was forced into temporary quarters on the Depot park until its new building on Broad Street could be made tenantable. C. W. Carlyle of Lebanon, N.H. did the brickwork, and the St. Johnsbury firm of Bragg and Morris did the woodwork for the new building. The morning after the 1894 fire the National Bank promised to provide adequate funds to rebuild the Lyndonville community, and its confidence in the village was rewarded by full repayment of all loans. Throughout its history the bank regularly declared a semiannual dividend of 3 percent.

The handsome lions guarding the entrance of the bank arrived in the early years of this century, a gift to the village by L. B. Harris.[7] They are replicas—cast in the original mold—of the Renaissance sculptor Donatello's famous Marzocco, or "Lion of the Republic," which guards the shield of Florence, Italy. When the bank building was remodeled in 1961–62, the lions were placed in relatively the same position as they had held previously.

The Lyndon Savings Bank was organized on October 15, 1884, by incorporators S. S. Thompson, L. K. Quimby, C. M. Chase, H. E. Folsom, L. B. Harris, I. W. Sanborn, J. W. Copeland, George W. Cahoon, Sewall Bradley, H. M. Pearl, and W. A. Densmore, all of Lyndon. At a later meeting additional members were elected: H. S. Root (Newport), George H. Blake (Barton), Chas. Harris (East Burke), and Charles Rogers (Wheelock). Elected trustees were S. S. Thompson, L. B. Harris, J. W. Copeland, I. W. Sanborn, H. E. Folsom, and H. M. Pearl. At a meeting of the trustees, the following officers were elected: I. W. Sanborn, president; C. M. Chase, vice-president; and Miss Ida Pearl, treasurer. The investment committee consisted of S. S. Thompson, H. E. Folsom, and H. M. Pearl.

The bylaws of the Passumpsic Bank at St. Johnsbury were adopted with little change. In order to encourage small savings by children, the trustees voted to receive any deposit regardless of size, rather than enforce a minimum of $1 as did the Passumpsic Bank.

Until 1889 the maximum deposit accepted was $500. At that year's June 17 meeting the trustees voted to accept deposits over $500 in "deserving and exceptional cases." The minutes of the trustees' meetings show that there were heavy investments in mortgages on lands in Missouri, Arkansas, Texas, and neighboring states. In 1896 the trustees voted that in future no homestead mortgage would be granted without the signature of the wife being attached.

The 1894 fire destroyed the offices of this bank along with those of the National Bank. In October 1896 the Committee on Investment voted "to purchase an undivided half of the Lyndonville National Bank building and vault with furniture, safe and fixtures therein, and pay for the same one half of their cost and the unpaid rent be made up on a basis of share and share alike." Almost without exception the Lyndon Savings Bank trustees declared a semiannual dividend of 2 percent and turned over from $100 to $5000 to its surplus fund at the same intervals. In 1903 President Sanborn died and was succeeded by Dr. J. W. Copeland.

On January 1, 1923, the National Bank and the Savings Bank merged to form the Lyndonville Savings Bank and Trust Company. Customers noted little change, for the two banks had long operated in the same building, and there was no change in personnel. Most notable in the history of the banks was the career of Miss Ida Pearl. After taking a job with the National Bank at its beginning in 1883, she was made treasurer of the Savings Bank at its start in 1885 and continued in that role until the merger in 1922, after which she served as assistant treasurer until her retirement in 1928.

On November 26, 1973, the Passumpsic Savings Bank of St. Johnsbury officially opened a branch at 27 Depot Street in Lyndonville; an open house had been held two days earlier. Assistant Treasurer Kendall Query first managed the branch. Its advisory board consisted of Gilman W. Ford, retired insurance agent (West Burke); H. Dale Gibson, vice-president and general manager of the Vermont Tap and Die Corporation, and a corporator of the Passumpsic Savings Bank; Stephen R. Astle, president of Maple Grove, Inc., also a corporator of the Passumpsic Savings Bank; and Howard Johnson, a retired farmer and longtime resident of Lyndon.

On July 16, 1973, the St. Johnsbury Merchants National Bank opened in Lyndonville in a building at the corner of South and Center streets that had been built for Dr. Bailey. Named as manager was Arthur J. Charland; the advisory board was Alfred A. Bona, owner and operator of the White Market; Harold E. Dresser, Jr., a local livestock dealer; and Cortland Ruggles of Barton, owner of the Pierce Pharmacy.

ᣱᐷ

Speedwell and Mountain View Farms

IN THE EARLY 1880s, Iphus H. Hall was a farmer living in Lyndon Center opposite the town hall. He was also a dabbler in real estate, and two of his sales of this decade had a profound effect on the history of Lyndon. In 1882 he encouraged his brother-in-law, Luther B. Har-

Calvin Bigelow Farm, T. N. Vail House, ca. 1888 (*Vail Museum, Lyndon State College*)

ris, to purchase the Joel Fletcher farm.[8] A friend of Mr. Harris, and long-time associate in both the mail service and telephone business, visited him soon after the purchase was made. This friend, Theodore Newton Vail, was so impressed with the location, the scenery, and the general atmosphere of the region that he asked Harris to have Hall secure the adjoining Bigelow farm for him. Thus, in February 1883, Vail came into possession of the Calvin Bigelow Farm of about 170 acres for a price of $10,000. For the first few years, the place was occupied only during the summer, but after 1889 it became the legal residence of the Vail family and remained so until Vail's death in 1920.[9]

The Bigelow house was a comfortable story-and-a-half farmhouse, typical of houses in the neighborhood. It became the nucleus for the construction of what the people in the village called "The Mansion" or, as Vail called it, "The House" or "The Residence." The first change was immediate: the addition of a wide piazza on three sides of the house. During succeeding years many further changes were made, at a total investment estimated at $2 million. Vail said that the only place preserved in its original condition was a stairway near the eastern entrance. In the process of these changes, Vail believed he had made the structure virtually fireproof through the use of mineral wool, metal lath, cork floors, and cork carpets. Eventually there were eighty rooms and twenty baths, with over 1000 electric lights and indirect heating.

In this north country, perhaps the most unusual feature of the establishment was the greenhouse built in 1894 on the south side of "The House." The main greenhouse was 175 x 24 feet; the annex was almost identical in size. The whole greenhouse was divided into three units, each heated by steam. Temperatures were maintained at the levels necessary to support the varied and luxuriantly beautiful plants. These provided food and decoration for "The House," and over the years they were generously shared with the people in the valley—especially invalids and shut-ins—and the churches.

The carriage house (west from "The House") was a model one, having a cement floor with a center drain so that vehicles could be washed indoors. It included carriage rooms for storage, harness rooms, and well-furnished rooms for the grooms plus their well-stocked library. The carriages and turnouts were many and varied. In Vail's personal carriage room were twenty vehicles, varying from Jack's (a welsh pony's) phaeton to the eight-horse tally-ho coach. Horses used for pleasure or business driving by Vail, his house guests, or the employees were kept in the adjoining barns.

In 1892, Vail purchased the Joel Fletcher farm from Mrs. Olive Harris, and in succeeding years he acquired nearly twenty farms along the ridge, so that his holdings totaled about 2500 acres plus a number of pieces of woodland and pasture in adjoining towns. The Fletcher-Harris farm became, and remained, the center of all farming activities.

On November 25, 1892, the Vail holdings consisting of the Bigelow farm, the Fletcher farm, and the General E. B. Chase property[10]—totaling about 750 acres—became "Speedwell Farms Inc.," with Vail as president and W. I. Powers as treasurer and manager of the corporation. The name was chosen to retain association with the Vail family's New Jersey heritage, the Speedwell Iron Works in Morristown.[11]

Immediately after establishing his family permanently on the Lyn-

Vail Mansion [Speedwell Farm] created from Bigelow Farmhouse, Lyndon, Vermont 1907 (*Vail Museum, Lyndon State College*)

don property, Vail began purchasing registered stock: horses, cattle, and sheep. The September 27, 1889, issue of the *Vermont Union* reported that "$100,000 worth of blooded cattle is pledged to appear at the Lyndon Fair next Wednesday, to say nothing of $75,000 worth of horses, and nearly as much value in other stock." The November 25, 1892, *Union* reported Vail's purchase of two Percheron mares weighing 2000 lbs., and a stallion weighing 2501 lbs., plus twelve French coach mares and a stallion; all these were bought from M. W. Dunham of Wayne, Ill., who was characterized as the "biggest owner of imported registered horses in the country." By 1894 the animal population of the farm was reported as "53 horses, 66 cows, 34 other cattle,

118 sheep, 27 hogs, everything is blooded, and the very best kind.
. . ." Despite a large auction sale of stock in 1895, the population in
1899 was listed as "140 cattle, including a dairy of 50 head, 90 horses,
350 Shropshire sheet, 50 Dorset sheep, 30 hogs, 500 hens." A large
proportion of the cattle were Jerseys, but some were Shorthorns and
Brown Swiss. The horses ranged from the little Welsh ponies headed
by Taffy and Jack (weighing less than 400 lbs. apiece), and the French
coach horses headed by Jenner, to the giant Percherons headed by
the stallion Vulcan.

The administration of the farms was a stupendous task, and over
the forty years of the estate's existence there were at least a half dozen
different managers.[12] W. I. Powers was the one to whom Mr. Vail
deferred in the greatest number of relationships; the last and longest-
serving (twenty-seven years) was W. N. Hubbard. Vail expected the
farms not only to show a profit, but also to provide all the forage
and feed for all the stock; he also insisted on using the most advanced
techniques, seeds, and machinery. In 1888 the harvest was reported
as 394 tons of hay, 12,000 bushels of turnips, and 3000 bushels of
carrots; 6 acres were sown to peas, 6½ to corn, 26 to wheat, and 90
to oats.

Vail was interested in setting an example for the farmers of the
region, by which the quality and quantity of produce and animals
in the whole Lyndon area would be materially improved. To this end
he spared no money in testing machinery, seeds, and procedures that
might facilitate the planting, cultivating, and harvesting of crops. On
the several occasions over the years that Speedwell Farms held auc-
tions of livestock, buyers included not only local residents, but also
people from the other New England states, New York, Pennsylvania,
and even farther away. Throughout its years, Speedwell sent stock
to local, regional, and state fairs, as well as the fairs in adjoining states;
the beasts always returned with an impressive collection of trophies,
honors, prizes, ribbons, and money.

In 1899 Vail purchased from George Ide the so-called Willey Springs
located on the Razee right and twenty-seven adjoining acres, where
he built a reservoir. This greatly improved the quality and quantity
of the drinking water, and provided an adequate supply for a fish

pond, which covered about two acres in a hollow southeast of "The House" on the west side of the highway. The pond was originally stocked with 1000 trout, which were fed regularly so they could furnish one of the luxuries of the table of "The House." It was also, in season, a spot of great beauty, with its cover of blooming aquatic plants, especially lotuses and lilies. In 1909 Vail purchased the Rogers farm and some land from George Jenkins in South Wheelock, thus acquiring the Chandler Pond property; pipes were run from the pond to the hill, thereby providing a fully adequate water supply for fire protection and other uses. The same year he purchased the Cushman-Rankin property and water rights,[13] and here constructed a power station capable of providing ample electrical power for Speedwell Farms and the Lyndon Institute property.

Vail keenly felt the need for rejuvenating agriculture in New England, and he was convinced that it could be accomplished only through the improvement of agricultural working and living conditions. His theory was succinctly stated in a letter to Governor Graham in 1917:

> . . . though agricultural colleges are many and good they have a different purpose, there is need of a training in actual farm operations, together with instruction as to why things should be done in a certain way and at a certain time which can be condensed into a couple of years of practical training and education on the farm and at high school, this opportunity should be within the financial reach of everyone. . . .[14]

In pursuit of these opinions, in 1910 Vail provided the finances to develop a program of agricultural training for boys and home economics for girls at Lyndon Institute. The boys' program became the Vail Agricultural School, which Vail gave, with substantial land and facilities, to the state in 1915. After Vail's death in 1920, the state abandoned the project, and the property reverted to Lyndon Institute, which over the years disposed of it.

The Fletcher-Sanborn-Harris farm was purchased by E. A. Lawson. Fire destroyed the barns in 1939; they were immediately rebuilt, but burned again in 1959. In 1965 E. A. Lawson's son, Robert, opened the eastern portion of the farm as a residential sub-division named "Speedwell Estates."

In the process of settling the Vail estate, the contents of "The House" were removed and, except for items kept by the family, sold at public auction in New York. Three sales were held of the library and art collections, from which a contemporary newspaper reported the proceeds as $131,865.25. Many and varied attempts were made to dispose of "The House." In fact, it did change hands a number of times, but was regained by default; none of the new owners was able to convert dreams into reality. In 1921 it was considered for a veterans' hospital. Later the same year D. I. Grapes exchanged it for the Grapes' block and his Corner Garage in Lyndonville, then sold a half interest to J. E. Manley of Brattleboro, and the next year Manley bought out Grapes. In 1923 the property was incorporated as "Manor Vail" to be developed as a "health resort"; the members of the corporation were Geraldine Farrar (the opera singer), Maj. Frederick De Tafford Craven (a retired British army officer), and two Boston doctors, Ralph Kendrick Smith and Owen B. Ames. Sometime after Manley's death in 1929, his sons and their wives formed "The Development Enterprizes, Inc." In 1944 and again in 1946 they formulated plans to make a resort, a summer school, a camp; but none of these varied schemes proved workable. "The House" was doomed to remain unwanted and unexploited, except by vandals, for another ten years before it was leased by the state to relieve the space problems of the Lyndon Normal School. It was used for offices and classrooms by the normal school and its descendent, Lyndon State College, but was finally destroyed as unsafe in 1974.

To a reader who did not know Vail, or Speedwell Farms in its prime, two quotations from Albert Bigelow Paine's biography of Vail, *In One Man's Life*, should be of interest. First, about the man:

> . . . I should like to make clear . . . something of the almost childlike simplicity in private life of this man, known to the public as one of the world's great captains, head of its foremost industry. To those who knew him but slightly he sometimes gave the impression of being austere, unapproachable, a sort of business czar. Nothing could have been further from the truth. He was, in fact diffident, easily embarassed, reluctant to meet strangers . . . in his home anyone could gain admittance. If an applicant of any sort called at his apartment, he would see him, listen patiently to what he had to say, and fre-

Will Aldrich, longtime coachman for T. N. Vail, with team and phaeton
(*Will Aldrich*)

quently grant a request that meant an outlay of time and money later
on. . . . He was easily moved, and his eyes filled at the relation of
any dramatic or pathetic circumstance. Romantic and soft-hearted,
full of good humor, with a tendency to mischief (blushing with confusion if detected in it), he never seemed more than a boy—a big
child, in fact—to those of his intimate daily circle. Great executive
force that he was in the world's business, to those about him—sharing
in his projects, his pastimes, and his humors—his daily personal life,
in its lighter register, lay somewhere between a joke and a sentimental
song.

And then about Speedwell Farms, his home:

It was on the evening before his 71st birthday that I arrived at Speedwell Farms. I had at this time never seen Mr. Vail, as he greeted me
in the entrance hall, the light on his snow-white hair, his great rosy
face smiling a welcome, I thought him the largest man I had ever
seen. It was not that he was so tall—a trifle more than six feet, I
think—but he had grown stout and stood so straight and carried
his weight so well, that he somehow seemed to tower above those

of his own stature. I believe that it was not really his physical proportions at all. It was his vigor, and more than that, the lofty intellect which one could not fail to realize from the moment of first acquaintance. . . .

I think what first impressed me was the size and abundance of everything—the spaciousness of the rooms, the large richness of their furnishings. It was all big, big and splendid, a proper setting for its owner—indeed a part of him. It was after the dinner hour, and presently the air became filled with music, mellow organ tones that seemed to come from no place in particular, and rose in a swell that vibrated and died away in waves of liquid harmony. The walls seemed filled with it, and this was, in fact, the case, for the reeds at different points were built into them, above stairs and below. The keyboard was in the gallery that encircled the room, and he was up there playing.

July 16, 1916, was a perfect summer day, and my first view of Speedwell out-of-doors could hardly have been under more favorable conditions. It was at its maximum of beauty: its lakes, its lawns, its trellised arbor across the hill, at their brightest and best; its spacious perennial gardens a riot of color; its great green-houses a store of hothouse fruits—gold and purple grapes, melons, nectarines, peaches, figs—all in abundance. Nothing was small, and nowhere was there scantiness.

The house itself seemed almost without end. When one imagined he had reached its limits it doubled back suddenly to the greenhouses or to a long veranda or to carriage house; there seemed really no way to compass its boundaries. It had grown and grown during the generations of its ownership—it was another part of himself. Facing it all, across the valley of the Passumpsic, was Burke Mountain and its purple range of supporting hills. Speedwell and its surroundings seemed to me, that golden morning, the most beautiful spot in all New England, perhaps in the world. . . .

Developing in the neighboring town of Burke at practically the same time as Speedwell Farms were the Mountain View Farms, which came to be an important force in the economic and social life of the Lyndon community also. In 1883 Elmer A. Darling purchased the Harley M. Hall farm of about 330 acres on the hill west of East Burke village. Within the next few years he added the Lemuel Walter farm

Burklyn Hall (*St. Johnsbury Atheneum*)

of 125 acres on the south and the William Belden farm of 127 acres on the north. His parents, Mr. and Mrs. Henry G. Darling, his brother Lucius and wife, and his sister Louise soon came to live on the property and administer the farm.

Elmer Darling had been associated with his uncle Alfred in the administration of New York's Fifth Avenue Hotel since 1872, and this relationship continued until 1908, when the hotel was sold. Therefore, Darling's direct contact with the farm was limited for several years largely to the summer and vacation periods. However, he still found time over these years to acquire the Humphrey Amidon, Joshua Bemis, and Arnold Bemis farms, creating a tract reported by some as 8000 acres in extent. These lands were immediately stocked with Jersey and Devon cattle, White Chester pigs, and Morgan horses.[15] A creamery was built, and much of its 70 pounds of cheese a day and 600 pounds of butter a month were shipped to the Fifth Avenue Hotel. The area was developed into a model farm.

In 1899 Darling purchased the grist and lumber mills in East Burke village. These provided a source of waterpower for the farm on the hill and processing lumber for construction. Begun in 1904 and finished in 1908, the residence of Darling and his sister Louise sat on the highest point within the farm holdings. The boundary line between the towns of Burke and Lyndon extended east to west through its center, and thus Darling named it Burklyn Hall. The builder was J. N. Foye of St. Johnsbury. The architects were Kent and Gardyne of New York, although Darling applied much of his own architectural training—acquired at the Massachusetts Institute of Technology—in making the plans. C. H. Goss Company of St. Johnsbury did the heating, roofing, and plumbing. The granite and lumber came from neighboring hillsides, and many local artisans were employed in the construction.

Soon after Darling's death in 1931, his brother Lucius and nephew Henry began disposing of the extensive holdings, and one by one the more distant parcels were sold. Finally, in 1933 Burklyn Hall and lands contiguous (1700 acres) were sold to Earle Brown of Minneapolis, whose specialties were Hereford cattle and Belgian horses. From this time this portion of the property came to be known as Burklyn Farms. The buildings and much of the land that had constituted the original Mountain View Farms (before the construction of Burklyn Hall) remained a unit and continued to retain that name.

Brown sold to C. H. Davis, president of Vermont Tap and Die Company, in 1948, and in 1957 Davis sold the Vermont Tap and Die Corporation and his Burklyn Hall and other holdings to the American Saw and Tool Company of Louisville, Ky. The new owners soon gave Burklyn Hall and eighty-six acres of adjoining land to the state of Vermont, which used the hall as a dormitory facility for Lyndon Teachers College.

Lucius and Henry Darling retained the property associated with the Hall farm, known as Mountain View Farm. However, for some years the house was unoccupied, as the family had moved to the H. E. Folsom place in Lyndonville. In early June 1960 the property—914 acres—was deeded to Mr. and Mrs. Nelson Pendleton of Lyndon. Mr. Pendleton's death in 1962 resulted in the sale of the property, as well as changes in the character of use of the property.

XI

Newspapers

The first newspaper in Lyndon was the *Vermont Union*, which began publication on February 10, 1865, under editor Charles M. Chase. A native of Lyndon, Chase had returned in 1864 from ten years' residence in Sycamore, Ill., and service in the Civil War. While away he had taught music, studied law, and worked as a newspaper correspondent; his return had been motivated by the illness of his father, Gen. Epaphras B. Chase.

Charles Chase purchased the plant of the *Newport News* and moved it to the Chase block opposite the Tavern in Lyndon Corner. The equipment included a Washington press for taking proofs and printing posters, a cylinder press, and a job press. The cylinder press was operated by hand power, and the job press by foot power; the person running the latter frequently shifted from one foot to the other, or stopped completely to rest two tired feet.

On the second page of the first issue of the *Union*, Chase stated the policies that would govern its publication for the next eighty years:

> Our Paper: There is a tendency, these days, among men of all parties to abuse and vilify political opponents, — as if there was but one side to political problems and those who can not see that side are either foolish or wicked. Men are apt to forget that the most positive in opinion are oftenest in error. The entire North today, with a very few exceptions, is loyal to the government, and would as soon sell their birthright as to suffer a dissolution of Union. All are agreed upon one thing—*This Union must be preserved*. Yet there is such a difference of opinion concerning the means of securing this object, that men desiring the same political result, array themselves on dif-

ferent sides, and treat one another more like deadly enemies than friends. The vocabulary of bad English is exhausted in finding terms of reproach to apply to political opponents. The result of this spirit is to divide and weaken the strength of the loyal States, at a time when every resource is needed. No one party can be accused of monopolizing the spirit of hate and intoleration, — (though candid Republicans will admit that as a party they have excelled in that direction), the evil pervades all parties and in some degree, influences all men. So far as *The Union* has any influence it will aim to check this intolerance in discussion and create a disposition for candid reasoning. Let men talk and not spat, — reason and not froth.

In politics the *Union* will be a conservative Democratic paper, but giving to the powers that be its support when they support the Constitution and the laws. To justify them in violating the Constitution would be as disloyal as to justify rebellion itself. The party has always been strictly law abiding and loyal. Not an instance can be cited where the party has rebelled against the law of the land, or even winked at its violation. That is what ails the party today; they believe, that within the limits of that sacred instrument, the rebellion can be put down, and Union restored. They want to see it done, and help do it. Is that papery? They will support war for the one purpose of restoring the Union. Can anything more be required?

But you say the Union can not be restored till slavery is destroyed — that we must wipe out that institution first and afterwards restore the Union on a firmer basis. If that be so, slavery will fall as a *consequence* of the war, and not as its *object*. If so, good. We shall not join the mourners. But supposing the rebels lay down their arms today, these rebelling, and come back into the Union. The constitution is in full force, protecting the whole sisterhood of States, and permitting each to regulate and rule her domestic institutions. Will you cease fighting then? Or continue the war for the abolition of slavery? If the latter, then you are disloyal — refusing to acquiesce in the laws of the land.

Better let the army crush the rebellion in the speediest way possible, then let the people decide what shall be done with slavery. When that question comes *legally* before them, in the form of a constitutional amendment, many who are now called copperheads will doubtless give it hearty support.

The last words of the great Douglass — "OBEY THE LAWS

AND THE CONSTITUTION" constitute the creed of the democratic party, from this creed it will never depart.

Our paper will be especially devoted to agriculture, supplying a
want long felt by the farmers in this and adjoining counties. We hope
they will consider it their own paper, and give it their hearty support.

At first the *Union* was a four-page weekly newspaper with seven
21¾-inch columns to the page. Its subject matter was political, agricultural, and miscellaneous; on its third page there was likely to be
a column or two of state and local happenings, not grouped under
any special headings. By 1869 the size of the paper was increased to
eight columns of twenty-four inches.

Early in the existence of the *Union*, Editor Chase made a great
effort to fill the paper with local news. To this end he spent at least
two or three days out of each week traveling in neighboring towns
collecting news and making friends; he soon had a mailing list of
2500, an unusually large number for that time in Vermont. He in-
itiated the custom of grouping local items under the heading of the
community in which they had occurred—the first publisher to do
this. The most prosperous days of the *Vermont Union* probably were
between 1870 and 1890, when the circulation reached 3000 copies
per issue. In those days there was no competition with the daily press.

Another novelty in the *Union* was the sequence of letters that Chase
wrote during trips to New Mexico, Florida, California, and elsewhere; frequently his absences were of a month or more in length,
during which he would send weekly "letters" reporting his experi-
ences and observations. Later some of these were collected and repub-
lished in paperback books as "The Editor's Run . . ."—each volume
concentrating on a specific locale—and sold at about $2 each. During
his last ten years, Chase frequently included articles, two or three
columns in length, reviewing happenings of previous years in town.

In November 1902 Charles Chase passed away after a period of
failing health; he had published the *Union* for thirty-seven years and
nine months. He had been an exceptionally keen, skillful editor, possessed of the ability of making newsworthy accounts out of events
of seemingly little importance, and also possessed of an enormous
gift of humor.

Following his death his son, John Bryant Chase, returned to Lyndon and assumed editorial responsibility for the *Vermont Union* for the next thirty-nine years. In 1905 John Chase purchased the *Lyndonville Journal*, the *Union's* chief competitor, and combined the two as the *Vermont Union-Journal*, producing the paper from the Lyndonville office of the *Journal*. One feature he added to the publication was a semieditorial "Just a Few Rambling Paragraphs," a mixture of his reminiscences and excerpts from early issues of the *Union*. He occasionally published another feature entitled "On The Street," a series of paragraphs commenting on contemporary events in the community. From 1929 to 1935, while Chase was a member of the Vermont legislature, the paper included weekly reports of its activities.

In May 1941 the *Vermont Union-Journal* was sold to the *Caledonian-Record* of St. Johnsbury. The report of the sale noted the new publisher's intention to continue it as a weekly newspaper. In 1945 the Caledonian Record Publishing Company sold the job-printing business and the *Union-Journal* equipment to Ross Stevens Advertising Agency, Inc.

During the seventy-seven-year history of the Chase publication, attempts—largely short-lived—were made to publish a competing paper. B. W. Farr launched one of the more successful ventures. In May 1886 he opened a job-printing office in the Fletcher block, and shortly announced that he would soon publish a newspaper called the *Lyndonville News*. In August the first issue appeared, named instead the *Lyndonville Comet*. According to the *St. Johnsbury Republican*, the *Comet* was "to be published semi-occasionally as the business interests of his advertizers may demand. It is a well-printed little quarto sheet, partly reading and partly advertising matter, is well patronized by the prominent business firms of the place, and has come evidently to stay." In September of the following year, however, it was reported as "having gone under." So far as this writer has been able to learn, no copies of any of the issues have survived.

Two years later the *Union's* only true competition came into being. Early in April 1889 H. B. Davis, for a quarter century a foreman in the *Caledonian* office, moved to Lyndonville to establish a printing office. In August the *Union* reported the publication of the first issue of the *Lyndonville Journal*, a seven-column paper. In his initial editorial, Davis outlined the policies of his paper:

> . . . we shall endeavor to chronicle all happenings that come to our knowledge in a truthful manner, to treat all classes and societies with fairness, granting to all the right of their own views and ask the same right for ourselves. Politically the *Journal* will be a temperance republican paper. We think the day has come in Vermont, as elsewhere, when all the strength of temperance people should be united, as a question of prohibition and high license is to be brought before the people. That wing of the Republican Party which had been a hindrance to good temperance work is now showing its hand in a more open manner by declaring for high license. . . .

On July 1, 1896, the *Lyndonville Journal* issued a "special" edition (volume 7, no. 48) titled "Lyndonville: The Hustling Railroad Village" and containing "sketches, illustrations of its leading industries, buildings, and citizens"; this issue is an invaluable historical treasure.

In 1902 the *Lyndonville Journal* was sold for $7000 to E. O. Leonard of Bradford, former treasurer of the Bradford Savings Bank and later proprietor of the *St. Johnsbury Republican*. A corporation of Bradford stockholders with $9000 capital formed the Journal Publishing Company. In July 1903 the *Journal* was sold to Allen S. Holbrook of Newport. Later in the year Holbrook received an appointment in the Government Printing Office, Washington, D.C., and E. L. Hopkins of Lyndon took his place in the *Journal* office. On November 1, 1905, John B. Chase acquired the *Journal* and its office in the west side of the Dodge and Watson block on Depot Street, which became the home of the *Vermont Union-Journal*.

XII

Catastrophes

LYNDON HAS HAD ITS SHARE of catastrophes, fire and flood coming most often and taking the heaviest toll in terms of life and monetary losses.

Fires

THERE HAS BEEN SCARCELY A YEAR in Lyndon's history that fire has not made a major change in the appearance of some part of the town. Of course, one thinks first of the fires of 1894 and 1924, because they were so devastating.

On November 27, 1894, about three o'clock in the morning, a fire was discovered in one of the back rooms of Webb's Hotel, located at the southwest corner of Elm and Depot streets. A very strong southeast wind was blowing and the hydrants were frozen, so although firemen from St. Johnsbury came promptly to the assistance of the Lyndonville men, by six o'clock both sides of Depot Street had been cleared from Main Street to the railroad station; one residence on Elm Street and two on Church Street had also burned. A total of twenty-three buildings, with thirty-four stores, shops, and offices, were gone, and twenty-eight families were homeless. Very little had been saved by anyone. The loss was estimated at $162,000 ($78,000 real estate, $84,000 personal property); insurance reimbursements totaled $130,000.[1]

The rapid spread of the fire is best described in the local newspaper account:[2]

> . . . W. A. Loomis, who lives in Dr. Davis' house, south of the hotel,

was awakened by a light shining into his window, discovered it and shouted the alarm, then rushed to the basement of music hall for the engine. A. E. Ruggles reached there at the same time and, in a few minutes there was a force enough to drag the machine to the fire where Loomis left it, ran to the church and spent a few minutes at the bell rope. When he left the engine it was fifteen minutes past three o'clock, and the fire was making rapid progress on the rear of the hotel. At twenty minutes past the engine had done nothing and was moved to the hydrant on depot park where water was obtained, but the bottom valve in the machine being frozen it was comparatively useless.

Meantime the fire was making rapid progress on the hotel, and the assistance of a strong south wind gained rapidly on the pail brigade. The flames soon enveloped the main building and from there was communicated to the three story Eaton block on the east, and when this big building got fairly under way it was perfectly evident that, with the strong wind to fan the flames, engine out of order, and hydrants frozen up, the street was doomed.

From the Eaton block the wind carried the flames across the street to the Nichols block which was soon in a big blaze. The wind apparently increased, switched to the west and from the Nichols block carried the flames to G. H. Weeks' post office block and from there swept everything on that side of the street . . . [to] Mrs. Parker's Millinery store, where the flames were stopped, saving the old Jenniss boarding house on the corner. . . .

On Church Street the flames swept north from the Weeks block and licked up the Weeks barn and from there communicated to the beautiful residence . . . owned by Dr. Cheney. . . .

On the east side of Church street, opposite the Cheney house, flames communicated from the Nichols block to the H. F. Woodard double tenement house, which was soon in ashes. Among the last to go was the Ide block. Water gave out almost entirely when this took fire, and at no time was the home engine able to send a stream above the second story windows.

While these buildings were going, the wind which was strongest from the south, would occasionally take a whirl around to the south, east, and west, or where ever it could find combustible material. From Eaton's block fire jumped to the Stern block, and to the long shed on the south, and from there to the four tenement Twombly house, south of the Stern's block. . . .

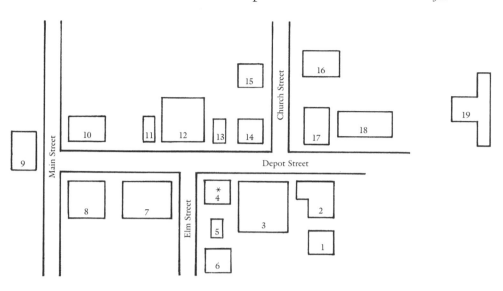

DIAGRAM OF BURNED DISTRICT AT LYNDONVILLE, 1894

1 Twombly Building	8 Silsby's Livery Stable	15 Cheney Residence
2 Stern Building	9 Pettigrew Building, not burned	16 Woodward Residence
3 Eaton Building	10 Boarding House, not burned	17 Nichols Building
4 Webb's Hotel	11 Parker Building	18 Ide Building
5 Hotel Barn	12 Cook Building	19 Depot, not burned
6 Howe Residence	13 Barber Shop	* Building where fire started
7 Hoyt Building	14 Weeks Building	

Depot Street 1894 fire, Lyndonville (*Caledonian Record*)

Back of the hotel, the hotel barn burned and communicated the flames to W. C. Howe's residence on Elm Street which was destroyed. West of the hotel and across Elm Street was the Hoyt block, occupied by D. M. Silsby which was soon in ashes, and completed the work of destruction, leaving nothing on the street except the old Parker boarding house. . . .

Special mention should be made of the snowball brigade. People used snowballs to save buildings a short distance from Depot Street. Whenever possible, water was poured on roofs, caught as it ran off, and used over and over again. The wind was so strong that it carried blazing shingles to the sides of buildings and held them there until the clapboards caught fire. It was at these places that the snowball

Depot Street, after 1924 fire (*Leo Hebert*)

brigades proved particularly effective. They are credited with saving several residences.

The second major fire occurred on January 21, 1924. It started in Stern's store shortly before eleven o'clock in the evening, beginning with an explosion of sufficient strength to break the plate glass windows on both the Broad Street and Depot Street sides of the store. Flames leaped up the sides of the building and spread so rapidly that there was no time for the occupants of the Stern block to dress. People from the third floor had to jump to the ground, since the fire escapes were soon cut off. Within a few minutes the flames had leaped across the street to the Ide block. The Eaton block by the Stern block, the Masonic block, and the hotel and livery stables were soon engulfed in flames.

The temperature was about twelve degrees below zero and a strong wind was blowing, complicating the efforts of the Lyndon firemen and their counterparts from St. Johnsbury—Chief McGill and his twenty-two firemen, who brought 2000 feet of hose. Many people performed heroically in helping those who were trapped. Special mention should be made of the telephone operators Mrs. Delia

McDuffee and Mrs. Forrest Grapes, who remained at their posts, working by kerosene lamps until forced to vacate by smoke and flames.

When it was over, every building had been burned on the south side of Depot Street from Elm Street to Broad Street, and on the north from Church Street to the railroad station. About 150 people, including thirty to thirty-five families, had to seek new homes. Destroyed were twenty-eight businesses employing sixty-one people. Property loss was estimated at $500,000, with $210,000 paid in insurance. Most important, the fire was more serious than its predecessor in terms of loss of life; seven people died in the conflagration.[3]

A Citizen's Relief Committee was promptly formed to cooperate with the Caledonia Chapter of the National Red Cross, of which Miss Laura Varney was executive secretary. This committee consisted of Dr. H. M. Smith, chairman; Mrs. C. L. Stuart, vice-chairman; W. E. Riley, treasurer; Mrs. H. A. Robie, secretary; Prof. O. D. Mathewson, corresponding secretary; and John L. Norris, H. W. Lyster, H. A. Squires, Albert Stern, L. D. Shonyo, Miss Laura Varney, Mrs. Annie Lane, and Mrs. John Cleary. Communities and individuals from the area and from far away made contributions to the relief fund totaling $16,763.94.[4]

The town fire that probably ranks third in seriousness occurred in Lyndon Corner. It was discovered early Monday morning, May 24, 1897, in the Lyndon House. By 8:00 a.m. the west side of Main Street south from York Street was in ashes except for Bryan's Ton-Teen at the lower end of the street. Not only were these buildings destroyed, but those on the east side of the street showed blistered paint and broken windows. The heaviest loser was George Warren, who had recently purchased the hotel from Curtis Stevens. Although all the destroyed buildings were seventy-five to ninety years old, the chief loss was the historic Lyndon House. It was ninety years old and for over forty years had been the leading tavern in this part of the state. Built by Capt. Alfred Fletcher, it was a square two-story building with a red hip roof; on the northeast corner was an old-time swing sign.

Fires have also struck single buildings of public significance. One of the first fires of any magnitude took place on November 28, 1867, when Walkers' Hotel was destroyed. This was located on a part of the lot later occupied by the Cobleigh Library and Lyndonville Hardware.

During the night of January 2–3, 1922, fire completely destroyed Lyndon Institute's Thompson Hall. While spectators stood watching the smoke rising from the ashes, they pledged more than $20,000 to rebuild. By the next day a building committee had been elected, and contributions poured in; a new building stood on the site before the year was out.

At 5:45 on Sunday morning, August 27, 1967, the alarm sounded for a fire in Lyndonville's First Congregational Church. By noon, when the fire was finally brought under control, the 1872 building was unsalvagable. Within two years, however, a new church had risen from the ashes.

The site in town where the largest number of destructive fires occurred was the Fletcher block, also known as Ide's block. The first took place in October 1888. This fire was of short duration, but water damage extended throughout the block, affecting the National Bank, Lyndon Savings Bank, LeBourveau's Drug Store, Parker's Grocery and Variety Store, Cahoon's Law Office, a barber shop, family rooms, and the Masonic Hall. On Wednesday evening, March 8, 1899, fire gutted the building, causing $2500 damage and destroying eight business concerns, four secret societies, and two family tenements. In October 1905 the explosion of the tank of Ira Davis' restaurant gasoline stove caused smoke, water, and fire damage. Early on the morning of February 24, 1910, fire broke out in the basement of Farrar's restaurant. It produced little damage but much concern and smoke. The summer of 1913 brought fire again. The building was finally destroyed in the massive conflagration of January 21, 1924.

Twice the Hall's Mills community of town was badly damaged by fire. On May 9, 1892, two dwelling houses were destroyed, one a double tenement housing four families. Only by the sheerest good fortune were the mills, lumber, and other dwellings saved. The second fire occurred on May 12, 1905, when sparks from a passing train apparently fell upon dry roof shingles. It was twice thought that the fire had been put out, but a stiff breeze revived it. The blaze not only completely destroyed the mills but also crossed the river onto the hill and became a sizable forest fire, one that threatened farm buildings on the hill as well as the Lyndonville Electric Light property.

Over the years other fires have destroyed private property and public business concerns, thus constantly changing the face of the community, but always the members of the community came together to aid those who were victims.

ᘓ⋙

Floods

THE NUMBER OF STREAMS in the town and the topography of the land have contributed to the frequency of "high water." Mini-floods have occurred at least annually and frequently more often, not only in the aftermath of melting spring snows, but also following especially heavy rains. The first occasion of serious high water of which record has survived was in 1802, when the town meeting voted to petition the General Assembly to permit the application for the special 2 percent assessment on town land to aid in the repair of town roads. According to the records of the Department of Agriculture, the Soil Conservation Service of Vermont has classified as "serious" the floods in the Passumpsic Valley occurring in 1828, 1866, 1869, 1896, 1899, 1913, 1927, 1933, 1935, 1936, 1940, 1950, 1952, 1968, 1969, 1972, and 1973. Of these 1869, 1927, and 1973 were designated as most damaging.

In 1869 the waters rose fourteen feet above normal. Twenty-seven public bridges, ten private bridges, and two railroad bridges in the town were washed away, and many others were badly damaged. A number of roads became impassable, and practically every road in town had washouts.

The flood of 1927 followed a rain storm that began about ten o'clock on Wednesday night, November 2. The downpour continued unabated until about noon on Friday, November 4. Although the rain

1927 flood, Lyndon Center looking east (*Ralph Hines*)

came at times in great volume like a cloudburst, most of the time it was steady with little let-up. It brought disaster to the whole state of Vermont, with damage being most serious in the western part of the state. Water on State Street in Montpelier was more than twelve feet deep. In Lyndon, water rose to eighteen feet above normal; sixteen bridges were carried away and eight others were badly damaged. Private property and business losses were enormous: for example, the Lyndonville Creamery lost 225 pigs and four work horses. The water rose so rapidly that many people were removed from their homes by boat, and because of ceiling-high flooding,[5] homes were not fit for occupancy for many days after the water receded.

Lyndonville people first became really alarmed on November 4. After daylight for three or four hours the water rose rapidly. It reached the Campbell house on the lower end of Main Street. At its highest point the entire length of Park Avenue was covered by two or three feet of water. Water was over two feet deep at Kreamy Ice Kream, where 900 gallons of ice cream was spoiled. The water rushed up School Street to within fifteen feet of Depot Street. At the upper end of Main Street five houses on the left and one on the right suc-

1927 flood, railroad track, Lyndon, Vermont (*E. Houghton*)

cumbed to the rushing water. The house on the right was the only one to feel the full force of the water. The ice pond on the West Burke road went out, adding to the rushing water.

At Lyndon Center no damage was done to the upper bridge, but north of it the water was very deep, extending almost to the Roundy farm. Water at the south end of the village reached past the Atwood house; it also reached up the back Center road.

The railroad track toward East Lyndon felt the full fury of the flood. Its track resembled a roller coaster, with portions twisted and suspended in midair. The Lyndon station was tipped on its side over a large hole at an angle of twenty-five to thirty degrees. The station platform was washed at least 100 feet down the track. The A. N. Wetherbee Novelty plant had water reaching almost to the ceiling of the first floor. Martial law was imposed for a few days to prevent looting, and members of Company C patrolled the area.

In his special message to the session of the General Assembly, convened in early December, Governor Weeks reported that 1258 bridges in the state had been destroyed or severely damaged and that the total estimated damage to roads and bridges amounted to $7,755,000.

1973 flood, North Main Street, Lyndonville [Rt. 5] (*Weekly News*)

The governor recommended a bond issue of $8.5 million, which the legislature approved. Eighty-four people had been killed, including Lieutenant Governor S. Hollister Jackson. The state Department of Agriculture estimated the farm loss of $7,622,145; about one-third of the maple trees usually tapped were lost. Caledonia County suffered serious losses, as did other parts of New England. Roads everywhere were blocked by fallen trees. Two creamery trucks had to go via Gorham, N.H., and Bethel, Maine, to Portland in order to get the early delivery to Boston.

In 1973 Lyndon suffered two instances of high water, both rated "significant" by state and federal agencies. The first occurred June 30–July 1. Over the course of the month of June 9.65 inches of rain had fallen, the highest ever recorded for June since records began to be kept in 1892. On the West Burke road, the Callender Brook rose some twelve feet and flooded Route 5, thereby putting sixteen inches of water on the first floor of the David Mitchell home. In Lyndonville the junction of north Main Street and Highway 114 was hardest hit. The mobile home park, Lynburke Motel, the Town and Country Restaurant, the service station, and the residences all were inundated with several feet of water. South of the village, along Memorial Drive, at least eight businesses and a dozen residences suffered major damage, with water four feet deep in the road. Water reached depths of three and one-half or four feet inside the Shop and Save market and three feet in the drive-in bank office. The Vermont Soil Conservation Service estimated the water level in the Shop and Save market would require a river rise of approximately seventeen feet above normal. Highway 122 was impassable in many places, especially at its entrance to the north end of Lyndon Center, and serious damage also occurred in Sheffield and Wheelock.

On December 21, 1973, Lyndon again suffered from high water, but not as seriously as in June. Again, the water was most threatening at the junction of Highways 5 and 114, damaging the Northeast Kingdom Trailer Park, Lynburke Motel, the Town and Country Restaurant, and upper Main Street residences. To the south of the village the water was high, but much less so than in June. The National Guard was activated and provided both trucks and manpower to assist the evacuees. Various state agencies and the Red Cross also rendered generous assistance.[6]

One instance of too much water occurred in 1911, it was a "flood" only in a small part of the town. Lyndon Center had its "Runaway Pond" when the dam on the pond back of Lyndon Institute broke. In the summer of 1910 as a part of Mr. Vail's repairing and remodeling of the school's property, the road back of Thompson Hall had been repaired and the course of the brook regulated. Early the next March, without warning, the water washed out the soil at the east end of the dam and rushed down the brook to the Passumpsic River,[7] flooding buildings in its path and "washing away" some livestock.

ᘒ☛

Storms, Cold, Quakes, and Bugs

OVER THE YEARS MANY WINDSTORMS have occurred, resulting in uprooted trees, roofs blown off buildings, buildings moved from foundations, and power lines downed.

Early one morning in July 1868 high winds swept through the area, unroofing several buildings and either moving barns or blowing them off their foundations. A severe thunderstorm accompanied by high winds was recorded in August 1914. A windstorm in September 1915 uprooted many trees and damaged telephone and light lines, especially in the Pudding Hill area. During a severe storm in May 1918 many shade trees in Lyndon were blown down. In Lyndon Corner, chimneys were blown off houses, holes blown in barns, and boards from Wetherbee's mill scattered in all directions. A large henhouse was blown completely off its foundation, landing about twenty feet away on electric light wires; numerous trees were felled, some in the village, others in sugar orchards.

One of the most destructive windstorms was the hurricane that swept through the area in September 1938. In three-quarters of the sugar places 70 to 80 percent of the trees were felled. Unharvested corn was a total loss; apples not harvested were also lost. One of the unusual features of this storm was that not a tree in Lyndonville's park was destroyed, although eighteen trees were downed on Main Street. The care given to park trees by the Village Improvement Society is credited with saving them. All over town trees were uprooted, some falling on buildings; power and telephone lines were downed, and roofs were ripped off buildings, including the roundhouse in the railroad yards. Once trees and power lines were cleaned up, the damage in the area was seen to be less severe than in other parts of New England.

At times over the years severe snowstorms have stopped all activity. One of the worst recorded was the blizzard of 1888, which dumped up to one and a half feet of snow. In October of 1925 a midwinter-type blizzard occurred, depositing six to ten inches of snow. Many autos were stalled, and any unharvested crops were destroyed. In February of the same year a foot or more of snow was deposited in the town, while high winds piled drifts several feet deep. It took snow-rollers two or three days to break open all the roads, and trains ran two or three hours late. Unlike many storms, the one occurring in April 1925 was thought to have been beneficial to the grass, according to the theory that melting snow sinks in better than heavy rains. One of the worst snowstorms to be recorded happened in February 1934. This storm, often compared to the blizzard of 1888, dropped up to a foot and a half of snow in this area.

Although winters are often accompanied by cold weather, two years produced particularly cold days. In January 1917 a four-day cold spell shattered all records, the mercury plunging to thirty and forty below zero. During the day on Saturday the temperature did not rise above ten to fifteen below zero. Many residents reported temperatures of fifty to fifty-eight below zero; at Rines store in Lyndon Center the mercury registered sixty-two below zero.

In 1943 the coldest February day ever recorded occurred, the temperature sinking lower than the limits of the official U.S. Weather Bureau thermometer. As late as ten a.m. temperatures of fifty-two below zero were recorded up and down Main Street in Lyndonville, and the Lyndonville Creamery recorded seventy below zero. It was so cold that telephone lines snapped, the northbound Red Wing ran four hours late, and bus service was curtailed; birds fell from the trees half-frozen and soon died. Cars were frozen solid. At three a.m. Eastman's Drug Store recorded − 44 degrees. Four hours later the fire station recorded fifty-four below zero, apparently the peak of the cold.

Few serious earthquakes have struck this area. In February 1925 one lasting from thirty to forty seconds occurred. At first it was accompanied by a roar like that of a high wind. Buildings rocked back and forth, cans fell from shelves, beds rocked, dishes rattled, and furniture moved without assistance. The quake was apparently centered in the Fundian Fault off the coast of Maine. In 1929 a mid-afternoon earthquake occurred; pictures rocked back and forth, dishes rattled, floors quivered, and buildings swayed, but many people did not even notice the tremors. In 1940 another mild earthquake shook the area, this one centered in Ossipee, N.H. In 1973 an earthquake centered in Beecher Falls, Vt., was felt in Lyndon. None of the shocks in the area resulted in serious damage.

In July 1895, after a long and severe drought, hordes of grasshoppers appeared in Lyndon. Hardest hit was the Egypt area of town, where all growing crops were destroyed. So thick were these grasshoppers that they roosted in trees, covering the trunks and limbs and eating the leaves. Finally a cool rain fell and put an end to the scavengers.

XIII

High-Spirited Happenings

ʒ☞

Fairs

THE FIRST "FAIR" IN TOWN was an agricultural exhibit held on the "parade ground" in Lyndon Center under the sponsorship of the Grange; the date and other facts about it are unknown. In early October 1877 the Grange held an agricultural exhibit in the Grove. The *Union* reported "317 entries in Floral Hall, 216 in fruits and vegetables, 51 in poultry and stock, 45 in mechanics, in all 629;" the "mechanics" included maple-sugaring evaporators and creamery equipment. Exhibits came from several neighboring towns.

In the fall of 1877 the Lyndon Park Association was formed with some forty or fifty stockholders controlling stock of $5000 divided into 200 shares of $25 each.[1] The directors were Robert Pettigrew, Henry Chase, Charles Folsom, W. A. Bemis, O. J. Quimby, H. W. Hall, C. T. A. Humphrey, Joshua Bemis, and Henry C. Mower. Officers were Robert Pettigrew, president; Henry Chase and W. A. Bemis, vice-presidents; E. S. Dunklee, secretary; Charles Folsom, treasurer; and W. A. Bemis, O. J. Quimby, and Henry Chase, finance committee. They purchased a twenty-eight acre piece of pastureland from Charles Folsom for $10 per acre, figuring that the site's levelness would make it possible to construct a racecourse that would be completely visible from a judge's stand.[2]

Work began at once, and the track opened on July 4, 1878. This was followed on September 5 and 6 with a horse fair and races at which $1000 was offered in premiums. Seating facilities for 1000 persons were prepared, and there were over 50 entries for the races; the occasion was considered a complete success. At a meeting on March

14, 1879, the stockholders—most of whom were farmers—voted to form an agricultural society rather than to continue to place the whole emphasis of the organization on horse racing. Fourth of July programs became regular occurrences, sometimes featuring wrestling matches, bicycle races, balloon ascents, and fireworks.

On September 18, 1889, the Northern Caledonia Fair Association was organized at a meeting in Webb's Hotel. Officers elected were L. B. Harris, president; H. B. Davis, secretary; A. W. Houghton, superintendent of grounds; J. W. Weeks, superintendent of agricultural halls; A. O. Harris, superintendent of cattle; D. W. Silsby, superintendent of horses; C. D. Bigelow, superintendent of swine; John Allen, superintendent of sheep; T. W. Parker, superintendent of poultry and pets; Charles Folsom, Joshua Bemis, Charles Ingalls, C. D. Hubbard, and Henry Chase, executive committee; and Mrs. W. H. Bowker, Mrs. C. D. Wilcomb, Mrs. A. L. Twombly, Mrs. H. E. Folsom, Miss May Harris, Mrs. W. S. Jeffers, and Mrs. Addie Cahoon, committee for Ladies' Floral Hall. The group appointed town committees in Burke, East Haven, Newark, Sheffield, Sutton, Kirby, North Danville, Concord, and South Wheelock, and set October 2 as the date for the first fair on the Trotting Park Association grounds.

According to the newspaper, the fair included 800 head of cattle, sheep, and horses; 40 entries of poultry; 700 entries in Floral Hall; and 124 entries of fruit, vegetables, butter, cheese, etc. The publicity concerning this first fair emphasized the point that there was no intent to compete with or detract from the Caledonia County Fair held in St. Johnsbury since before midcentury.

In 1890, after several meetings of interested persons, a group decided to form a permanent organization with a capital stock of $1000 issued in $10 shares.[3] The organization further agreed to rent the grounds of the Park Association for annual fairs, and stipulated that any improvements made or buildings constructed would revert to the association if and when the fairs were discontinued. One of the resolutions unanimously adopted with the constitution prohibited all gambling, games of chance, and intoxicating liquors on the fairgrounds (over the years this was frequently reaffirmed). Officers elected were L. B. Harris, president; Henry Chase and W. H. Bemis, vice-presidents; H. B. Davis, secretary-treasurer; and Isaac Sanborn, assistant secretary. The executive committee consisted of representatives of neighboring towns and Lyndon members Joshua Bemis, Joel Sanborn, A. W. Houghton, S. W. Russell, A. T. Evans, A. O. Harris, Charles Folsom, Charles Ingalls, and J. T. Gleason. The territory covered by the organization included Caledonia County and portions of Essex and Orleans counties. In preparation for the fair on September 22–23, 1890, the group proudly announced:

> The grounds are being put in fine shape to properly accommodate all exhibitors and visitors. A new floral hall 120 x 30, a dining hall 60 x 24, and a barn 50 x 30 giving 20 stalls, a part of which are double, are being added by way of building. The floral hall occupies a place on the flat east and a short distance from the main entrance, we believe a much more desirable location than formerly. The dining hall stands on the site of the old floral hall. . . .[4]

In addition to the exhibits and races, the Lyndonville Silver Cornet Band was in attendance, assisted on the second day by Will A. Cushing, an expert cornetist from Boston. On the first night of the fair the Lyceum Concert Company of Boston appeared at Music Hall; the Lyndonville Band gave a half-hour concert in front of the hall before the Lyceum concert and played for a promenade in the hall afterwards. There were ten divisions of exhibits, with nearly 1000 animals being shown in the stock divisions. The approximately 120 exhibitors came from Lyndon, Wheelock, Sheffield, Glover, Island Pond, Greensboro, Newark, East Haven, Kirby, and St. Johnsbury. The judges of the races were J. W. Copeland, A. W. Houghton, D. S. Winter, and G. E. Clark, with W. H. Weeks as clerk.

Beginning at the December 1890 meeting, the stockholders of the Lyndon Park Association and the Northern Caledonia Fair Association met at the same time and place. Throughout the next ten years the two organizations worked closely together, and there were frequent rumors of intended union. The *Vermont Union* of February 2, 1900, reported the accomplishment of this union under the name of "The Lyndonville Fair." The officers of the new association were C. M. Darling, president, and C. L. Stuart, clerk; directors were L. B. Harris, T. N. Vail, A. O. Harris, G. M. Campbell, Elisha

Bigelow, Charles Rogers, W. I. Powers (all of Lyndon), L. A. Darling (East Burke), and O. C. Woodruff (West Burke).

On May 15, 1891, the Northern Caledonia Fair Association held its first "Stallion Parade" at which seventy animals—including a few colts paying honor to their sires—were exhibited. Animals were brought from Newbury, Barnet, St. Johnsbury, Danville, Wheelock, Lyndon, Burke, Sheffield, Island Pond, Barton, and some other towns. These exhibits were conducted annually in May or June for five successive years.

Not only were certificates and small cash awards given to exhibitors at the fair, but local merchants provided special premiums. Here are a few taken from the 1891 premium list.

> H. L. Parker offers a large Webster dictionary for the best lot of garden vegetables.
>
> J. C. Eaton offers (1) a patent strainer pail for the best tub of sugar, (2) a galvanized bottom pail for the best specimen of maple honey, (3) an agate teapot for the best stirred sugar.
>
> J. L. Watchie offers a 56 lb. sack of dairy salt for the best print of butter.
>
> C. B. Dodge offers an improved English sweeper and window brush for the best specimen of wheat bread.
>
> Geo. Grow of St. Johnsbury offers a $2.50 safety lantern to the person that wins on a safety bought of him in the bicycle race.
>
> H. Bulavis offers a copy of the Lyndonville *Journal* one year to the person showing the best Jersey stock.
>
> H. J. Dwinell offers (1) a handsome pair of celluloid plaques for the best oil painting, (2) a special prize will be given for the best trained steers driven by a boy 15 years or under.
>
> Mrs. A. L. Twombly offers a stylish fall hat to the girl of 12 or under who makes the best display of cut flowers.
>
> F. W. Silsby & Co. offer a dozen fine napkins to the person having the best lot of pastry.
>
> Eastman and Eaton offer a large stone china platter for the best display of fruit.
>
> Taylor and Wadley offer a copy of *Europe, Illustrated* for the best specimen of needle work.
>
> J. W. Cass offers a copy of White's *Modern Method for the Cabinet Organ* for the best crayoning.

In 1891 a group of horsemen in the vicinity subscribed to keep the track in condition for the winter training of their horses. At the annual meeting in 1894 the organization voted to invite the Fifteenth Vermont and other veterans to hold their reunions during the fair again. At a later meeting the group planned a tournament for the fair in which half a dozen bands competed.

In 1900, to solve the problem of inadequate receipts, the fair organization adopted a policy whereby the ladies of the Lyndonville Epworth League would pay $25 for a monopoly on the sale of fruit, F. E. Winslow would pay $10 for the cigar trade, Herman Squires would monopolize the popcorn trade for $10, and the Universalist ladies would pay $50 to use the dining hall. In 1901 the St. Johnsbury Fairground Company proposed that the Lyndonville Fair Association abandon its fall agricultural show in favor of a Fourth of July exhibition of sports, racing, etc. in which St. Johnsbury would participate. The proposal did not receive favorable action, and the usual fairs were held for two more years.

In the winter of 1931–32 Charles E. Willoughby proposed the idea of a community fair. The community approved of the project, and officers were elected: C. E. Willoughby, president; C. M. Darling, vice-president; Archie E. Donahue, secretary; Lawrence B. Wood, treasurer; and David I. Grapes, Willis C. Conner, and Harold H. Stone, directors. Volunteers removed the horse sheds from the old St. Johnsbury fairgrounds and rebuilt them on the old Lyndon fairgrounds. On July 4, 1932—the fifty-fourth anniversary of the first use of this territory by the Lyndon Park Association—the new "Community Fair Association" reopened the grounds with a successful day of sports and entertainment. The first Community Fair of September 1–2, 1932, opened with a parade of floats, followed by baseball games, other competitive sports, and horse races. A cavalcade of horses and cattle took place in the afternoon of the second day, and the Lyndonville Military Band provided music both days. The next year poor weather forced the fair's postponement for two days, but the occasion was nonetheless a real success, with all aspects of the program and entertainment of both days originating in the community.

At a special meeting of the association on March 30, 1938, the name "Lyndonville Community Fair" was changed to "Caledonia County

Fair." Before the 1939 fair, three new buildings were constructed: a poultry house (16 x 36), a draft horse barn (80 x 36), and a 4-H building (50 x 22); and at this fair the midway made its appearance. In anticipation of the 1947 fair a new grandstand was built seating 1200 people. That year the track record was broken Friday afternoon and again the next day.

In the early spring of 1963 there were twenty-five horses "in training" at the fairgrounds in anticipation of the early opening of the racing season. Kenneth Stone, with nine in training, had the largest group; also represented were Guy Birchard, Harold Stone, Murray Learmouth, Robert McNally, Percy Lynaugh, and Wendell Blake. At the 1963 fair, for the first time, the fair was extended to four days, with the last day being Sunday. As a concession to the strong opposition of the churches of town, the gates were not opened until a minute after twelve o'clock.

༢☚

A Horse Named Kendall

THE SHADOW OF A BAY COLT named Kendall extended across Lyndon for a half century in the form of the winter races on Main Street.

In the late years of the 19th century, interest in horses and horse racing ran high in the town. A number of men regularly entered their horses in the races at the Barton and St. Johnsbury fairs, as well as the one in Lyndonville when that was held. In 1895 Henry Mower's "Lyndon Boy" was in his prime, and Mower had planned to continue the horse's training with John Moulton, a reputedly skillful trainer, who had been with the Utton brothers in Morrisville. When Moulton's negotiations for stable space in Barton fell through, the Lyndon Building Company—W. I. Powers, president; J. T. Gleason, clerk and treasurer; and Mower and his son-in-law John LeBourveau—paid Alvah Brockway $350 for the old Universalist Church and im-

A horse named Kendall, owned by Lucien LeClerc (*Charles LeClerc*)

mediately remodeled it into "John Moulton's Training Stable."[5] According to the *Vermont Union*, in September 1896 a "dozen or more owners of good steeds" formed the "Lyndonville Driving Club." Fred Gorham, M. L. Stearns and C. S. LeBourveau were "appointed a committee to consult with the horsemen at St. Johnsbury Fair to see what arrangements could be made for two days of races the first week in October with purses amounting to $1000." No more information on the club has been found.

The story of Kendall begins earlier. In 1891 Lucien LeClerc, a seventeen-year-old Canadian boy, went to work for John Utton in Morrisville; without doubt the Uttons were Vermont's ablest horse trainers of the time. The son of a blacksmith and amateur "hoss-doctor," Le-

Clerc had already shown a knack with horses, and he was given responsibility for a partly broken colt, bay with a white hind foot, named Kendall after Kendall's Spavin Cure. The boy and the horse became devoted to each other during the seven or eight months of LeClerc's stay.[6] A few years later LeClerc came to Lyndon to work for John Moulton in his training stable, where one of Moulton's charges was this same Kendall. LeClerc stayed for six years, and the attachment between man and horse steadily increased to near devotion.

In the spring of 1907, Lucien LeClerc was almost beside himself with joy when he discovered that his horse-friend, Kendall, was for sale in Dover, N.H. The horse was then at least eighteen years old; though he had established a trotting record of 17¼, he had been idle for two years. LeClerc and his brother-in-law, George LaPointe, bought the horse for $219. When LaPointe got him home, he found that Kendall's long period of idleness had resulted in a bad case of lymphangitis. LeClerc knew that the best treatment for this was exercise, so he began using him on the delivery cart of the LaPointe Brothers Meat Market. At first Kendall was stiff, but his condition gradually improved. After a little while LeClerc planned his deliveries so that he would be returning from upper Main Street when the men would be coming out of the shops at noon. They provided the needed inspiration and encouragement, and soon Kendall was regaining his youthful speed; both he and his driver appeared to enjoy their races down Main Street.

In early December 1907 a group of horsemen—LeClerc, Roger Ladd, Charlie Lee, and Edd Meginnis—discussed the idea of racing on Main Street in winter. The chairman of the village trustees, Elisha Bigelow, granted permission, telling them, "police the corners and you may race as long as you like." The first race was scheduled for the next Saturday afternoon. In preparation, a dozen men met in the office in Charles Darling's barn on Main Street and formed the "Lyndonville Driving Club", and all twelve—LeClerc, Ladd, Lee, Meginnis, Darling, Dr. D. R. Brown, Everett Ruggles, Frank Trefren, Austin Houghton, Mr. Perry, Peasley Randall, and Dutchy Lee—drove in that first day's races. In her *Vermont Life* article "Kendall Runs Again,"

Main Street Races, Lyndonville (*Charles LeClerc*)

Tennie Toussaint described the preparation for that first day and the event itself:

> . . . Austin Houghton . . . volunteered to scrape Main Street. . . . His offer was accepted and he proceeded to make a scraper of two old car sills from the Railroad shops.
>
> On Friday evening before the race about thirty men turned out to get the "track" ready for the next day. Houghton began to scrape the street and there were plenty of volunteers armed with snow-shovels to shovel out the driveways of residents where the "scraper" had filled them up. LeClerc and some helpers measured off the quarter-mile track with a tape, and Roger Ladd kept the count. . . .
>
> A big crowd turned out that cold snowy Saturday in December 1907, and the twelve men who formed the Driving Club started their horses. . . .
>
> The race was started with a red flag instead of a bell, and Aldis Barber was the first starter, and held that position for several years. Russell Griswold and Albert Ruggles were the judges and timers.
>
> All stores and shops in the village were closed at two o'clock, when

the races began, and continued the practice for years. In spite of the extensive preparations of the night before the "track" was still ankle deep with snow, and most of the racing gear was of the old Lyndon egg-shell sleigh model, then being made in Lyndon Corner, so not very fast time was clocked.

Everett Ruggles won the race at around a 2:38 or 40 clip much to everyone's surprise, including LeClerc (who came in second). Ruggles horse was a four-year-old mahogany-bay colt with black points, called C. E. R., out of "Rogene," and sired by Charles Darling's "Red Elm" . . . .

Everett and Albert Ruggles operated the Ruggles Brothers Meat Market in the village, and Everett had been peddling meat with C. E. R. on the meat-cart. . . . The horses who raced those first years led a double-life, on week-days they were just any old work horse, but on Saturdays—well, that was different.

During the next 50-plus years many names were added to the roster of the Driving Club. It continued to meet regularly on Thursday evening during the "season," when the chief business was arranging the program for the Saturday races. Main Street was not wide enough for three horses to race, so it was necessary to arrange the classes in pairs of comparable speed, with the win decided by the best two out of three heats. On many occasions four or five heats were needed to make a decision possible. The winner of Class A (the fastest) took on the winner of Class B, and the two losers were left to race each other. In general, this procedure was carried out to as many alphabetical listings as there were entries; the following Saturday's pairings were based on the results of the preceding week's races. The Driving Club continued to meet in Darling's barn until 1916, when the club rented a room in the Ruggles block that became something of a social center for the members. In 1920 they moved to the basement of the Hotel Lyndon and changed the meeting time to Friday evening.

The racing season depended largely on the weather. The Driving Club usually held its fall meeting and elected officers in late November, and the first Saturday race frequently occurred in late December—on occasion, on Christmas Day afternoon—but certainly took place by New Year's or soon after. Most often the season closed with major races held on Washington's Birthday, and the event was capped by a special banquet that evening. Usually 150 to 200 persons attended; there were nearly always visitors from neighboring communities, and a pleasing program of music and speeches was offered. The first of these banquets was held in Masonic Hall: oyster stew and its trimmings at 25¢ per plate! In later years, more formal banquets were held in the various halls of the community or rotated among the church dining rooms, with the women of the respective church serving the meal. Finally, they were held in hotels or were professionally catered.

In the first years the horses pulled Lyndon sleighs and, later, sulkies, and some years runners were attached to the sulkies. Various procedures were tried in preparing the track: sometimes workers laid down a six- or eight-inch bed of snow, sometimes they flooded the street to produce bare ice, and on occasion they covered the ice with a thin layer of snow; but scheduled races were run even if the track was covered with slush, mud, or water. In most seasons horses ran the quarter mile in the neighborhood of 30 to 32 seconds; the record of 28½ was made in 1934 by Angus Mack, owned by O. Harvey of Passumpsic, and equaled by E. A. Lawson's F.E.W. (*Faster Every Week*). Many felt that Angus Mack would have broken his record if he had not drowned in the windstorm of 1938.

Driving clubs were formed in Glover, Barton, Newport, and St. Johnsbury, and representatives often joined in the Lyndon Saturday races. They participated most often in the February 22 events, to which they were especially invited. On several occasions Lyndon horses were taken to Glover, Barton, or Newport to participate in racing events, and the drivers enjoyed the banquets that usually followed.

Although the races usually occurred on Saturday afternoons, they sometimes took place on other days. For a time in 1938, races were held Wednesday evening under the Main Street lights. During the 1940s some races were held at the fairgrounds, but they seemed less well supported, so the program drifted back to Main Street for the February 22 meet, and then for all the others. Throughout the years the community supported the races on Main Street. Newspaper reports frequently referred to the cold raw weather, but always noted

Lyndonville Creamery (*Pauline Connors*)

a generous turnout of spectators—often a thousand and in several instances 1500 to 2000, plus a goodly audience in the windows of the houses along the street.

To attract more attention in 1911, there was an automobile exhibit. Fifteen autos rolled down the track: three Mitchells, one Regal from the Goss Garage, three Buicks from the Union Garage, one Hupp from Wright's Garage—all from St. Johnsbury—and three Fords from the local Blodgett's Garage. In 1929 the races were part of a carnival, and the Glover Driving Club was specially invited. A morning parade featured over twenty teams of draft horses furnished by Lyman Brown, Will Brown, Charles Hoyt, Philo Lang, Ted Lawson, John Watkins, Lee Easterbrooks, Ira Hunter, the Allen brothers, Frank McClellan, A. W. Edmunds, the Lyndonville Creamery, A. E. Donahue, and W. Arthur Simpson; each team drew an attractive float depicting some phase of farm life. The Corner Garage presented the Reo Speed Wagon, and at the rear of the parade rode a number of youngsters on ponies. Philo Lang, in charge of the parade, received high praise for its excellence, particularly given the short notice on which he had organized it. At eleven o'clock there was a spirited tug-of-war in front of the Darling Inn between the railroad employees and men representing the town. At noon Miss Dorothy Cutting was crowned "Queen of the Carnival." The usual races occurred in the afternoon, followed by a saddle-horse race, a Studebaker footrace, and a tug-of-war between the men at the Corner Garage and the Creamery boys. The annual banquet was at the Darling Inn, and the Washington Ball was held in the new Corner Garage because the Music Hall had been damaged by the bursting of the water tanks—all this in the year when the Driving Club leaders were so discouraged they nearly gave up having any races at all.

Given the number of races held, it is little short of a miracle how few accidents occurred. The only really serious incident was not even the result of an accident: on January 23, 1940, George Prue (age sixty-one) dropped dead of a heart attack while trailing his sulky prior to driving a second heat. In 1935 George McShane's horse balked and fell, spilling McShane, and in 1938, when McShane was Driving Club president, he took another spill when the belly girt broke on the harness of his horse, letting the thills up into the air. In 1938 a Glover horse ran away, broke his sulky, and shook up Donald Beau (for many years a Lyndonville resident). In 1945 a couple of drivers, Harold Stone and Clifton Drew, were thoroughly soaked by spills while warming up their horses. In 1947 Dean McDowell of Sheffield was thrown from his sulky on to an automobile parked near the track. In 1948 Dale Roundy's sulky skidded on the icy track.

In 1940 Earle Brown awarded a couple of silver cups: one for the most consistent winner of the season, and one for the fastest horse at the Washington Birthday races. The Dr. Robert Burke Trophy for the fastest time by a pacer in the final day's events was established in 1948. Other gifts were awarded to honor the special contributions of a few people. In 1910 the Driving Club gave Charles Darling a loving cup six inches tall in appreciation of the many things he had done for the Club; in 1914 the group presented Frank Lynch with a gold-headed cane and George Macdonald with a silver cup and saucer in appreciation of their services as president and clerk, respectively; and in 1938 the club gave Charles M. Darling a loving cup inscribed "Presented by Darling Inn to Charles M. Darling—the grand man of harness racing 1938."

The races begun in December 1907 continued annually through 1956 with the exception of the one winter of 1918, during World War I. During World War II racing here was not affected because it qualified as "amateur" and did not involve motor transportation of the animals. This winter racing program brought publicity to Lyndon through several avenues: (1) It was recorded in 1937 in Fox Movietone pictures; (2) pictures appeared during World War II in the *London Times* and the European edition of *Stars and Stripes*; (3) in 1945 both *Life* magazine and the Associated Press took pictures; (4) the *Saturday Evening Post* of January 17, 1948, carried Lloyd Mann's "Snow Time Derby"; and (5) the 1949–50 winter issue of *Vermont Life* contained Tennie Toussaint's "Kendall Runs Again."

In several ways the races were unusual and perhaps even unique. Especially during the early years, many of the horses were no longer young: Kendall raced until he was twenty-four (he died at twenty-nine), Silver Direct (owned by Frank Carr and later by Norman Healey) was past thirty, Red Logan (owned by Donahue) and Harvest Queen were over twenty-five, and Nina Dillon (owned by Charles Darling) was twenty-three. Many of the drivers had also passed their youth: Charles Darling drove his last race at the age of eighty-six; Frank Carr drove in 1943 at seventy-eight; George Drew — precise age unknown — was certainly no longer young; and Herbert Rugg, who came from Lowell, Mass. many times to drive, was eighty-four in 1936. The races carried no purses; usually blue ribbons for first place, red for second, and white for third were given out as part of the Washington's Birthday banquet program. There were none of the trappings of the great race tracks: silks and fancy numbers were unknown, and for many years the horses were started by the ringing of a hand bell. Perhaps most astonishing, a main thoroughfare in the center of a community was closed to traffic each Saturday for eight or ten weeks without any protest from the community.

Chautauqua

THE CHAUTAUQUA MOVEMENT derived from an adult education program founded in Chautauqua, N.Y., in 1874. Organized commercially in 1912, the movement came to Lyndon in 1915, when the town became part of a six-community circuit with Saranac Lake and Plattsburgh, N.Y., Woodsville, N.H., and Hardwick and Montpelier, Vt. This circuit was organized by the Redpath Bureau, a Boston booking agency that had for years supplied performers to Lyndonville's Lecture Course (described in "Village Improvement Societies"). There were thirteen circuits in all, each possessing eight tents and maintaining eight crews; each of the six towns in the circuit had its own "crew"—ushers, scene shifters, maintenance men, and directors—sometimes numbering as many as twenty-five. These crews were usually young college men, or teachers—people with a free summer. R. N. Northrup of Scranton, Pa., had the reputation of being the ablest of the circuit superintendents, and Lyndon had the privilege of his services for several of its fifteen seasons.

Each community formed a citizens' sponsoring committee of at least fifty members who accepted responsibility for the minimum overall cost of the season's program. At least half the sum had to be in hand before the season's first event. In Lyndon this guarantee was $1500. A transferable ticket covering all programs of the six days cost $3, but the Lyndon committee was permitted to sell 750 advance tickets at $2.25 ($2 in the first year or two of the circuit). Tickets for individual programs were available at the door for a slightly higher price. Rarely was attendance at any program under 500, and 1200 was reported as the top.

A day or so before the series began, the big round brown tent (seating 800–1000 people) and the other physical equipment arrived, in the first years by train and later by truck. In Lyndonville the crew pitched the tent on C. M. Darling's meadow at the south end of Main

Street; his red barn nearby supplied dressing rooms for performers and storage for equipment. The performers, arranged in advance by the management, arrived daily and, after presenting their share of the week's program, moved on to the next community on the circuit. One of the most striking features of the week's programs was the intense, almost mechanical efficiency with which they were administered. The entertainment itself, however, was often lively and always varied: plays, operas, dramatic readings, vocal and instrumental performances, and lectures.

Throughout the years, Chautauqua week was one of the outstanding events of the year. Out-of-town people visited their friends and relatives, or neglected all kinds of tasks at home so as to be free to attend all the Chautauqua programs. In the first years there were three programs every day; in later years, however, the morning program was omitted and its cost added to the expenditure for the evening, when attendance was greatest. Perhaps the most important member of the staff of directors was the one in charge of the junior program, to which local young people usually provided assistance. When the weather permitted, much of it was conducted in Powers Park.

It was a matter of much satisfaction to the people of Lyndon that many of the entertainers repeated their appearances through the years of Chautauqua or had first appeared (and perhaps more than once) on the Lecture Course platforms of earlier years. Among these performers were the Ben Greet Players (giving Shakespeare plays), the Boston Opera Singers, Dr. Russell H. Conwell, Dr. S. Parker Cadman, Miss Katharine Ridgeway (reader), Edward Amherst Ott, Knight McGregor (Scotch-Canadian baritone), William Jennings Bryan and his daughter Ruth Bryan Owen, Judge Ben Lindsay, and Vierra's Hawaiians (instrumentalists and vocalists).

Whenever the Chautauqua program was so arranged that Sunday fell within its local calendar, the local Protestant churches canceled the morning worship services, and all the pastors and choirs cooperated with the Chautauqua superintendent in a union service in the tent. These were always well attended and greatly enjoyed by the community.

The gradual decline in attendance and final demise of circuit

Chautauqua, like that of the Lecture Course, was hastened by the development of motion pictures, radio, and television; by the rise of the automobile, which allowed people to travel further for entertainment; and by the onset of the Great Depression in 1929.

౭౦

Lyndon's Anniversaries

THE TOWN APPROPRIATED $1000 toward the expenses of observing the centennial anniversary of its first town meeting—July 4th, 1791. At the 1891 town meeting the selectmen were directed to appoint a committee of five to make the necessary arrangements for the occasion. Those appointed were E. W. Sanborn, D. S. Winter, W. E. Ranger, J. M. Pearl, and C. M. Chase; Chase later resigned and was replaced by J. W. Weeks. The general committee in turn appointed nine subcommittees involving about fifty persons, as follows: antiquarian room, decorations, horribles, modern trades, ancient trades, centennial companies (the last four being divisions of the parade), games, fife and drum corps, and fireworks.

The committee planned a program centered in Music Hall and the Grove in Lyndonville. Extending over two full days, it was attended by an estimated 8000 to 10,000 people. George N. Beals of Boston oversaw much of the decoration of the streets and of both public and private buildings; he began the process a full week in advance of the occasion, giving the whole community "a gala appearance never before worn."

The real celebration began with a concert Friday evening by Sherman's Military Band of Burlington and the Cecilian Quartette of St. Johnsbury. After a night of noise, there was a thirteen-gun salute at sunrise followed by the ringing of all the bells in town. Rain soon followed, and the downpour continued through the forenoon. In spite of it, a part of the parade formed and, though drenched, carried through its duties. Further efforts during the forenoon were abandoned, but when the rain stopped in the afternoon the participants whose displays had not been completely spoiled joined a parade representing more than fifty businesses or organizations.[7] The parade disbanded at the Grove, where many people had assembled, and here the addresses of the day were delivered. Walter E. Ranger, principal of Lyndon Institute, was presiding officer. C. M. Chase paid tribute to the founders of the town, Elwyn G. Campbell read a portion of the federal constitution, Wm. L. Quimby of St. Johnsbury, a son of Lyndon, spoke of Vermont's declaration of independence and its declaration of rights, the Hon. Albro J. Nichols related some of the events of the preceeding hundred years, the Hon. H. H. Powers retold the history of Vermont town meeting, and the governor of Vermont, Hon. Carroll S. Page, complimented the community on the excellence of the occasion.

On Saturday evening there was a concert in Music Hall by the Mahogany Quartette and Monarch Banjo and Guitar Club of St. Johnsbury, assisted by Sherman's Military Band, which "drew a packed house and created great enthusiasm." After the concert, Louis V. Green of Rutland supervised a display of fireworks from the Tuttle Company of Rutland which was described as of "great variety and first class in quality." During the evening events, Chinese lanterns hung in front of some buildings and across some streets, contributing to the festive appearance of the community.

The Sunday service in Music Hall, attended by about 1000 people, provided an appropriate ending to the centennial ceremonies. Sherman's Military Band opened the program, followed by a chorus under the direction of Professor J. H. Humphrey with Royal M. Howe at the piano. Then came the invocation by Rev. John Hoffman, a response by the chorus, a reading of Scripture by Rev. L. Dodd, a prayer by Rev. E. J. Beach, and further music by the band. Principal Ranger, again master of ceremonies, made brief comments on the significance of the occasion. Rev. John H. Hoffman (Peterboro, N.H.), a son of Lyndon, then delivered an address entitled "The Religious Life and Work of Lyndon for One Hundred Years" in which he traced the development of local churches and named many of the Lyndon youths who had made places for themselves in the religious life of other communities. Rev. J. C. Bodwell gave the final address. The exercises closed with singing by the chorus and a benediction by Reverend Nason.

At the 1898 town meeting the selectmen were instructed "to have prepared and published the proceedings of the Town's Centennial Celebration of 1891. The same to be sold to pay the expense of publishing, and a certain number to be deposited in the Town Clerk's Office."[8]

On September 4, 1909, the community observed the 100th anniversary of the construction of the meetinghouse by holding a day-long picnic at the site. During the forenoon several guides identified points of interest in the cemetery, at noon a picnic luncheon was held on the Common, and by 1:30 p.m. people had congregated in the town hall for a historical program arranged by Mrs. C. T. Walter. The presiding officer was Rev. J. W. Burgin. Mrs. Walter gave the "History of the Lyndon Town Meeting House." E. M. Campbell read "A Day in Church in 1840," written by Mrs. Curtis Stevens; the Lyndon Methodist Choir sang a hymn; and E. M. Campbell read "Early Hotels," written by Mrs. E. B. Chase. There followed a prayer by Rev. E. G. French, remarks by Rev. W. H. Lyster, an original 100-line poem entitled "Centennial" by Rev. W. C. Clark, and a recitation by Mr. Pillsbury. The occasion closed with the audience singing "Auld Lang Syne."

In 1941 the 150th anniversary of the first town meeting was observed as part of the annual town meeting day. The organizing committee, appointed by the selectmen, consisted of W. C. Conner, Mrs. Daisy Baldwin, H. G. Shonyo, and P. R. Griswold. The business of town meeting was transacted in the forenoon; after the noon recess the historical program began with a selection of the Lyndon Institute orchestra under the direction of Miss Ruby Blaine. John B. Chase related historical facts and told stories concerning early Lyndon, P. R. Griswold gave the history of the town house, and Rev. A. Ritchie Lowe of Johnson reviewed the life of Ethan Allen.

Postscript

NUMEROUS DAYS HAVE BEEN SPENT in a futile effort to locate the original home of Benjamin Sanborn. Two sites seemed to offer the most promise.

One set of circumstantial evidence comes from records of 1890. On August 1, of that year the railroad company sold to Mrs. C. S. LeBourveau, Jr., a one-acre tract of land on Center Street east from West Street (now Park Avenue), "together with the buildings thereon."[1] On September 3 the railroad sold Mrs. LeBourveau an additional 63 feet on West Street extending north from her earlier purchase; this piece extended 10 rods east from West Street. On September 4, 1891, Mrs. LeBourveau purchased from N. A. McDonald a 54-foot lot facing Center Street and lying to the east of her previous purchase.[2]

The July 10, 1890, issue of the *St. Johnsbury Republican* reported that Stephen Eastman had "purchased from C. S. LeBourveau one of the barns on the old *Sanborn place* and moved it to his lot as a carriage house" (italics added). The August 28, 1890, issue of the same paper added that "E. H. Stone was in the place last week moving the building from the lot recently purchased by Mrs. C. S. LeBourveau, Jr., of the Railroad Company."

On September 2, 1890, Editor Charles Chase reported in the *Vermont Union* that C. P. Chase "has bought the Hume House, moved it, and is putting it in repair." (The Hume house is at 9 Park Avenue and was for long years occupied by Mr. and Mrs. N. A. Norton). When Editor Chase reported (August 22, 1890) the beginning of construction of the LeBourveau home, he referred to it as on the *old*

Sanborn site. An intensive search of the Lyndon land records failed to justify calling this building "the Hume House" (Miss Susie Hume taught in the public school for some years), nor did it uncover any evidence of Sanborn habitation. Were the references merely casual and figurative?

The second lead is found in 1868 records. On February 1 of that year the railroad company sold to one of its engineers, Henry Mower, a one-half acre tract of land on Center Street, "it being the same land deeded by I. W. Sanborn to Wm. H. Hoyt June 12, 1866."[3] Hoyt had conveyed this land and "the buildings thereon" to the company by a deed of November 10, 1866.[4] The description of the land notes that it was "bounded northerly and easterly by land formerly owned by Benjamin Sanborn, southerly by the highway." The large covered bridge that was moved in 1960 to cross the river back of the Lynburke Motel on North Main Street was always known as the Sanborn Bridge. The western boundary of the land sold to Hoyt was the Passumpsic River; it excluded the Sanborn meadow lying on the south side of the highway.

In my childhood, Henry Mower, the grandfather of two of my schoolmates and a personal friend of my own grandfather, lived in a house, now destroyed, that stood in front of where Dr. Howe has built his house; that is, on the top of the rise of ground a couple hundred feet west of the junction of Center Street and Park Avenue. Therefore, taking into consideration the above deeds, it is possible that the house next to the river was the home of Mr. and Mrs. Benjamin Sanborn. Elden Hovey owned this house for many years; when he attempted to make some repairs, he found that the house's planks proved it to be very old. Some have wondered if this house were built to fulfill "settling duty." Although its measurements are consistent with that view, it is apparently located within Right 30; and if that is the case, William Rhodes gave the forty-acre "setling duty grant" to William Fisher, who built his home in the northern part of Lyndon Center.

Neither of these "leads" bore conclusive evidence, nor was it possible to find any succession of deeds or other evidence to provide an unquestionable identification of any other site. It is the hope of this writer that someone will be interested in continuing this quest, building on this beginning, and finally be successful.

Notes

PREFACE

1. *A Gazetteer of the State of Vermont, containing a brief general view of the state, & historical and topographical description of all the counties, towns, rivers, &c together with a map and several other engravings* (Montpelier: Zadock Thompson and E. P. Walton, 1824).

2. *History of Vermont, Natural, Civil, and Statistical* (Burlington: Chauncey Goodrich, 1842).

3. *A Gazetteer of Vermont, containing descriptions of all the counties, towns, and districts in the state and of principal mountains, rivers and waterfalls, harbors, islands and curious places, to which are added statistical accounts of its agriculture, commerce, and manufactures with a great variety of other useful information* (Boston: Tappan, Whittemore, and Mason, 1849).

4. Town Records, Minutes III, pp. 31–34, 40–41 (March 2, 1852). The original of this report is among the MSS of Mrs. Mathewson from the Sanborn Papers, handwritten and signed by Roberts, Houghton, and Cahoon. Also among those papers is the original of the acknowledgment from Reverend Greenleaf. Reverend Greenleaf had been a summer supply pastor in the Congregational Church at Lyndon in 1841–43 while vacationing in Lyndon and living at the home of Jude Kimball.

5. Hamilton Child, *Gazetteer of Caledonia and Essex Counties, Vermont, 1764–1887* Syracuse, N.Y.: Syracuse Journal Company, 1887.

6. A shed-chamber was usually a room over the kitchen.

7. Some of these documents were scraps 1½ x 3 inches or smaller in size, while others were several legal-size pages in length.

8. Reverend Tabor's report of having performed the marriage ceremony of this writer's grandparents was on one of the smallest of these scraps of paper, but its entry in the town records has not been found.

9. One of these is the sexton's report noted above.

10. His son and successor, John B . Chase, told this writer that his father's interest in things historical developed from his being asked to present the history of the Congregational Church at Lyndon on the occasion of the observance of its seventy-fifth anniversary.

CHAPTER II

1. See Matt Bushnell Jones, *Vermont in the Making, 1750–1777* (Cambridge, Mass., 1939); and Allan R. Raymond, "Benning Wentworth's Claims in the New Hampshire–New York Controversy: A Case of Twenty-Twenty Hindsight," *Vermont History* 41, no. 1 (Winter 1975): 20–43.

On January 31, 1770, a petition from Lawrence Kortright, Peter Van Schaact, John Woods, Hubert Van Wagenen, and thirty-two associates requested a patent of 36,000 acres from Cadwalder Colden, governor of New York, to be the township of "Besborough." This tract must have included a large part of what later became the towns of Lyndon and St. Johnsbury. *State Papers of Vermont*, VII, "New York Land Patents, 1688–1786," pp. 116–20(ed. Mary Greene Nye).

2. The choice of this name proved unfortunate as the western lands, along the Susquehanna River, that were claimed by Connecticut were designated "New Connecticut." Therefore, the name "Vermont" was soon used universally, though it was not actually adopted until the meeting in Windsor in June 1777.

3. Resolutions passed by Congress in June 1780 in condemnation of the Vermonters' declaration of independence were interpreted by Governor Chittenden and his Council as constituting in reality a declaration of war. Consequently, the October 1780 General Assembly put Vermont on a war footing.

4. Perhaps the most active of these agents were Ira Allen, Elisha Payne, Jonas Fay, and Abel Curtis. Evidence can be found in the James Madison *Papers*, in the *Letters of the Members of the Continental Congress*, and in the *Journals of the Continental Congress*, that Jonathan Arnold was more than casually interested in Vermont even while he was the representative of Rhode Island in Congress.

The following bill provides proof of his activity after the end of his term of service to Rhode Island (1782–84):

> 1789 August   To my time 13 days in the service of the State as Agent to
>   the Congress of the United States   10£ 6s 10d
> Errors excepted
> [notation at the bottom of the bill]
> "Paid Jan. 15, 1791"

MMS Vermont State Papers, Old Series, Treasurers, p. 292, Office of the Secretary of State, a bill from Jonathan Arnold. See also *State Papers of Vermont*, III, "Journals and Proceedings of the General Assembly, 1781–83," II, pp. 81, 106.

5. R. C. Benton, *Vermont Settlers and New York Speculators*, p. 143.

6. Vermont Historical Society *Collections*, I, p. 393.

7. E. T. Walton, ed. *Records of the Governor and Council of the State of Vermont*, II, p. 63. A resolution passed October 14, 1780, provided "a Committee of Five to join a Committee from the Council . . . to take into consideration the situation of ungranted lands within this State which can be settled, and the several petitions filed in the Secretary's office praying for grants of such ungranted lands: and

report their opinion what lands can be granted, and *what persons will most conduce to the welfare of this State to have such grants. . . ."* (emphasis added).

8. Many petitions have survived and been published in *State Papers of Vermont*, V, "Petitions for Grants of Land, 1778–1811" (1939), ed. Mary Greene Nye. Lyndon is not among these, however. The speculative nature of the project is emphasized by the fact that Daniel Cahoon, Sr., was the only proprietor to reside in the town for any length of time (1793–1811). Asa Kimball lived here perhaps three years, then moved to Barton, where he also had land.

9. Walter H. Crockett, ed., *State Papers of Vermont*, III, "Journals and Proceedings of the General Assembly," I, p. 149.

10. E. T. Walton ed., *Records of the Governor and Council of the State of Vermont*, II, p. 50. It is interesting to note that this was a "floating grant"; that is, it was to include the Great Falls even if a change of location was necessary.

11. Franklin H. Dewart, ed., *State Papers of Vermont*, II, "Charters Granted by the State of Vermont, p. 129ff. It has not been possible to identify all the men named in the charter as proprietors. Some were certainly distinguished citizens. Many had been officers in the Revolutionary army, and the list also included the current governors of both Rhode Island and Vermont, the president and several trustees of Rhode Island College (later Brown University), two former lieutenant governors of Rhode Island, professional men, and merchants. Several names also appear on lists of men involved in the Winchester Furnace venture. Since the names of several Lyndon proprietors appear among the names of proprietors of other towns, they must have possessed money. See the appendix for the list of proprietors.

12. MSS Proprietors of the Town of Lyndon, Book of Reccord, 1781 (hereafter cited as Proprietors' Book of Reccord). This original manuscript record book is in the possession of the Lyndon town clerk. It contains convincing evidence that these multiple rights were a matter of purchase, thus refuting the oft-repeated opinion that they were a gift, a reward for service in the American Revolution. Of the six men who acquired multiple rights only Jonathan Arnold had rendered war service. The records show that ex-soldiers were permitted a discount of 1£ 10s in their payments per right.

13. This date is *not* in error; see the charter.

14. Proprietors' Book of Reccord. Three meetings were held: January 1 and 2, 1781, August 2, 1781, and February 2, 1784. The actions taken are carefully recorded in the MSS, including the result of the drawing for the rights. The volume also contains a treasurer's record of the obligations and their fulfillment by each proprietor. From some parenthetical entries it appears that a "day book" existed; if it were now available perhaps it would clarify some other entries.

15. This threat seems to have been rather pointless, since the date of the Charter is November 20, 1780, and contains the full fifty-three names; or was it written later and back-dated?

16. Daniel Cahoon became the third member of the committee.

17. It is well established tradition that they climbed Prospect Hill and sited what appeared to them a most desirable spot. The tract was very heavily wooded. The Great and Little Falls promised generous waterpower. Assurance of rich farmlands was given by the two rolling valleys created by the five streams. These water systems came together not far north of the falls to form the fluid corkscrew, the Passumpsic River.

18. The committee designated the college and county grammar school rights on the northeast corner of the town. The members chose to divide each of the other three rights into three parts rather than designating a single right to each of the other three purposes. Because of the relation of the Little Falls to the town boundaries, two rights were reserved bounded by rights 12, 14, 15, 16, 11, 4, 3, and 2. The mill right occupied one-third of one of these rights and two-thirds of the other, so school lot 1 was assigned the remaining one-third, with the minister and church lots occupying the two-thirds of the other right. lot 2 of school, church, and minister is bounded by rights 31, 34, 32, and 21; lot 3 of school, church, and minister is bounded by rights 50, 55, 49, and 43.

So far as this writer knows, no school building has ever been located on any of the so-called school lots except that at Red Village; likewise, neither has a church been built on a church lot. For some years the Methodist parsonage at Lyndon Corner was located on the so-called minister lease land.

19. Proprietors' Book of Reccord, p. 7. It is interesting to note that there was only one drawing of Lyndon lands, whereas in many towns there were several drawings, the process in some cases extending over a period of years. In some townships, the pasturage, wood lands, and tillage were held "in common" for several years before being divided among the respective proprietors.

20. In both instances these amounts appear to be residual balances due after each man had advanced money for obligations related to the settlement of the township. Therefore it would not appear that these sums could be considered as the full amount paid to either of them.

21. No evidence has been found that this task was performed.

22. Capt. James Monro paid 8£ 10s for his right. In one place he is referred to as "mariner," so his title was probably not related to any Revolutionary War service. The name of William Arnold appears in the charter list and in the list in the Proprietors' Book of Reccord of those to whom rights were drawn on August 2, 1781, but it does not appear in Winsor's accounts. Why?

23. Until after 1925 there has always been at least one, and sometimes two, mills on this site, near the north end of the bridge at the west end of York Street. The mills have been known by various names, including Chamberlin—the most persistent—Paris, Whitcomb, and Nadeau.

24. Town Record Deed Book A, pp. 25–26 (March 7, 1796), p. 34 (March 6, 1797). These mills appear to have already been begun before this action was

taken, perhaps in fulfillment of the Cahoon agreement with the proprietors, as recorded on p. 9 of the Proprietors' Book of Reccord.

25. In recent years this has been confused with the original log house built in 1788 by Daniel Cahoon, Jr. on the west side of the Passumpsic. The descendants of the Cahoon family who still occupy it (1975) believe construction of the residence was begun by Daniel Sr. about 1802 and finished by his son William in the neighborhood of 1825.

CHAPTER III

1. Surveyor General File, I, part I, p. 81, Office of the Secretary of State of Vermont. When the town survey was completed the north and south boundaries were 6½ miles, and the east and west boundaries 6¼ miles in length; there were also numerous variations in boundaries of the individual rights, a fact readily apparent from careful examination of the town map. Since Lyndon was surveyed before the neighboring towns, it is symmetrical whereas many of the others are not.

Surveyor's Field Book of Lyndon 1789, Office of the Secretary of State of Vermont (MMS notes of the surveyor.) Whitelaw became deputy to Surveyor-General Ira Allen in 1783, and the second surveyor-general of the state in 1794.

2. Orange County Land Records (Chelsea, Vt.), Book C, p. 118, March 31, 1788. Both men were then residents in Winchester, Cheshire County, N.H. The big island at the foot of the Great Falls was excluded from this sale as it had been sold to Jonathan Arnold on August 2, 1782.

3. Speaking with this writer about the cellar hole, as he saw it in his youth, John Chase said it was about 100 yards north of the St. Johnsbury–Lyndon line on the east side of the highway as it then existed. In "J. B. C. Rambling Paragraphs" in the *Vermont Union Journal* of January 15, 1941, he reported that a 100 years after the Davis tansy bed was planted, remnants of it still were visible.

4. The identity of the persons accepting "settling duty" responsibilities on about half the rights of the town has been established, as shown by Table I facing p. 8. Though Jonathan Arnold never lived in town, in addition to his own five rights (2, 7, 45, 53, and 60) he assumed "settling duty" for rights 6, 9, 11, 21, 22, 43. Likewise Lyndon Arnold, a nonresident took on settling duties for rights 41 and 42, and Daniel Reniff, resident, for rights 24, 29, 31, and 35.

5. *First Census of the United States*, "1790 Heads of Families, Vermont," p. 31.

6. *State Papers of Vermont*, IX "General Petitions, 1788–92," pp. 122–23 (petition filed October 21, 1789).

7. Vermont Historical Society Library, Whitelaw MMS.

8. *State Papers of Vermont*, I, p. 9 and footnote.

9. There is no date on the map, but Daniel Cahoon, Jr., was town clerk and

selectman from 1791 to June 11, 1793, and Daniel Cahoon, Sr., held both offices from 1793 to 1804.

10. Each of these roads would have connected with the road from St. Johnsbury, for there is excellent reason to believe that the road from the south came into Lyndon through Route 5 and not, as at present, through Route 3.

11. The writer was told in the early 1970s this road could be traced in many places along the crest of these hills, and that there were still evidences of old homes alongside.

12. Later known as Sanborn Hill, Tuttle Hill, Telephone Hill, Harris Hill, and, later still, as Vail Hill.

13. Usually the potash was converted to pearlash because it was more valuable and a great deal lighter for transport; nearly all was exported. Dorothy Canfield Fisher in *Vermont Tradition* makes several interesting comments about this trade: "In 1791 a thousand tons of potash were sent out of Vermont" (p. 163). ". . . in 1770 potash to the value of $290,000 was exported" (p. 168). By the year 1790 the sum "has risen to the value of $840,000" (p. 168). "It took a good deal of time to transform a big elm tree into five tons of wood, then burn the wood into ashes, then to extract lye from the ashes and thence, by evaporation, to produce thirty-nine pounds of potash" (p. 171). "By 1807 the value of exported potash and pearlash made from wood ashes was $1,490,000. In 1810 (after removal of the embargo) the value was $1,579,000. But in 1813 it slid down to $204,000 and thereafter slid to zero." (p. 183). The chief use of potash and pearlash was in the "finishing" of wool; the major markets were, in succession, Florence (Italy), the Low Countries, and England. Accounts in Lyndon have been found showing that $4 or $5 a hundredweight or $100 to $120 per ton were considered good prices.

14. John Johnson is reputed to have been the first to send teams to Boston sometime before 1800. Using two yoke of oxen, he allowed a month for the trip.

15. This was located on the southwest corner of what is now Main and York Street, Lyndon Corner. It was reputed by some to have been the first frame house in town. Fletcher took a lease on the building to secure payment for his work.

16. *Vermont Union*, January 25, 1867: "In the winter of 1866–67 . . . G. H. and J. M. Weeks shipped from the station at Lyndon Corner, 60 carloads of potatoes. Allowing 350 bushels to the car, it made 21,000 bushels of potatoes purchased in this section. . . ."

17. *Vermont Union*, September 3, 1873: "Mrs. Jonathan Hunter has tested the relative qualities of the Early Rose and the Brooks Seedling potatoes. From 60 pounds of Early Rose she gets seven pounds of starch and from 25 pounds of the white seedlings she gets 3½ pounds of starch, showing the seedlings to be much superior."

18. In 1964 the late Dale Roundy told the writer that he had leveled off several

potato pits on his farm that would have held 15,000 to 20,000 bushels of potatoes. These would have been near the Whipple starch factory.

19. One of the men engaged in the Winchester Furnace venture, as well as one of the original proprietors of Lyndon, drawing Right 52.

20. This site later was, in succession, the residence of Isaac Fletcher, Gen. E. B. Chase, L. K. Quimby, Dr. A. S. Haskins, Dr. E. K. Merley, and Drury Vinton.

21. Town Record Deed Book C, p. 385; Book D, pp. 12–15. Bounds were set again in 1868 and 1898.

22. This stream has been known at different times as "The Branch," "South Branch," "Wheelock Branch," and "West Brook."

23. Town Records, Minutes I, p. 34 (March 6, 1797).

24. This was the first schoolhouse in Lyndon Corner (District 1). It burned in 1837 and was replaced by the "West School," which was built beside the Congregational Church farther east on York Street.

25. This was always known as the "New Mill." In 1880 an extensive addition was made.

26. This partnership lasted thirty-six years, four months, and five days, ending only with Eaton's death.

27. Eaton had previously bought out J. F. Thompson, who had built his shop at the southeast corner of Elm and Depot streets. Editor Chase reported, long years after the event, that Captain Thompson's was the first business sign hung (1868) in the New Village.

28. Raeia Harris and Elizabeth Harris Brown, "Square Pegs in Round Holes," *Vermont Life VIII*, no. 1 (Autumn 1953): 54–57.

29. Purchased from Abel A. Pierce and Jenny H. Applebee for $2000 in August 1876.

30. This was eventually acquired by Mr. and Mrs. L. D. Hall as a residence; it was burned August 24, 1931. For the last few years the Halls had entertained summer boarders, and the place had been known as "The Wilders."

31. This must have conveyed more than this one right, as the original total acreage in a right was $329\frac{1}{7}$ acres, and of this, $9\frac{1}{7}$ acres were reserved for roads and highways and so could not have been sold.

32. Town Records, Minutes I, p. 245, from a special town meeting held on February 13, 1812: "Abel Carpenter chosen moderator, immediately voted to adjourn to the Marsh Co. store." One wonders if the unheated meetinghouse was too cold for comfort.

33. Late in 1975 this writer learned there was once a coffin factory and a silversmith located in Lyndon Center, but no further information has been available.

34. Town Records, Minutes II, p. 78. The original manuscript from which this was copied into the Town Records is among the Sanborn Papers of Mrs. Mathewson.

35. No date has been found for its building, but the Walling map of 1858 shows

it in this place; a deed of 1853 appears to cover a three-acre piece of land in this location.

36. The deed to the land is dated March 19, 1849; from its text it is evident that the chapel had already been constructed.

37. For more information on the Angel Gabriel, see "The Universalist Church."

38. A proud example was Henry Mower's black gelding, making one half mile in 1:15 and a full mile in 2:36.

39. Several liens were placed on it, and legal proceedings were begun against H. M. Nichols for collection of wages for work done in building it. These actions are a matter of record in the town deed books under various dates of 1857 and 1858.

40. The row of large elms cut during the summer of 1971 from the back yards of the houses along Broad Street were in a direct line with the west side of the wider street near the present post office and the bank, thus making it evident the trees had been the west boundary of the street in 1869.

41. On several occasions this writer heard John B. Chase quote his father, Editor Charles M. Chase, as having made this statement. It also appears in the *Vermont Union* of January 11, 1895, in an item of reminiscent character.

42. *Vermont Union*, November 16, 1866.

43. The *Vermont Union*, August 12, 1870, reported that the company had purchased a new spring from Cyrus Newcomb, paying $200 for it.

44. *Vermont Union*, July 31, 1868.

45. Perry's house was sold to Emmons Raymond, who in turn sold to S. S. Thompson; it passed via his estate to D. I. Grapes.

Hubbard Hastings sold his house to Robert Pettigrew. After his death it was sold to his daughter, Mrs. Julia Pettigrew Hutchins. She sold it to W. I. Powers, who willed it to his daughter, Mrs. Theia Powers Watson.

Horace Alden's house passed from the hands of Jeremy Pearl to his daughter, Ida, who sold to Dr. A. N. Leonard.

46. This was one of the 1971 victims of Dutch elm disease. After its death the curbing and park were removed, and the space was paved over to provide parking space.

47. These came from the pen of Franklin Horatio Smith, who had a clothing store in the Mathewson block in the early 1880s.

48. President Keyes resigned in 1870 and was succeeded by Emmons Raymond; in 1871 Superintendent Perry resigned. Though Harley Folsom, a native son, was appointed superintendent of the division in 1875, his letter books show that he functioned according to the dictates of the officials in Boston. By 1876 the last of the members of the board of directors from this area had vanished, even though S. S. Thompson came onto the board in 1879 for a short time. In 1881 Hubbard Hastings, the cashier, resigned.

49. The five largest community lists were Burlington, thirty-eight; Barre, thirty-two; Rutland and Brattleboro, twenty-seven each; and St. Johnsbury, eighteen.

50. In 1964 for the first time the aluminum crown of red and blue electric bulbs was suspended over Depot Street, taking the place of the strings of multicolored lights that had been used for some years. The crèche on the lawn of the library first appeared in the 1950s. Both the crown and crèche were the work of Paul Aubin.

51. According to Robert Lawson, his parents and their three children arrived on July 4, 1923, from Newport after staying overnight in Barton. They brought thirty-six cows, a bull calf, two horses, and an express wagon. Bob celebrated his second birthday on the way.

CHAPTER IV

1. Lyndon was chartered as part of Orange County. Caledonia County was incorporated in 1792; by an act passed October 27, 1795, "the present jurisdiction" of Orange County was continued until December 1, 1796.

2. On town highway 31, on the north side of the rise south of the bridge across Miller's Run, a granite marker was set in 1906. In a recess in the north side of the marker, a plate bears this inscription: "Here stood the house of Daniel Reniff where was held the First Town Meeting in Lyndon July 4, 1791 L. B. Harris 1906." The marker was made and set by Harris. As late as 1977 the bounds of the Reniff house were still discernible.

3. Elder Hines and Daniel Cahoon remained moderator and clerk, respectively, until 1793. Daniel Cahoon, Sr., arrived in town with his family about a month before the death of his son, Daniel Jr.; thus, it is not strange that he should follow his son in his many public responsibilities. Daniel Jr. was the first incumbent in the following offices, and continued in them until his death on June 11, 1793; town clerk, selectman, lister, justice of the peace, and representative from the town. Daniel Sr. served as town clerk the next fourteen and one half years, selectman the next ten and one half years, lister the next nine years, and town representative the next eight years.

4. In 1791 twelve men subscribed 1£ 16s 6d to purchase needed record books; in 1801 Nathaniel Jenks gave his personal note to Capt. Job Sheldon for part of his six-acre "gift" to the town.

5. The first evidence found of a bond for the constable and collector was in 1815. The next year the bond was $1000, and each bondsman was liable not only for his equal share but for the full amount of the bond. The constable was Samuel Hoit, and his bondsmen were Joel Ross, James Sherman, William McGaffey, Nathan Weeks, and Elijah Graves. This bond is among Mrs. Mathewson's Sanborn Papers.

6. When this money was spent and the record books acquired is unknown, but it is interesting to note that the minutes of the first nine town meetings were not recorded until 1795. Daniel Cahoon, Jr., the first town clerk, died in 1793, so these must have been recorded by his father, Daniel Cahoon, Sr., the second town clerk.

7. In his diary Sanborn noted that town meeting was held on March 2, 1858, but did not mention that he was elected town clerk. His entry for the next day includes "Today moved the safe and books belonging to the Town Clerk's Office." Although it does not state where he moved them. The entry for February 16, 1858, notes his twenty-fifth birthday.

8. *Vermont Union*, May 20, 1904, Lyndonville items: "The town has leased for ten years the store in the John L. Norris block [Mathewson Block] formerly occupied by G. F. Wheeler. At the rear of the building and connected with the office, Mr. Norris will build a fireproof vault, 8 x 10 and 7 ft. high. The vault will have walls 19 inches thick, double walls 8 inches thick, with an air space of three inches. The office will be thoroughly repaired, a steel ceiling put up, and the rooms otherwise put into first class condition.

9. *Vermont Union*, January 18, 1867.

10. Josiah Henry Benton L.L.D., *Warning Out in New England 1656–1817* (Boston: W. B. Clarke Co., 1911); Mrs. Winifred L. Holman, quoted by the late Dr. Arthur Peach in *Vermont History* XXXIV, no. 1, p. 93; Katherine E. Conlin, "Warning Out in Windsor 1779–1817," *Vermont History* XXIII, no. 3, pp. 244–47; Louis A. Lamoureaux, "Victory in St. Johnsbury," *Vermont History* XXII, no. 4, p. 56 — he cites the Fairbanks family as one warned out of town.

11. Town Records, Minutes I, pp. 184–85, March 14, 1808.

12. *Vermont Union*, February 17, 1899.

13. For the village's boundaries, see "The Settlement of the Town: Lyndon Center," p. 34.

14. Records of the General Assembly of Vermont, 14th biennial session, pp. 235–39.

15. Acts of General Assembly, 1900, p. 216, approved November 24, 1900.

16. Acts of General Assembly, 1935, p. 299, approved February 14, 1935.

17. Village Charter, Section 8.

18. Town Records, Minutes V. pp. 48–50.

19. *Vermont Union*, June 12, 1896.

20. It is not clear how the legislature was involved in this decision.

CHAPTER V

1. Town Records, Minutes I, p. 143.

2. Sanborn Papers.

3. Sanborn Papers.

4. Among the Sanborn Papers of Mrs. Grace Mathewson. There were other similar bonds in her collection.

5. Sanborn Papers.

6. Sanborn Papers.

7. Sanborn Papers. Also in possession of Robert F. Pierce, Sr.

8. Town Records, Minutes II, pp. 66–67.

9. Town Records, Minutes II, p. 94.

10. Town Records, Minutes II, p. 203.

11. Sanborn Papers, Mrs. G. H. Mathewson.

12. *Vermont Union*, March 5, 1875.

13. From the Sanborn Papers we learn that the rates allowed for labor in 1800 were 66¢ per day. In 1824 the price of labor was 10¢ per hour from May 1, to July 1, and 7¢ per hour the rest of the year. Oxen cost 67¢ per day until July 1, and 50¢ thereafter; a cart was 28¢ a day, a plow 25¢, an ox shovel 34¢. In 1825 $1.25 per day. In 1881 a two-horse team, equipped, cost $1.50 per day, a one-horse team $1.00 per day; a two-ox team with cart or plow was $1.50 per day.

14. In the early 1900s there were at least twenty-eight public covered bridges in Lyndon.

15. The 1928 Lyndon Town Report lists the road commissioners "Flood Account" as totaling $121,520.82.

16. The 1923 inventory of town tools showed eight snow rollers valued at $480.

17. Custom of putting snow on bridges for use of winter sleds.

18. In contrast to many neighboring towns, neither tangible nor legendary evidence indicates the existence of any private cemeteries within the limits of the town of Lyndon. In a mortgage deed of Silas Gaskell to Daniel Quimby (Town Record Deed Book G, p. 67, January 16, 1841), a part of the northern boundary of the tract covered by the deed is given as "the burying ground"; this could well have been the "Sutton South Ridge" cemetery, which is located on the south line of Sutton and so on the north line of Lyndon, on the west side of the "County Road." It is possible that citizens of Lyndon residing on Pudding Hill were buried there. No known burial list has survived, however. Most of the graves are unmarked, and most of the remaining grave markers have been vandalized.

19. In the *Vermont Union* of July 23, 1897, Editor Chase reported that "we had a short call last week from an old resident of Lyndon Corner, way back in 1830 and before, G. M. Ramsdell now 77 years old." Chase then recounted some of Ramsdell's reminiscences, among them the following: "Mr. Ramsdell remembers distinctly the original Lyndon Burying Ground, on the flat half acre, south of the Cahoon Cabin, marks of a few graves being still seen north of the opening leading to the Wilder Pulp Mill [now Lyndonville Electric Plant]. He remembers in 1829 of seeing Abram Houghton and Gen. William Cahoon, the Congressman, excavate the remains of the first settler Daniel Cahoon [brother of Gen. Cahoon], and take them to the Lyndon Centre Cemetery."

20. Town Records, Minutes I, p. 206.

21. The subscription list is headed with this statement: "To perpetuate the memory and virtues of that noble band, whose efforts contributed to secure to us the blessings of civil, political, and religious liberty and to whom, under Providence,

we are chiefly indebted for our prosperity and happiness and the very means, even, which now enable us to express such testimonial of our warmest gratitude; to rescue from oblivion the names of those heroes of the Revolution, whose remains are now sleeping, ingloriously, in our church-yard, in graves unmarked by even headstone or slab, we desire to erect an appropriate monument in the common burying at Lyndon Center. Gratitude to them prompts it—respect to ourselves demands it—duty to posterity recognizes it and patriotism sanctions it. For the accomplishment of such purpose, therefore, we the subscribers, mutually promise each other to pay on demand to such committee as shall be appointed by ourselves, the sums annexed to our several names."

22. Town Records, Minutes II, pp. 241–43.

23. *Vermont Union*, November 20, 1874: "The Bullock boys are building a hearse house west of the school house. The Town purchased 40 feet front of land, paying $40.00 for the site, and pay $57.50 for doing the work on the house." The building was 32 x 22 feet.

24. 1828, selectmen; 1843, Silas Houghton, Stephen McGaffey, and Otis Evans; 1844, Job Randall, Stephen McGaffey, and William McGaffey; 1845, Edw. S. Mattocks, A. J. Willard, and William McGaffey; 1851, the sexton.

25. Thanks to Mrs. Mathewson's Sanborn Papers, James McGaffey's MMS report as sexton has survived (1852). He reported that in accordance with action at the 1851 town meeting he had secured a book in which he had put a plan of the burying ground. The old part had been laid out in 53 ranges varying from 7 to 18 feet, and the new part had been divided into lots 13 by 18 feet, numbered from 1 to 180. He reported that there were 198 graves without stones, markers, or other identification. In Range 37 was the stone of Eunice, wife of Moses Evans, a Revolutionary soldier. An unmarked grave nearby McGaffey assumed to be the burial place of Moses. So far as possible, McGaffey also recorded in this book the names of all persons buried, age at death, and grave location.

26. Until at least well into the 20th century, this was known locally as "Reservoir Hill."

27. Town Records, Minutes IV, pp. 138–40.

28. In the Sanborn Papers among the Mathewson MSS is an undated, fragile scrap about 3¼ x 4 inches in size, with writing in several directions: "Dementions of a Pound Erected at the Centre of Lyndon s^d Pound to be 27 feet Square same height as the old one Post and Sills of E8 Inches square plates the same Railing to be Spaced the Same as the old one Braced with 2 Braces at Each corner accept the Dore corner and that to have one With a Suitable gate or Dore hung and fit for use the Same to be Done in a workmanlike Manner thirty-two of the old Rails to be considered fit to go into the new one With suitable Stone under Each Post."

Written across the paper in the opposite direction is this: "Dementions of A pound to be erected at the Centre of Lyndon to be twenty-eight feet square the same hight as the old one Posts ten inches square."

On the reverse is the notation "the Building the Pound sold at Public Auction and struked off to David McGaffey at Twelve Dollars and to be Completed by the twentieth of October next. [Signed] "A Carpenter vendue master"

29. *Vermont Union*, December 27, 1895.

30. The village report of 1895 contains an extensive report from the water commissioners describing in some detail the efforts to create a water system to meet the needs of a community of 4000 people "during the forseeable future."

31. While working here, these men lived in temporary tent shelters on the north side of the Wheelock Road, a little north of the present exit from I-91. Ralph and Howard Allen supplied part of their meat by giving them all the woodchucks they could kill, as Howard told the story seventy-five years later.

32. Lyndonville Water Works adopted water rates, rules, and regulations September 13, 1895.

33. The water commissioners were C. B. Grapes, R. F. Pierce, and P. F. Baraw.

34. This agreement was nullified by the enlargement of the water system through the purchase of the Birchard property.

35. At this time the Mathewson, Chandler, and Woodworth water systems were retired to a "standby" status. The Copeland system continues to supply the Powers Park swimming pool. The East Street artesian well pump is activated weekly, and so is available if needed.

36. According to the *Vermont Union* of August 1, 1884, subscribers were Robert Pettigrew, $200; H. M. Pearl, $200; Dr. J. W. Copeland, $100; I. W. Sanborn, $100; Lyndonville Band, $100; H. E. Folsom, $50; W. A. Densmore, $25; and S. Stern, $10—total, $785.

37. The Baxter house is the large two-story house still standing (1975) immediately back of the Lyndonville Post Office and facing Center Street.

38. At the turn of the century there were nineteen other halls in Lyndonville.

39. *Acts and Resolves of the General Assembly of Vermont in 1894*, pp. 31–37, Act 37: "Act to promote establishment of Free Public Libraries." This act provided for the governor to appoint a Board of Library Commissioners, five in number, and authorized the board to spend $100 for books for any town without a library. The act obligated the town to (1) elect a library board of five members, which board was to petition for this expenditure, and (2) make annual contributions for maintaining the free library, the sums—not less than $15 or more than $100—to be based on the size of the town grand list. Compensation of board members was prohibited, but $300 could be used for necessary expenses in any one year.

40. *Vermont Union*, February 7, 1896.

41. The contributors and their donations were as follows: T. N. Vail, 2,333.33; Mrs. H. E. Folsom, 800; Eber Cobleigh, 666.67; C. M. Darling, 400; D. M. Silsby, 290; H. E. Folsom, W. I. Powers, G. M. Campbell, L. B. Harris, C. G. Norris, J. L. Norris, J. P. Webster, J. C. Eaton, Mrs. S. S. Thompson, and Dodge & Watson, 100; and C. L. Stuart and wife, W. S. Jeffers, A. D. Paige, H. L. Parker,

Ruggles Bros, Mrs. J. F. Webber, W. H. Ford, and H. W. Lyster and wife, $50.

42. Subjects included the Venus de Milo, the Cathedral of Notre Dame, Rembrandt's *Syndics*, Fresco's *Phoebus and Aurora*, Cobraggio's *The Holy Night*, Gainsboro's *Portrait of Mrs. Giddeons*, and the Canterbury pilgrims (three paintings).

43. After the death of John B. Chase (successor of C. M. Chase as editor), a sizable portion of his unbound file of the *Union* and the *Vermont Union-Journal* were deposited in the library.

44. This was the first house on the east side of Main Street north of Depot Street. It was destroyed in 1974 to make way for the White Market parking lot.

45. In 1971 this case, which had been stored in the basement, was loaned to Lyndon State College "for as long as needed."

CHAPTER VI

1. *Lyndonville Journal*, May 6, 1891. The bylaws are given in full.

2. *St. Johnsbury Republican*, May 14, 1891.

3. In 1921 this chore was repeated.

4. *Vermont Union*, June 2, 1893.

5. Dr. J. W. Copeland was one of the most loyal of these, leaving at his death $1000 to the society.

6. The society had minimal dues in the hope of securing a large membership. Once for a year they were 50¢, but membership decreased, and the dues were returned to the earlier level of 25¢, at which they have remained.

7. There is confusion about the Universalist parsonage located west of the church. Some sources indicate that this was not given to the society; others say that it was, and that it was sold after a period of being unsuccessfully rented under the name of the "Harrison Cottage."

8. The one known exception was the solicitation of funds for the town clock, which struck its first chimes on November 9, 1894. Jennie Folsom and Austin Houghton were the moving spirits in the solicitation of the necessary $600, and T. N. Vail made the final contribution.

9. The *St. Johnsbury Republican* of November 12, 1891, reported that this park had been named "Park Benjamin." Possibly this was in honor of the late Benjamin Sanborn, whose home faced the spot.

10. Before the village streets were paved, the society had made and regularly maintained a triangular flower bed at the junctions of most streets, thus providing a traffic sentinel of beauty. One of the most attractive of these was at the junction of Main and Center streets.

11. Made by Albert Russell and Sons Company, Newburyport, Mass.

CHAPTER VII

1. Town Records, Minutes I, pp. 68–69, special meeting.

2. Town Records, Minutes I, p. 70, January 5, 1801.

3. Town Record Deed Book B, p. 38.

4. Town Records, Minutes, I, p. 80, May 30, 1801. By vote, the town treasurer was "Directed to give his note to Job Sheldon for $24 for two acres of the Meeting House Lot and pay the same out of the Treasury as soon as the money for the Tax for that Purpose is paid into the same." It is to be remembered that Sheldon *gave* to the town four acres of land, and that the town purchased two acres, making the total of the six covered by his deed. The G. H. Mathewson MMS contains the original note of Nathaniel Jenks, town treasurer, to Job Sheldon. Town Records, Minutes I, p. 42 contains an entry—in a list of many payments made—dated July 1, 1799, "To paid Job Sheldon for land for Meeting House 24 dollars." This may be an error in dating the entry, for when the Jenks note was authorized only 20¢ was reported in the treasury.

5. "To Sund^ry orders in fav^r of persons for Clearing Meeting H Lot $56.89" and "June 5 To order in fav^r of Eben Peck Clearing Do 66¢."

6. Town Records, Minutes I, pp. 200–202, March 13, 1809, and adjourned meeting of April 1, 1809.

7. Town Records, Minutes I, p. 205.

8. Town Records, Minutes I, p. 218. The original copy of this committee report is in the Sanborn Papers.

9. Town Records, Minutes I, p. 256.

10. Town Records, Minutes I, p. 271.

11. Town Record Deed Book C , pp. 477–78.

12. The original copy of this report is in the Sanborn Papers.

13. Pew 5, James Sherman; 6, Nathan Weeks; 7, E. Graves estate; 8, Abner Smith estate; 10, M. Haskell estate; 11, H. Field; 12, W. W. McGaffey estate; 21, Walker & Winsor; 22, S. Fletcher estate; 23, Jude Kimball estate; 24, Wm. Cahoon estate; 26, D. Emery; 27, James Knapp estate; and 28, Asa Smith.

14. Town Records, Minutes IV, p. 101, November 3, 1874. These sheds extended along the line between the town house and the cemetery on the west, as well as along the north line of the town house property.

15. Town Records, Minutes IV, pp. 184–87. The article was dismissed without action.

16. The only authority for this statement is an entry in the MMS First Book of Record of the Baptist Church in East Burke.

17. Town Records, Book 2, p. 27.

18. Local tradition maintains that this building was later moved westward and used as the Pudding Hill schoolhouse. After many years of such use, the vaulted ceiling of this "Quimby church" was lowered for more effective heating. In 1969

this building was sold, moved eastward, and renovated for use at the regional airport. A grandson of Daniel Quimby, however, stated that the building was torn down by his father. No records exist to confirm either version.

19. Whether these were loans or gifts is not known, no reference to, or proof of, repayment has been found.

20. Later the site of Sanborn Hall, the dormitory of Lyndon Institute.

21. Town Record Deed Book V, p. 358, November 1, 1898. The following subscribers associated themselves as a corporation named the Lyndon Center Free Baptist Church: E. J. Quimby, Geo. A. Downey, Freemont L. Pugsley, Grace B. Pugsley, Edna O. Quimby, H. W. Lyster, C. K. Hubbard, Mrs. C. K. Hubbard, Jennie L. Hoyt, Leila Chaplin, Etta M. Currier, Mary R. Currier, W. H. Lyster, C. P. Lyster, John I. Welch, A. A. Batchelder, A. E. Batchelder, Amos Morse, W. F. Stoddard, Ester M. Clement, R. Amelia Downey, Mrs. M. Stone, Mrs. A. S. Stoddard, Mrs. L. A. Welch, Mrs. Emma Campbell, Mrs. Melia S. Batchelder, Orpha A. Farmer, Daisy M. Sherburne, Loren J. Prescott, D. B. Stoddard, Mrs. L. J. Prescott, Frances H. Winter, Mrs. Susan Briant, I. H. Hall, I. H. Hall, Jr., Mrs. I. H. Hall Jr., L. Ingerson, Myra Irena Bean, Helen Louise Bean, Lila Marion Hoffman, Lena Davis, and L. S. Easterbrooks. The document was dated November 25, 1898, and signed by the deputy secretary of state.

22. Sutton later joined this group, and the name was changed to "Northeast Parish."

23. Town Record Deed Book J, p. 704, August 3, 1855. Luther Morrill and wife (Cynthia) Hubbard Field sold a tract of land to the church for $14, which it had used for twenty years. The church also bought a piece of land—1488 square feet—to the rear of the church.

24. Town Record Deed Book J, p. 83 (July 9, 1851), refers to the Congregational Church as a landmark along with Tavern Stand in reference to the fact that land on which the church was built was sold to the Congregational Society by Dr. Hubbard Field.

25. The boss workman was William Slyfield, who lived at the foot of Pudding Hill. The *Vermont Union* of March 13, 1872, noted that the same people who built the South Wheelock church helped build the Lyndon Congregational Church: Andrew Edgeton, master workman; and T. J. Cue, Rosewell Farr, Zebec Hoyt, and Curtis Bond.

26. Hubbard Hastings, Mrs. Betsey Hastings, Miss Mary Hastings, Mrs. Lucinda Carpenter, Mrs. Roxana Ayer, Edward Goss, George H. Weeks, Mrs. Martha Weeks, Abram Hicks, Mrs. Caroline Hicks, Luther Russell, Mrs. Maria Russell, Mrs. Aurora Randall, Mrs. Annie M. Goss, Mrs. Julia M. Morse, Mrs. Amelia K. Washburn, Mrs. Betsey H. Randall, Rev. P. B. Fisk, Mrs. Hattie L. Fisk, Lyman S. Dewey, William H. Fletcher, Mrs. Emma S. Fletcher, Silas Wheeler, Mrs. Jane F. Wheeler, Joseph Morrison, Mrs. Mary G. Morrison, Mrs. Miriam H. Merrill, Mrs. Jan D. Wright, Mrs. Matilda Hoyt, J. B. W. Butterfield, James

B. Carpenter, Miss Katie Moore, Miss Mary Taylor, Lucius M. Kent, Mrs. Emeline F. Kent, William D. Babcock, Mrs. Hattie G. Babcock, George H. Morrill, Mrs. Sally Green, and Mrs. Sarah Cowley.

27. Town Records, Minutes II, pp. 250–51.

28. Town Record Deed Book 8, p. 300.

29. This contract is among Mrs. Mathewson's Sanborn Papers. Note that the agreement predates the land deed, a further indication that the chapel was built before the land was acquired.

30. At the time the identity of the culprits was either unknown or carefully concealed. On September 12, 1963, the late Dorothy Walter told this writer that as a child, she remembered hearing her father (the late Charles T. Walter) retell the story of the difficulties he and Bernie Owen (son of Rev. E. Owen, pastor of the Baptist Church at the time) had in removing the angel because of the noise made in cutting the rod. Then they had difficulty in disposing of it when it was down, finally; they left it under the store. Owen spent the remainder of the night with Walter so that his parents would not know how late he had stayed out. On October 9, 1964, the late H. J. Hubbard told this writer that long years after Gabriel came down, he and Elwyn Nichols found the angel buried in the shed cellar back of the Nichols store. The gilt was still bright, and though the horn was badly bent it was fully recognizable.

31. For more information on the chapel's private use, see "The Settlement of the Town: Lyndon Corner."

32. Town Record Deed Book 34, p. 156, May 1, 1930.

33. The condition of this grant was that he would "settle with us as a minister of the Gospel on or before the 1st day of July next (1812)." The selectmen were to secure a written statement from Elder Peck promising to "continue a preacher of the Gospel in Lyndon for five years if not disabled." Town Records, Minutes I, p. 245.

34. The *Vermont Union Journal* of February 28, 1917, reported that while the new parsonage was open for public inspection, a short program was held in the church. During this program George E. Riley and Mrs. Lillian M. McArthur were married in the parsonage, thus having the honor of being the first couple married there.

35. Now Powers Park. See "The Village Improvement Societies."

36. John S. Michaud, "The Diocese of Burlington," *History of the Catholic Church in the New England States*, ed. William Byrne (Boston: Hurd & Everts Co., 1899), II, pp. 523–24; Joseph Paquet, "Questions for Historical Sketch," [1898] (in Archives, Diocese of Burlington; hereafter referred to as Archives), on which Bishop Michaud's section on the Catholic Church in Lyndonville is based; anonymous notes, probably a draft for this section, which gives additional information, e.g., the story of the hemlock tree (in Archives). Trudelle is also spelled Trudel or Trudell.

37. "Diary of Very Reverend Louis de Goesbriand, Bishop of Burlington, 1853–1899" (in Archives), p. 5. Hereafter referred to as "Diary."

38. Ibid., p. 9.

39. Ibid., p. 13. On Father Danielou and the church in St. Johnsbury during its early days, see Michaud, II, pp. 559–560.

40. Michaud, II, p. 524; Paquet.

41. "Diary," p. 66.

42. Ibid., p. 78. On Father Boissonnault see William Goss, "St. Johnsbury's Builder Priest, Rev. Jean A. Boissonnault, 1841–1909," *Vermont Catholic Tribune*, July 20, 1979, pp. 3, 16; William H. Jeffrey, *Successful Vermonters* (East Burke, Vt.: Historical Publishing Co., 1904), pp. 46–48.; Edward T. Fairbanks, *The Town of St. Johnsbury, Vermont* (St. Johnsbury: Cowles Press, 1914), pp. 310–11; "Faithful Priest Called Home," *Caledonian*, March 10, 1909, p. 1; March 17–1909, p. 4.

43. Town Record Deed Book P, p. 29; *Vermont Union*, August 13, 1975, p. 3.

44. Paquet; *Vermont Union*, September 17, 1975, p. 3; November 5, 1875, p. 3.

45. *Vermont Union*, November 19, 1875, p. 3.

46. Reports of Church of St. Martin of Lyndonville, 1875 (in Archives). The title and format of these reports, which were submitted annually by the pastor, changed periodically. Hereafter referred to as Reports.

47. Ibid.

48. Ibid., 1877.

49. Ibid., 1877, 1888.

50. Parish Register. See also "St. Elizabeth's Parish, Lyndonville, Vermont," *Our Sunday Visitor* (Vermont Edition), May 16, 1948, p. 4A.

51. Reports, 1875.

52. *Vermont Union*, December 17, 1875, p. 3.

53. Paquet; Michaud, II, p. 524.

54. "Diary," p. 108; *Vermont Union*, May 28, 1880, p. 3.

55. "Diary," p. 121.

56. Reports, 1882.

57. Ibid., 1876, 1877, 1881, 1882.

58. Town Record Deed Book R, p. 85; *Vermont Union*, June 17, 1881, p. 3.

59. Town Record Deed Book S, p. 332, U, p. 309.

60. *Vermont Union*, July 22, 1881, p. 3; Paquet; Reports, 1881.

61. Paquet; anonymous notes; *Lyndonville Journal*, September 4, 1889, p. 3, September 2, 1891, p. 3.

62. Reports, 1881–92; Paquet states that the school served the lower grades.

63. Reports, 1884.

64. Ibid., 1888–90.

65. Ibid., 1889.

66. *Vermont Union*, July 12, 1889, p. 3.

67. Ibid., December 20, 1889, p. 3; April 25, 1890, p. 3; Reports, 1890.

68. On Father Marceau see Parish Register; Jeffrey, p. 46; *Caledonian-Record*, June 11, 1927, pp. 1, 5; *Burlington Free Press*, June 13, 1927, p. 8.

69. "Diary," p. 164; *Lyndonville Journal*, August 12, 1891, p. 3.

70. On Father Paquet see *Lyndonville Journal*, July 1, 1896, p. 8; *Vermont Catholic Tribune*, August 12, 1977, p. 15; *Burlington Free Press*, February 20, 1940, p. 15.

71. Reports, 1891.

72. Town Record Deed Book U, p. 12; Reports, 1892.

73. *Vermont Union*, May 6, 1892, p. 3.

74. *Lyndonville Journal*, February 3, 1892, p. 3; February 17, 1892, p. 3; *Vermont Union*, February 5, 1892, p. 3; Reports, 1892.

75. *Lyndonville Journal*, February 17, 1892, p. 3; February 24, 1892, p. 3; March 23, 1892, p. 3; April 13, 1892, p. 3; May 4, 1892, p. 3; *Vermont Union*, August 5, 1892, p. 3; February 3, 1893, p. 3; February 17, 1893, p. 3, May 19, 1893, p. 3; Reports, 1892, 1893; Paquet; anonymous notes.

76. *Vermont Union*, May 26, 1893, p. 3; June 2, 1893; *Our Sunday Visitor*, May 16, 1948, p.4a; Paquet; anonymous notes.

77. *Vermont Union*, May 26, 1893, p. 3.

78. Ibid., July 28, 1893, p. 3; September 8, 1893, p. 3; November 17, 1893, p. 3; December 15, 1893, p. 3.

79. Paquet, anonymous notes; *Lyndonville Journal*, July 1, 1896, p. 8.

80. Reports, 1895, 1896; Paquet; Elizabeth was the name of Father Paquet's mother.

81. Reports, 1893. Insurance was carried on the school until 1907. Reports, 1893–1907. The move, whose exact date cannot be verified, is described in Harriet Fisher, "Catholic Church Marks 100 Years in Lyndonville," *Weekly News*, November 12, 1975, pp. 12–13, 15.

82. Reports, 1894–98.

83. *Vermont Union*, April 7, 1893, p. 3; April 21, 1893, p. 3; May 26, 1893, p. 3; October 27, 1893, p. 3; November 17, 1893, p. 3; November 16, 1894, p. 3. See Harriet Fisher, "Town Clock Has Been Ticking for 90 Years," *Caledonian Record*, March 6, 1985, p. 13.

84. Memorandum of Agreement, October 22, 1894, signed by A. W. Houghton, J. P. Webster, and H. L. Parker, village trustees; and Memorandum of Agreement, November 2, 1894, signed by A. W. Houghton, H. L. Parker, and J. Paquet (in Archives).

85. *Vermont Union*, April 13, 1894, p. 3; April 20, 1894, p. 3; April 27, 1894, p. 3; May 25, 1894, p. 3; February 1, 1895, p. 3; July 26, 1895, p. 3; January 8, 1895, p. 3; February 19, 1895, p. 3; April 2, 1895, p. 3; December 31, 1895, p. 3. Documents from Alphonse J. Aubin, including Alphonse Ouellette to Aubin, St. Johnsbury, February 17, 1943, and enclosure: Thomas R. Hesney to Ouellette, Chicago, February 12, 1943. On the Foresters in Vermont, see Arthur F. Stone, *The Vermont of Today* (New York: Lewis Historical Publishing Co., 1929), II, pp. 662–63.

86. *Vermont Union*, December 21, 1894, p. 3; March 29, 1895, p. 3; November 11, 1898, p. 3; Reports, 1896, 1898.

87. *Vermont Union*, September 29, 1899, p. 3.

88. *Vermont Catholic Tribune*, August 12, 1977, p. 15.

89. Reports, 1899, 1900. An obituary, source not indicated, is in the Archives. He died on July 9, 1914.

90. On Father Pontbriand see *Burlington Daily News*, December 5, 1944, n.p.; *Vermont Union-Journal*, June 30, 1926, p. 5; *Caledonian-Record*, November 20, 1950, p. 1.

91. Reports, 1900–1906.

92. Ibid., 1910; interview with Gerald Aubin, December 7, 1975, and November 29, 1984.

93. Reports, 1914; *Vermont Union-Journal*, April 29, 1914, p. 3.

94. Reports, 1915; *Vermont Union-Journal*, January 9, 1918, p. 3; January 30, 1918, p. 3; February 6, 1918, p. 3; March 6, 1918, p. 3; December 24, 1919, p. 3.

95. Reports, 1900–1932; *Vermont Union-Journal*, August 27, 1924, p. 3; October 28, 1925, p. 3.

96. *Burlington Daily News*, December 5, 1944, n.p.; *Vermont Union-Journal*, December 24, 1919, p. 3. Interviews with Leo Hebert, November 5, 1975; Gerald Aubin, December 7, 1975; and Frances Proulx, March 3, 1985.

97. Reports, 1910–27. A new format for the annual report, which indicated number of individuals rather than families, was adopted in 1910. Three Italians made their appearance in 1911.

98. Interviews with Rev. Gerard O. Duford, S.S.E., November 14, 1975, and Gerald Aubin, February 26, 1985; *Burlington Daily News*, December 5, 1944, n.p.: *Vermont Union-Journal*, January 16, 1935, n.p.

99. *History, Year Book and Church Directory of St. Elizabeth's Church, Lyndonville, Vermont* (1934), p. 4.

100. *Vermont Union-Journal*, December 20, 1933, n.p.; *Caledonian-Record*, December 14, 1933, p. 1; November 20, 1950, p. 1; *Burlington Daily News*, December 4, 1944, p. 8B; December 5, 1944, n.p.

101. Obituary, July 10, 1974 (in Archives).

102. Reports, 1936; correspondence between Sevigny and the Chancery Office, November 1935–September 1936 (in Archives).

103. Reports, 1938, 1941; Sevigny to Rev. Charles A. Towne, chancellor, September 22, 1941 (in Archives).

104. The list of names is displayed in the church vestibule.

105. Reports, 1946, 1948; Sevigny to chancellor, January 15, 1948 (in Archives).

106. Father Trahan's life is detailed in *Vermont Catholic Tribune*, July 7, 1978, p. 11; *Burlington Free Press*, September 17, 1983, pp. 5A, 8A; and *Caledonian-Record*, August 15, 1984, p. 3 (obituary).

107. Reports, 1953 to 1965; Trahan to Bishop Ryan, November 11, 1955 (in Archives).

108. Trahan to Bishop Robert F. Joyce, October 28, 1961 (in Archives).

109. Reports, 1958–65.

110. Town Record Deed Book 45, p. 488.

111. Ibid., Vol. 48, p. 339.

112. Trahan to chancellor, November 21, 1954; Trahan to Rev. Barry Fontaine, assistant chancellor, January 31, 1955 (in Archives).

113. *Caledonian-Record*, May 14, 1958, p. 8; *Vermont Catholic Tribune*, May 23, 1958, pp. 1, 11; Reports, 1957, 1958; Trahan to Joyce, May 9, 1957; March 9, 1958; Trahan to Fontaine, n.d.; Joyce to Carrieres, March 11, 1958; "*De Consecratione Trium Altarium*," March 17, 1958 (in Archives).

114. Reports, 1955, 1956, 1961, 1962; correspondence between Trahan, the Chancery Office, and the Diocesan Building Commission, November 1955–April 1961 (in Archives).

115. Reports, 1960, 1962, 1963; correspondence between Trahan, the Chancery Office, and the Diocesan Building Commission, May 1960–December 1962 (in Archives).

116. Biographical information from Society of St. Edmund. Hereafter referred to as biographical information.

117. Correspondence between Trahan and the Chancery Office, May 1965.

118. Reports, 1959.

119. Reports, 1967, 1968.

120. Biographical information; *Caledonian-Record*, September 9, 1966, p. 6; August 15, 1984, p. 3; *Vermont Catholic Tribune*, July 7, 1978, p. 11; August 31, 1979, p. 1; *Burlington Free Press*, September 17, 1983, p. 5A.

121. Biographical information; *Caledonian-Record*, September 9, 1966, p. 6.

122. Biographical information; *Burlington Free Press*, December 30, 1981, p. 2B (obituary).

123. Biographical information; *Vermont Catholic Tribune*, March 29, 1968, p. 1; *Caledonian-Record*, April 12, 1968, p. 11; Reports, 1968–70.

124. *Caledonian-Record*, June 12, 1974, p. 3.

125. Biographical information.

126. *Caledonian-Record*, October 17, 1973, p. 1; October 24, 1973, p. 14; St. Elizabeth Parish Bulletins, September 1973–January 1975.

127. *Caledonian-Record*, November 23, 1974, p. 10; Reports, 1974; St. Elizabeth Parish Bulletins, September 1973–January 1975; St. Elizabeth Parish Building Committee, Final Report, February 11, 1975.

128. *Caledonian-Record*, November 23, 1974, p. 10.

129. Annual Financial Report, Calendar Year 1974; Reports, 1974, 1975; St. Elizabeth Parish Bulletin, May 30, 1976.

130. *Caledonian-Record*, November 7, 1975, p. 4; November 15, 1975, pp. 1, 10; *Weekly News*, November 12, 1975, pp. 12–13, 15; November 19, 1975, pp. 13–14; *Vermont Catholic Tribune*, November 12, 1975, p. 8; November 26, 1975, pp. 2, 8.

131. *Burlington Free Press*, July 6, 1976, p. 2B; *Caledonian-Record*, July 7, 1976, p. 2.

132. Interview with Father Citti, February 28, 1985.

133. *Caledonian-Record*, May 21, 1985, p. 10; *Weekly News*, May 22, 1985, p. 4.

134. Lyndon Vital Statistics; Lyndon Institute Alumni Office; *Our Sunday Visitor*, May 16, 1948, p. 4A.

135. Town Record Deed Book U, p. 391.

136. Village Record Deed Book 39, pp. 299–300.

137. The society's articles of association are dated January 26, 1942. Officers were Marion P. Sutton, clerk and treasurer; Charles Chaffee, second reader; and Anne M. Eastman, first reader.

138. Village Record Deed Book 67, pp. 401–3.

139. Much of the information on the Christian Science Church was taken from the church history written by Helen Coolidge, signed by Irene E.Stimson, and loaned by Marion Sutton.

CHAPTER VIII

1. Town Records, Minutes I, pp. 40–41. It is practically impossible to identify positively the location of these six districts. An examination of the pre-1800 deeds on record leads one to think the great majority of these people were squatters and had no legal title to the land on which they lived. A venturesome guess would make these districts the equivalent of the following: 1, Lyndon Corner; 2, Cold Hill; 3, Squabble Hollow; 4, Pudding Hill; 5, Red Village; 6, Bemis Hill.

2. There may have been exceptions. Only four district minute books have been available: 7, Lyndonville; 12, Mt. Hunger; 13, Egypt; and 14, Fletcher. Otherwise it has been necessary to depend on reminiscences and similar sources. Even in these four minute books, no teachers are named.

3. By 1868 there were 120 heads of families and 122 scholars between the ages of four and eighteen in District 1. *Vermont Union*, February 21, 1868.

4. The East School was also known as the South School and as the Ledge School. Among the John B. Chase papers is a manuscript report of the prudential committee of District 1, dated April 7, 1857, which contains this sentence: "You have paid for a new school house and fixtures $549.70. . . ." In this report mention is made of the "south school house"; perhaps the "new" school house was that known later as the West School? The East School was located on the east side of Main Street just south of the big ledge at the side of Route 5. According to the *Vermont Union* of May 10, 1872, the building was sold at auction to Andrew J. Goodell for $200. It was remodeled into a residence, which it has continued to be to the present time (1975).

The West School was located slightly west of the Congregational Church, on the south side of York Street. At the auction above noted, it was sold to Charlie Colley for $221; he used it as a paint shop until 1905, when his widow sold it to

Enterprise Grange 16 Patrons of Husbandry. They remodeled it and used it for ten years for their various activities. It was next sold in 1915 to Dorman Stockwell, who had it moved (by J. A. Russell, St. Johnsbury) to the west side of Main Street, nearly opposite the post office, and made into a tenement house.

5. The school opened with an attendance of 140 pupils in two departments of four grades each; the ninth through twelfth grades were in the "Academy."

6. *Vermont Union*, February 23, March 1, and March 8, 1872.

7. The building was converted into a private home and is still (1976) an attractive part of the Speedwell Estates community.

8. Their attendance at this school may not have been constant, for the 1897 town report includes the entry "$16.50 paid to Ed Randall conveyance 1896." By the 1903–4 report he received $39.50 for the year. In the 1907–8 report similar payments totaling $71.45 were made to six people for "transportation" or "carrying scholars," which implies similar service for other districts. In the same report the state transportation payment is $71.19.

9. In 1944–45 there were three children at East Lyndon and thirteen at Red Village.

10. This schoolhouse has perhaps the most unusual history of any in town. About 1816 Elder Daniel Quimby constructed a small church from lumber cut on his farm on Pudding Hill. Legend has it that this building was later moved, for use as a schoolhouse, to a point about midway on the crossroad (#13) to the County Road (#11). Mrs. Howard Allen (Ethel Gaboree) told this writer that when she began teaching in the Pudding Hill School (1955), the vaulted ceiling was intact, but later this was lowered by the installation of a false ceiling so as to provide more effective heating of the room. Her husband, Howard, hearing her reminiscence, remembered that Hugh Eastman (1882–1964) had told him of having participated in the destruction of the "Quimby church" horse sheds when he was a young boy; all had been destroyed but two left for storage of wood for the school stove. One may guess that this moving had occurred during the late 1880s.

11. The old building was sold to Fire District 3; it was later taken over by the town and used for storage purposes by the cemetery staff.

12. Pp. 25–27. Reverend Henderson was not only a member of the Yearly Meeting for many years and a beloved pastor (1857–66) of the Lyndon Center Church, but also a member of the seminary location committee—credentials that lend a high degree of authority to the story.

13. Henderson, *Historical Sketch*, p. 27: "The site occupied by the school building is the same selected by the Yearly Meeting Committee thirteen years before but not approved by the Conference for the reason of ineligibility."

14. Evidently the plans were modified, for the two ells and the wooden building at the rear did not materialize, nor did the basement apartment.

15. Hopkins, a Civil War veteran, died in September 1872.

16. No record has been found of the building being officially named "Thompson Hall"; it may have been a popular designation.

17. In later years this was succeeded by "Jottings," and in 1924 the "Cynosure," a yearbook, began to be published.

18. So far as this writer has been able to find, it continued to function under this name until 1907.

19. *Lyndonville Journal*, March 11, 1891: "Today the building stands completed ready for the furnishings, and is a building that adds much to the location where it is situated, neatly finished and conveniently arranged for the purpose. The main building faces north and is 100 x 34 feet, three stories high with an ell 39 x 25 feet two stories high. On the first floor is an entrance 12 x 12 finished in oak with outer doors of oak and polished plate glass, four parlors, two suites of rooms, six sleeping rooms, and a main hall running the entire length. On the second floor there are 16 sleeping rooms, 12 x 12, two water closets, and main hall. On the third floor are 14 sleeping rooms, two kitchens, for self-boarders, and main hall. The main hall has a partition in the center from cellar to attic, dividing the building so the parts are as separate as though they were not under the same roof. The ladies are to occupy the west end and the gentlemen the east end. Each sleeping room has a wardrobe. In the ell part the first floor contains dining room, kitchen, pantry etc, with all essential fittings for convenience. On the second floor are two sleeping rooms for students, and four for help, divided off with partitions so there is no communication between the ell and the main part except by way of the dining room. In the basement there are waterclosets with cemented floors. A brick partition divides it. The cellar extends under the whole building, with vegetable cellar under the ell. The inside walls of the building are finished throughout in hard finish and the rooms painted in a variety of colors. It is built for warmth, being back plastered and lined with paper under the clapboards, and the roof is covered with cedar shingles, and we believe stands a credit to the builders. . . ."

20. The minutes of the October 13, 1890, meeting of the trustees (Book I, p. 122) have this entry: "On motion it was voted to grant I. W. Sanborn the right and privilege of naming the new boarding hall on condition that he pay $500 to pay for the building lot or otherwise."

21. In 1929 the trustees approved names for the buildings in the central part of the village owned by the Institute. For the most part the names were those of the people occupying the buildings when they were acquired by the school: Pearl Place (Vail purchased this from I. H. Hall, who in turn had bought it from Jeremy Pearl, for many years a trustee) Thompson Cottage (the residence of S. S. Thompson even before the school was built), Y. Olde Tavern, Smith Cottage, Collison Cottage, Bean Cottage, Cutting Cottage (tenants in the former David Willey home), and Willey Cottage.

22. Accepted by the Vermont secretary of state on May 27, 1921.

23. It is interesting to note that these new bylaws contain no allusion to any relation between the school and the members of the Baptist Church, despite the fact that the original bylaws (1868) provided that this article "shall never be changed."

24. This school motto was adopted at the meeting of the trustees on July 12, 1922.

25. In 1955 this second house was destroyed and the barn remodeled to create attractive quarters for the homemaking department. Previously, the various elements of this program had been so widely dispersed around the campus as to impede the department's efficiency.

26. This was the "parade ground" as designated by the Job Sheldon 1801 deed to the selectmen. The lease has been renewed periodically since 1929; the Institute plans to fence it in 1934 were soundly defeated at a special and vociferous town meeting.

27. The committee chairmen were Gerald Aubin, president, alumni association; Winifred King, historical gallery; Norris Elliott, loyalty letter and program; John Norris, Jr., and Roy Christophersen, music; Maurice Hill, reviewing stand; Harriet Fisher, publicity; Marion Wakefield, yearbook and history; Herbert Gallagher, advertising; and Bertha Koury, parade.

28. In listing the graduates of Lyndon Institute in 1896, notation was made that six students had completed the one-year "teachers course."

29. Though the building was declared unsafe, the wrecking crew broke several cables before defeating its resistance.

30. This building has been known by many names. During the most prosperous era of Speedwell Farms, it was the residence of I. Q. Vail, (the brother of T. N. Vail and his farm manager). At one time it was called the Harris home, reminiscent of its being the residence of the L. B. Harris family, it was known earlier as the Charles Sanborn home and as the Joel Fletcher place during their respective periods of occupancy of the farm. In more recent times it has been almost universally called the Ted Lawson place.

31. Records of enrollment or graduation are unavailable. The picture of the June 1912 class shows twenty-five persons; that of the June 1914 graduation group shows twenty-eight persons. A conservative estimate of total enrollment is 300 students.

CHAPTER IX

1. In 1933 a roster of Vermont soldiers in the War of 1812 was prepared and published under the direction of Herbert T. Johnson, adjutant general of Vermont. However, this list rarely gives the soldiers' place of residence.

2. These names are on record in the office of the Vermont adjutant general.

3. Editor Charles Chase described June training in the *Vermont Union*, January

13, 1893; O.D.M. in the *Vermont Union Journal*, April 14, 1929; Anthony Marro in *Vermont History* XL no. 1, pp. 28–42 (winter 1972).

4. Town Records, Minutes III, p. 186.

5. A later issue reported the proceeds of these entertainments as $32.75.

6. The following regulations were issued by the regional Committee on Domestic Fuel Economy. "Householders: 1. Not to use coal for heating before the 1st of Nov. or after the 1st of May, unless the house temperature is below 60; 2. To burn wood whenever possible; 3. To use small oil heaters when it is necessary to keep certain parts of a house at a special temperature; 4. To reduce coal used in the stoves, do your cooking at one part of the day, use wood whenever you can; 5. To be economical with gas; and with electricity where it is generated by coal-using plants. Turn off house lights when not needed, if only for a few moments. To those who control office bldgs., hotels, apt. houses: 1. Not to use coal for heating before the 1st of Nov. or after the 1st of May, unless the temperature of the bldg. is below 60; 2. Not to heat bldgs. in excess of 65; 3. To bank fires at all practicable times, and when bldg. is to be only partially used to turn off heat whenever feasible. Business bldgs. not used after 6:00 p.m. should bank fires at 4:00 p.m.; 4. To reduce to the barest necessities all illumination by gas or by coal-made electricity."

7. My Tuesdays are meatless
My Wednesdays are wheatless
I'm getting more eatless each day
My home is heatless
My bed is sheetless
They're all sent to the Y.M.C.A.
The bar rooms are treatless
My coffee is sweetless
Each day I get poorer and wiser,
My stockings are feetless
My trousers are seatless
My God, how I hate the Kaiser
—*St. Albans Messenger*—

8. Pits of peaches, plums, apricots, prunes, cherries, and olives; shells of Brazil nuts, walnuts (English or native), hickory nuts, and butternuts; and date seeds.

9. This writer has not found the material necessary to reconstruct a record of the service rendered by Lyndon men and women during World War I.

10. The general committee comprised Chairman G. M. Campbell, and members Dr. F. E. Dwinell, George W. Pierce, C. L. Stuart, H. A. Squires, C. M. Darling, H. C. Wilson, G. W. Macdonald, Homer Watson, U. S. Grant, Fernald Ladd, C.W. Clark, and B. A. Hines. Specific duties were assigned as follows: compilation of honor roll, George W. Pierce; banquet, H. W. Squires; carnival, Dr. F. E. Dwinell; dance managers, A. E. Donahue, W. H. Parker, Myron Eastman,

Geo. Batchelder, Joe Gates, Wm Durgin, George Akley, C. E. Willoughby, P. R. Griswold, R. P. Aldrich, Thomas Wark, and D. J. Vallier.

11. Snare drums: U. S. Grant, E. C. Grant, H. F. Johnson, Walter Nichols, Isaac French, C. H. Whitcomb, Joel Whitcomb, and B. A. Hinds; bass drum: James Nichols; fifer: Allen Morse.

12. From a booth here, ice cream, cigars, and cigarettes were available without charge to servicemen.

13. The menu consisted of tomato soup, roast pork, roast beef, chicken pie, mashed potatoes, vegetables, pies, doughnuts, ice cream, cake, and coffee, plus a pack of cigarettes for each serviceman. The waitresses (dressed in white, wearing caps of national colors) were Beatrice and Agnes Ouellette, Mary Hebert, Alice Norton, Eva Breason, Ida Charron, Maude Wetherbee, Ida Flower, Eva Wood, Erma Pierce, Ruth Blodgett, Adelaide Brewer, Carolyn Darling, Emma and Blanche Cusson, Edith Lewsey, Eunice Silsby, and Flora Barber. Mrs. G. M. Campbell was in charge of food, and Mrs. H. J. Hubbard in charge of the dining room.

14. A special town meeting held July 12 appropriated $1000 to provide suitable medals for each of the servicemen, with any unspent balance to be returned to the town treasury. The committee—O. D. Mathewson, chairman, and M. E. Daniels, F. E. Dwinell, H. C. Wilson, and N. H. Norton—purchased 160 medals at a total cost of $277.20.

15. B. A. Hinds, Clifton Wilkie, Philip Rheaume, Malcom Macdonald, Wesley Colby, Maynard Pease, Allen Lynaugh, John and James Beattie, and Frank, James, George, and Loff Greenwood. The soloist was Philip Rheaume; Allen Lynaugh and the Greenwood boys gave a first-class exhibition of clog dancing. James Beattie entertained with an excellent bit of jig dancing. Loff Greenwood played the violin and Reginald Bigelow the piano.

16. The chairman of the banquet committee was Mrs. Robert Wishart, who was assisted in the kitchen by Mrs. Ross Bennett, Mrs. Cyde Brooks, Mrs. Edgar Kelloway, Mrs. Joseph Breason, Mrs. Harold Miller, Mrs. John Goodsell, Mrs. William Dahlbeck, and Mrs. Perley S. Harris; and in the dining room by Mrs. Olive Wishart, Mrs. Merle Pierce, Mrs. Waltena Harris, Miss Angie Duford, Mrs. Althea Harris, Mrs. Grace Bigelow, Miss Joyce Gilman, Miss Josephine Ross, Mrs. Vera Hughes, Miss Agatha Smith, Mrs. Blanche Sylce, Miss Freda Boardman, and Mrs. Marian Bassett.

Seated at the head table were Maj. R. F. Pierce, Lt. W. J. Hughes, Lt. E. G. Andross, Lt. Dean Emerson, Lt. Lyndon Squires, Lt. Willard Harris, Lt. George Martelle, toastmaster L. D. Shonyo, Rev. J. D. Staffeld, Rev. N. C. Webster, Rev. A. M. Markey, and Rev. G. E. Jaques.

17. The author of much of the material in the preceding pages on World War II is not known; it comes from a folder handed to this writer by the late Sherburn Lang, then town clerk. From the evidence of other items in the folder, it seems

likely that it is the report sent by P. R. Griswold, town clerk to the State History Commission, in answer to its request for a "community history" of the war period.

18. This writer is deeply indebted to L. H. Buss, Chief, Officer of History, Peterson Air Force Base, Colorado, and Maurice Lustig, Chief, Real Estate Division, Corps of Engineers, New York District Department of the Army, New York, for their gracious assistance.

19. Perhaps held at the Baptist Church, since Reverend Perkins was pastor there.

20. On March 5, 1900, terraces seventeen and eighteen of section eight in the town cemetery were deeded in trust to Farnsworth Post No. 106 (G.A.R.), Farnsworth Post No. 67 (Women's Relief Corps), and Lyndon Camp No. 75 (Sons of Veterans). This plot has been the center of Memorial Day ceremonies in the cemetery ever since.

L. B. Harris' correspondence on file in the Vermont State Historical Society Library would lead one to think that the cannon on the lot is a U.S. Navy "condemned cannon" and that the shells at either side come from the same source.

21. The members of this band were W. C. Johnson, 1st E-flat cornet; W. H. Bowker, 2d E-flat cornet; J. M. Murch, 3d E-flat cornet; F. D. Leonard, B-flat cornet; James Mooney, 2d B-flat cornet; H. L. Parker, 3d B-flat cornet; Ira W. Bemis, alto; Alonzo Newton, 2d alto; N. K. Tracy, 3d alto and cymbals; A, L. Pushie, trombone; E. M. Campbell, B-flat tenor; E. C. Potter, baritone; W. A. Knapp, 1st B-flat bass; Frank Bowker, 2d B-flat bass; A. S. Bowker, E-flat bass; J. G. Sanborn, clarinet; B. G. Morrison, tenor drum; and James Ritchie, bass drum.

22. The writer is deeply indebted to the Aubins for their assistance in preparing this piece.

CHAPTER X

1. *Vermont Union*, February 1871, and May 28, 1899.

2. The Tavern was located at the southwest corner of the junction of the present Main, York, and Chapel streets. It was frequently credited with being the beginning of the community, since the earlier buildings had been constructed at the west end of York Street, where the road of that day came from the south into the community of Lyndon.

3. This was on the east side of the main road through the village, about half way between the turn to Fletcher Hill and the turn to the east side of the river, where Lyndonville developed.

4. Apparently Hubbard used the site for the construction of the home he occupied until his death.

5. The Nichols' home was built here and remained the family residence until after Nichols' death. T. N. Vail purchased the property in 1912 and remodeled the

building into the village store and post office; after the store was discontinued the building continued as the post office.

6. The Cobleigh Public Library received the register from the estate of Luther B. Harris.

7. See Village Records, Minutes I, p. 19, for the letter of this gift.

8. Literature relating to this property has located it on Fletcher Hill, Sanborn Hill, Tuttle Hill, Harris Hill, and Telephone Hill—locally best known as Vail Hill.

9. This was located on the original Right 22 of Stephen Jenks.

10. Known in recent years as Paul's Wayside Furniture.

11. Stephen Vail, grandfather of T. N., acquired the New Jersey property in 1804. Here was built the engine of the first steamship to cross the Atlantic, the *Savannah* in 1819. Stephen Vail gave generous financial support to Samuel F. B. Morse to aid his work on the telegraph, a project in which his son, Alfred Vail, was actively interested. It was on the New Jersey Speedwell Estate that the first practical demonstration of the telegraph was set up.

12. Albertus Allen, Mr. Moulton, L. B. Harris, George Howatt, W. I. Powers, I. Q. Vail, and W. N. Hubbard.

13. Lyndon Mills, earlier known as Little Falls and as Cahoon Falls; it is now Lyndonville Electric Plant Station 2.

14. Letter of January 15, 1917, printed in the *Vermont Union-Journal* of January 31, 1917.

15. Mr. Darling was president for more than 20 years of both the American Jersey Cattle Club and the American Morgan Horse Club.

CHAPTER XII

1. From Editor Charles Chase's account of the fire in the *Vermont Union* of November 30, 1894.

2. Ibid.

3. From Editor John Chase's account of the fire in the *Vermont Union-Journal* of January 24, 1924.

4. The village report of 1925 gives a full accounting of the disposition of these funds on pp. 42–45.

5. From the account by Editor John Chase in the *Vermont Union-Journal* of November 6, 1927.

6. Over the next three years the Federal Disaster Assistance Administration reimbursed the town 100 percent for these costs.

7. *Vermont Union-Journal*, March 8, 1911; *Caledonian Record*, March 8, 1911.

CHAPTER XIII

1. *Vermont Union*, October 12, 1877.

2. Many years later it was given the name "Mountain View Park."

3. The constitution was adopted on August 23, 1890, and the association was incorporated in September.

4. *Lyndonville Journal*, September 10, 1890.

5. The company sold the building in 1904, after which it served as a livery stable under two successive owners. The present cemetery toolhouse was for about forty-five years the Lyndon Center schoolhouse, and the stable was 15 or 20 feet east of it. One of this writer's most vivid childhood memories is of dodging the horses coming out of the sheds every time I went to or left school.

6. He worked for $7 per month and board, and slept in the barn.

7. The parade marshall was Capt. H. E. Randall (born in Lyndon, resident in Island Pond); his assistants were A. H. Hale (Island Pond) and W. F. Stoddard and S. G. Collison (both of Lyndon).

8. This writer has been unable to find a copy, if in fact any were printed. The *Vermont Union*, *Lyndonville Journal*, and *St. Johnsbury Republican* printed extensive reports of the occasion. All the addresses are available from one or the other of these publications.

POSTSCRIPT

1. Town Record Deed Book S, p. 255.

2. Town Record Deed Book S, p. 343.

3. Town Record Deed Book M, p. 564.

4. Town Record Deed Book M, p. 299.

Bibliography

Books and publications in this bibliography do not represent all the material read during the twenty-five years of research for this book. They are representative of the books researched in the pursuit of information about Lyndon.

Arnold, Samuel Greene, 1860. *History of the State of Rhode Island and Providence Plantations*. Vol. I, 1636–1790; Vol. II, 1700–1790. New York. Appleton.

Bartlett, John Russell. 1864. *Records of the State of Rhode Island and Providence Plantations*. Vol. IX, 1780–1783. Providence, Rhode Island. Alfred Anthony.

Benton, Josiah Henry LLD. 1911. *Warning Out in New England 1656–1817*. Boston. W. B. Clarke Company.

Benton, Reuben Clark. 1894. *The Vermont Settlers and the New York Speculators*. Minneapolis. Housekeeper Press.

Bogart, Walter Thompson. 1950. *The Vermont Lease Lands*. Montpelier, Vermont Historical Society.

Bowen, Richard LeBaron. 1957. *Massachusetts Records: A Handbook for Genealogists, Historians, Lawyers and other Researchers*. Reheboth, Massachusetts. Privately Printed.

Carleton, Hiram. 1903. *Genealogical and Family History of the State Vermont & a Record of the Achievements of Her People in the Making of a Commonwealth and the Founding of a Nation*. New York & Chicago. Lewis Publishing Company.

Dawson, George C. *Vermont Post-Offices 1733–1966*. Montpelier, Vermont. Lloyd T. Hayward.

Fairbanks, Edward T. 1914. *The Town of St. Johnsbury, Vermont*. St. Johnsbury. Cowles Press.

Fisher, Dorothy Canfield. 1953. *Vermont Traditions*. Boston. Little Brown Publishing Company.

Burgess, Rev. G. A. and Rev. J. T. Ward. 1889. *Free Baptist Cyclopedia: Historical and Biographical*. Free Baptist Cyclopedia Company.

Chadwick, Hon. Albert G. 1883. *Soldiers' Record of the Town of St. Johnsbury, Vermont in the War of the Rebellion 1861–5*. St. Johnsbury, Vermont. C. M. Stone and Company.

Child, Hamilton. 1887. *Gazetteer of Caledonia and Essex Counties, Vermont: 1764–1887*. Part I. Syracuse, New York. Syracuse Journal Company.

Crockett, Walter Hill. 1921. *Vermont: The Green Mountain State*. New York. Century History Company, Inc. 4 volumes.

Greenleaf, Rev. Jonathan. 1852. *Sketch of the Settlement of the Town of Lyndon in the County of Caledonia and State of Vermont*.

Hayward, John. 1849. *A Gazetteer of Vermont*. Boston. Tappan, Whittemore and Mason.

Henderson, M. C. 1890. *An Historical Sketch of the Vermont Yearly Meeting of Free Will Baptists from 1808–1889*. St. Johnsbury. Republican Press.

Hill, R. N. 1950. *Contrary Country*. New York. Rinehart.

Jeffrey, William K. 1904. *Successful Vermonters*. East Burke, Vermont. Historical Publishing Company.

Johnson, Virginia W. 1891. "The Bronze Boar." Chap. XV. in *Florence: The Lily of the Arno*. Boston. Dona Estes Company.

Jones, Matt Bushnell. 1939. *Vermont in the Making 1750–1770*. Cambridge. Harvard Press.

Lewis, Elder John. 1852. *The Life, Labors and Travels of Elder Charles Bowles of the Free Will Baptist Denomination*. Ingall's & Stowell's Stream Press.

Lovejoy, David S. 1958. *Rhode Island Politics and the American Revolution, 1760–1776*. Providence, Rhode Island. Brown University Press.

Michaud, John S. 1899. *The Diocese of Burlington, History of the Catholic Church in the New England States* (ed. Wm. Byrne.) Boston. Hurd & Everts Company.

Paine, Albert Bigelow. *In One Man's Life*. New York. Harper Rowe.

Robbinson, R. E. *Vermont, A Study of Independence of American Commonwealths*. New York. Houghton Mifflin.

Sosin, Jack M. 1867. *The Revolutionary Frontier*. History of the American Frontier Series (ed. Roy Billington). New York. Holt, Rinehart & Winston.

Stone, Arthur F. 1929. *The Vermont of Today*. New York. Lewis Historical Publishing Company.

Thompson, Charles M. 1942. *Independent Vermont*. New York. Houghton Mifflin.

Thompson, Zadock. 1824. *Gazetteer of Vermont*. Montpelier. Zadock Thompson & E. P. Walton.

———. 1842. *History of Vermont: Natural, Civil, & Statistical*. Burlington. Chauncey Goodrich.

Van de Water, Frederic F. 1941. *The Reluctant Republic: Vermont 1724–1791*. New York. John Day Company.

Williamson, Chilton. 1949. *Vermont in Quandary 1763–1825*. Montpelier. Vermont Historical Society.

GOVERNMENT

Annals of Congress—Debates & Proceedings of Congress. 1789–1824 Letter involving Jonathan Arnold Nov. 25, 27, 1782. Ref. Madison Papers.

Journals of the Continental Congress. 1774–1789, XXII 1782, XXV 1783.

Letters of Members of Continental Congress—References to Vermont begin in volume I and continue through the whole 8 volumes.

National Archives:

Force, Peter—Papers.

General Services Administration.

1950. List of National Archives microfilm publications.

1840–80 Census Schedules.

1830 Census.

Records of Veterans Administration. Rol #105. Vermont Veterans Census.

American State Papers Class VIII. Public Lands. 8 Volumes for Vermont Controversy.

First Census of the United States. 1790 Heads of Families. Vermont.

Office of the Secretary of State, Vermont:

Acts and Resolves of the General Assembly of Vermont 1894, 1900, 1935.

Agency of Development and Community Affairs, Educational Service by the Division for Historic Preservation. Montpelier, Vermont. State of Vermont.

Thomas, Peter A. & Lauren A. Kelley. "An Archaeological View of Vermont's Past."

———. "The Preservation of Vermont's Archaeological Resources."

Public Laws of the State of Vermont relating to election of town officers. Montpelier. 1939.

Records of the Governor and Council of the State of Vermont II. (ed.)
E. T. Walton.

Records of Governor and Council III. Appendix I. Resolutions of Congress hostile to Vermont. Dec. 5, 1782 & Related Documents. Appendix II. contain much correspondence.

State Papers of Vermont. II. Charters Granted by the State of Vermont. (ed.) Franklin H. Dewart.

State Papers of Vermont III. Journals and Proceedings of General Assembly (ed.) Walter Crockett.

State Papers of Vermont III. Journals & Proceedings of General Assembly. 1781–83.

State Papers of Vermont. Journals and Proceedings III. Part II. Reports Jonathan Arnold read in General Assembly.

State Papers of Vermont V. Petitions for Grants of Land 1778–1811. (ed.) Mary Green Nye. Brattleboro.

State Papers of Vermont VII. New York Land Patents 1688–1786. (ed.) Green Nye.

State Papers of Vermont IX. General Petitions. 1788–92.

State Papers of Vermont XI. General Petitions. 1797–1799.

Surveyor's Field Book of Lyndon 1789.

Surveyor General File, I., Part I.

Vermont Agency of Transportation. Montpelier, Vermont.

   Thomas, Peter A. & Pamela Bumsted. 1979. "Phase I Archaeological Assessment for St. Johnsbury RS-0113 (14) — "Benedict's Curve." Prepared by Department of Anthropology, University of Vermont, Burlington for the Vt. Agency of Transportation. Montpelier. Report No. 18, Aub. 1979.

Vermont State Papers, Old Series, Treasurers. MMS.

New Series of Documents.

   Grand Lists 1801, 1810, 1812, 1813, 1830–55 inc., 1865, 1867, 1869–1913 inc.

Quinquennial Appraisal for 1865.

Railroad Appraisal for 1878.

War Bonds Held in Lyndon 1865.

   Roads. Vol. 44, 45, 46, 47, 48, 80.

   Lyndon Bank Petition. Vol. 63 1833.

   Annexation to Kirby Vol. 64.

   Memo from Inhabitants of Lyndon. Vol. 65. 1837.

   Incorporation of Bank Vol. 75—1835.

Lyndon Book of Reccord 1781, Proprietors of the Town of Lyndon.

Lyndon Cemetery Records.
Lyndon Center Village Charter.
Lyndon Center Village Minutes.
Lyndon Road Records.
London Town Charter.
Lyndon Town Record Deed Books.
Lyndon Town Records, Minutes.
Lyndon Town Reports.
Lyndon Village Records.
Lyndonville School Districts Minutes.
Lyndonville Village Reports.

MANUSCRIPTS
Depositories for manuscripts given when known.
* Indicates present location not known.

Angell, Col. Israel. Diary.*
Atwood, Hale. Diaries: 74 volumes. Town Clerk's Office.
Aubin, Alphonse. Documents.*
Baptist Church, East Burke, First Book of Records.
Chase, Charles. Scrapbook II. Great Flood of Oct. 1869, Papers. Lyndonville
    Savings Bank & Trust Company.
Chester, Fenton. Envelope on Lyndon Area.*
Christian Science Church of Lyndon Records.*
Diocese of Burlington Archives (Catholic Church):
    Correspondence, Diocesian Building Commission 1955–1965, St.
    Elizabeth Catholic Church of Lyndonville.
    Diary of Very Reverend Louis de Goesbriand, Bishop of Burlington
        1853–1899.
    Paquet, Joseph. Questions for Historical Sketch 1898.
    _____. Reports—St. Elizabeth Catholic Church, Lyndonville.
Farnsworth Post 106, G.A.R. Lyndon Town Office.
Freewill Baptist Church. Lyndon Center. Records. At Church.
Houghton, Paul. 1899. Program Lyndon Congregational Church Reun-
    ion.*
Houghton, W. P. Diaries, Account Books, Papers.*
Kropski, Mrs. H. Account Book—Lyndon Store.*
Lang, Charles. Diaries, Account Books of Joseph Burrington.*
Lyndon Congregational Church Records.

Lyndonville Congregational Church Records.

Mathewson, Grace. Papers believed to be in those taken to Vermont Histori-
    cal Society:

  Hoyt, Charles Estate. Papers and Clippings.

  Chase, E. B. & Isaac Fletcher. Correspondence 1836–1840.

  General Orders #18. 1841, Militia Laws 1837–1839, Organization 1838.

  Grand List of Lyndon 1844.

  Jones, Stephen Mathewson. Diaries: 1858, 1860, 1861.

  Sampson Scrapbook.

  Miscellaneous Papers.

Methodist Church Records From Rev. Barney:

  Vital Statistics Lyndon Methodist Church 1871–1901, 1899–1918, 1962–65.

  Vital Statistics, Lyndonville Church. 1906–1943, 1944–On.

  Records of Ladies Aid. 1937–1951.

Paris, Murray. Reminiscences: Paris Mill Activities.*

Society of St. Edmund (Catholic). Biographical Information.*

St. Elizabeth's Parish (Catholic). Lyndonville:

  Building Committee Final Report 1975.

  Annual Financial Report 1974.

  Parish Register.

  History, Year Book, Church Directory.

Stone, Madeline McCann. Scrapbook.*

St. Peter's Episcopal Church Records, Lyndonville.

Universalist Church Records, Lyndonville.*

Village Improvement Society, Lyndonville. Minutes, Papers, Clippings.

Walter Collection.* D. P. Hall Estate, Papers of Dudley P. Hall, Letters, Old
    Lyndon Academy 1914.

PAPERS, NEWSLETTERS, CATALOGUES

Burlington Daily News, Burlington, Vermont.

Burlington Free Press, Burlington, Vermont.

Caledonian-Record, St. Johnsbury, Vermont.

The Institute Chimes, Lyndon Institute, Lyndon Center, Vermont.

Lyndon Institute Cynosure, Lyndon Center, Vermont.

Lyndon Literary & Biblical Institution Catalogue 1874.

Lyndonville Journal, Lyndonville, Vermont 1889–1903.

Lyndonville Union-Journal, Lyndonville, Vermont 1905–1941.

Our Sunday Visitor (Vt. Ed.) St. Elizabeth's Parish, Lyndonville, Vermont.

St. Elizabeth's Parish Bulletin, Lyndonville, Vermont.

St. Johnsbury Republican, St. Johnsbury, Vermont.

Vail Agricultural School Catalog, Lyndon Center, Vermont 1918.

Vermont Catholic Tribune, Burlington, Vermont.

Vermont Life, Montpelier, Vermont.

The Vermont-Union, Lyndonville, Vermont 1865–1905.

Weekly News, Lyndonville, Vermont.

VERMONT HISTORY MAGAZINE
Montpelier, Vermont

Allen, Morse. "Connecticut and Vermont Town Names" 22.4. Oct. 1954.

Coolidge, Guy Emerson. Bibliography: Index to the French Occupation of the Champlain Valley 6:3 Sept. 1938.

Davis, Robert. "Some Characteristics of Northern Vermont" 5:4 Dec. 1937.

Felton, Harold W. 1962. "A Horse Named Justin Morgan" New York. Dodd Mead Company (Rev. 30:4 Oct. 1962).

Fox, Dixon Ryan. "Yankee and Yorkers" 9:2 June 1941.

Gorham, Alan. "Federal Court Records Pertaining to Vermont: Sources For Study: 36:3 Summer 1968.

Gould, Mary Earle 1965. "The Early American House" Rutland. Charles Tuttle Company. (Rev. 36.2 April 1966).

Hetch, Arthur. "Postal History of Vermont in 1795." 25:2 April 1957.

Hendricks, Nathaniel. "A New Look at the Ratification of the Vermont Constitution of 1776" 34:1 Jan. 6 1966, 34:2 April 1966.

Holbrook, Stewart. 1961 "Yankee Loggers." New York. International Paper Company (Rev. 29:4 Oct. 1961).

Hoyt, Edward A. "Editorial about Manuscripts belonging to State of Vermont" 19:4 Oct. 1951.

Mellin, Jeanne. 1961 "The Morgan Horse" Brattleboro, Vermont Stephen Greene Press (Rev. 29:4 Oct. 1961).

Richardson, A. H. "Haldemand Negotiations" 9:2 June 1941.

Squires, Duane. "Review of History of Brandon" 31:1 Jan. 1963.

Spargo, John. "Iron Working & Smithing in Bennington 1786–1842" 6:4 Dec. 1938.

Stevenson, Noel C. "Search & Research, Researchers Handbook" 27:4 Oct. 1959.

Stillwell, Lewis D. "Migration from Vermont, 1776–1860" 5:2 June 1938.

Thurber, Harris E. "Some Values of the Vermont Community" 25:3 July
    1957, 25:4 Oct. 1957.
Vermont Historical Society Staff. "Personal Narratives of the Civil War in
    Collection of Vermont Historical Society" 31:2 April 1963.
———. "Bibliography of Vermont 1964, Articles and Books" 33:2 April 1965.

Index

Printed at
Meriden-Stinehour Press
Lunenburg, Vermont

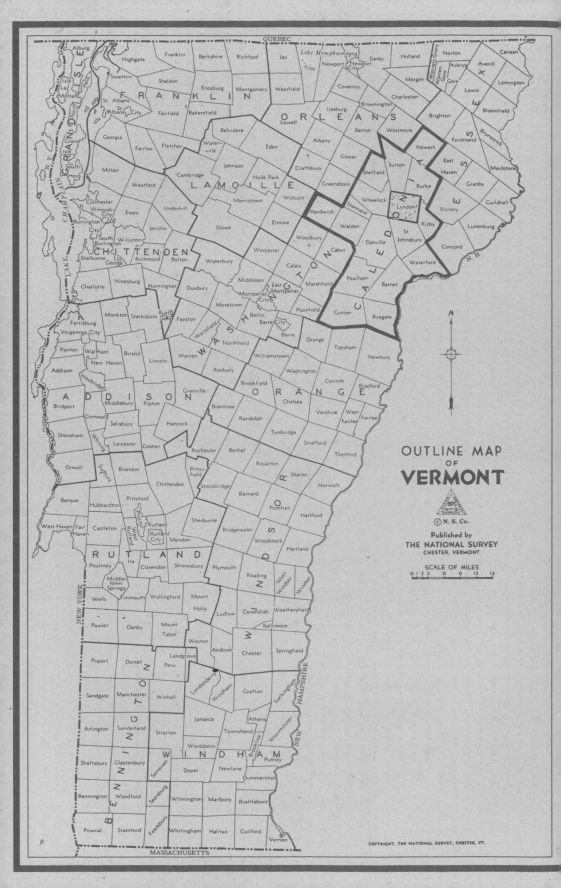

OUTLINE MAP OF VERMONT

Published by
THE NATIONAL SURVEY
CHESTER, VERMONT

SCALE OF MILES
0 1 2 3   6   9   12   15

© N. S. Co.